Company Law in the New Europe

CORPORATIONS, GLOBALISATION AND THE LAW

Series Editor: Janet Dine, *Director, Centre for Commercial Law Studies, Queen Mary College, University of London, UK*

This new and uniquely positioned monograph series aims to draw together high quality research work from established and younger scholars on what is an intriguing and under-researched area of the law. The books will offer insights into a variety of legal issues that concern corporations operating on the global stage, including interaction with WTO, international financial institutions and nation states, in both developing and developed countries. Whilst the underlying foundation of the series will be that of company law, broadly defined, authors are encouraged to take an approach that draws on the work of other social sciences, such as politics, economics and development studies and to offer an international or comparative perspective where appropriate. Specific topics to be considered will include corporate governance, corporate responsibility, taxation and criminal liability, amongst others. The series will undoubtedly offer an important contribution to legal thinking and to the wider globalisation debate.

Titles in the series include:

Human Rights and Capitalism
A Multidisciplinary Perspective on Globalisation
Edited by Janet Dine and Andrew Fagan

Company Law in the New Europe
The EU *Acquis*, Comparative Methodology and Model Law
Janet Dine, Marios Koutsias and Michael Blecher

Company Law in the New Europe

The EU *Acquis*, Comparative Methodology and Model Law

Janet Dine

Director, Centre for Commercial Law Studies, Queen Mary College, University of London, UK

Marios Koutsias

PhD Candidate, University of Essex and Research Assistant, Centre for Commercial Law Studies, Queen Mary College, University of London, UK

Michael Blecher

Senior Counsel for legal development projects for German Technical Co-operation (GTZ), EU and World Bank

CORPORATIONS, GLOBALISATION AND THE LAW

Edward Elgar
Cheltenham, UK • Northampton, MA, USA

Published by
Edward Elgar Publishing Limited
Glensanda House
Montpellier Parade
Cheltenham
Glos GL50 1UA
UK

Edward Elgar Publishing, Inc.
William Pratt House
9 Dewey Court
Northampton
Massachusetts 01060
USA

A catalogue record for this book
is available from the British Library

ISBN 978 1 84542 415 2

Typeset by Cambrian Typesetters, Camberley, Surrey
Printed and bound in Great Britain by MPG Books Ltd, Bodmin, Cornwall

Contents

Preface

In times when the political and legal 'battle' surrounding the project of a new EU Constitution has demonstrated the fragility of the 'joint European project' and its underlying parameters of social construction, this book considers the influence that the prospect of EU membership has on transition countries in general and specifically on the drafting of commercial law, and in particular company law, in transition economies. In order to understand the extent of this influence the enlargement of the Union is examined in its historical context, looking at the political, economic and security reasons for the imposition of ever more complex conditionality over the years. The focus is on the political, economic and security reasons underlying the decision of the Union to extend its membership from the initial six members to the current 25 and potentially to 27 or more.

The 'values' informing this conditionality are critically considered. Philosophies underlying property rights and human rights have a controversial heritage and the authors do not feel that they can just be taken for granted in the way that countless pre-accession programmes and projects have done. The study reveals that the question 'what kind of Europe do we want?' is strongly related to the question 'transition to what?'. Once we set aside the membership question, parallels can also be drawn with the EU development discourse from Lomé to Cotonou which has applied the same underlying philosophies to the relations with ACP countries. The third question is therefore 'development of what?', and it shows that the EU project's parameters of ('internal') social construction are strongly linked to those which should guide the economic, political and legal making of a global society.

The book claims that alternatives to the criteria applied by the EU transition and development discourses are necessary in order to create a sustainable democratic European and global society which takes into account the social, legal and institutional traditions and potentials of their changing local environments. As regards the construction of a commercial law which fits into such a project, the book moves on to suggest how, using a risk assessment method, an alternative methodology for commercial law drafting can be developed. Such a method needs to take account of the EU *Acquis* if EU membership is at stake, while, at the same time, making sure that a law can be properly embedded in the local social and economic context. There is no space for pure transplantation.

The second part of the work sets out a complete draft of a model company law for transition (and development) economies, drafted following this methodology. It would, of course, need fine tuning to particular societies but the authors hope that it might be considered a starting point for discussion.

Marios would like to express his deep gratitude towards his parents for their love and support. Janet would like to thank her co-authors for their help and forbearance and Keith for his support. Michael extends thanks to his co-authors for their co-operation. Michael and Janet thank Elizabeth Leiss and GT2 for their support while drafting the model law. The authors are also grateful to Luke Adams and all at Edward Elgar for their assistance during the development of this project.

PART I

The challenge of enlargement

Contents of Part I

1. The EU and the recent enlargement: opportunities and challenges

INTRODUCTION

This book deals with particular aspects of the process of enlargement and more specifically with the tools available in the hands of the EU to influence and determine the nature of the reforms taking place in a given society of a candidate country anticipating its imminent enlargement. The EU has discovered in its accession strategy and the enlargement procedure and, most significantly, in the entrance criteria it has decisively established a very effective strategy that enables it to reshape fundamental parts of the candidate countries' societies. This is a process that affects every single aspect of the national life in the countries to be included in an enlargement wave. This became particularly evident in the framework of the recent enlargement encompassing the eight Central and Eastern European Countries (CEEC) along with Cyprus and Malta. In particular the former had to undergo radical reforms that transformed their economic and political life and introduced a major shift in the administrative patterns that had been in force at least during the second half of the last century throughout the Eastern part of the continent. Of course it was not the first time that the EU had dealt with the experience of enlargement and with the necessity to incorporate new countries in its body, but the nature of the recently accepted countries, their divergent political past, their fundamentally different economic system, their diverse political orientations in addition to the isolation between the Western and Eastern parts of the continent that emerged as a direct consequence of the Cold War, created a wholly new landscape within which both the EU and the new candidates had to find new balances and to shape new compromises. It is especially important to note that the CEEC emerged from communist rule into a *post-national* situation and had immediately to deal with the implications of multi-level governance.

The context and the conditions under which the recent enlargement has taken place will be analysed, the process shaped by the EU to be followed in the case of accepting new members will be considered along with reflections over the far-reaching impact of such a process in the societal systems of the countries aspiring to join. Emphasis will be given to the area of company law because it occupies a central part in the field of the economy and its shaping reflects the particular ideological approach adopted in the respective field by the countries in question. Thus, the transformation of the centrally planned economies of the CEEC into Western European type liberal free market economies had a strategic character and signalled a radical reform of the markets in the part of the continent lying east of the Danube. In this context the way a country decides to regulate the companies operating in its borders is directly linked with the orientation it wishes to afford to its economy and consequently society. Therefore, the importance of this issue and of the influence exercised by the EU in the direction of aligning the Company Laws of CEEC with the Western European patterns is evident. Thus, this book examines the issues stemming from the interaction between the two partners: the EU on the one hand, and the candidate countries on the other.

THE DYNAMICS OF ENLARGEMENT: WHY HAS THE EU DECIDED TO ENLARGE TO THE EAST?

The recent expansion is not the first time that the EU has extended its borders to encompass countries that are relatively poorer or less advanced than its current members and the examples of Ireland in 1973, Greece in 1981 and Spain and Portugal in 1986 serve as a proof of that. However 'these enlargements involved mainly Western European States, whereas the current enlargement involves countries that do not necessarily hold the same historical experience or shared objectives of Western Europe'.[1] In the words of the Commission this enlargement 'finally heals a rift in Europe opened up by World War II, the East-West confrontation and the Cold War'.[2] Moreover, the recent enlargement almost completed the process of gathering the continent's countries under the same institutional roof as, apart from the Western Balkan countries, the rest of the continent appears to enjoy a piece of the stability and prosperity afforded by participation in one of the world's most successful economies: the European Union. Of course this argument is directly linked with the ongoing discussion concerning the actual limits of Europe and consequently of the size of the catalogue of future aspiring members, but at the moment it is not feasible to foresee the conclusion of such a debate. The focus will rest on the recent enlargement for an additional reason. The latter rests on

---

1 Clements W. Carson, 'A More Perfect Union? Eastern Enlargement and the Institutional Challenges of the Czech Republic's Accession to the European Union', *Syracuse Journal of International Law and Commerce*, 29, 2002, p. 402.

2 See the European Commission publications on Enlargement at: http://europa.eu.int/comm/publications/booklets/move/41/en.pdf, accessed 5 June 2005.

the premise that apart from the benefits brought to the EU by the recent enlargement to the East, the challenges faced by the enlarged Union of 25 members with sometimes fundamentally different ideals, aspirations and objectives stemming of course from widely divergent political and economic historical experiences, are greater than at any other enlargement round. The referendums held in France and in the Netherlands on 29 May 2005 and on 1 June 2005 respectively and the role that the enlargement to the East or the potential inclusion of Turkey in the EU played in the negative outcome of both, revealed political problems that might have been effectively hidden below the surface for some time but found their way out through a significant popular vote in a rather dramatic way. Thus, after discussing the benefits that the EU has reaped from the enlargement to the East, the challenges arising from the same event will be fully analysed.

ECONOMIC REASONS

It was realised at an early stage that the enlargement to the East would offer new opportunities for trade and businesses across Europe. With the inclusion of ten new countries 'the expanded EU will be the world's largest frontier free market economy'[3] and with the addition of almost 100 million new citizens from Eastern Europe it will now comprise 470 million consumers boosting economic growth and creating new jobs both in the 'old' and in the 'new' Europe.[4] The dynamics from creating such a big barrier free market encompassing countries that can be viewed as prosperous or wealthy are enormous and render the view that 'joining the EU has no alternative in economic and geopolitical terms'[5] dominant, although, as we shall see, the political alliances came under strain, particularly during the controversy over the Iraq war. The economic dimension of the enlargement cannot be isolated from the accompanying processes of political and administrative reforms that are stimulated by the need to comply with the EU norms. Thus, reforms such as the ones related to property ownership in the CEEC were of course motivated by the passing to a new era when the free market liberal economy would stand at the

[3] Jill Parker, 'Comment: West Meets East: A Discussion of European Union Enlargement and Human Rights', *Tulsa Journal of Comparative and International Law*, 11, 2004, p. 603.

[4] See the European Commission site at: http://www.europa.eu.int/comm/enlargement/arguments/index.htm#Benefits, accessed 5 June 2005.

[5] Antoeneta L. Dimitrova, *Driven to Change, The European Union's Enlargement Viewed from the East*, Manchester University Press, Manchester, 2004, p. 2.

core of the transformation to a democracy in accordance with Western European standards; however they cannot be viewed solely from this strictly economic angle. They are organically connected to a fundamental change in the nature of the political system and the constitutional and administrative culture of a country. The wide limitations placed upon the role of the State in the market economy do not solely encompass economic factors but, in the transition from a centrally planned to a market economy, reflect also the nature of the constitutional choices that a country aims to adopt at a given historical moment. And the historical moment when the stimulus was provided for a radical change in the economic and constitutional foundations of a range of Eastern European countries was reached when the aforementioned countries were brought by the EU on track for enlargement. This is more evident in the case of the CEEC where the centrally planned economy systems coincided with the Communist regimes in charge of the respective economies. Lack of transparency and accountability affected both the efficiency of the economic policies pursued and the quality of the constitutional model, which lacked basic democratic elements. Thus, for the Eastern European nations the dictatorial regimes dominant for 45 years and the notion of an economy wholly arranged centrally by the State, which assigned itself the role of the absolute leader, were found to be closely related to each other, if not in complete coincidence. Therefore, for them the passing to an economy where several actors are encouraged to compete freely with domestic or foreign producers was not only a change of a purely economic character, but also a significant shift to a different type of constitutional arrangement that enabled and promoted a greater sense of personal freedom. Consequently, it is evident that the economic motivations cannot be viewed in isolation from motivations of a distinctive and especially of a political nature. And the costs and benefits of the enlargement stemmed of this pressure; that through the process of coming closer to the EU, the candidate Eastern European countries had to decisively and radically change their economic systems and consequently the whole set of constitutional arrangements in force up to that point in those countries. Parallel with the pressure exerted by convergence there was pressure from individuals asserting their rights. This work concentrates on the institutional changes demanded by the EU; it is accepted that this by no means provides the whole picture.

The situation was not the same for all countries as not all of them began from the same starting positions. However, the carrot of eventual membership forced even the most problematic candidates, especially at an initial stage, to overcome resounding difficulties stemming from 45 years of Communism and be ready along with the rest of the candidates to enter the EU. The Czech Republic and Hungary were seen as the countries in need of most radical reform, but also in a position to join the EU more rapidly than others if they pursued an effective choice of policies. However, 'if states of Eastern Europe had merely to rearrange their existing economic systems to work on the foundations of a market economy Latvia and the other Baltic States had to create their own system of economy with its basic elements: national currency, budget, infrastructure of economy'.[6] Thus, especially in those states that were not only in the socialist sphere but were incorporated as an integral part of the Soviet Union the road towards the EU did offer significant challenges but also an important set of motivations to initiate the reforms necessary if not to reach at least to align themselves with the standards acceptable by the EU of the 15. The objective of the pre-enlargement process is exactly that, to encourage the countries which wish to join the EU to do so after they have succeeded in bringing their systems or standards into compliance with EU requirements. The EU does not require that the candidate countries should have reached its level of institutional or economic development but that the new members have initiated and implemented the reforms necessary to be able to pursue such an objective as soon as they have entered the Union. 'Economic convergence will take longer than the CEEC are willing to wait for admission to the EU',[7] so the pace and level of institutional alignment inherent in the concept of a notion central to the EU enlargement strategy, *acquis communautaire*, which is considered later, are deemed as sufficient prerequisites for entry.

Irrespective of the painful reforms necessary to bring those countries into line with EU standards, the prospect of membership was deemed a very powerful factor for the promotion of the far-reaching economic reforms agenda and emerged as the crucial magnetic pull that attracted the CEEC in the direction of successful economic transformation. 'The influence that the EU can exercise on the other European countries is due most of all to their hopes to become its members'.[8] Only after such a transformation could the new member states stand as members of the internal market, which constitutes the Union's greatest achievement at least so far. The latter functions on the basis of a range of directives and regulations and unless the newly arrived countries had adopted the entirety of such a body of legislation they would not have been able to compete within the framework of the internal market while their presence would have created certain distortions that would put in peril its

---

6 Baranovs Olegs, in *East European Transition and EU Enlargement, A Quantitative Approach*, Wojciech W. Charemza and Krystyna Strzala, Physica Verlag, Heidelberg and New York, 2002, p. 39.

7 Victoria Curzon Price, Alice Landau and Richard G. Whitman, *The Enlargement of the EU, Issues and Strategies*, Routledge Studies in the European Economy, London, 2000, p. 25.

8 Loukas Tsoukalis, *What Kind of Europe?*, Oxford University Press, Oxford, 2003 and Potamos, Athens, 2004, p. 266.

very existence. Thus, there was a variety of important economic interests at stake on both sides. The CEEC had to achieve the necessary consensus at national level to implement far-reaching reforms aimed at changing the fundamentals of the economic and political life of the countries involved and the EU had to closely monitor such a process because its greatest achievement could otherwise be threatened by malfunctions. Furthermore, the CEEC were aware of the significance of these reforms in relation not only to the ultimate goal pursued, which was their much desired membership, but also to their ability to deal with the competitive pressures within the framework of the common market after their integration in the EU. The importance of this principle is such that it constitutes one of the criteria to be fulfilled in order to enter the Union. So the CEEC also had to focus on the period after their actual entry when all remaining barriers to trade and competition would be removed and they would have to face stiff competition both from the current member states and from other newly arrived countries that had been more successful in their preparation for the post-entrance period.

The CEEC had certain obvious advantages to offer such as their low-cost labour and fewer social protection regulations, but investment kept flowing not only because of these factors, but also because the countries in question were gradually becoming an integral part of a larger European market. And as they were countries considered relatively poor, usually with large agricultural sectors, they were looking forward to substantial financing through certain of the Union's much publicised policies such as the Common Agriculture Policy or the Structural and Cohesion Funds. The earlier enlargement to include Ireland, Greece, Spain and Portugal provided an attractive example of generous Community funding that is however unlikely to be repeated in the future. Moreover, it will give them the highly significant ability to co-determine future EU legislation on the internal market in a direction more suitable to their own national interests and expectations.

It has to be noted, however, that there are also additional costs for the CEEC in the course of their adjustment as they are obliged to introduce higher standards of environmental protection as required by the respective EU legislation, an extra cost for their governments and industry representatives that will not be easy to bear. The costs of restructuring their administrative capacities to deal with the demands of the participation in the internal market are not negligible either. These can vary from the training of public servants to be employed in government departments dealing with EU-related issues to the complete reorganisation of certain administrative directorate generals.

Furthermore, within the framework of interaction with the EU there is the possibility of further regulation from Brussels related for example to the duration of a working day or stricter conditions for the employment of labour that might remove some of the competitive advantages currently offered by the

CEEC. The political storm caused by the infamous Bolkenstein Directive on the liberalisation of services at pan-European level and the debates preceding the referendums in France and the Netherlands, dealt with later, proved that the road towards future integration and adjustment will not always be smooth and have shed light in a dramatic way on the potential negative repercussions of the enlargement project. The negative results of the referendums served as a stark reminder to the majority of Europeans, at least to those residing in the 'old Europe', that along with the positive aspects of the enlargement, the EU has to deal with and provide satisfactory answers to the challenges that derive from the extension of the Union to ten new member states.

POLITICAL AND SECURITY REASONS

The recent enlargement of the EU was prompted mainly by strong motives of a political nature. There was a concerted effort to reunite the continent and bring to an end the divisions that had dominated Europe for more than half a century. It was perceived as the healing of the rift between the two parts that had assumed protagonist roles in the framework of the painful Cold War. On 9 November 1989 the Berlin Wall collapsed and along with it Europe changed for good. The triumphal spirit prevailing in most Western European capitals due to ideological and political victory in the Cold War which had just come to an end was interrupted abruptly by the side effects of the collapse of the highly symbolic Wall that had divided Europe into its free Western part and the Soviet-dominated Eastern European countries for 40 consecutive years. A whole system of political governance was shredded into pieces, economic theories dominant in the Eastern part of the continent were suddenly found unsuitable for the new era that was approaching unexpectedly quickly and new countries were emerging on the borders of Western Europe. This happened either in a peaceful manner, the velvet divorce that split Czechoslovakia into the Czech Republic and Slovakia serving as an example of a rather successful segregation of a former unified state, or more importantly in a way that led to bloody and violent wars such as those in the Balkans, which left their intense imprint both in the nations that experienced them and on the rest of Europe that felt that security in the continent could not be taken for granted but had to be assured and consolidated through common action. The wars in the Balkans and the subsequent accusations of mass murders, ethnic cleansing and genocide that took place in the framework of the armed confrontation of the nations involved, reminded the rest of the Europeans that there is at least a part of Europe where collective memories of war atrocities and mutual cruelties do not wholly belong to the past as was initially believed and widely hoped for but can be revived as nationalism re-emerged as an important feature of public life. The wars in the Balkans were accompanied by a sense of unrest in most of Eastern Europe, as the recently liberated societies of that part of the continent were entering a phase of transition into something at that point still unknown and they were in the course of re-establishing and clarifying their identity as nations with a common heritage and trying to adjust to the expectations of their Western counterparts. The sudden fall of many Eastern European regimes and the call for radical reform in the respective societies might have been an event heavily supported by the majority of public opinion but it naturally did not cease to be a source of insecurity for the future and uncertainty over the present. The war in Bosnia in 1992 and the turmoil in Russia in 1993, which brought the country to the brink of a serious constitutional crisis with President Yeltsin facing an open rebellion of citizens in the streets that ended in bloodshed, reminded the Heads of the EU member states that action had to be taken immediately in order to entrench stability in Eastern Europe. The European leaders were very well aware of the fact that instability in the Eastern part of the continent entailed certain challenges for the security of the Western part.

In this context of visible challenges to the security of Western Europe, the European Council convened in Copenhagen in 1993 decided to agree on a principle that paved the way for the historic enlargement to the CEEC. 'The European Council today agreed that the associated countries of Central and Eastern Europe that so desire shall become members of the European Union. Accession will take place as soon as an associated country is able to assume the obligations of membership by satisfying the economic and political conditions required'.[9] The final sentence refers to the criteria for membership shaped at the particular Council that have gone down in history as the 'Copenhagen Criteria' and constitute up till now the codification of the basic values on which the EU is constructed and which have to be adhered to by new members in order for the EU to open its doors to them. The criteria include an economic criterion referring to a functioning market economy and the ability to cope with competitive pressure in the internal market, a political criterion signalling respect for the rule of law, minorities, democracy and human rights and, last but not least, the ability to assume the obligations of membership widely known as the *acquis communautaire* or the whole existing body of EU law and regulations. The Copenhagen Criteria are considered in Chapter 3. Here it should be noted that the stated criteria must be considered with some scepticism, as the analysis of their origins set out in Chapter 4 emphasises. Using such criteria to justify dominance is not unknown and the EU should be

---

[9] Presidency Conclusions, Copenhagen European Council, 21–2 June 1993, see: http://www.europarl.eu.int/enlargement/ec/pdf/cop_en.pdf#search='copenhagen% 20%20council%201993', accessed 6 June 2005.

wary that it is not adopting convenient criteria in order to embellish its own power.

Just before the Copenhagen European Council, in 1990, only months after the dramatic events of 1989, the Heads of the EU member states expressed at the Dublin European Council their aspiration to 'overcome the divisions of Europe and restore the unity of the continent'.[10] However, it was still too early to contemplate full membership. In October 1990 in Rome the European leaders made a further step in that direction by emphasising that 'the European Council is aware of its special responsibility towards these countries at a time when they are pursuing structural adjustments . . . in these circumstances the Community has a duty to help and consolidate and develop the general process of reform being undertaken in these countries'.[11] Again, the European Council in Rome in December 1990 confirmed that in anticipation of the signing of the Europe Agreements assistance will take the form of financial aid.[12] The Maastricht European Council finally invited every European country whose system of governance is based on the principle of democracy to apply to become a member.[13] The Essen European Council in 1994 noted in the same spirit that 'the European Union is making an essential contribution to overcome the legacy of past divisions, and promote peace, security and stability in and around Europe' and that 'the European Council confirms the conclusions of the European Councils in Copenhagen 1993 and Corfu 1994 that the associated States of Central and Eastern Europe can become members of the European Union if they so desire and as soon as they are able to fulfil the necessary conditions'.[14] The Heads of States in Essen set out four priority areas for the EU for the years to come, one of which had been 'ensuring the lasting peace and stability of the European continent and neighboring regions by preparing for the future accession of the associated countries of Central and Eastern Europe'.[15] It is obvious that the objectives to be achieved by the

---

10 Dublin European Council, Presidency Conclusions, 25 and 26 June 1990, see: http://www.europarl.eu.int/summits/dublin/du1_en.pdf, accessed 6 June 2005.

11 European Council in Rome, 27 and 28 October 1990, Presidency Conclusions, see: http://www.europarl.eu.int/summits/rome1/ro1_en.pdf, accessed 6 June 2005.

12 European Council in Rome, 14 and 15 December 1990, Presidency Conclusions, see: http://www.europarl.eu.int/summits/rome2/rd2_en.pdf, accessed 6 June 2005.

13 Maastricht European Council, 9 and 10 December 1991, Presidency Conclusions, see: http://www.europarl.eu.int/summits/maastricht/ma1_en.pdf, accessed 6 June 2005.

14 European Council in Essen, 9 and 10 December 1994, see: http://www.europarl.eu.int/summits/ess1_en.htm#ext, accessed 6 June 2005.

15 Ibid.

enlargement to the East were heavily related to issues that the EU found particularly important such as the safeguarding of peace and stability in the continent. Thus, stability and security appear to be the principal reasons that underlie the choice of the recent enlargement. The importance of this objective for both parties was obvious also from the fact that in parallel to the EU another international organisation whose principal aim up to that point was to act as the pillar for Western European security, namely NATO, decided to adjust to the new European and international political landscape as it had been radically transformed and accept new members from the bloc that used to constitute its primary enemy. In 1995 NATO issued its Study on Enlargement[16] in which it stated its desire to include countries from the former Soviet bloc as a means of contributing to enhanced security and stability for all. Therefore, Poland, Hungary and the Czech Republic were invited to begin accession talks by the Madrid Summit in 1997 and in 1999 they became members of NATO. Thus, security functioned as the principal objective for the integration of the CEEC in what used to be up till then solely Western European organisations. Initially NATO, with its scope of activities limited to security issues, and subsequently the EU, which offered an even more significant sense of political stability and economic development, advanced the integration of the CEEC countries.

Thus, the allure of the EU as a guarantor of security played a massive role in attracting many applications from countries with recent experiences of oppressive regimes or even occupation. The newly discovered principles of democracy and sovereignty were widely appreciated and their safeguard through the integration into a Union that is actually based on these principles seemed an objective of fundamentally vital importance for the new republics of Eastern Europe. The EU could anyway offer 'successful examples of democratisation in Greece, Spain and Portugal, which have successfully managed the difficult transition from authoritarian rule towards democracy'.[17] It is a matter of universal agreement in the societies of the southern European countries that participation in the EU has played a profound if not the principal role in consolidating democracy in the aforementioned nations. The CEEC were aiming to achieve exactly the same goal.

The importance of the existence and maintenance of democracy in the EU framework is underlined by the fact that it constitutes one of the criteria for entry. Furthermore, apart from the mere consolidation of the newly established

---

[16] See: http://www.nato.int/docu/basictxt/enl-9501.htm, accessed 6 June 2005.

[17] Christian W. Haerpfer, *Democracy and Enlargement in Post-Communist Europe, The Democratisation of the General Public in Fifteen Central and Eastern European Countries, 1991–1998*, Routledge Advances in European Politics, London and New York, 2002, p. 2.

democratic and representative institutions, other Eastern European countries such as Latvia, Lithuania and Estonia viewed the EU as the harbour that could safeguard their independence. The three Baltic republics were not only members of the Eastern Bloc but also formed a part of the Soviet Union, in the territory of which they were incorporated for decades. So it was only natural that they would turn to the EU as an important alternative sphere of influence to balance that of Russia. Like Finland in the past, the 'former Soviet republics wanted to embed themselves as much as possible in the European security framework'.[18] In this case, escaping Russian influence was put at the centre of the countries' considerations for entering the Union.

Thus, the safety and stability that EU participation can entail has lured countries with previous experience of political turmoil into its ambit. The EU is based on a set of 'fundamental values: stability, democracy, rule of law, and a free market economy. These values are the real source of solidarity between its members. These values illustrate how expansion is a natural and logical process of reintegrating the Central European nations into the Euro-Atlantic community. The Central European nations share a commitment to these values and have the ability to defend them'.[19] The highly expressive tone of the Romanian Ambassador to the USA emphasises the importance of the security parameter of the application on behalf of the CEEC. It is evident that the entry of a country into the EU is mostly a political choice. The same can be said about the EU, which of course places maximum importance on economic criteria and the ability to assume the responsibilities stemming from membership including the obligations inherent in the framework of the internal market. However, political considerations and the urgent need to extend the zone of stability from Western Europe to the whole of the continent, with the exception of the Balkans, was of a purely political nature. The EU had estimated that the instability that was a feature of the Eastern European countries could be exported to the EU if the latter did not act to prevent this. The 15 member states of the EU could not live in complete isolation from their direct neighbours and if the latter were in constant political turmoil this was inevitably going to adversely affect them in one way or another. Therefore, extending peace and stability in the whole continent and ensuring that all European nations would enjoy the same level of security was an absolutely necessary precondition for the development of the continent as a whole. Europe's economy could not grow without the stability necessary for

---

[18] Maria Green Cowles and Desmond Dinan, *Developments in the European Union*, Palgrave, New York, 2004, p. 9.

[19] Geoana Mircea, Eighth Annual Philip D. Reed Memorial Issue: Essay 'Romania: Euro-Atlantic Integration and Economic Reform', *Fordham International Law Journal*, 21, 1997, p. 12.

economic development and investment. The fundamental projects of the EU, especially the internal market and the Common Agriculture Policy, could not proceed after a massive and uncontrolled influx of immigrants from an unstable Eastern Europe. The Common Foreign and Security Policy of the EU would have been put under pressure by the need to find common workable solutions for dealing with problems that could be transferred to within the EU itself. Hence, it was a matter of absolute priority for the Union to pursue a policy that would foster democracy and stability in an area that cannot be viewed in isolation from the previous group of the 15 member nations. As the brutality of the wars in the Balkans as recently as in 2000 have clearly demonstrated, security and stability in Eastern Europe are organically connected with security and stability in Western Europe. There might have been divergent historical experiences in the respective parts of the continent but their interlinked future can hardly be in doubt. As Romano Prodi, the former Prime Minister of Italy and President of the European Commission, had put it 'as an instrument of a stability policy that has been successful in all senses, opening up a reliable prospect for Eastern Europe, enlargement has been an unparalleled success story. It represents the triumph of stability in Europe, the extension of democracy and above all our common European values . . . only by opening up to the East, could the EU durably stabilise the Continent, secure its own interest . . . and accept its historic responsibility'.[20]

And of course when the EU required as a prerequisite for entry the existence of democracy it actually meant 'Western type of democracy',[21] which is an important parameter that should not be neglected. The EU realised at an early stage that the accession procedure especially through its entry criteria, which as mentioned before required the existence of institutions based on the principle of democracy, constituted a very essential tool in its effort to influence developments in the new republics. The EU, using the magnetic pull of its membership, was in a powerful position to actually dictate the model of institutional, constitutional and administrative reform to be followed by aspiring new members. Thus, creating a whole geographical zone based on relatively similar institutional structures founded on the same political principles was of obvious importance for the current member states, which wished to somehow be in a position if not to influence at least to have a say in the rapid changes occurring in the Eastern part of the continent. Moreover, accepting already well-functioning democracies into the EU framework would be beneficial for the EU as the latter would not have to deal with the existing political problems of the new member states such as the malfunctioning of internal

---

[20] Romano Prodi, 'Reform and Proximity', in *Desperately Seeking Europe*, Susan Stern and Elisabeth Seligmann, Archetype Publications, London, 2003, p. 266.

[21] See Tsoukalis, supra note 8, p. 277.

institutions that can cause public dissatisfaction or even the treatment of national minorities and relations with neighbouring countries. The EU could operate more smoothly as cooperation between relatively homogeneous states in terms of political organisation can be more easierly pursued. Thus, it was an opportunity for the Union to extend its institutional standards and models to a new array of states that were just emerging right next to its borders. As the Commissioner responsible for the Enlargement noted, the 'enlargement is one of our best security guarantees. It reflects the essence of the EU as a civilian power, extending the zone of peace and stability, liberty and democracy across the continent. The EU has used its soft power to shape post communist Central and Eastern Europe in its own image of liberal democracy and social market economy, ensuring stability during the difficult and potentially dangerous years after the fall of the Berlin Wall . . . by extending the zone of peace and democracy the EU has achieved far more through its gravitational pull than it could have by a stick or a sword'.[22] In any case, as Walter Hallstein, the first President of the European Commission 'made it clear, the founders of the Community had all of Europe in mind: We share one wish above all others, which is to overcome the division of Europe between East and West'.[23]

The political reasons which persuaded both the EU and the CEEC that membership would be a target worth achieving also included a moral aspect, an aspect imbued with a sense of symbolism rather than any tangible political interest. 'EU leaders often mentioned historical and moral debts as key reasons for expansion. They appeared uncomfortable with the idea that they have left their neighbours on the other side of the Iron Curtain, impoverished and under Stalin's brutal control. After the wars in former Yugoslavia, the EU leaders felt an additional moral debt towards the Western Balkan victims'.[24]

This sense of 'moral duty' towards the fellow Europeans from the East was a result of collective guilt towards the partition of Europe during the Cold War and remained as a post-war legacy that always left the Western European leaders with a sense of an uncomfortable blame. After World War II the two parts of Europe had grown almost in isolation from each other and the dramatic

---

[22] Olli Rehn, member of the European Commission, responsible for Enlargement, 'EU Enlargement under Stress: The Policy of Consolidation, Conditionality and Communication', Speech at the Institute for European Policy, Berlin, 12 July 2005. SPEECE/05/438. Accessed also at: http://europa.eu.int/comm/commission_barroso/rehn/speeches/pdf/s05_438.en.pdf.

[23] Reinicke H. Wolfgang, *Building a New Europe, The Challenge of System Transformation and Systemic Reform*, The Brookings Institution, Washington, DC, 1992, p. 5.

[24] Bartol Letica, 'Reflections on a New Europe, Europe's Second Chance: European Union Enlargement to Croatia and the Western Balkans', *Fletcher Forum of World Affairs Journal*, 28, 2004, p. 210.

differences in the quality of life and standards of democracy experienced on the two opposite sides of the Wall were revealed after its collapse. The incorporation of Eastern Europe was consequently seen not just as an economic opportunity or a significant chance to create political stability in the whole continent but as a wonderful chance to heal the wounds of brutal separation and live together under the same – albeit already predetermined – institutional roof. In this sense it created issues of identity linked with the so-called 'Europeanness' of the new member states. In the words of Pat Cox, the President of the European Parliament, 'the changes following the fall of the Berlin Wall have made the widening of the EU a moral and political necessity'.[25]

Andrei Plesu, a former Romanian minister of foreign affairs, stated that 'when we say Europe in Eastern Europe we usually think about something in the past something we lost and have to regain . . . it is something in an old faded photograph, the world between the two World Wars, a nostalgia, a longing. In the West Europe is a project, in the East, it is a memory'.[26] Milan Kundera 'emphasised that to a Hungarian, a Czech or a Pole the word "Europe" is not a geographical expression but a spiritual notion synonymous with the word "West" '.[27] Thus, for the CEEC the issue of joining the EU became an important focus for the move to redefine their identity through the common European angle and re-establish themselves as countries participating in the mainstream of European political life. In a sense it was a struggle to reinvent the European part of their history that was thought to have been abandoned during the obscure decades of Soviet domination. 'The return to Europe discourse called for the symbolic return of these states to their rightful cultural and civilisational spheres as well as their entry into the economic and political institutions of the EU'.[28] To this end they were even willing to sacrifice part of their hard-won national sovereignty. Participation in the EU served purposes obviously even more important than that. On the other hand there was no particular alternative, as if a country chose not to surrender the part of its sovereignty necessary for accession, it risked finding itself once again marginalised on the periphery of Europe between the current member states and Russia, a scenario that the Eastern European elites dreaded and worked successfully to avoid.

25 Pat Cox, 'Europe's Constitution in the Making', in *Desperately Seeking Europe*, supra note 20, p. 277.

26 Bartol Letica, supra note 24, p. 216.

27 Stefan Elbe, *Europe, A Nietzschean Perspective*, Routledge, London and New York, 2003, p. 4.

28 Nicole Lindstrom, 'Rethinking Sovereignty: The Politics of European Integration', *Fletcher Forum of World Affairs Journal*, 24, 2000, p. 31.

The rationale behind the recent enlargement can also be traced to a 'sense of common identity and involvement in a common project the reconstruction and recreation of Europe, which is not purely instrumental or guided by self interest . . . the EU membership with its newly articulated conditionality has become a goal for almost every emerging and newly stabilising European state, and an instrument of economic, political and legal change beyond its boundaries'.[29] As a post-war remnant 'the term Eastern Europe conjures up gray, looming images in most Western minds. Thus, one cannot invoke this geographical designation without confronting these persistent negative connotations. . . . the idea of Eastern Europe as a work of cultural creation, of intellectual artifice, of ideological self interest and self promotion clearly precedes the Cold War'.[30]

As Giuliano Amato and Judy Batt have observed: 'The division of Europe has left its mark on perceptions in the West, reinforcing long standing prejudices about the East as "backward" and less "civilised" than the West, not fully "part of Europe". The prospect of enlargement to the East has brought these prejudices to the fore, further contributing to the tendency to portray the increasing diversity that it entails as a new and uniquely threatening challenge for the EU'.[31] Thus, entry into and membership of the EU, leaving aside the obvious economic benefits already analysed are closely linked with the issue of national identity and the re-establishment of links with the pre-Cold War past. The latter is viewed as the reshaping of the links with the common European past as a whole. The Cold War and the subsequent deprivation and isolation are perceived as the factors that abruptly interrupted the natural relation between Eastern and Western Europe and their common European credentials. Therefore, enlargement has greatly assisted the Eastern Europeans in dealing with 'a residual cultural problem. The new Europe has always identified itself in opposition to the others; to the other Europeans that lie beyond the remnants of the Berlin Wall, to those who lie across the Mediterranean'.[32] Maybe in the EU framework Europeans will not try to define themselves in contrast to each other but in conjunction with the several common elements of shared heritage across the continent and in harmony with 'the European way: peace and reconciliation'.[33]

---

29 Marise Cremona, 'EU Enlargement: Solidarity and Conditionality', *European Law Review*, 30(1), 2005, p. 9.

30 Helen E. Hartnell, 'Subregional Coalescence in European Regional Integration', *Wisconsin International Law Journal*, 16, 1997, p. 117.

31 Excerpt taken from Peter Mair and Jan Zielonka, *The Enlarged European Union, Diversity and Adaptation*, Frank Cass, London, Portland, Or., 2002, p. 3.

32 Ian Ward, *Temple International and Comparative Law Journal*, 15, 2001, p. 252.

33 Olli Rehn, Commissioner responsible for Enlargement, 'The Balkans, Europe and Reconciliation', Debate in Sarajevo University, Sarajevo, 11 July 2005, SPEECH/05/434, accessed also at: http://europa.eu.int/comm/commission_barroso/rehn/speeches/pdf/s05_434.en.pdf.

CHALLENGES STEMMING FROM THE ENLARGEMENT TO THE EAST

The recent enlargement has provided the grounds for a new round of debate in the EU over significant issues related to its identity, its basic goals, the reshaping of its institutions, its foreign policy objectives and the ideological values on which the Union is thought to be based. The new countries, as analysed above, joined the Union with new aspirations, different historical experiences and widely divergent levels of political and economic development. Therefore, although the enlargement took place in a glorious atmosphere of triumph with the European leaders gathering in Athens in 2003 to sign the Treaty of Accession with a feeling of having written the final conclusion in the historical chapter of European divisions, however the reality, as the war in Iraq which erupted just before the signing of the Treaty of Athens[34] had already indicated, has proved a little bit less exciting than that. The challenges stemming from the enlargement can be classified mainly in two categories; challenges of a political nature and challenges of an economic nature.

THE POLITICAL CHALLENGES

One of the basic challenges stemming from the recent enlargement is related to an element fundamental both for the common European construction and for individual nations around Europe: the issue of identity. The identity issue is very important because it is closely linked with the particular characteristics a certain nation possesses, the notion of belonging to a group whose members share if not identical at least similar cultural habits and characteristics. It is very much connected with the position a nation wishes to preserve in the international order, the nations it feels closer to for cultural and historical reasons and of course it provides the rallying point that defines and determines its goals for the future and principles and values that should remain uncompromised or widely preserved. In a Union of 25 member states with different political agendas reflecting a variety of policy objectives and national expectations, the shaping of a common list of priorities at the EU level is likely to be more challenging in the future. Defining the basic objectives of Community initiatives can become more demanding as now there would be 25 countries (or even more in the imminent future) with interests and concerns that need to be reconciled and addressed. Finding a balance between widely divergent

---

[34] See its content at: http://europa.eu.int/eur-lex/en/archive/2003/l_23620030923en.html, accessed 9 June 2005.

national approaches and directly opposed political considerations might involve one of the Community's basic tasks. For example the demands of the CEEC upon the Structural and Cohesion Funds, the respective needs of the Southern European countries on this front and the increasing reluctance of the net contributor member states to increase their funding may create a political framework that encourages a confrontational atmosphere in the EU especially as the latter reaches a point where it is becoming difficult to serve different interests.

In the area of foreign policy widely distinctive perceptions of the national or 'common European' interest may also lead to uncomfortable situations like the one that Europe experienced in 2003 with the war in Iraq. Especially now that the EU comprises countries such as Poland or the Baltic republics that share a common border with Russia, its relations with the former superpower may be influenced by a potential lack of consensus between those like France and Germany eager to find fields of cooperation and those more suspicious for historical reasons like the Eastern European member states, where the experience of Soviet domination remains fresh and vivid. The potential inclusion of Turkey, which shares common borders with the Middle East including Iraq, Iran and Syria, will create a whole new series of challenges for EU foreign policy makers. Furthermore, tensions might rise as the Convention for drafting the Constitution for Europe and the negotiations taking place in Nice in 2000 proved over the distribution of power in the Community institutions. The inclusion of countries which, with the exception of Poland, fall into the category of either medium sized or mainly small states has created concerns in bigger member states, especially Germany, that the EU will depend to an unacceptable extent on the representation capacity afforded disproportionately to smaller states by the current EU regulations. Thus, the issue of legitimacy came onto the Community agenda. The issue became the subject of wild negotiations in Nice and led to a compromise that was criticised for granting excessive power to countries such as Spain and Poland. The discontent evident on the German side was one of the reasons that promoted a new arrangement of the power distribution at the EU level, the outcome of which could be read in the pages of the Constitutional Treaty. However, the rejection of the relevant document by an overwhelming majority of the French and Dutch electorates brought the EU back to the arrangements introduced by the Treaty of Nice.

Thus, in a Union of 25 member states based on the principle of assigning a piece of their national sovereignty to central institutions that take decisions greatly affecting the life of all their citizens, it is extremely important that consensus can be reached and compromises can be made. If the latter is not possible then the EU will be doomed to suffer from malfunctions and inefficiency. Problems stemming from granting Brussels competence over a greater range of issues that used to be at the discretion of the national legislator were a popular source of discontent at the EU level long before the eight CEEC entered the EU. Other European governments had also expressed in the clearest possible manner (the example of the UK remains the most prominent so far) their dissatisfaction with the gradual shift of power from national capitals to Brussels. Apart from the obvious problems that the concentration of powers could cause and had caused in the bureaucratic mechanisms of the Union at administrative or organisational level, the whole issue was also seen as linked with a sense of identity. Governments felt that the granting of additional areas of competence to Brussels placed in peril certain elements of their sovereignty that touched the sphere of the unacceptable. And sovereignty forms a part of an identity of a nation, especially when the latter has recently fought hard to acquire it. The eight CEEC, which have recently joined the EU, fall within this category. The majority of them achieved independence only at the beginning of the previous decade after 45 years of either occupation or open foreign interventions to the extent of complete erosion of the principles of self-governing and sovereignty. It comes as a natural implication that the aforementioned nations, comfortable in their recently achieved sovereignty, would not want to dismiss but part of it necessary for their participation in the EU. Thus, they are not as enthusiastic for the 'ever closer union' principle stated in the Treaties as France or Germany or other most continental European countries. This has caused a sense of unease between different parties in the EU. Countries that were previously feeling the pressure to move forward towards the goal of achieving further integration, such as the UK, Denmark and Sweden, now feel more comfortable as their lack of enthusiasm is shared by many in the Eastern part of the continent. Different perceptions of what should be the national future objectives or how the national interest itself can now be better served vary to a significant degree within the EU framework.

Due to the completely different historical context within which Western and Eastern Europe evolved in the second half of the 20th century they ended up forming different national aspirations and divergent perceptions over the future direction of the European construction. Of course the distinction between Western and Eastern Europe is not one that can be easily and precisely drawn. As mentioned above, Western European countries such as the UK, Denmark and Sweden do tend to share the same or similar vision as most of the CEEC on Europe and its future direction. Thus, there is a conflict in the EU framework that starts from the basic premise of how to shape the future Europe and ends in differences over specific policies to be pursued at Community level.

Sovereignty is not the only issue which falls within the notion of identity. More important are the basic ideological principles so significant for a given nation as to form part of its collective identity. Problems may occur when these principles come into direct conflict with the core principles of other nations participating in the Union. This contrast can have fundamental repercussions if the issues involved are related to conflicting societal or economic models. Entry into the EU involves acceptance of the whole range of EU laws and policies so this problem appears to have been minimised. However, the referendums in France and the Netherlands on 29 May and 1 June 2005 proved that each nation remains strictly attached to its own cultural affiliations, including its own perception of the model to be followed in the organisation of its society and the development of its economy. The insistence of the French on their own societal and economic model in conjunction with the perceived threat from the 'Anglo-Saxon' economic model, and the notion that the latter is marching through Europe with the support of the Eastern Europeans, threatening the model of the social market economy championed by many continental European countries with France and Germany at the forefront, was one of the basic reasons for the French 'non' to the Constitutional Treaty. France felt that its economic model based on the existence of a generous welfare state would be put in peril by the domination of an absolute free market economy pioneered not only by the UK but also by the new entrants. This was perceived as a threat to France's basic societal values; a threat to its identity. 'The national identity is multiple and supersedes several factors, regional, national but also European . . . there is a crisis of the European identity of the French'.[35] Thus, enlargement was seen as a factor placing or accelerating the appearance of threats to the country's social model. The negative vote, apart from the other factors that definitely motivated it such as a wish to condemn the current political establishment in France with President Chirac as the main target, was, thus, among other reasons linked to the recent enlargement. 'One of the outcomes of the French referendum is that the enlargement of the EU is not popular anymore to the Europeans'.[36]

In the Netherlands the Constitutional Treaty was rejected also because the Dutch wished to hold onto their social model based upon liberal policies such as the decriminalisation of soft drugs and gay marriage deemed to be under threat from Brussels.[37] As the Prime Minister of the country Jan-Peter Balkenende has sincerely admitted, 'we understand there were worries about the loss of sovereignty, the speed of European integration, our financial contributions to the EU and the loss of national identity'.[38] 'Europe in general has

---

[35] *Le Monde*, 'La Persistence de l'attachement à l'Identité Nationale', 3 June 2005.

[36] Geremek Bronislaw, former minister of foreign affairs of Poland, *The Wall Street Journal*, 30 May 2005.

[37] *Le Monde*, 'Les Néerlandais ont rejeté massivement la Constitution européenne', 2 June 2005.

[38] *Independent*, 'What Now for Europe', Stephen Castle and Colin Brown, 2 June 2005.

more than a communication or image problem to grapple with. It has a real identity problem'.[39] The Prime Minister of the Netherlands himself and 80% of the members of the Parliament were active supporters of the Treaty, but 'fears of sovereignty and the imminent Turkish accession'[40] proved superior to trust in elected political representatives. According to the polls that analysed the vote, the Dutch felt that Europe had become 'so big that the status of countries such as the Netherlands in the framework of – a disparate membership of[41] – 25 would be diminished'[42] in a Europe engaged in a 'range of changes'[43] that appeared too fast to follow. People felt that somehow the basic principles underlying their collective identity had been put in peril.[44] 'It is time to pause and digest the addition of 10 countries last year, most of them poorer ex communist nations . . . what is wrong with standing still for a few years, rather than always rushing? All countries are becoming the same; we are losing our language, identity and traditions'.[45] 'The Dutch are on a train that is moving forward, but they don't know where the train is heading to'[46] noted characteristically the leader of the Dutch Labour Party Wouter Bos. Michiel van Hulten, a former MEP, declared that 'the message from France and the Netherlands is that they are unhappy with the way Europe is built . . . the enlargement of the EU was agreed in 1993, but it was only when it happened that the debate began'.[47] 'The vote represents an inarticulate nervousness about the expansion of the EU . . . a startled sense of how big the Union now is'.[48] The Dutch were one of the most

---

39 Schaeffer Ute, 'A Small Chance for Europe', *Deutsche Welle*, 1 June 2005, see: www.dw-world.de/dw/article/0,1564,1602667,00.html

40 *Financial Times*, 'Dutch Join French in Rejecting EU Treaty', Ian Bickerstone, 1 June 2005. See also: *Washington Times*, 'French Voters Reject EU Treaty', Nicholas Kralev, 30 May 2005.

41 *International Herald Tribune*, 'Politicus: After French "No" Vote, All Bets are Off on EU', John Vinocur, 31 May 2005.

42 *Le Figaro*, 'Le non des Pays Bas, nouveau choc européen', François Hauter, 2 June 2005.

43 *El Mundo*, 'Holanda rechaza la Constitutción Europea con un no aún más rotundo que Francia', 2 June 2005. See also the editorial of the Dutch newspaper Trouw, 2 June 2005, stating that the Dutch among others are 'seriously concerned about the development of Europe'.

44 *Le Monde*, 'Une révolte contre une Europe qui va trop vite, trop loin et coûte trop cher', 1 June 2005.

45 *Washington Times*, 'Politicians Try to Turn Tide for EU Constitution', David Rennie, 1 June 2005.

46 *Le Monde*, 'Le rejet de la Constitution par 61.6% des Néerlandais révèle l'ampleur du fosse qui separe l'Europe des citoyens', 2 June 2005.

47 See: http://news.bbc.co.uk/1/hi/world/europe/4601731.stm accessed 1 June 2005.

48 *The Times*, 'Goodbye Treaty, Goodbye Chirac but Europe will Muddle on', Bronwen Maddox, 30 May 2005.

fervent supporters of European integration but recently their enthusiasm has showed signs of entering a cooling off period due to 'the fear that the EU will interfere with the Dutch social model and . . . the imminent entry of Turkey in the EU'.[49]

Miguel Ángel Moratinos, the minister of Foreign Affairs of Spain, although he recognised the importance of enlargement for establishing peace and security in Europe, agreed that 'the enlargement of the EU to ten countries the previous year along with the perspective of further enlargement including Turkey, have generated many fears and questions to the European public opinion'.[50] Dominique de Villepin, the prime minister of France, after noting in his inauguration speech before the French Parliament that the French rejection of the Constitutional Treaty was not an overall rejection of Europe and its ideals, emphasised that the people 'want to know where it [Europe] goes. The rapid enlargement of the continent surprised our compatriots. Let's give ourselves the time to better know each other and build together with the new countries'.[51] He also added that: 'the 25-nation bloc's rapid expansion had "surprised" the French and made them fearful of the economic and social consequences'.[52] It is now a fact: a new concept of 'enlargement fatigue' may be in the course of emerging and it has to be addressed and dealt with immediately by European leaders.

Furthermore, additional pressure is also exercised by the future enlargement of the EU to include countries with controversial European credentials such as Turkey. This emerged as a factor that influenced the rejection vote in the two referendums. The new set of values that Turkey would bring to the EU, in the event of a successful entry has become the subject of disputes around Europe with public opinion in most countries in serious doubt over the necessity of such a choice that could see an end to any project of future integration and deliver a decisive blow to Europe's social model. In this context Angela

---

[49] *La Libération*, 'Le fosse qui s'élargit entre les nantis et les autres est un vrai débat', Nathalie Dubois, 2 June 2005. See also: *Abc*, 'Francia rechaza la Constitución europea y sume a la UE en una crisis sin precedente', Juan Pedro Qiuiñonero, 30 May 2005. See also: *Le Figaro*, 'Ankara pèse les consequences du rejet français', Marie Michèle Martinet, 31 May 2005. See also: *Guardian*, 'Dutch Say Devastating "No" to EU Constitution', 2 June 2005.

[50] *El Mundo*, 'Moratinos cree que el no holandés y francés a la Constitutión va a afectar a la ampliación', 2 June 2005.

[51] See the whole speech at: http://www.latribune.fr/Tribune/Articles.nsf/ArticlesWeb/ID05196A7503538215 C125701A00492BC3?OpenDocument, accessed 8 June 2005.

[52] *International Herald Tribune*, 'Villepin Unveils Plan to Cut Jobless Rates', 8 June 2005, see: http://www.iht.com/bin/print_ipub.php?file=/articles/2005/06/08/europe/ we.0608villepin.php.

Merkel has insisted that 'we must finally define the borders of the EU',[53] proposing a 'privileged relationship' with Turkey rather than full membership, an idea firmly opposed by Ankara but increasingly popular in European political circles. Taking into account the intensity of the relevant debate generated by the differing approaches to the issue along with the duration of Turkish preparations for potential entry that may take up to ten or fifteen years it is impossible to make a prediction at this stage in this book about the possible outcome of Turkey's efforts to join the EU.

Thus, the enlargement has accelerated changes already in train in the EU framework and exacerbated tensions that had been lying below the surface for some time now. 'This enlargement is therefore the start of an ongoing process that will change the character of the EU and challenge its fundamental values'.[54] The scale of different approaches to the same issues ranging from identity elements to the choice of a certain economic model and from foreign policy objectives to whether or how to proceed in future integration initiatives has been without precedent in EU history.

As stated above, this divergence in approaches over the basics of European integration has already been reflected in many aspects of the common European activities. Foreign policy objectives can serve as examples of recent expressions of an inability to perceive the 'common European interest', if of course we take for granted that such a widely constructed interest can indeed exist. The initial hesitant reaction of the EU towards the Ukrainian revolution in 2004 was shaken by the dynamic intervention of mainly Poland and other CEEC, which were quick to provide support both for the demonstrating opposition and for the future prospects of Ukraine as a member of the EU, while most of the other European countries were less willing to openly challenge President Putin's stance on the issue and risk entering into a new phase of uncertainty with Russia. Poland had no similar hesitations. The CEEC, once again due to their recent historical experience tend to view the United States as their natural ally guaranteeing their security from Russia, which they still view, if not as a threat, at least as a source of potential security challenges in their region. Therefore, they are more eager to be included in the category of European nations known in the international press as 'Atlanticists', namely the nations that share many of the common aims of US foreign policy and usually support in one way or another the related US foreign policy initiatives. The war in Iraq in 2003 and the rift between 'old and new Europe', as Donald Rumsfeld succinctly called it, proved that forming a common European stance in international affairs can be an issue that

53 *Le Figaro*, 'L'Europe assommée par les deux non', 3 June 2005.
54 Marise Cremona, supra note 30, p. 8.

stimulates vibrant debates between different European nations, provides grounds for open collision between European governments and leads to admittedly embarrassing situations for Brussels and a troubled sense of European unity. The perception currently dominant throughout Europe is that consensus would be more difficult to achieve amongst countries with such divergent historical experiences and therefore national interests. This serves as one of the most interesting features of the recent enlargement and has led to a certain degree of disenchantment with the EU (partly expressed also through the referendums) and with its ability to reconcile different approaches and emerge with a compromise solution providing sufficient guarantees to all conflicting sides.

THE ECONOMIC CHALLENGES

Social Policies

The urgency of the need to deal with the economic challenges stemming from the enlargement was clearly and spectacularly demonstrated by the outcome of the referendums in France and the Netherlands. It was proved that the recent enlargement had generated fears among the population of the EU of the 15 whose exact nature and scope was not perceived by European governments and policy makers at least at the initial stage. The enlargement to include poorer countries had raised concerns among a significant proportion of the population of the EU of the 15 related to reform of social policies and the nature of the social state across Europe, deregulation of labour markets, concerns over engaging in a 'race to the bottom' over the level of social and labour protection with the less protective Eastern European countries and fears of social dumping, a shift in spending on the Common Agriculture Policy and of course radical changes to the general structure and direction of the EU budget that would now have to accommodate the needs of the new much poorer member states from the East.

The governing elite of the EU and the member states that comprise it failed to prepare adequately the structures of the EU on the one hand and the public opinion on the other over the consequences of enlargement to the East. They failed to adjust EU policies, especially those of a budgetary and economic nature, to the new reality which had been radically altered by the introduction of ten new countries into the Union and nor did they promote the reforms necessary to encourage the smooth adaptation of European societies to the new post-enlargement political and economic landscape. The lack of debate about the decision to enlarge and the lack of willingness to adapt the policies necessary to allow the Western European countries to adopt to competition stemming not only from the Eastern part of the continent but also from the USA and the emerging powers of Asia such as India and China led to growing discontent among the wider public with the governing political powers across the continent and to an ever increasing disenchantment with the EU as a whole. The impact of the enlargement was frequently viewed as tantamount to a threat to the model of advanced social protection enjoyed by the citizens of many Western European countries. The sensitivity of the issue and its subsequent importance is high since it is related to the actual quality of life to be enjoyed in a certain society. This is due to the definitional scope of the term 'social policy', which includes the regulation of the labour market, social security, the welfare state, labour mobility, level of employment, the creation of new jobs, taxation and the financing of public services. In simple terms it rests on the foundations of the organisation of a society and it is strictly defined by the basic features of the life of its citizens. That is the reason why any real or perceived threat to it can create intense tensions and reactions on behalf of a great part of the public.

The model of increased social policy expenditure is jeopardised by both the adverse demographic trends in Europe and the competition from the Eastern European countries, which offer cheap labour, deregulated markets and greater freedom for employers to hire and fire employees. These parameters in combination with the lower tax rates introduced in many Eastern European countries that can function as a magnetic pole for Western European enterprises that rush to switch their business to the East have created a sense of insecurity among large sections of the public. Unless this problem is addressed now it may lead to reactions like those expressed through the referendums for the Constitutional Treaty. The stagnation which the euro area currently suffers and the contrasting dynamic growth rates in the Eastern part of the Union provide a conflicting image: an old Europe rallying to avoid being faced with the challenges of the future, aiming to preserve its wealth and consequently seriously doubting the necessity of choices such as the enlargement that could undermine the aforementioned objective. And a new Europe that is highly ambitious to cover the gap that still divides it from its Western counterparts. 'Many EU citizens question the governmental bodies' motives for wanting to achieve enlargement. They are wary that enlargement will not be in their best economic interest'.[55]

The construction of a welfare state was one of the central features of the European economic model, an important distinctive parameter that Europeans view as a part of their culture, an important societal principle that provides the

---

[55] Peter Katz, 'The Treaty of Nice and European Union Enlargement: The Political, Economic, and Social Consequences of Ratifying the Treaty of Nice', *Pennsylvania Journal of International Economic Law*, 24, 2003, p. 226.

basis on which the American and the European models can be distinguished from each other. The Europeans like the Americans have chosen to organise their societies on the basis of a capitalistic system founded on the concept of free market and liberal financial policies. However, the existence of a greater sense of social protection accompanied by a lower degree of labour insecurity on the continent is what has distinguished the two models. America is characterised by greater labour mobility, a deregulated labour market, fewer restrictions on the actual amount of time for which an employee can offer his services and a wider freedom to increase or decrease the number of employees in a given enterprise. This model has led to low unemployment rates and an increasing number of new jobs especially in the services sector in countries adhering to it. However, it has also contributed to the widening of the gap between the wealthiest and the poorest sections of society and is accompanied by low tax rates to public services that fail to meet the expectations of the public. In contrast, the European model based on a more advanced level of protection granted to employees, higher tax rates to businesses, a more regulated labour market that determines, sometimes in a rigid manner, the duration of employment and the conditions under which an employee can lose his job have led to a European workforce that enjoys more security in its personal professional prospects, more benefits, better social welfare and social security and more advanced public services due to increased public spending. However, it has also led to higher rates of unemployment, a factor which appears to be the price to be paid for sustaining a model that guarantees a certain quality of life but fails to provide the flexibility necessary for the creation of new jobs.

Europe was not presented with dilemmas over reform of its welfare state in the post-war years, because high growth rates in conjunction with favourable demographic tendencies made the functioning of its social security system possible. Europe managed to provide the funds necessary for the preservation of a model that allowed the inclusion of all segments of the society in on-going economic activities and the distribution of wealth to all individuals who had been employed for the necessary period of time through a generous social security and pension system. However, as we are heading towards the second decade of the new millennium, there are new challenges that, as mentioned above, can pose a threat to the continuity and sustainability of such a model.

The first is the adverse demographic trends that appear to be the dominant characteristic in the majority of European societies. These pose a threat to the financing of the system as they upset the ratio between the active employees who should be financing the welfare state through their contributions and the actual pensioners, who after a lifetime of employment are now the net receivers of several social security and pension schemes. The growing number of people of pension age in Europe in conjunction with the decreasing number of individuals of working age has shaken the whole welfare system construction to its foundations as it places great doubt over its future existence.

The second factor is growing competition from China, India and recently Eastern Europe. Competition with low wage and low tax countries will not be easy for the EU, which apart from promoting its competitiveness aims simultaneously to preserve its ability to guarantee an advanced level of social protection for its citizens. It should be noted at this point that the model of the 'social market economy' championed most prominently by the French has not been immune to criticism even from members of the French political establishment. Nicolas Sarkozy famously commented that 'the French social model is not a model because it does not create jobs'. Similarly, Patrick Devedjian, a former minister, commented that 'the French social model is not a model because no-one wants to emulate it. It is not social because it causes record unemployment'.[56] Thus, the main criticism stems from what appears to be an inability of the French economy to generate employment, something reflected in French unemployment rates of 10.2% in May 2005.

Tax, Wages and Unemployment

'Western European countries are having to reconsider the foundations of their economies as a low tax revolution in Eastern Europe gains momentum'.[57] The result of this is that investment flows and consequently jobs will be lured to the new member states away from old Europe. This system is based on imposing a common rate for income tax, company tax and VAT, which leads to a great simplification of the national taxation system. Slovakia introduced a flat tax rate of 19% in 2003 that encouraged large car makers such as Volkswagen to shift their industrial base there from Germany. The flow of investment to the country and the subsequent job creation in sharp contrast to the high unemployment rates observed in Western Europe with France and Germany as the principal examples have persuaded more countries to consider such solutions. Romania, which is set to join the Union in 2007 or 2008, has introduced a flat tax of 16%, which in combination with cheap labour and the prospect of membership has attracted investments fuelling a growth rate of 8% for 2004.[58] In the last quarter of 2004 Slovakia has seen its economy grow by 5.8%, while

---

[56] *The Times*, 'Blair puts Boot in Over Rebate by Marching to Moral High Ground', Charles Bremner, 15 June 2005.

[57] *The Times*, 'Flat Tax Revolution shakes up Europe', Anthony Browne, 19 March 2005.

[58] See the relevant data at: http://www.factbook.net/GDP_Comparison_data.htm, accessed on 12 June 2005.

France in the respective period grew by 2.3%, Germany by 0.5% and Italy by 0.8%.[59]

From being one of the three biggest economies of the euro zone, Italy slid into recession in 2005 as its GDP decreased by 0.2% in the first quarter of the year. The dynamism of the new members reflected in higher growth rates and the stagnation in the euro zone is a factor of concern for countries like the continental Western European countries, which retain social policies at the core of their economic planning. Thus, the new challenge for the rich high tax countries of the West is to successfully deal with the pressure exercised by the policies implemented in the new member states. Such policies, characterised by lower tax rates and cheaper labour, can attract many investors from the West, who can decide to transfer their activities to the more business friendly and less regulated and protective entrepreneurial environment in the new member states. The latter would generate higher unemployment in the euro zone, which would further undermine the ability of the relevant countries to finance their generous welfare schemes. The proposals for reform in the direction of deregulating labour markets using the American or the British model as a standard have been met with disbelief and spurred public unrest as 'to many in the rich high tax countries of western Europe, all of this smacks of the dreaded race to the bottom, long forecast by those who feared enlargement of the EU would lead to a loss of jobs and an erosion of the welfare state'.[60] The significance of the issue was underlined by the ongoing debate in the EU over harmonisation of tax around the EU. Consensus on the issue can only be agreed on the basis of unanimity as the Treaty of Nice has left the decision making for the approximation of tax outside the qualified majority voting process due to the absolute objection by the UK and Ireland to agree to such a solution. Harmonisation of tax across Europe is now even less likely to be passed since a growing list of Eastern European countries will join forces to prevent a decision that would deprive them of an effective competitive advantage. The issue has fuelled political tensions, with Joschka Fischer, the former minister of foreign affairs of Germany, arguing that the only reason that countries such as Slovakia can afford such tax cuts is the subsidies that they receive from Brussels, which are partially funded by Germany. According to Mr Fischer, Germany is actually providing the finance necessary to render such a system of tax cuts sustainable. Hence, he found it a paradox that Germany

---

59 See the Eurostat news release 12 May 2005, accessed at: http://epp.eurostat.cec.eu.int/pls/portal/docs/PAGE/PGP_PRD_CAT_PREREL/PGE_CAT_PREREL_YEAR_2005/PGE_CAT_PREREL_YEAR_2005_MONTH_05/2-12052005-EN-AP.PDF

60 *Economist*, 'The Impact of Central Europe's Tax Revolution', 5 March 2005.

should assist policies of other member states, which lead to investment and jobs being directed out of Germany to neighbouring low tax and low wage countries. Nicolas Sarkozy, current minister of Internal Affairs of France and an aspiring presidential candidate for the elections of 2007, has voiced similar concerns and embraced the fairness of reducing aid to countries which use it to preserve their low tax arrangements. Their proposals were quickly shelved by the EU,[61] but they revealed the tensions related to fiscal dumping that lie just below the surface.

The flow of investment eastwards and the creation of jobs in the respective countries by the transfer of businesses from the West is also accelerated by the enormous difference in wage levels in the two parts of the continent.[62] A survey conducted by the Federation of European Employers on wages across Europe revealed sharp differences among the current EU member states and shed light on the magnitude of the competitive challenge facing the Western European countries, especially those on the continent. In February 2005 weekly private sector earnings in France were €465, in Germany €749, in Italy €631, in the UK €635 and in Spain €433. In contrast to those figures, in flat tax Slovakia the weekly private sector wage amounted to €115, which is equal to 15% of the respective wage in Germany; in Romania €52, 7% of the wages in Germany; in the Czech Republic €143, 19% of the German wage; and in Bulgaria €35, an astonishing 5% of the respective German wage.[63] Moreover, according to the Eurostat, in 2003 minimum wage rates around Europe differed significantly from €56 in Bulgaria to €1369 in Luxembourg. In Romania and Slovakia the minimum wage was set at €73 and €118 respectively, while in France it was set at €1154 and in the UK at €1105.[64] The issue of productivity plays a very important role here; however, the degree of wage differences across the Union reveals the magnitude of the challenge to be

[61] See coverage of the event: http://news.bbc.co.uk/1/hi/world/europe/3705032.stm, accessed 5 June 2005 and http://www.lexpansion.com/art/26.0.78068.0.html.

[62] This is also reflected in the wide differences in GDP per capita in purchasing power standards in the EU. According to the Eurostat news release 164/2005–20 December 2005, GDP per capita in the EU ranged from 43% of the average EU25 in Latvia to 227% in Luxembourg. Estonia stands at 51% of the average, Lithuania at 48%, Poland at 49% and EU hopefuls Bulgaria at 30%, Romania at 31% and Turkey at 29% of the average. At the same time Slovenia left Portugal behind managing to achieve 79% of the average GDP EU25 per capita, while Portugal is at 72%.

[63] See the survey of the Federation of the European Employers at: http://www.fedee.com/payinasia.shtml, accessed 12 June 2005.

[64] See the Eurostat report at: http://epp.eurostat.cec.eu.int/cache/ITY_OFFPUB/KS-NK-03-010/EN/KS-NK-03-010-EN.PDF#search='minimum%20wages%20and%20EU', accessed 12 June 2005.

faced. Thus, a country such as Germany, France or Italy should find an adequate policy strategy to counterbalance the competitive advantages of the Eastern European countries, namely low tax regimes and low wages to promote the further development of their own industries. Such countries with a traditional adherence to the notion of the welfare state[65] will need to assume the initiatives necessary to tackle unemployment, stimulate growth, prevent the transfer of domestic industries to Eastern Europe and shape a delicate and effective balance that can simultaneously guarantee the existence of their social policies. Or they will have to deal with the realisation that achieving all of the aforementioned goals might prove impossible and therefore they will need to make choices that may prove painful for their societies such as introducing certain limits on the generous welfare systems enjoyed by continental Europeans from the post-war period to the present. It has to be accepted however, that enlargement has played a role in bringing all these debates to the forefront of political dialogue as competing with countries with such competitive advantages in the framework of the internal market will prove to impose great challenges to the Western European political world.

A practical example of this was recently offered by an incident in the small provincial area of Schirmeck in France, which managed to attract national attention and through headlines made its contribution to creating the national mood that led to the rejection of the Constitutional Treaty on 29 May 2005. A small transformer factory fired nine employees and announced its intention to move its business to Romania. It provided them, however, with the chance to be re-employed if they were prepared to move to Romania and assume the same positions under a revised salary of €110 'about a tenth of what they had been earning in France'.[66]

This incident, albeit on a small scale concerning a small provincial area of France, served as an indication of the nature of the future challenges for the EU, or at least for some of its members, and played its role in reinforcing the parties campaigning for a 'non' to the Treaty. Whether there was an actual link between the document and the post-enlargement economic reality remains to be seen; however public concerns especially of such a wide scale do have to be fully taken into consideration. The latter relate mainly to public doubts over the size and timing of the enlargement at a point where the candidate countries had not reached a sufficient level of economic development to allay fears of

---

65 See also the European Social Charter signed in the framework of the Council of Europe for 'the purpose of safeguarding and realising the ideals and principles which are [its members'] common heritage and of facilitating their economic and social progress', http://conventions.coe.int/treaty/en/treaties/html/163.htm.

66 *New York Times*, 'Fear of Regression in a Growing EU', Craig S. Smith, 19 May 2005.

social dumping 'within the Community's own limits'.[67] This rift between citizens' everyday life concerns and the political considerations of the European elites behind the EU decision making mechanisms culminated in the rejection of the centrepiece of the Union's integrative initiatives during at least the last couple of decades.

The significantly lower wages and taxes in the new member states together with their deregulated labour markets, which tend to impose fewer restrictions on labour mobility and fewer employment guarantees, have created a more 'flexible' or otherwise 'less protective' regulative regime that serves as a magnet for businesses already established in the more protective and regulated countries of the West such as France and Germany, where they are subject to higher tax. The phenomenon of the transfer of business from the more heavily regulated countries to the new member states in order to profit from the more business friendly institutional arrangements has gradually emerged as one of the most prominent issues on the political agenda of several European countries. It provided the basis for a wide range of disputes and counter-arguments which had a significant impact on the results of the referendums on the Constitutional Treaty. Fears of what large sections of the public and the opinion makers called 'social dumping' led a significant portion of the electorate to reject a Treaty that was viewed as the document that institutionalised and approved such tendencies. The fear of unemployment generated by the relocation of business in the EU framework and the undermining of labour rights and safeguards that European employees in certain areas of the continent consider part of their long-held privileges has led to a rift between large sections of the society and the governing elites. The issue in question was also very much related to the preservation of a certain societal model, which placed social policy at the core of its existence. As explained before, adverse demographic trends and the threat of 'social dumping' function as the main perceived challenges to the social model chosen as the preferred model by various European continental countries. And while public opinion cannot perceive as an imminent threat to its well-being the declining birth rates across the continent, the image of the 'Polish Plumber'[68] marching towards Berlin, Paris, Rome or Amsterdam was certainly more tangible and definitely more menacing.

---

67 Financial Newspaper, *Naftemporiki*, 30 May 2005.

68 *Le Figaro*, 'Le Fabuleux destin du petit plombier polonaise', Arielle Thedrel, 31 May 2005. Polish daily *Zycie Warszawy* talked about the 'petrifying effect of the Polish plumber in France', 30 May 2005. Greek daily *Kathimerini*, 'The Myth of "Polish plumber" has Proved more Convincing to Voters than the end of Europe', Konstantinos Kallergis, 29 May 2005.

The 'current member states fear the new members may apply lower social standards in the workplace . . . resulting in social dumping'.[69] These concerns were also taken into consideration at the signing of the Treaty of Athens on the accession of the new member states in 2003 resulting mainly in some restrictions on the free movement of workers from the eight CEEC to the EU.[70] Cyprus and Malta, probably due to a combination of reasons related to their relative wealth and small size, were effectively exempt from the restrictions. So, the old member states 'fearing social dumping and welfare tourism'[71] resorted to transitional restrictions on the movement of labour around Europe. Welfare tourism refers to the tendency of certain individuals to move to a country with a generous welfare state in order to intentionally profit from the benefits granted therein. These restrictions appeared to appeal mainly to the concerns voiced especially by the electorates of Germany and Austria over the imminent increase in the influx of migrant workers from the CEEC rather than resulting from any rational estimation of a potential flood of workers to the West. The respective governments pressed hard for such safeguards to be inserted into the Treaty and the European Council consented. Traditionally the fears of large-scale immigration from new member states to the old ones have assumed a central position in the pre-enlargement debates that tend to focus more on aspects of the enlargement that appear closer to populist outcries rather than on a full-scale analysis of the balance of benefits and challenges flowing from a given widening initiative. Such a detailed public debate over the enlargement to the East was wholly absent in the old member states and this amounts to a serious charge against the governing elites, which failed to present the European nations with a full account of the advantages and potential disadvantages of such a historic choice. The scale of the recent enlargement, which encompassed an unprecedented wave of ten countries, rendered a more responsible approach necessary. The EU sponsored a dialogue that was taken up with the decision to adopt measures only to appease wide public fears of a wave of immigration, which would have been very unlikely to occur anyway. The same fears were spectacularly publicised before the accession of Greece, Spain and Portugal only to be found to be exaggerated in the following years.

---

69 Jill Parker, supra n. 3, p. 610.

70 For the relevant provisions that set the restrictions see Annexes V–XIV in Part Four of the Act of Accession, Title I, Transitional Measures. Access the document at: http://europa.eu.int/comm/enlargement/negotiations/treaty_of_accession_2003/treaty_accession_28.htm.

71 Christophe Hillion, 'The European Union is Dead. Long live the European Union, A Commentary on the Treaty of Accession 2003', *European Law Review*, 29(5), 2004, p. 597.

The failure to launch a debate on the issue before the enlargement had actually taken place and the challenges emerging in the post-enlargement period linked mainly to fears of unemployment have incited public dismay as openly expressed in France with the opportunity of the referendum on the Constitutional Treaty. All the press articles at that time attributed the rejection of the Treaty to enlargement-fuelled economic and social fears linked principally to unemployment and social dumping without of course underestimating other factors such as those related to a rejection of national and Brussels-based political elites and the perceived threats to the notion of national identity already analysed above. The quest by the French electorate for 'another Europe . . . is a last cry to protect France's social system . . . France's central economic fear is decolonisation: the loss of jobs to low cost central and eastern Europe . . . fears of low wage workers embodied by a mythical Polish plumber flooding to France to undercut its wages and steal its jobs'.[72] 'Call it social dumping, outsourcing or the Bolkenstein proposal for the liberalisation of services in the EU, the subject is always the same: the fear of unemployment'.[73]

Thus, the relevant fears were further stimulated by the proposal for a directive on the liberalisation of services in the EU,[74] one of the most famous pieces of EU legislation up to now, which passed into history as the Bolkenstein Directive or under the vitriolic term 'Frankenstein Directive' that was effectively turned into the flag of the campaign against the Treaty in France. The proposal caused a storm in France and other European countries due to its aim to liberalise services across the EU and subject certain key public services to EU-wide competition. The basic provision that provided the grounds for the public backlash was the so-called country of origin principle, which constituted one of the main features of the proposed directive. According to the clarifications provided by the Commission itself, 'The country of origin principle means that when a service provider wants to provide his services into another member state without a permanent presence there, he has, in principle, to comply only with the administrative and legal requirements of his country of establishment. This means that Member States may not restrict incoming cross-border services from a provider established in another Member State by applying its own administrative and legal regime in addition to the requirements the service provider is already subject to in his Member State of estab-

---

72 *Economist*, 'A severe crise d'identité', 28 May 2005.

73 *Le Monde*, 'La crainte pour l'emploi est la raison principale du rejet de la Constitution par les Français', 30 May 2005.

74 See the proposal at: http://europa.eu.int/eur-lex/en/com/pdf/2004/com2004_0002en03.pdf, accessed 13 June 2005.

lishment'.[75] This provision assumed a central position in the campaign that preceded the referendum in France. The reason for its importance was the fears over social dumping and the consequent erosion of social policies. If service providers are to comply only with the legal requirements of their place of establishment, that can lead to countries such as France, Germany, Sweden or Belgium, characterized by a developed system of social protection and a notion of the welfare state central to their social structure, accepting that companies originating from Eastern European countries have to meet much lower standards related to wages, working time or labour protection. The effects of such a policy would be profound for the future of both the domestic industries of the relevant countries that would simply switch to the less regulated CEEC and of their welfare states that would suffer a severe blow from the relaxation of protection that would emerge as an effect of competition with the East or a race to the bottom as the proposal critics have called it. Thus, in the run-up to the French referendum and with the polls signalling the victory of the 'no' campaign fuelled by the relevant directive proposal, the European leaders decided to drop the proposal in its current form and agree to a far-reaching revision. President Chirac called it 'unacceptable for France and other European countries notably Germany, Belgium and Sweden' while the Swedish Prime minister Goran Persson commented that 'there is agreement to have a far reaching revision of the proposal which is in line with the social European model'.[76] Fears of undermining social protection and promotion of social dumping played a key role in the shaping of the tough stance on the issue taken by many European leaders.

The French no vote thus had 'cast a huge doubt on the entire direction of the EU' as the split between the British[77] and French leaders over whether the

---

75 See the details provided by the DG Internal Market of the European Commission at: http://europa.eu.int/comm/internal_market/services/services-dir/faq/200410-faq-point06_en.htm#63, accessed 13 June 2005.

76 See the BBC coverage of the meeting at: http://news.bbc.co.uk/2/hi/europe/4374007.stm, accessed 13 June 2005. *Guardian*: 'Chirac Takes Aim at EU Liberals in Race to Win Yes Vote', Nicholas Watt, David Gow, 24 March 2005. *International Herald Tribune*: 'Chirac Urges French to Back EU Charter', Graham Bowley and James Kanter, 24 March 2005. *The Times*: 'Liberalisation of EU Services hits Political Delays', Aine Gallagher, 27 March 2005.

77 The differences between the way the British and the French have approached the very same document are well documented. Although the French saw it as a document imposing the more liberal Anglo-Saxon model in Europe, the British, as the ambassador of the UK in Paris explained, saw it in a quite conflicting manner: as a document 'full of too social measures'. Although his personal opinion is that the document is 'neither liberal nor social' it is revealing of the contrasting approaches over the nature of the Constitution and the future direction of economic policies in the EU. The interview with Sir John Holmes can be read in *La Tribune*, 2 June 2005.

emphasis should be on free market economics or on granting importance to high social protection in the same framework 'is increasingly being seen in Brussels as a battle for the soul of the EU'.[78] Tony Blair of Great Britain was right to comment in the aftermath of the referendum that 'underneath all this there is a more profound question, which is about the future of Europe and in particular, the future of the European economy and how we deal with the modern questions of globalisation and technological change'.[79] This is further illuminated by claims that 'the result of the referendum showed that the majority of the French people did not reject Europe per se, but the neo liberal policies that influenced its construction and have been constitutionalised by this Treaty'.[80] In fact, when asked, 57% of the people that voted 'no' replied that they were not in principle opposed to further 'evolution of the European construction'.[81] They were, however, worried about the current direction that the particular construction had taken.[82] Exit polls also indicated that 'two thirds of people were voting on European issues; two fifths against unemployment and poverty. The linking theme appears to have been fear . . . that the Union's expansion to the east will destroy jobs in France'.[83] The question of enlargement 'played a key role in the referendum . . . with the risks of outsourcing, the Bolkenstein directive proposal and the Polish plumber . . . invoked by the supporters of no . . . so intensively that . . . at some moments there was the impression that the referendum was over the enlargement'.[84] Thus, the negative vote might have been driven by the more sentimental feeling of fear[85] for the future and its challenges but this statement does not invalidate the claim that along with other reasons the rejection of the Treaty entailed 'the rejection of the enlarged Europe that the Treaty embodied'.[86] The refer-

---

78 *The Times*, 'As Luxembourg Wavers, Poles and Czechs Wobble', Anthony Browne and Rosemary Bennett, 2 June 2005.

79 *New York Times*, 'French No Vote on European Constitution Rattles Contitnent', Elaine Sciolino, 31 May 2005.

80 *Le Monde*, ' "Trop liberal, trop inégalitaire", la Constitution a été rejetée par le nombreux enseignants', 31 May 2005. *Libération*, 'La Hollande, l'autre pays du non', Nathalie Dubois, 1 June 2005.

81 See the survey conducted by Canal Ipsos, at: www.ipsos.fr/ CanalIpsos/articles/1608.asp?rubId=19, accessed 30 May 2005.

82 Germany's leading paper *Die Welt* commented that the French rejection is in fact a 'good day for Europe' as the French had effectively rejected 'not Europe itself but, a wrong idea of it'.

83 *The Independent*, 'Chirac Seeks to Overcome Rejection with New Cabinet, John Lichfield, 31 May 2005.

84 *Le Monde*, 'Le non souligne les difficultés de l'élargissement', 30 May 2005.

85 Hungarian newspaper *Nepszabadsag*, saw it as a 'victory of fear over globalisation and fear of competition with Eastern Europe'.

86 *Kathimerini*, 'Why the French said "No" to Chirac', 31 May 2005.

endum turned 'into a judgment on the European Union as a whole'[87] and its central features such as the single market, which was 'excellent when it was first agreed, but the context has been changed by the enlargement to much poorer countries such as Poland and Slovakia'.[88]

The rejection of the Constitution has led to a so-called 'period of reflection' in the EU which will be used to absorb the outstanding effects of the popular vote and find solutions to the problem of the institutional adaptation of the Union after consecutive enlargements. The 'period of reflection' however has turned into a period of inaction during which, apart from some sporadic suggestions over the fate of the Treaty, the European institutions and the main European countries have remained without any visible plan for Europe's future direction. The Austrian Presidency for the first half of 2006 declared its intention to revive the efforts to deal with this issue, preferably by continuing the ratification process. The latter seems rather futile after its rejection by two of the founding members of the EU but such a plan seems to enjoy the approval of Angela Merkel, who would support the addition of a Protocol on the social dimension of Europe to the current text and its reintroduction for popular or parliamentary approval. The chances of such a proposal being successfully implemented remain bleak as it ignores the significance of the no vote for the internal political order of the two aforementioned countries. It also sends the wrong signal to the European peoples on how much their voice and opinion are valued in Brussels. Therefore, it did not come as a surprise that the Dutch Foreign Minister was quick to respond to these plans by bluntly declaring the Constitution as simply 'dead'. Similarly, Jacques Chirac basically declared the constitution dead, at least in its present form. He proposed so-called 'cherry-picking' from the text, basically the separation of the institutional part of the text from the rest and its implementation after approval by national parliaments, an idea not very popular in Berlin. President Chirac accompanied this view with his frequently expressed proposal to create 'pioneer groups' of countries to move forward ahead of others towards faster integration. In January 2006 the European Parliament expressed its view on how to overcome the 'constitutional crisis'. The Parliament based its report on the fact that no enlargement can take place after Romania and Bulgaria in 2007 or 2008 since the Treaty of Nice currently in force provides only for the enlargement of the EU to include those two Balkan countries. Therefore, Parliament proposed a wide public debate on the issue and a Constitution for

87 *The Economist*, 'So whose Bright Idea was the Constitution in the first place?', p. 52, 28 May 2005.

88 Laurent Fabius, former prime minister of France in *The Economist*, supra note 73, p. 52.

2009 to be submitted to public approval.[89] It is not clear whether the text of the Treaty will undergo changes or whether it will remain identical but with the addition of further protocols on issues related to voters' basic concerns so as to allay their fears and win back their support. In this sense this approach appears close to that of the current German leader.

Budget

Enlargement poses significant challenges to the drafting of the new budget of the EU. Taking into account that the new countries are poorer than the current members, there is significant pressure to redistribute Community funds. The delicate political issues flowing from such obvious need include the shaping of a balance with the previous net beneficiaries of the Union's financing, notably Spain, Portugal, Ireland and Greece and with the related political imperative on the wealthier members to reduce their budget contributions. Moreover, there is a need to redesign the allocation of funds from the Structural and Cohesion Funds to include the Eastern European regions, a great part of which is now eligible for funding. The conflicts between major political actors within the EU that preceded the European Council on 16 and 17 June 2005 underlined the existing differences and revealed the magnitude of the challenges which the enlarged Union has to deal with. The Presidency, at that time Luxembourg, proposed to dedicate 1.14% of European gross national income to the Community budget but this initial proposal met stiff resistance from the budget's main contributors, namely the Netherlands, Sweden, Austria, Germany, the UK and France, which insisted the proportion should be 1%. Although the Presidency felt that the amount initially proposed was necessary for the efficient development of EU policies aimed at meeting the new demands stemming from the incorporation of ten new countries, the group of the six main contributors rejected the idea of raising national participation in the funding of the EU budget. Some of the contributing countries, with France and Germany being the most emphatic examples, were facing domestic problems in dealing with excessive deficits infringing even the limits set by the Stability and Growth Pact, while other countries found no rationale behind their increased contributions. This created internal disputes reflected in the case of the Netherlands in the surprisingly overwhelming rejection of the Constitutional Treaty.

Within this context and with the spectacular 'no' votes in France and the

---

[89] See the Parliament's position at: http://www.europarl.eu.int/news/public/story_page/005-4526-16-1-3-901-20060119STO04525-2006-16-01-2006/default_en.htm, accessed 20 January 2005.

Netherlands to serve as a recent indicator of massive public discontent with many aspects of EU policies such as enlargement itself, the EU appeared to find it increasingly difficult to reach a consensus on the budget issue. Moreover, more thorny issues were threatening to exacerbate the process of reconciling contrasting approaches which was already in disarray. French President Jacques Chirac, having been faced with a recent embarrassment as the French electorate effectively rejected the Treaty (29 May 2005), had absolutely no scope for political manoeuvre and was not eager to demonstrate the necessary flexibility to compromise on issues essential for French public opinion such as finance from the Common Agriculture Policy (CAP). Furthermore, in an obvious attempt to divert attention from the loud French 'non' to the British side, he played a central role in emphasising the 'obsolescence' of the British rebate and its impact on the budget. His central argument was that the UK should abandon its rebate and thus, render any further major budget reform unnecessary.

On the other hand, the leader of the other major European country Chancellor Gerhard Schroeder was heading towards the summit significantly undermined by his heavy defeat in the state elections in North Rhine-Westphalia (22 May 2005), Germany's most populous state and his party's stronghold for the last 39 years. The magnitude of the defeat and the impact on his personal credibility was such that he was urged to call for early elections to be held in September 2005. With the polls predicting a comfortable victory for his political opponent, the Christian Democrat Angela Merkel, his presence on the European political stage was at that moment rather weak and evidently enfeebled. He dismissed proposals to reform the CAP before the budget agreement and positioned the considerable weight of his country in the same direction as France: against the British rebate.

Meanwhile, Tony Blair, deprived of the unfortunate commitment to refer the already rejected Constitutional Treaty to his own electorate and significantly reinforced by his recent re-election as Britain's Prime Minister for the third consecutive term (5 March 2005), rejected any demand to scrap his country's rebate (worth between 25 to 30 billion euros for the period 2007–13 to be covered by the new budget) as wholly unjustified since Britain contributed significantly to the EU budget without receiving substantial funding from the CAP in sharp contrast to France, which reaps the benefit of the Union's most expensive policy.[90] Mr Blair placed the reform of CAP as one

---

90 See: *The Times*, 'Europe Turmoil as Treaty Collapses', Philip Webster, David Charter and Anthony Browne, 14 June 2005. *Independent*, 'Blair Rejects EU Rebate Freeze', Jon Smith, 14 June 2005. *Guardian*, 'Sharp Disagreement at Blair Chirac Talks', Matthew Tempest, 14 June 2005. *El Mundo*, 'Blair dice que existen intensas diferencias sobre los presupuestos se l'Unión Europea', 14 June 2005. *Le Monde*,

of his top priorities, first because he thought, and he was not the only one, that dedicating 40% of the Community budget to agricultural expenditure mainly in the form of direct subsidies constituted a choice with a doubtful economic or political rationale. Secondly, Britain appeared to benefit from the CAP to a significantly lesser degree than other European countries even of much smaller size or economy. Furthermore, Mr Blair certainly did not forget the bitter European summit in Brussels in October 2002 when, outmanoeuvred by Jacques Chirac, he was forced to accept a limited reform of CAP well suited to meet French demands and interests pre-agreed between the French President himself and Gerhard Schroeder. The two leaders met privately before the actual summit and agreed on the financing of the CAP up to 2013 at around current levels, an outcome that Mr Blair viewed as a damaging blow to the developing world, although it did involve some reduction in the subsidies granted to current members states as the same budget would now have to be distributed to the newcomers as well. The fury of Mr Blair and his row with President Chirac during the summit went down in history as one of the most evocative moments at the usually grey European conferences due to the nature of the accusations and words exchanged between the two leaders, which made the entente traditionally binding the two countries distinctly less cordiale while it led to the postponement of the Anglo-French summit scheduled for December of the same year.

However, it should be stated that in the light of enlargement and the lack of willingness on the part of the net contributing member states to raise their budget contributions as shown at the European summit in Luxembourg in June 2005, further calls to reform the CAP are definitely to be expected. Furthermore, another significant EU country, Italy, was heading into elections in 2006 with its Prime Minister Silvio Berlusconi in agony over his electoral performance as the country entered the final year before the national elections. Thus, he was not ready to show any flexibility on issues of such importance for his electorate as the aid Italy received for its poorest regions, the Mezzogiorno in the south of Italy. He, therefore, appeared determined to veto proposals involving a significant decrease in the structural funds his country receives from the EU.

Spain, albeit a beneficiary of the EU funds, was alone in appearing surpris-

---

'Tony Blair parle d'un profond désaccord sur le budget européen', 14 June 2005. *Le Monde*, 'Budget de l'UE : Tony Blair juge "inacceptable" un gel du rabais britannique', 14 June 2005. *Le Figaro*, 'Budget UE : Blair parle d'un "désaccord aigu" avec Chirac', 14 June 2005. *Le Figaro*, 'Blair ne cède rien sur l'Europe et s'attaque au tandem Chirac-Schröder', 14 June 2005. *International Herald Tribune*, 'Blair Calls for Debate on Direction of EU', 14 June 2005.

ingly eager to compromise and receive decreased Community funding.[91] Spain demonstrated its European credentials in a rather hostile European political environment, caused by the rejection of the Treaty, which at the very end only the Spanish electorate approved by referendum, albeit with a feeble participation of only 42%. The Zapatero government, however, was swift to link its flexible position with a related flexibility on behalf of the British over the issue of their rebate. Despite the early signs of flexibility, Spain eventually was among the countries rejecting the proposed compromise (along with the UK, the Netherlands, Finland and Sweden) as they chose to do what almost the whole of the European Council did: defend their strictly defined national interests. María Teresa Fernández, the vice president of the Spanish government, declared that 'it is always better to return without an agreement than with a bad agreement for the interests of Spain'.[92]

In this context the Presidency proposed a compromise of 1.06% of EU income, a percentage significantly reduced from the previous 1.14%. Although Germany hinted at approving this proposal, the British and the Dutch remained firm in their insistence not to go beyond the set 1% threshold. The Luxembourg Summit on 16 and 17 June 2005, therefore, went down in history for two spectacular failures. The first was linked with the ambiguity over the status of the rejected Constitutional Treaty, which although it was not pronounced officially dead for reasons of a purely political nature, was put into a coma as a 'period of reflection' was chosen by the anxious European political leaders as the preferred solution to the recent electoral storms. However, it was mainly the second political failure that confirmed the view that Europe has entered one of the most crucial phases in its history. The lack of political will and ability to reach an agreement on such a fundamental issue for the Union as the budget was a source of great embarrassment for a Union that increasingly seemed to lose momentum. The whole discussion was characterised by mutual accusations, without precedent in the summit history of the EU, the vigorous safeguarding of strictly national interests and the demonstration of personal animosity, especially between the leaders of the UK and France. It was the latter two countries that placed themselves at the centre of the diplomatic arena by actively promoting the two most controversial issues of the summit; the rebate on behalf of the UK and the agricultural subsidies on the part of France. Mr Blair placed the reform of CAP as one of his top priorities, first because he thought, and he was not the only one, that dedicating

---

91 Spanish secretary of state for the European Union, Alberto Navarro, 'Spain will Accept EU Cuts if UK Rebate Pared', *Financial Times*, Leslie Crawford, 9 June 2005.

92 *El Mundo*, 'El gobierno considera que es major volver sin acuerdo que con uno que perjudique a España', 18 June 2005.

40% of the Community budget to agricultural expenditure mainly in the form of direct subsidies constituted a choice with a doubtful economic or political rationale.[93]

At the end it was obvious that some countries, notably Sweden and the Netherlands, did favour a reform of the CAP. However, it was recognised that it was impossible to agree upon such a reform during a two-day summit and without any previous preparation.

The proposals for reform, albeit popular in some European capitals, were largely viewed as the main tool that the British government would use in Luxembourg as a counter-argument to abandoning the rebate. As European diplomats put it, Mr Blair 'did have quite a few allies on the points he raised, but you cannot suddenly demand a fundamental review of the EU budget three days before the meeting'.[94] Thus, at the very end, the British rebate emerged as the greatest source of disputes at the EU level, leading to tensions between traditional 'rival parties' in the EU context such as the UK on the one hand and France, Germany and Luxembourg on the other, but also to a surprising rift between the UK and many Eastern European countries, which found themselves rather disillusioned by the diplomatic stance adopted by the British prime minister at the summit.

The stakes were particularly high for the CEEC, which aimed to receive for the first time after joining generous funding from the EU budget, a perspective that now appeared highly improbable. Their discontent became more evident when they viewed the UK, the country that strongly supported them during their accession preparations and throughout their initial period after their entry, as having become one of the central factors for the summit's failure.[95]

---

93 However, in an article published in the Greek newspaper *Kathimerini* the European Commissioner for Agriculture Mariann Fischer Boel dismissed these statements as 'irrational and detrimental'. 'The Danish commissioner points out that the CAP absorbs 40 percent of the EU's budget as it is the *only* policy that is funded exclusively by the Commission. The policy's actual cost does not surpass 0.43 percent of the EU's gross domestic product (GDP) – a figure that is set to drop to 0.33 percent over the next eight years. This is a small price to pay if one considers that the EC uses the CAP to avert the widespread desertion of rural areas, to ensure the production of quality foodstuffs, to offer incentives to farmers to protect the environment, as well as to protect the natural landscapes which play such a significant part in the lives of all Europeans', Mariann Fischer Boel in *Kathimerini*, 17 July 2005, the English edition accessed at: http://info.ekathimerini.com/4dcgi/news/content.asp?aid=934254

94 *Independent*, ' "Pathetic, Tragic, Embarrassing". And then things got really nasty', 19 June 2005.

95 See Polish newspaper *Rzeczpospolita*, 'London does Not want to Pay for the Expansion of the EU', 19 June 2005. Hungarian paper *Nepszabadsag*, 'It is Unacceptable that New EU Member States should be among those Financing the Rebate', 17 June 2005.

Consequently, in a rather dramatic gesture, the Polish Prime Minister, Marek Belka, headed a group of new Eastern European member states in offering to give up a part of their funding in order to reach a deal. In this context, Mr Juncker shaped the final proposal to be presented to the British prime minister, one that the latter could not reject as he unsuccessfully predicted. The foundations underlining the rebate (the fact that Britain receives back two thirds of the difference between what it pays to the EU and what it gets in return) would be sustained. The difference would now lie in the fact that money reserved for the CEEC as part of the Structural Funds would not form part of the amount from which the actual size of the rebate is determined. Mr Blair rejected the final compromise on the basis that the deal does not entail any change in the structure of the budget, especially in relation with the agricultural subsidies. This choice brought him into collision with traditional allies in the European context and the related statements were among the EU's most confrontational moments. Bertie Ahern, the Irish prime minister, called British arguments 'simplistic . . . and the spectacle pathetic and embarrassing . . . hating to see grown men bickering like that'.[96] 'Pathetic'[97] (and even more colourfully 'tragic') was the word that the always expressive French President chose in his effort to describe this situation. Mr Chirac does not rank among Mr Blair's political allies, of course, quite the opposite; thus, his outburst is viewed within the framework of his willingness to seize the opportunity provided by the open demonstration of dismay in the ranks of the CEEC and bring Mr Blair into the difficult position of defending his choices to countries politically allied to him.

Furthermore, Mr Juncker of Luxembourg, the President of the European Council at that moment, did not only feel as outraged as his French counterpart, but also 'ashamed as he heard the new member states the one after the other say that in the interest of the agreement they would be ready to renounce part of the money they are due'.[98] He also emphatically and rather sarcastically noted that 'he would hand over the presidency to Mr Blair without comment and advice, because clearly his advice is not appreciated'.[99] He is determined to stick to his decision even in the light of his statement that the EU is 'in a deep crisis'.[100] Etele Barath, the European affairs minister of Hungary, warned that the blockage would lead to 'extremely serious consequences', Jaroslaw Pietras, the

96 *Independent*, ' "Pathetic, Tragic, Embarrassing". And then things got really nasty', 19 June 2005.

97 *Guardian*, 'Rebate Row Wrecks EU Summit', Nicholas Watt and Patrick Wintour, 18 June 2005.

98 *International Herald Tribune*, 'Shame and Anger as EU Budget Talks Collapse', Elaine Sciolino, 20 June 2005.

99 Ibid.

100 *Der Spiegel*, 'Brussels in Crisis, EU Summit Collapse in Historic Failure', Hans-Jürgen Schlamp and Frank Dohmen, 20 June 2005.

Polish counterpart, stated that such consequences were made 'greater by the fact that the large, rich member countries weren't prepared to budge an inch on the amount they want to pay into the EU budget'[101] and blamed 'national egoisms'[102] for that.

Meanwhile, the foreign minister of Germany, Joschka Fischer, warned 'that the EU could become a conflict ridden bloc, unable to compete successfully in the global marketplace if the member states did not work together'.[103] Even more pessimistically, Michel Barnier, the former minister of foreign affairs of France, removed by Mr Chirac after the rejection of the Constitutional Treaty by the electorate, acknowledged the delicate point that the EU had now reached and concluded that 'the risk of the disintegration of the European project is very big'.[104] Wolfgang Schüssel, chancellor of Austria, was less dramatic and more realistic in recognising that 'it is certainly the question of the concept. The British want a different Europe. They want a more market orientated Europe, a large market but no deeper union'.[105]

This statement is closer to the main question that the EU will finally have to address: its future form. Will it proceed on the basis of a common market approach according to the British and Scandinavian idea of Europe, or as a group of countries politically coordinated in accordance with the Franco-German vision of Europe? Such a fundamental issue has to be resolved as soon as possible and indications of the way Europe will choose to evolve in the future can be found in the budget, as the latter includes the central projects to be funded by the EU. It comprises the central political aims of the EU to be funded by the member states.

The ongoing debates caused anxiety not only to the main beneficiaries of Community funding up to that point but also to the new entrants, as they realised that, in the hostile post-referendums EU political landscape, reaping the benefits of membership would not be as easy as initially perceived. It was evident that the EU was facing a new era with many of its central political choices in serious doubt. As an alarming confirmation of this, the EU Presidency decided not to make any reference to the enlargement plans of the Union in its Summit Conclusions. Although this may prove to be only

---

[101] *Independent*, 'New Members Review Relations with Britain after Rebate row', Stephen Castle, 21 June 2005.

[102] *Financial Times*, 'Poles Hit Out at National Egoism', Jan Cienski and James Blitz, 19 June 2005.

[103] *International Herald Tribune*, 'German Minister Warns of a Conflict Ridden EU', Judy Dempsey, 22 June 2005.

[104] *Le Monde*, 'Le risque de détricolage du projet européene est grave', interview with the former minister of foreign affairs, 21 June 2005.

[105] *International Herald Tribune*, 'Rival Views on the Future of Europe', Judy Dempsey, 21 June 2005.

symbolic, it serves as an indicator of the controversy accompanying future projects to enlarge in many European countries and was met with disbelief by future EU hopefuls.[106]

It was not until the European Council of 15 and 16 December 2005 that the European leaders agreed upon the financial perspectives of 2007 to 2013. After a dramatic meeting with several debates and intense negotiations, an agreement was reached and the budget for the next seven years was shaped.[107] The debate was fuelled once again by the UK's demand to maintain its annual rebate at acceptable levels, by France's openly asserted position not to renegotiate any further reform of the CAP before 2013 and by the wish of other countries, notably Germany and the Netherlands, to reduce their net payments to the common EU budget. Although the failure of the ongoing negotiations was hailed as highly possible by part of the European media, the sense that such a development would have triggered a massive crisis in the EU framework as the lack of funding would have lead to a halt to further enlargement and the rapid disillusionment of the current newly admitted Eastern European members, the European leaders were urged to reach a compromise. London feared alienating the eight new member states, which would have suffered to the greatest extent from the lack of an agreement in December as they would not have been able to fund the policies and projects necessary to converge with their Western European partners. These fears played a central role in reaching an agreement. The UK sensed that causing a rift with the new member states with which it shared common views on issues such as the need for economic reform or the future of the European structure would not be in its long-term interest. Therefore, it was more willing to give up part of the rebate, allowing a deal to be reached. Furthermore, during the summit Europe experienced the inauguration of Angela Merkel as the new leader of Germany. The latter made a rather impressive appearance in the summit acting as an 'honest broker' mainly between the UK and France[108] and contributed significantly to reaching

---

106 See http://euobserver.com/?aid=19314&rk=1, 13 June 2005.

107 The text of the agreement is found at Document 15915/05, Council of the European Union, Brussels, 19 December 2005, CADREFIN 268, Financial Perspectives 2007–2013.

108 The latter through its Foreign Minister Philippe Douste Blazy linked the agreement on the budget in December with granting candidate status to the Former Yugoslav Republic of Macedonia. France, at an EU foreign ministers' meeting preceding the European Council, refused to consent to grant FYROM candidate status for fear that it would send the wrong political signal to its public, namely that a new round of enlargement was imminent. Apart from trying to capitalise on the unpopularity of further enlargement especially to include the Balkans, the French linked the case of FYROM to a budget agreement in December. As initially anticipated, after an agreement was reached Paris retreated from its initial position and accepted the granting of candidate status to FYROM albeit with no set date for opening negotiations. The

the much needed agreement as she successfully proposed a spending ceiling while she reversed part of the cuts initially planned for Eastern European nations, paving the way for consensus. Her role as an honest mediator between conflicting parties was widely praised[109] and led to speculations over the future political position of Germany on European affairs as the close relationship with France appeared to have reached its limits.

Under the agreed compromise EU spending will not exceed 1.045% of the Union's GNI. This amount is equal to 862.363 billion euros. Tony Blair ceded €10.5 billion from the British rebate of the 2007–13 period, securing in return a commitment on behalf of France and the rest of the Union that the European Commission will institute a wide ranging review of the budget as early as in 2008 or 2009. This review will be focused on reducing, possibly radically, the agricultural spending of the Union, which currently stands at 40% of the EU budget and the Union's resources including the British rebate. This was a significant political success for Tony Blair, the extent of which is, however, limited by the need to achieve unanimity in passing such changes to the structure of the budget. Therefore, Tony Blair has secured the re-opening of a wide debate in 2008 over the future priorities of Europe that deserve funding from its budget but has not in any way managed to render these changes compulsory. Reaching unanimity in 2008 over potential budget reform means that the consent of France and other countries which enjoy significant benefits from the CAP would be absolutely necessary for an agreement. Otherwise, the negotiations would have to be repeated in 2013 and then all the issues ranging from the CAP[110] to the actual structure of the whole budget would be open,

---

European Commission had recommended the offering of such status to FYROM in November 2005. See: Communication from the Commission, Commission Opinion on the application from the former Yugoslac Republic of Macedonia for membership of the European Union. Brussels, 9 November 2005, COM (2005) 562.

109 Chancellor Wolfgang Schussel of Austria stated that 'she played an extraordinary important role behind the scenes' (see Graham Bowley, 'Deal Gets EU Out of Doldrums', *International Herald Tribune*, 19 December 2005) and Anders Fogh Rasmussen, the Prime Minister of Denmark noted that 'she has played an immensely positive role in the negotiations in part by contributing in relations to both France and Poland and in part by at a key moment showing flexibility when it came to the overall expenditure ceiling'. See the BBC report with leaders' statements at http://news.bbc.co.uk/2/hi/europe/4537304.stm, accessed 17 December 2005.

110 The trade deal reached by the 149 countries of the WTO in Hong Kong on 17 December 2005 is highly relevant here. As a part of that deal farm export subsidies will be progressively phased out by 2013. Obviously, Peter Mandelson as the representative of the EU consented to that date as a starting point of reform of the CAP as well. It is not a coincidence that the agreement in Hong Kong came 24 hours after an agreement was reached in Brussels. The substantial reduction in export subsidies will be an aspect to be taken seriously into account when the European leaders reshape CAP in 2013. It now constitutes an obligation of the EU towards the rest of the WTO members.

leaving the European leaders able to shape a new set of parameters for the function of the Union, implement radical reforms on its current policies or even change its future political orientation.

Therefore, it is evident that although the 2007–13 budget debate is now over[111] the battle for the future direction of Europe has actually just begun. If in 2008 or more likely in 2013 the European leaders decide to radically reform the structure of the budget shaping a new list of priorities for the Union, this would constitute a political choice which would herald a new era for the EU, setting its function on a completely different basis. Paving the way for future reform was at the very centre of the debate in Brussels in the first place. The actual amount of the budget that the UK proposed setting at €862.4 billion was not much lower than the €871 billion that Luxembourg had proposed in June only to cause a storm in most European capitals. Six months later Luxembourg warmly welcomed the new budget proposal. The amount of €9 billion, albeit definitely important, was not the factor that sank the previous proposal and plunged the EU into a new crisis. It was the lack of any certain timetable for change that enraged those countries in Europe that sought change and reform. The new budget provides for just that, signalling the beginning of a new era for the EU. As Jose Manuel Barroso[112] stated, 'the budget provides the means for the realisation of our common goals' and actually defining which goals are to be considered as common at European level will be at the centre of the debate in 2008. Will the EU promote more integrationalist policies or will it evolve in a different direction? Will it be focused on facing the challenges of globalisation by introducing more liberal policies with the UK or Eastern Europe as its pattern or will it continue with reforms in the path of social Europe?[113] Will it continue to work as a group of 25 or 27 along with the states

---

[111] As expected, however, the European Parliament rejected by an overwhelming majority the text of the budget agreement consistent with its previous decision to reject the Council proposal for the Financial Perspectives of 2000–2006 as well. Back then it managed to get more funding from the EU leaders but at the moment with stagnation in much of the euro zone and discontent in the Netherlands such a compromise is not as possible. Negotiations between the Parliament and the Council are to start soon and it is hoped a solution can be found before July. See the Parliament's position at: http://www.europarl.eu.int/news/expert/infopress_page/034-4219-37-2-6-905-20060112IPR04218-06-02-2006-2006—false/default_en.htm, accessed 13 January 2006 and http://www.europarl.eu.int/news/expert/infopress_page/034-4415-18-1-3-905-20060118IPR04414-18-01-2006-2006—true/default_en.htm, accessed 20 January 2006.

[112] See his article in Greek newspaper *Kathimerini*, 'European Union: A Budget Fair for All', 4 December 2005.

[113] Jacques Chirac writing in *Kathimerini*, noted that the most adequate model for Europe is 'the social economy of the market. Its commitment is freedom with solidarity, public powers as guarantor of the general interest . . . the rejection of such an ideal

of Bulgaria and Romania or will it comprise groups of countries working more closely on certain areas while others choose to abstain, having the euro or the Schengen areas as obvious examples? These are absolutely fundamental questions that will have to be considered in the next seven years.

Structural and Cohesion Funds

The lack of consensus at the level of the European leaders on the issue of the budget is disappointing taking into account the gravity of the problem the Union faces. The new member states, which entered the Union with strong aspirations of raising the quality of life of their citizens and creating the infrastructure necessary to fund their development, have based their policies on the expectation of receiving certain financing from Brussels. According to new Council Regulation 1260/1999 on the Structural Funds,[114] the latter (including the European Regional Development Fund (ERDF), the European Social Fund (ESF), the European Agricultural Guidance and Guarantee Fund (EAGGF), Guidance Section, and the Financial Instrument for Fisheries Guidance (FIFG)),[115] will contribute among others things to 'promoting the development and structural adjustment of regions whose development is lagging behind',[116] the so-called 'Objective 1' regions. The European regions falling within the crucial definition of the 'Objective 1' regions are those 'whose per capita GDP, measured in purchasing power parities and calculated on the basis of Community figures for the last three years available on 26 March 1999, is less than 75% of the Community average'.[117] The areas falling within the 'Objective 1' areas will receive the lion's share of the Community funding. Between 2000–2006 the 'Objective 1' areas received 70% of the Structural

would be a betrayal of European heritage. For these reasons France will never accept the transformation of Europe into a free trade zone. This is the reason why we should promote the plan for a political and social Europe based on the principle of solidarity . . . we should allow the countries which wish to cooperate in fields falling out of the common policies to do so. Countries that possess the political will and means should have the chance to form pioneer groups . . . such as the Euro area or the Schengen group . . . the members of the Euro zone will have the ability to further deepen their political, social and economic integration'. See Jacques Chirac, *Kathimerini*, 26 October 2005.

114 Council Regulation (EC) No 1260/1999 of 21 June 1999 laying down general provisions on the Structural Funds, *Official Journal* L 161, 26/06/1999 P. 0001 – 0042. It can also be accessed at: http://europa.eu.int/eur-lex/lex/LexUriServ/LexUriServ.do?uri=CELEX:31999R1260:EN:HTML

115 Article 2(1) of the Regulation.

116 Article 1(1) of the Regulation.

117 Article 3(1) of the Regulation.

Funds 195 billion euro budget.[118] 'Objective 2' areas include areas with 'structural problems whose socio-economic conversion is to be supported and whose population or area is sufficiently substantial. They shall include in particular areas undergoing socio-economic change in the industrial and service sectors, declining rural areas, urban areas in difficulty and depressed areas dependent on fisheries'.[119] 'Objective 2 areas can receive funds only from the ERDF and ESF, while the respective 'Objective 1' areas can receive funds from all the Funds involved. Finally, the areas defined as 'Objective 3' are those not covered by 'Objective 1'[120] and are funded mainly by the European Social Fund. Thus, it is easily understood that the threshold of 75% is of maximum importance for defining the regions which will be the recipients of significant financial aid on the part of the EU. The interesting point is that after the entry of the eight Eastern European countries, which were poorer than the existing members, the average Community income has dropped significantly. Therefore, various regions in Spain or Greece, which received significant Community funding, were now found to exceed the threshold and hence, were instantly rendered ineligible to receive future funds. This rapid shift in the catalogue of areas now eligible to benefit from the Structural Funds has created concerns over a potential sharp increase in the financial means allocated to the funding of the relevant projects and also spurred reactions from the citizens of the countries previously benefiting who viewed the imminent interruption of funding as a serious obstacle in regional development. Some example of the differences to be brought by the insertion of the new regions in the 'Objective 1' catalogue can be viewed by the research undergone by the Eurostat.[121] Taking into account that the EU-25 average volume index of GDP per inhabitant in Purchasing Power Standards (PPS) is 100 the following indicative findings were produced:

---

118 See the European Commission site at: http://europa.eu.int/scadplus/leg/en/lvb/l60014.htm, accessed 14 June 2005.

119 Article 4(1) of Regulation No. 1260/1999.

120 Article 5 of the Regulation.

121 Eurostat, Regional Breakdown of GDP per capita, percentage of EU-25 average, at: http://epp.eurostat.cec.eu.int/portal/page?_pageid=1996, 39140985&_dad=portal&_schema=PORTAL&screen=detailref&language= en&product=sdi_ed&root=sdi_ed/sdi_ed/sdi_ed_inv/sdi_ed1130, accessed on 14 June 2005. See also the Eurostat news release 47/2005 of 7 April 2005 on the Regional GDP per Capita in the EU-25. According to that the five lowest regions in the ranking were all in Poland with a GDP per capita ranging from 32% to 36% of the EU-25 average. The catalogue of the lowest ten was completed by two regions from Hungary, one from Slovakia, one from Latvia and one more from Poland. Their GDP per capita stood at 37% to 39% of the average.

Table 1.1 GDP per inhabitant in purchasing power standards

	1995	1996	1997	1998	1999	2000	2001	2002
Région de Bruxelles-Capitale/ Brussels Hoofdstedelijk Gewest	243.3	243.8	239.6	240.4	240.3	238.2	238.6	234.5
Praha	128.5	130.6	133.3	137.7	138.7	139.1	149.6	152.8
Strední Cechy	54.1	55.5	54.3	53.6	54.4	53.9	53.8	55.3
Jihozápad	66.6	69.1	66.1	62.4	60.8	60.3	59.8	61.1
Severozápad	66.5	67.2	62.0	58.0	55.3	53.5	52.5	53.9
Severovýchod	60.3	61.7	60.4	56.8	55.6	55.1	54.9	56.7
Jihovýchod	62.5	64.7	61.5	59.0	57.3	56.6	58.0	59.8
Strední Morava	59.3	60.7	59.0	54.7	53.0	51.8	51.9	52.4
Moravskoslezko	66.0	69.4	65.0	59.7	56.4	54.2	55.1	56.5
Estonia	35.5	37.1	40.5	41.8	41.1	43.4	44.7	46.6
Kentriki Makedonia	70.1	73.4	74.8	73.5	73.3	73.8	74.7	78.9
Sterea Ellada	107.8	110.0	107.7	105.0	99.6	102.7	104.2	108.9
Peloponnisos	64.9	64.3	68.3	69.3	69.0	71.0	72.6	77.3
Attiki	77.8	74.2	73.8	73.8	74.9	76.4	78.0	82.3
Voreio Aigaio	60.0	60.5	63.9	63.7	66.4	69.7	73.6	79.3
Notio Aigaio	77.9	80.7	85.1	83.0	85.2	85.3	86.7	91.0
Kriti	71.0	72.3	71.9	70.7	71.4	70.5	71.0	75.1
Castilla-la Mancha	71.8	72.4	71.8	73.3	74.3	73.8	74.3	76.0
Comunidad de Madrid	115.2	115.2	115.8	119.6	123.1	122.8	124.4	126.7
Campania	73.0	71.9	72.3	73.1	72.2	71.3	72.2	71.9
Puglia	74.3	74.4	72.1	72.9	73.5	72.5	72.6	72.5
Basilicata	78.1	79.8	79.2	80.3	81.6	78.9	77.4	76.4
Calabria	68.2	67.5	67.6	67.9	68.5	67.6	68.5	67.7
Sicilia	74.1	74.0	73.3	73.6	72.2	71.9	72.8	71.3
Sardegna	84.6	84.0	84.1	84.3	84.0	82.1	83.6	82.3
Cyprus	85.4	84.2	83.0	83.7	84.6	85.7	88.7	82.9
Latvia	29.8	30.8	32.8	33.8	34.2	35.5	37.4	39.0
Lithuania	34.1	35.4	37.2	39.1	37.7	38.5	40.7	42.4
Luxembourg (Grand-Duché)	178.7	177.6	184.7	192.9	208.1	218.4	213.0	212.7
Közép-Dunántúl	44.9	45.4	48.5	50.7	49.3	52.0	53.1	51.8
Nyugat-Dunántúl	51.0	51.9	53.2	57.1	60.4	60.8	59.5	60.8
Dél-Dunántúl	40.5	39.6	39.3	39.9	40.9	39.7	41.5	42.8
Észak-Magyarország	36.1	34.2	34.0	35.1	34.9	34.3	36.6	37.3
Észak-Alföld	35.3	34.8	34.9	35.0	33.7	33.8	37.3	37.7
Dél-Alföld	41.2	40.2	39.4	39.4	39.2	38.0	39.9	40.4
Malta	69.8	70.9	72.0	71.9	77.6	77.8	73.4	73.2
Lódzkie	37.4	36.8	39.5	39.9	41.7	41.7	41.3	41.3
Mazowieckie	51.4	57.6	60.9	66.1	68.4	67.1	69.6	69.5
Malopolskie	35.9	37.7	39.5	40.6	40.5	41.0	39.1	39.5
Slaskie	49.7	50.5	51.5	49.9	49.9	51.2	50.1	50.6

	1995	1996	1997	1998	1999	2000	2001	2002
Lubelskie	31.5	32.2	32.9	32.9	32.1	32.3	32.4	32.0
Podkarpackie	31.2	32.3	33.7	33.9	33.2	32.9	32.9	32.6
Swietokrzyskie	32.0	32.8	33.6	34.5	35.4	36.3	35.4	35.7
Podlaskie	31.0	33.0	35.0	34.7	33.5	34.8	35.2	35.1
Wielkopolskie	39.9	42.2	45.8	47.3	47.8	49.1	48.4	47.1
Zachodniopomorskie	42.3	43.8	44.6	44.4	46.2	47.7	46.2	45.1
Lubuskie	40.2	39.5	40.8	41.3	41.6	42.3	41.2	39.9
Dolnoslaskie	42.2	44.3	45.5	44.8	46.5	48.3	46.9	47.4
Opolskie	39.8	39.4	40.2	40.1	38.5	39.6	37.9	37.4
Kujawsko-Pomorskie	40.5	40.0	40.3	41.6	40.6	41.9	41.8	41.6
Warminsko-Mazurskie	32.4	33.8	34.9	34.7	35.6	35.8	34.3	34.1
Pomorskie	41.6	42.2	43.9	44.9	46.8	46.6	45.3	45.5
Norte	62.2	62.1	61.8	62.2	63.4	62.6	61.7	61.5
Centro (PT)	59.7	59.8	59.8	60.7	62.6	63.2	63.0	63.0

The figures include some of the new areas added into the 'Objective 1' list, while some previously funded regions, especially in Greece, Italy, Portugal and Spain, are now found to be beyond the threshold and are therefore ineligible to receive aid from the EU.

Similar issues are raised over the allocation of the Cohesion Funds. According to Regulation No. 1164/94,[122] 'the Fund shall contribute to the strengthening of the economic and social cohesion of the Community'.[123] 'The Fund shall provide financial contributions to projects, which contribute to achieving the objectives laid down in the Treaty on European Union, in the fields of the environment and trans-European transport infrastructure networks in Member States with a per capita gross national product (GNP), measured in purchasing power parities, of less than 90 % of the Community average which have a programme leading to the fulfilment of the conditions of economic convergence referred to in Article 104c of the Treaty'.[124] Furthermore, 'an indicative allocation of the total resources of the Fund shall be made on the basis of precise and objective criteria, principally population, per capita GNP and surface area; it shall also take account of other socio-economic factors such as deficiencies in transport infrastructure'.[125] Thus, 'until the end of 1999, only

[122] Council Regulation (EC) No. 1164/94 of 16 May 1994 establishing a Cohesion Fund, *Official Journal*, L 130, 25/05/1994 P. 0001–0013. Accessed also at: http://europa.eu.int/smartapi/cgi/sga_doc?smartapi!celexplus!prod!DocNumber&lg=en&type_doc=Regulation&an_doc=1994&nu_doc=1164.

[123] Article 1 of the Regulation.

[124] Article 2 of the Regulation.

[125] Article 5 of the Regulation.

the four Member States which currently meet the criterion regarding per capita GNP referred to in paragraph 1 shall be eligible for assistance from the Fund. Those Member States are Greece, Spain, Ireland and Portugal'.[126] However, 'total annual receipts from the Cohesion Fund under this Regulation, in combination with assistance provided under the Structural Funds, should not exceed 4% of national GDP'.[127] 'If the GNP of a Member State benefiting from the Cohesion Fund rises above the 90% threshold, it may no longer receive funding for new projects or new project stages . . . if a review establishes that a Member State is no longer eligible, financial support from the Cohesion Fund will cease'.[128] Thus, it is possible that when the next review takes place the current countries which benefit from the activities of the Cohesion Fund will no longer be eligible to receive the relevant financing, while the inclusion of the eight Eastern European countries will create a considerable burden on the general finances of the EU. Currently, according to the provisions of Regulation No. 1264/1999, the Cohesion Fund has been granted 18 billion euros for the period 2000–2006.[129] The same Regulation states that 'In the event of a member state becoming ineligible, resources for the Cohesion Fund will be reduced accordingly'.[130] According to Annex I of the relevant Regulation, Spain receives the lion's share of the funds: 60% of the whole. The inclusion of the new countries has created new parameters that need to be fully taken into account. Therefore, the Commission has opened the debate for the 'future of the Cohesion Policy over 2006'[131] in order to adjust it for the post-enlargement period and the challenges therein.

---

126 Article 2(2) of the Regulation.

127 Article 5 of Council Regulation (EC) No. 1264/1999 of 21 June 1999 amending Regulation (EC) No. 1164/94 establishing a Cohesion Fund, *Official Journal* L 161, 26/06/1999 P. 0057–0061, accessed also at: http://europa.eu.int/eur-lex/lex/LexUriServ/LexUriServ.do?uri=CELEX:31999R1264:EN:HTML See also: Council Regulation (EC) No. 1265/1999 of 21 June 1999 amending Annex II to Regulation (EC) No. 1164/94 establishing a Cohesion Fund, *Official Journal* L 161, 26/06/1999 P. 0062–0067. Accessed also at: http://europa.eu.int/smartapi/cgi/sga_doc?smartapi!celexplus!prod!DocNumber&lg=en&type_doc=Regulation&an_doc= 1999&nu_ doc= 1265

128 See European Commission site on the Cohesion Fund, http://europa.eu.int/scadplus/leg/en/lvb/l60018.htm, accessed 14 June 2005.

129 Article 4 of Regulation 1264/1999.

130 Ibid.

131 See contributions to the debate at: http://europa.eu.int/comm/regional_policy/debate/contri_member_en.htm. See the relevant Conclusion of the Italian Presidency in Rome, 20 October 2003: http://europa.eu.int/comm/ regional_ policy/ debate/document/futur/ member/rome_201003.pdf, accessed 14 June 2005.

THE FUNDAMENTAL QUESTION: WHAT KIND OF EUROPE DO WE WANT?

European integration has up to now been mainly a choice made on behalf of the European peoples by the political elites. This statement does not deprive it of its democratic legitimacy as aspects of it have been approved by electorates in several instances especially in national elections or in the elections for the European Parliament. The majority of public opinion in most European countries has approved or seemed to consent to the central choices made at EU level, a tendency that apart from national elections has also been confirmed by opinion polls and referendums on European issues, like the ones on the Treaty of Maastricht paving the way for the common currency which constitutes the cornerstone of integration efforts in the last half of the 20th century. The political parties supporting further integration at EU level enjoy mainstream status in most European countries, while the related political initiatives are supported by parties across the whole range of the political spectrum as European integration has emerged as the central area of consensus between the centre right and social democratic political forces across the EU, with limited exceptions, the most prominent of which remains the Conservative Party in the UK. Usually, anti-European political forces received political credit only during the (usually low profile) elections for the European Parliament.

Thus, public consent to central choices such as the issuing of a common currency, the abolition of cross-border controls initiated by the Schengen Treaty and most recently the enlargement and the unfortunate Constitutional Treaty was taken for granted on the basis of an admittedly limited debate within the framework of all or of the significant majority of the European societies involved. However, the decision to set the people aside, avoiding a vibrant public debate on European-related issues and presuming that public apathy equals consent has reached its absolute limits as the spectacular rejection of the Constitutional Treaty by the French and Dutch electorates – and probably by more nations if further referendums were to be held – has painfully proved. Central choices with a massive impact on the life of European citizens such as the rapid enlargement to encompass ten new countries at once and the issuing of a document with the aim of embodying the Constitution of the European Union cannot continue to be undebated and unchallenged at the public opinion level.

The EU has recently proved that it does suffer from a democratic deficit, a favourite term in the relevant literature for more than 20 years, since it failed to connect its central policy goals to public aspirations and therefore failed to match the expectations of the European peoples. The latter remain more confused than ever as the Union moves forward at an extremely rapid pace while failing to explain to the electorates involved the rationale behind its policies and objectives. The recent enlargement was a victim of the Union's lack of a communication strategy. It fails to explain its political agenda to the people and to provide them with a convincing explanation of its presumed necessity. Furthermore, the tendency of the national governing elites to attribute necessary but usually painful and therefore politically costly economic or political reforms to Brussels has significantly eroded the image of the latter in the public view. The tendency of national governments to refuse to take responsibility for the reforms introduced and to link them to the demands stemming from membership have discredited both national governing elites and the European Union as a whole in the eyes of the electorates.

The political situation in France preceding the referendum serves as a revealing indication of an enfeebled political leadership failing to convince its public over one of its central choices. The electorate lacked confidence both in its national leaders and in the Union's decision to enlarge without providing substantial information on the actual benefits from such a choice and without actually engaging in the adjustment necessary to achieve the smooth inclusion of new members in the already stagnation-hit EU. The transition that the economies of the West needed to experience in order to be in a position to compete with the emerging powers in Asia, the USA and of course with the Eastern European countries was not as bold as it should have been, the relevant reforms produced limited results and were blamed by the national elites on Brussels. Consequently, the credibility of the actors involved received a decisive blow and the European nations, when called on to vote, grasped the unique opportunity to effectively express their legitimate concerns over fundamental choices already made by the EU and its future direction.

If the European Commission was sincere in its aim of engaging the people in the ongoing European debates and fighting apathy, it should be proud that at least it managed to do just that: stimulate public debate over political issues and provide the people involved with an opportunity to voice their concerns, express their views and in the end, unluckily for the Union's top executive body, reject some of the centrepieces of its policy: the Constitution (the landmark achievement of the 'deepening' process to date) and through that the enlargement to the East and the possibility of future enlargement especially involving Turkey (the greatest initiatives in the framework of 'widening').

Now, that the EU is faced with the outcome of the public's decision and with the initial failure to agree on a budget at the Luxembourg summit in June 2005, it should deal with what is the most essential issue: its future identity and role. What exactly does the EU aspire to be, what are the foundations on which it is going to base its future structure and what will be its basic policy objectives? The Union cannot afford another public backlash. It needs to clearly define its political agenda and set its future plans openly and with the consent of the peoples involved. Far-reaching initiatives such as large-scale enlargement on the one hand and constitutional experiments at the highest possible level on the other, pursued simultaneously seem to have become increasingly unacceptable to large parts of European society. This is not necessarily discouraging as the EU has proved immensely successful in extremely significant fields such as consolidating democracy, security and stability on the continent, fostering economic development and establishing an effective framework of bilateral cooperation between the countries of the continent. These achievements have vast historical importance and it would be unfair for the hugely important role of the EU in achieving what 50 years ago seemed inconceivable to go unrecognised. However, this historical circle has reached its end and the EU leaders should now take crucial decisions on the future directions of the common European construction.

The recent crisis proved that the balance between the EU itself and the nation states that comprise it must be clearly shaped. The final resolution of this fundamental question is a prerequisite for Europe to rediscover its dynamism and reinvent itself as an influential international actor. The public debate over the budget is very significant not only due to strictly practical issues such as the allocation of specific funds but also because the main priorities of the economic policy pursued usually reveal the main priorities of the Union itself. The role that social policy initiatives are going to play in the new enlarged Union reflects the place one of the most important features of the culture of individual member states, namely social policy, will assume at EU level. Thus, the so-called conflict between the model of the free market pioneered by the UK, the Netherlands and Eastern European countries and the social economy of the market championed by France, Germany and other continental countries has to be dealt with. Both models present certain advantages and negative aspects and it is a matter for the societies involved to elect the model they perceive as the most suitable in accordance with their needs but, since this issue has assumed such importance in the recent EU context it should at least be a subject of discussion between leaders or institutions. Of course, at this point no prediction over the possible outcome of such a debate can be made, since other parameters may be introduced, the most significant of which remain government changes in member states after national elections and the political leaders at any given moment. It cannot be judged at this moment whether a German government under the Christian Democrats will remain as faithful to its adherence to costly social policies as the Social Democrats and the emergence of Mr Sarkozy as a President of France might signal a change in the country's policies whose extent cannot be appreciated at this stage. Nevertheless, it is a matter of great importance for the EU to discuss its economic agenda, its economic priorities for the future. This debate will be heavily linked to a discussion over how Europe perceives its future role as it will reveal its main objectives and ideals. Economic policy objectives have always been at the core of a country's cultural perceptions as evidenced by the emergence of the Common Agriculture Policy as the most important piece of Community action for 50 consecutive years.

Furthermore, the European political leaderships should clarify their future vision of Europe. They have to take delicate but crucial decisions such as where will the source of power in the Union be located. This question is linked to the exact nature of the relationship between the individual member states and the Union. It reflects the identity problem that Europe currently has. In simple words it is essential to find an answer to the question: what does Europe want to be in the future? Several parties in the EU supported the emergence of the Union as a counterbalance to the USA in the framework of a multi-polar world. However, the vision of a United States of Europe was buried along with the Constitution in May 2005, when two of the founding members of the EU rejected a much more minimalist version of the aforementioned ambition. The importance behind the French rejection lies not only in the importance of the country but also in the realisation that France was actually the country that pioneered the vision of Europe that was set aside with the rejection of the Treaty. It is the model of a federal Europe with strong supranational institutions and common policies on the economy, taxation and foreign policy that has received a painful blow with the negative vote. The referendum on the Constitution in France and the relevant debate at the very end urged people 'to ask themselves, what the EU should be?'[132] A subsequent question was related to whether the Treaty was taking the Union's future in the desired direction. Obviously the French viewed the liberal and not sufficiently integrated Europe, which according to mainstream opinion in France emerged as the central choice in the document, as not their desired version of a European future. Ironically enough, the rejection of the Constitution has been hailed as a victory for the parties within the EU that favoured exactly that vision of the European future; a vision of Europe as a large bloc of countries loosely connected with each other, mainly at intergovernmental level, within the framework of a common market. Therefore, France's rejection of the Constitution was viewed by many as a 'triumph for Britain',[133] because of its embrace of the common market vision and managed to 'blunt the drive towards European political union; and prevent Franco-German domination of European politics'.[134] The major political aim of promoting this vision of Europe has been decisive behind Britain's efforts to encourage the enlargement of the Union to eight Eastern European members, which politically and

---

132 *The Wall Street Journal*, 'Europe Revisited', 31 May 2005.

133 *The Economist*, 'How Britain Unexpectedly Emerged Victorious from Votes on the EU Constitution', 4 June 2005.

134 Ibid.

economically stand much closer to the British vision of Europe[135] rather than the Franco-German states as 'they tend to be more Atlantist in instinct and put greater onus on free markets and competition than social protection'.[136] 'An eastwardly enlarged EU of 25 or more member states, on this view, would create a structure of such size and heterogeneity . . . wider would necessarily imply shallower'.[137] And conversely the lack of enthusiasm on the part of France, inherent in the negative vote on the Constitution, over the recent and future enlargements is attributed to the realisation that the new members share divergent ideals.

After the negative vote in France, it was reported[138] that Gerhard Schroeder offered Mr Balkenende, the Dutch Prime Minister, 'a chance to take part in an inner circle of EU founding members, who could forge ahead'.[139] He was, thus, proposing to him a revival of the idea of a 'core Europe' initially perceived as comprising the six founding members of the EU, which could move towards closer integration faster, more effectively and without the need to acquire other members' consent. The others would remain outside this inner circle without the ability to shape the integrative policies of the founding six. The idea of a 'core' or 'multi speed' Europe is not new, it is present in everyday Community vocabulary, 'since Willy Brandt, former Chancellor of the Federal Republic of Germany, launched the idea in Paris in 1974, that the Community might progress faster if its economically stronger member states were allowed to develop more quickly'.[140] A similar notion is that of 'Europe à la carte', where 'member states can determine which Union obligations they wish to undertake or in which initiatives they would like to participate with only a minimum of a common base which all members must accept'.[141] Related to that is the notion of a 'variable geometry Europe', which refers to 'the idea of a method of differentiated integration which acknowledges that there are irreconcilable differences within the integration structure and therefore allows for a permanent separation between a group of Member States and

---

135 *The Economist*, 'Tony Blair's Battle for Europe', 28 May 2005.

136 *Independent*, 'Which Way for Europe', 31 May 2005.

137 Neil Walker, 'Constitutionalising Enlargement, Enlarging Constitutionalism', *European Law Journal*, 9(3), Blackwell Publishing, July 2003, p. 375.

138 The *Euobserver*, 'Core Europe Idea Resurfaces, Honor Mahony', 2 June 2005, see: http://www.euobserver.com/?aid=19224, accessed 2 June 2005.

139 Ibid.

140 Claus Dieter Ehlermann, Director General of Legal Service, European Commission, European Community, 'How Flexible is Community Law? An Unusual Approach to the Concept of "Two Speeds" ', *Michigan Law Review*, 82, 1984, p. 1274.

141 Daniel T. Murphy, *Georgia Journal of International and Comparative Law*, 31, 2003, p. 272.

a number of less developed integration units'.[142] Finally, there is also the model of 'Europe of concentric circles' according to which 'Europe is structured out of subsets of states which have achieved different levels of integration. It is not confined just to the integration structure of the European Union, and the idea has been expanded upon by a number of prominent figures. Some of them talk of "the circle of shared law" (the Union's Member States), the "adjacent circle" (the countries outside the Union waiting to join it) and "more select circles" for the purpose of greater cooperation (the currency circle, the defence circle and so on)'.[143] It should be noted that already different states have chosen to participate in different aspects of the EU's policies and refrain from becoming integral participants of others. The euro zone serves as an example of a set of countries moving towards monetary union without the consensus of the rest of the member states (UK, Denmark, Sweden), which chose to abstain from such initiatives. The Schengen Treaty is another prominent example of such a model (UK, Ireland and Denmark do not form a part of the Schengen system). At this stage it is impossible to define Europe's future shape precisely, but it can be confidently stated that Europe needs and will engage in such a debate especially after the rejection of the particular model shaped by the abandoned Constitutional Treaty.

---

[142] The site of the European Union: http://www.europa.eu.int/scadplus/glossary/variable_geometry_europe_en.htm.

[143] Ibid. See: http://www.europa.eu.int/scadplus/glossary/concentric_circles_en.htm.

2. Enlargement: the story so far

WIDENING V. DEEPENING

The interaction between widening and deepening reflects one of the fundamental parameters of the evolution of the EU project. In the preamble to the founding treaty, the Treaty of Rome, it was stated that the signatory parties were 'determined to lay the foundations of an ever closer union among the peoples of Europe'.[1] It can be deduced that the signatory parties were aiming at further consolidating the ability of the Community to expand its activities in areas of policy which were not initially covered by the founding Treaty. The 'ever closer union' signals their ambition to entrench their cooperation in all fields possible and achieve a level of integration unforeseeable at that time. The second part of the phrase reads 'among the peoples of Europe' and reveals the other basic objective of the Community: its enlargement to encompass the other nations of the continent. Thus, integration and enlargement were from the very beginning viewed as two of the foundations of the common European construction. The evolution of the latter is historically based both on the 'transfers of sovereign power from the member states to the Community . . . and the moving of fields into progressive policy coordination',[2] which set the foundations of 'deepening' and on the extension of the 'territorial applicability of the Treaty framework'[3] and along with it of the whole set of EU principles and policies which stand at the core of 'widening'. Subsequently, when looking at 50 years 'of history of the European Communities we see a process of alternating deepening and widening of European integration'.[4] Many political or academic parties support the theory that the two trends usually relate to each other in a conflicting manner but it can be argued that, on the contrary, deepening is historically seen to be decisively encouraged by previous widening

1 Treaty of Rome, accessed at the European Union site at: http://europa.eu.int/eur-lex/en/treaties/selected/livre2_c.html.

2 Markus G. Puder, 'Constitutionalising the EU', *Fordham International Law Journal*, 26, 2003, p. 1566.

3 Ibid.

4 Reinhard Rack and Judith Schwarzbauer, in *Changing Borders: Legal and Economic Aspects of European Enlargement*, Renate Kicker, Joseph Marko, Michael Steiner and Peter Lang, Frankfurt, 1998, p. 123.

initiatives. The most important integrative projects of the EU were adopted in the period preceding an enlargement or immediately after it. It appears that the adoption of further integration measures serves as the element that guarantees the balance between the supporters of integration and the adherents of a Union characterised more by a greater variety and less by full coordination at all political levels. Hence, the decision to grant full membership status to additional countries is accompanied by the expression of political willingness to further deepen common European action in certain fields and promote further decision making at supranational level. Each time the Union decided to enlarge, it simultaneously decided to integrate further as well.

The almost 50-year-old history of the EU provides us with a generous catalogue of examples. In the early years Jean Monnet, Robert Schuman, Alcide de Gasperi and Konrad Adenauer, who pioneered European integration and established the theoretical foundations for the development of European construction, chose the coal and steel industry as the preferred first step for European cooperation. They effectively rejected the structure of political balance in post-war Europe and projected a new Community based on the principles of shared sovereignty and close interstate coordination of actions in carefully selected fields. The foundation of the European Community of Coal and Steel became a reality in 1952[5] paving the way for the most important development on the continent during the second half of the twentieth century: the birth of the European Economic Community. Robert Schuman in his monumental declaration of 9 May 1950 (now celebrated as the 'day of Europe') stated that Europe 'will be built through concrete achievements which first create a de facto solidarity . . . the pooling of coal and steel production should immediately provide for the setting up of common foundations for economic development as a first step in the *federation* of Europe, and will change the destinies of those regions . . . in this way, there will be realized simply and speedily that fusion of interest which is indispensable to the establishment of a common economic system; it may be the leaven from which may grow a wider and deeper community between countries long opposed to one another by sanguinary divisions'.[6] Thus, fusion of interest, Robert Schuman claimed, would ensure that European countries were bound into a common future and a new war between them would be not only inconceivable but basically impossible.

The European Economic Community[7] was born with the Treaty of Rome

---

5 See the Treaty at: http://www.europa.eu.int/abc/obj/treaties/en/entoc29.htm, accessed 25 June 2005.

6 See the declaration at: http://www.europa.eu.int/abc/symbols/9-may/decl_en.htm, accessed 25 June 2005.

7 See the Treaty establishing the European Community at: http://europa.eu.int/abc/obj/treaties/en/entoc05.htm.

in 1957[8] and along with it a common market and a customs union between the founding six members.[9] Moreover, the founding Treaty signalled enhanced cooperation at a supranational level in the areas of agriculture with the establishment of a common agriculture policy (articles 38 to 47), trade with the promotion of a common trade policy (articles 110 to 116) and transport (articles 74 to 84). The first integration projects of the Community were in the course of realisation as a new chapter in European history was effectively opened. Article 235 of the Treaty read, 'if action by the Community should prove necessary to attain, in the course of the operation of the common market, one of the objectives of the Community and this Treaty has not provided the necessary powers, the Council shall, acting unanimously on a proposal from the Commission and after consulting the European Parliament, take the appropriate measures'. Thus, further deepening initiatives could be taken on the basis of agreement between the parties involved.

THE FIRST ENLARGEMENT

In 1961 the first enlargement of the Community was under way with the applications of the UK, Denmark, Norway and Ireland. The UK had rejected the invitation to co-found the EC and opted instead for participation in the European Free Trade Association founded in 1960 by Austria, Denmark, Norway, Portugal, Sweden, Switzerland and itself. It was realised at an early stage by the government in London that the EC was an ambitious project likely to influence Europe in a fundamental manner and it, therefore, decided to apply for membership. As the UK did not participate in the Community from its very beginning it saw membership as an adequate tool with which it could now influence the future shaping of the Community. The application of the UK provided the grounds for a new round of Anglo-French disputes culminating in President Charles de Gaulle's veto of the British application, but it also led to the shaping of an early phase of an entry procedure that 'established the framework within which future applicants would operate'.[10]

Charles de Gaulle vetoed British entry twice, once in 1963 (after the application of the Conservative Government of Harold Macmillan) and in 1967 (after the application of the Labour Government of Harold Wilson). In his statement on 16 May 1967 he said: 'Britain – who is not continental, who

---

8 Furthermore, in the same year the European Atomic Energy Community was founded, again in Rome. See the relevant treaty at: http://europa.eu.int/abc/obj/treaties/en/entoc38.htm.

9 France, Germany, Italy, the Netherlands, Belgium, Luxembourg.

10 Carson W. Clements, supra note 1, p. 404.

remains, because of the Commonwealth and because she is an island, committed far beyond the seas, who is tied to the United States by all kinds of special agreements – did not merge into a Community with set dimensions and strict rules. While this Community was taking shape, Britain therefore first refused to participate in it. Then she tried to negotiate in order to join the Community, but in such conditions that the latter would have been suffocated by this membership . . . This is true, for instance, of the agricultural regulations. . . . The idea, the hope which, from the beginning, led the Six continental countries to unite . . . of acting one day politically by itself and for itself toward anyone. Considering the special relations that tie the British to America, with the advantage and also the dependence that results for them; considering the existence of the Commonwealth . . . (the UK is) distinguished from the continentals'.[11]

As was obvious from the statement of the French President, a central issue in the refusal of France to consent to the entry of the UK, apart from the fear of the latter potentially challenging its political supremacy, was the objection the British had to adhering to the CAP. At a time when the CAP absorbed most of the Community's budget, with France emerging as the principal beneficiary due to its large agricultural sector, the UK's reluctance to appear enthusiastic was justified. Its relatively small agricultural sector would lead to significantly fewer benefits from the CAP, leaving France as a net beneficiary and rendering itself at least initially a net contributor. Therefore, France was fervent in its 'insistence that accession for the new members could only be on the basis of acceptance of the complete *acquis communautaire*. This was to ensure that Britain did not try to slip out of the uncomfortable budgetary position into which the French believed that they had manoeuvred it'.[12] Although this statement contributes greatly to the understanding both of the sources of current disputes over the British rebate and the disagreement with France over the CAP and of the subsequent confrontational impact of the European project in the British society,[13] it is important for an additional reason. It is obvious that the seeds of the current enlargement procedure existed from the very first attempt of the EC to extend its membership. A current member, France, insisted that a future member, the UK, could not choose to opt out of a substan-

---

11 President Charles de Gaulle at his fifteenth press conference on 16 May 1967, access at: http://www.fordham.edu/halsall/mod/1967-degaulle-non-uk.html or http://www.cartage.org.lb/en/themes/GeogHist/histories/histdocts/Biblio20/A20/deGaulle/1967-degaulle-non-uk.html.

12 Stephen George and Ian Bache, *Politics in the European Union*, Oxford University Press, Oxford, 2001, p. 408.

13 See: Hugo Young, *This Blessed Plot: Britain and Europe from Churchill to Blair*, Macmillan, London, 1999.

tial part of the Community's policies and therefore, in order for a future member to accede it needed to fully accept the entirety of the principles and policies of the Community up to that point. The latter established as the '*acquis communautaire*' still serves 40 years afterwards as one of the main criteria to be fulfilled in order to achieve membership. Hence, the main principle that newcomers have to accept the Union's policies and priorities *before* their entry appears to apply from the very first enlargement.

The Hague Summit on 1 and 2 December 1969 convened with the objective to 'examine the problems arising for the Community principally in the matter of its completion, its consolidation and its enlargement'.[14] In his address to the European Parliament on 11 December 1969, M. Jean Rey, the president of the Commission, stated that 'it is no longer the member states meeting in an intergovernmental conference, which are to negotiate with Britain, Ireland, Denmark and Norway but the Community as such . . . the Heads of the Governments have indicated their agreement to the opening of negotiations between the Community on the one hand and the applicant State on the other. This is a tremendous progress. It would be incomprehensible if negotiations concerning the common policies at present in operation in the Community were to be pursued other than by the Community as such . . .'.[15]

In contrast to the pattern of negotiations pursued during 1961–63 at the time of the first British application when individual member states held negotiations with the British government, at the second British application the Community negotiated through its common institutions and not through the competent national authorities. Thus, the principle adhered up until the recent enlargement, which entails the involvement in negotiations of the Commission on the one hand and the applicant on the other, was introduced at the first enlargement of the EC. The procedure which the EC at the beginning, and the EU later on, followed when assuming the decision to enlarge is a product of decades of integration and the development of policies. In the Final Communiqué of the Summit on 2 December 1969, it was stated that 'the member states reaffirmed their agreement on the principle of enlargement in accordance with Article 237 of the Treaty of Rome . . . in so far as the applicant countries accept the Treaties and their political aims, the decisions taken since the entry into force of the Treaty'.[16] The agreement on enlargement was linked to the previous acceptance by the applicants of the Treaty and all the decisions therein.

Finally, the Commission in its memorandum to the Summit of November 1969 clarified its position by declaring that 'the Commission considers that the

---

14 The Hague Summit, Bulletin of the European Communities, No. 1 1970.
15 Ibid.
16 The Final Communiqué of the Summit on 2 December 1969, paragraph 13.

strengthening and the enlargement of the Community should go hand in hand'.[17] Thus, from the very first enlargement it was made clear by the basic institutions of the Community that widening and deepening, enlargement and further strengthening and integration go hand in hand. In the Paris Summit of 19 to 21 October 1972 the EC Head of States decided to complete Economic and Monetary Union, to deal with major regional imbalances by the promotion of a regional policy (one of the Union's central projects in the following years) to coordinate policies for employment and the environment,[18] to assume common initiatives in the framework of the Community's external relations, to enforce the role of the Parliament by introducing new procedures and election of its members by universal suffrage[19] and to convert all the relationships between member states into a European Union.[20] Thus, the EC decided to accept the UK, Denmark and Ireland[21] as full members and simultaneously extended its scope of competence to additional fields of policies and activities while further consolidating interstate cooperation in the areas already within the framework of the Community's scope.

THE SECOND AND THIRD ENLARGEMENTS

The second enlargement of the Community took place in 1981 with the inclusion of Greece. The 1981 enlargement was the only one in EC history to involve only one country. The enlargement to include Greece is usually viewed in conjunction with the respective expansion to include Spain and Portugal in 1986 as both widening initiatives involved countries of Southern Europe. Furthermore, the three countries had common historical experiences due to being ruled by dictatorial regimes in the recent past and therefore shared similar political aspirations from their membership in the EC; the latter included the consolidation of their newly established democratic regimes, access to a larger European market, the benefits of receiving generous Community funding in the framework of policies such as the regional policy or the common agricultural policy since all three countries had a relatively sizeable agricultural sector and, in the case of Greece in particular, for reasons of national security in relation to neighbouring countries especially Turkey

---

17 European Commission Memorandum to the Summit on 19 November 1969, paragraph 4.

18 By taking advantage of Article 235 among others.

19 The first European Parliament elections took place in 1979.

20 Paris Summit on 19 to 21 October 1972, Bulletin of the European Communities, No. 10 1972.

21 In a referendum on 25 September 1972 53.5% of Norwegians rejected entry to the EC and therefore Norway failed to accede with the rest of the applicant countries.

and to a lesser degree the communist Balkan states. Moreover, they were all countries with capitalist economies, despite a relatively extensive public sector generated economy and albeit poorer than the current nine members of the EC, they were still a part of the West during the Cold War, within the framework of which the EC decided to extend to the South.

The entry of Greece into the EC presented certain particular issues. Apart from being the only country that entered the EC unaccompanied by other applicants, something that is attributed to the success of the Greek delegation in disestablishing any link between the Greek application and those of Spain and Portugal, an additional unique feature in this enlargement is that it was historically the only time that the Council decided and effectively set aside the opinion of the Commission on the issue of an applicant's entry. In its opinion on the Greek application the European Commission noted that although 'the Community must now give a clearly positive answer to the Greek request . . . and the consolidation of Greek democracy is fundamental . . . also for the Community and its members . . . and a clear affirmative reply must be given and negotiations for Greek accession be opened'[22] Greece should be subject to a pre-accession transition period before full integration in order for the necessary economic reforms to take place. 'It would be desirable to envisage a period of time before the obligations of membership, even subject to transitional arrangements, are undertaken'.[23]

The opinion of the European Commission was 'swept aside by the European Council led by the French President Giscard d'Estaing who played an influential role in pushing membership. Political reasons were to the fore in the EU taking in the southern new members'.[24] Although Portugal was found to be 'a society and economy with major structural weaknesses in all sectors of activity',[25] the application was also accepted and Portugal was to become a member of the EC in 1986. Although Spain was found to be 'less economically developed than the present Community, its economic weight and growth potential was found to be much greater than that of Greece or Portugal'.[26]

---

22 Opinion on Greek application for membership, transmitted to the Council by the Commission on 29 January 1976, COM (76) 30 final, Bulletin of the European Communities, Supplement 2/76.

23 The same.

24 Fraser Cameron, *Europe, Integration and Enlargement*, Routledge, London, 2004, p. 4.

25 Opinion on Portuguese application for membership, transmitted to Council by the Commission 19 May 1978, COM (78) 220, Bulletin of the European Communities, supplement 5/78.

26 General Considerations on the Problems of Enlargement, Communication sent by the Commission to the Council 20 April 1978, COM (78) 120 final, Bulletin of the European Communities, Supplement 1/78.

Problems emerged especially in relation to Spanish agricultural products but were soon dealt with after granting transitional periods to assist in the harmonisation of standards around the Community.

It should be emphasised that the new southern European member states, although at that time less economically advanced, proved to be supporters of further European integration and because of the nature of their European aspirations they heavily supported initiatives such as the creation of a dynamic EC regional policy, the reallocation of the CAP funds and the shaping of a Cohesion Fund to deal with growing regional disparities at pan-European level. Furthermore, viewing this enlargement from a geostrategic point of view, the EC extended its borders to the Iberian peninsula and the south-east of Europe, exporting its stability and democratic traditions to what used to be the periphery of the EC. The impact of EC membership on the three states is universally praised as highly successful as it cemented democratic institutions and practices, brought constant political stability, stimulated economic development and granted the societies concerned a level of prosperity unprecedented in their respective histories.

However, the European Commission at the time of enlargement noted that because of the 'accession of Greece, Portugal and Spain . . . the Community will have lost much of its homogeneity by a two phase doubling of its membership[27] . . . so . . . the Community [shall] complete the common market, move towards economic and monetary union and formulate common policies on energy, regional development and tax harmonisation'.[28] Thus, after widening, deepening should now be pursued.

The enlargement to the South stimulated further integration as it led to some of the most historically important steps in such a direction. The most important of such integrative initiatives has admittedly been the Single European Act, entering into force on 1 July 1987. In 1981 the plan drafted by Hans Dietrich Genscher, the German Minister for Foreign Affairs and his Italian counterpart, Emilio Colombo, 'called for the progressive transformation of the Community into a new entity to be called European Union'.[29] The plan led to the solemn declaration of Stuttgart of 19 June 1983, which was accepted by all member states.

The Heads of States had agreed that 'a united Europe was more than ever necessary . . . that the Community should strengthen its cohesion . . . and

---

27 From the six original members the Commission jumped to twelve with the enlargements taking place between 1973 and 1986.

28 Enlargement of the Community, transitional period and institutional implications, Bulletin of the European Communities, COM (78) 190, supplement 2/78.

29 David O'Keeffe, 'Current Issues in European Integration', *Pace International Law Review*, 7, 1995, p. 5.

develop a European social policy . . . speak with a single voice in foreign policy . . . transform the whole complex of relations between their States into a European Union'.[30] In 1984 the momentum was seized by the European Parliament, whose Committee on Institutional Affairs under the inspiration of the Italian federalist Altiero Spinelli prepared a draft of a Treaty establishing a European Union. The latter was overwhelmingly approved by the Parliament on 14 February 1984. The impact of the approval of the draft Treaty by the Parliament was such that in the Fontainebleau European Council of 25 and 26 June 1984 a committee comprising representatives of the Heads of State was formed inviting the Council to convene an intergovernmental conference on the issue of the negotiation of a Treaty on European Union. Finally, the Milan European Council of 28 and 29 June 1985[31] proposed convening an intergovernmental conference which opened under the Luxembourg Presidency on 9 September 1985 and closed in The Hague on 28 February 1986.

More significant for the promotion of further integration was the appointment of Jacques Delors, 'a dynamic, far sighted and politically adroit'[32] personality to the Presidency of the European Commission. Under his guidance the White Paper on the Internal Market of 1985[33] was produced. This identified 279 legislative proposals necessary to remove obstacles to trade within the Community and put forward a schedule for the creation of the Internal Market by 31 December 1992. The European leaders shaped the strategy for accession and clearly articulated that 'the key element in the strategy to narrow the gap is preparation of the associated States for integration into the internal market of the Union'.[34]

The preparations for adjusting smoothly to the internal market assumed a central position in the accession process, and therefore, the White Paper as the document aiming at 'approximating the legislation of the pertinent associated

30 Solemn Declaration on European Union, European Council, Stuttgart, 19 June 1983. Bulletin of the European Communities, No. 6/1983.

31 European Council, 28 and 29 June 1985 in Milan, Draft Concerning the Reform of the Treaty establishing the European Economic Community, Bulletin of the European Parliament, 8 July 1985. Alternatively access at: http://www.europarl.eu.int/summits/milan/mil_en.pdf.

32 Roger J. Goebel, 'The European Union Grows: The Constitutional Impact of the Accession of Austria, Finland and Sweden', *Fordham International Law Journal*, 18, 1995, p. 1100.

33 Commission of the European Communities, COM (85) 310 final, Brussels, 14 June 1985, Completing the Internal Market, White Paper from the Commission to the European Council, Milan 28–9 June 1985. Alternatively at: http://europa.eu.int/comm/off/pdf/1985_0310_f_en.pdf.

34 European Council, 9 and 10 December 1994, Essen, Presidency Conclusions, Bulletin of the European Communities 12/1994.

States with the Community norm relative to the internal market'[35] was of great practical importance. The White Paper, albeit significant, was a non-binding document and therefore presented 'the important advantage of flexibility being a simple guide or a general reference document'.[36] The whole process culminated with the passing of the Single European Act[37] that came into force in 1987, which constitutes a milestone in the history of European integration and is one of the most significant constitutional documents of the EC. The Single European Act paved the way for massive political and institutional developments at the EU level and accelerated reform and integration at a pace unknown up till then. According to Article 18 (ex Article 8a) the EC assumed the obligation to complete the formation of the internal market by 31 December 1992. Even more importantly a new Article 95 (ex Article 100a) introduced a change to the voting system in the Council. Article 95 constituted a derogation from Article 94, which demanded unanimity in the Council for the passing of directives for the approximation of laws relating to the internal market. The new Article 95 established qualified majority voting for internal market legislative initiatives and paved the way for greater flexibility as it facilitated the adoption of the relevant decisions at the Council level. The Single European Act (SEA) provided a legal basis for European Political Cooperation as a form of consultation on foreign policy matters between the member states with reference to the opinion of the European Parliament, whose role was substantially enhanced by the Act as a means to entrench the Community's democratic legitimacy. Finally, it introduced new areas of Community competence such as economic and social cohesion, research and technological development and environmental policy. Thus, the SEA gave significant impetus to the integration process at a period when the EC was also dealing with its southern enlargement. The SEA was successfully put to voters in a referendum in Denmark in February 1986, while the Prime Minister of the UK at that time, Mrs Thatcher, did not raise any objections to this important deepening initiative.

Meanwhile, Austria's application for EC membership was made on 17 July 1989 by the then Minister for Foreign Affairs, Alois Mock. This was followed

---

35 Eritja Mar Campins, 'The New Accessions to the European Union from the Central and Eastern European Countries: The Strategy of Accession and its Implications on the Environmental European Community Policy', *ILSA Journal of International and Comparative Law*, 6, 2005, p. 618. See also: Mike Pullen, 'The Accession of Central and Eastern States to the EU, The Background and some Observations', *International Trade Law and Regulation*, 4(3), p. 70.

36 Marc Maresceau, *Enlarging the European Union, Relations between the EU and Central and Eastern Europe*, Longman, London and New York 1997, p. 46.

37 See its text at the European Union site: http://europa.eu.int/abc/obj/treaties/en/entoc113.htm.

by Cyprus on 3 July 1990, Malta on 16 July 1990 and Sweden on 1 July 1991. These applications underlined the inevitability of a new round of enlargement for the EC. In addition to that, the collapse of the Berlin Wall in November 1989 and the subsequent reunification of Germany with the incorporation of the German Democratic Republic into the Federal Republic of Germany on 3 October 1990 constituted yet another enlargement of the EC, albeit in the form of the unification of an existing member state with a neighbouring state, putting an end to the divisions created by post-war arrangements. This signalled imminent future developments for the EU. The European leaders 'warmly welcomed'[38] German reunification and stated that the 'unification . . . will be carried out without revision of the Treaties'.[39] The issue of the incorporation of the Democratic Republic into the Federal Republic was treated rather as an internal affair of Germany than as a further expansion of the EU, irrespective of the fact that Eastern Germany was the size of a middle-sized European country when it entered the EU through the German unification. The combined size of the unified Germany was now significantly bigger than France, the UK and Italy with whom Germany had shared the same status for the previous 40 years. Therefore, although a revision of the Treaties would have been justified, a further increase of Germany's voting rights in the Council did not occur, probably for political reasons linked to political concerns over the re-emergence of Germany as the biggest country in Europe. Germany continued to enjoy the same voting weight in the Council as the other three big member states; France, the UK and Italy. However, the EU leaders agreed in 1992[40] to upgrade Germany's presence in the European Parliament allowing the country to have the biggest parliamentary representation starting from the euro-elections of 1994. With the reunification of Germany and the collapse of the Wall, the Cold War came to a final end and Europe was entering a permanent new historical phase. What seemed inconceivable at the beginning of 1989 was a fact in 1990. Communism had collapsed and a new range of Eastern European countries searching for new systems of governance compatible with the Western European ones were about to apply for membership to the EU, which now had no reason to confine itself to the Western part of the continent. The expansion to the Eastern part of Europe passed within one year from the sphere of the unimaginable to a project that had to be carefully planned. Thus, with the four aforementioned applications already on the table, with Finland applying on 18 March 1992,

---

38 Special Meeting of the European Council, Dublin 28 April 1990, Bulletin of the European Communities, No. 4/1990, Presidency Conclusions, paragraph 1.3.

39 Paragraph 1.5.

40 European Council in Edinburgh, 11 and 12 December 1992, Bulletin of the European Communities 12/1992, Presidency Conclusions, paragraph 26.

Norway on 25 November 1992 and Eastern Germany paving the way for the rest of the Eastern European countries, the EU had to consolidate its deepening before it engaged in an unprecedented round of widening. In this context the Treaty on the European Union (TEU) or the Treaty of Maastricht was signed on 7 February 1992.

The Treaty of Maastricht[41] constituted a significant further step in the process of integration, something that can be easily deduced from the name given to the document: the Treaty on the European Union. The Treaty regulated the passing to a new stage; the European Community became European Union. The Treaty initiated the necessary regulatory framework for the future adoption of the common currency, introduced the three pillar structure of the EU, the European Communities being the first, the Common Foreign and Security Policy, an evolution of the European Political Cooperation promoted by the SEA, the second and Justice and Home Affairs the third. Thus, issues such as criminal and judicial cooperation and asylum and immigration came into an area where the EU could encourage coordination of member state policies. The TEU reconfirmed the Union's adherence to the principle of subsidiarity,[42] introduced the concept of European Union citizenship[43] and a Committee of the Regions was founded.[44] Furthermore, it can be argued that the TEU initiated a certain degree of flexibility providing for some 'opt-out' choices for member states unwilling to assume certain obligations, the most notable being the refusal of the UK to accept the Social Charter[45] and the opt-outs of Denmark after the negative result in its first referendum in June 1992.

Therefore, the enlargement to the South, apart from its success in introducing reforms in the societies of the countries involved, and stimulating further development, provided the basis for a radical reform of the Community, which not only seized the opportunity to become a Union but also a much more integrated one. The factors that accelerated such a development were the magnitude of the enlargement as the EC membership grew from nine to twelve countries between 1981 to 1986, the nature of the candidates involved, which were absolutely confident of their European credentials and favoured further integration in the EC context, the existence of a dynamic European Commission embodied in the personality of its President, Mr Jacques Delors, and the ability of the European leaders of that period, notably François Mitterand of France and Helmut Kohl of Germany, to convince European public opinion at the time of the necessity of implementing the vision of a united Europe.

---

41 See its text at: http://europa.eu.int/eur-lex/en/treaties/dat/EU_treaty.html.
42 See Article B.
43 See Part Two, Article 8.
44 See Chapter 4, Article 198a.
45 See Protocol on Social Policy annexed to the TEU.

The existence of leaders with a certain degree of craftsmanship has always been a significant parameter of historical developments and Europe's dynamic leadership in the 1980s certainly played a decisive role in the rapid integration achieved in this period. This can be contrasted with the failure of today's leaders to convince their electorates of the rationale behind their recent choices and to link the future of the Union with the everyday concerns of the citizens. The results of the referendums on the Constitutional Treaty revealed the dangers looming when there is a distance between the choices of the ruling political elites and unconvinced electorates.

THE FOURTH ENLARGEMENT

The fourth enlargement of the EU took place on 1 January 1995, the date on which Sweden, Austria and Finland entered the Union. Norway failed to join the fifteen European countries, which comprised the EU in 1995, because its electorate rejected such a prospect for a second time in a national referendum held in November 1994. The referendums in the other three countries provided the respective governments with the popular consent necessary to engage in the common European project. The EU leaders at the European Summit in Corfu in June 1994 welcomed the prospect of the imminent admission of the relevant countries (although the Norwegian negative reply was not foreseen) and cheerfully stated that 'the European Council welcomes in this connection the additional impetus coming from these countries which are in the vanguard of the efforts to promote environmental and social protection, transparency and open government, areas considered essential by a large part of the Union's citizens'.[46] This phrase revealed the main future contributions of the new member states to the EU edifice. The new countries were distinguished by their level of open and transparent government, high level of social protection and public services and high standards of environmental protection. Consequently, the EU was for the first time admitting a group of new member states, all of which enjoyed equal if not superior levels of quality of life, economic development and institutional transparency. Apart from some challenges in relation to further institutional adaptation to accommodate the newcomers and efforts to reconcile the compatibility of certain aspects of common European policies such as the Common Foreign and Security Policy with the traditional status of neutrality enjoyed by some countries such as Austria or over the compatibility of various community policies with the

---

[46] Presidency Conclusions, European Council at Corfu, 24–5 June 1994. See the conclusions at: http://www.europarl.eu.int/summits/cor1_en.htm#into.

higher standards of environmental protection in Scandinavian countries, this event was a widening initiative that evolved rather smoothly for the EU. The latter was further assisted by the fact that the new countries had already acquired knowledge of the European institutions' function as they were members of the European Economic Area. Additionally, they had experience of participating in an organisation with economic aims (although the EU had already effectively evolved into something much more than that) as they had been members of the European Free Trade Association since 1960.[47] However, the new developments on the continent with the collapse of the Eastern bloc and the blurring of the distinction between West and East rendered revisiting their national strategy necessary. Austria had no reason to remain neutral in a continent where animosity between the two different camps had finally ceased to exist. Moreover, membership in the EFTA became increasingly less strategically important, since economic cooperation within the framework of the EU was deeper, rendering their membership substantially more influential.

Meanwhile, in 1994 the applications of Hungary (31 March) and Poland (5 April) followed in 1995 by the applications of Romania (22 June), Slovakia (27 June), Latvia (13 October), Estonia (24 November), Lithuania (8 December) and Bulgaria (14 December) and in 1996 by the Czech Republic (17 January) and Slovenia (10 June) signalled a new enlargement on the political horizon for the EU, this time involving countries with a bigger population than the Scandinavian countries and Austria, presenting far greater challenges for the Union than at any time in the past. In this context the Commission noted that 'because of its scope and its diversity, this enlargement will be different from previous ones: an extended Europe is bound to be more heterogeneous and therefore more complex. As the number of Union members increases, it creates a risk of the Union being watered down. As one Head of State put it, we have to avoid the situation where, as the last applicant country arrives, it joins something which no longer exists. Enlargement must be undertaken with safeguards for the achievements of forty years of European integration. These achievements are the basis of the Union's solidarity with the new Member States'.[48] Therefore, the Heads of State agreed to hold an Intergovernmental Conference, already envisaged by

47 However, Finland became an associate member of EFTA in 1961 and a full member only in 1986.

48 European Commission Opinion on the Intergovernmental Conference in 1996, Reinforcing Political Union and Preparing for Enlargement, 28 February 1996, accessed at: http://europa.eu.int/en/agenda/igc-home/eu-doc/commissn/avis-en.html, 28 June 2005.

the Treaty of Maastricht,[49] to deal with the needs of a Union with a growing membership.

With the enlargement to the North already implemented and with new plans to enlarge to the East of the continent at the planning stage there came the realization that the EU had to confirm its basic principle that widening should not undermine deepening. The EU member states had to introduce reforms in order to consolidate further integration just after a further expansion of the group to three new countries and just before a new much more radical expansion to the East. The European Commission emphasized its view that 'the forthcoming conference will be a crucial one: the deepening and widening of the Union are intertwined. The Commission expects of the Intergovernmental Conference (IGC) that it strengthen the Union so as to prepare enlargement around a clear political project'.[50] In the Corfu European Summit in June 1994 the European leaders decided to set a Reflection Group[51] to prepare for the 1996 Intergovernmental Conference in order to 'elaborate options in the perspective of the future enlargement of the Union'.[52] The European Parliament fully endorsed the imminent IGC and with its Resolution[53] it provided the Union with its views on the priorities of its reformist agenda. The latter were basically the provision of a definition of European citizenship, respect for human rights, internal security, economic and social cohesion and transparency issues.

Therefore, the Treaty of Amsterdam[54] was finally agreed upon and was signed in 1997. The changes brought about by the Treaty were particularly significant as the EU made the clear political choice to become more active in fields of a purely political nature such as judicial cooperation or justice and home affairs and that constituted a serious step on the way to further integration.

---

49 'A conference of representatives of the governments of the Member States shall be convened in 1996 to examine those provisions of this Treaty for which revision is provided, in accordance with the objectives set out in Articles A and B'. See Article N(2) of the Treaty of Maastricht.

50 European Commission Opinion, supra note 30.

51 See its Report on a Strategy for Europe, Brussels 5 December 1995, at: http://europa.eu.int/en/agenda/igc-home/eu-doc/reflect/final.html, accessed 28 June 2005.

52 European Summit in Corfu, 24–5 June 1994, Presidency Conclusions, access at: http://www.europarl.eu.int/summits/cor1_en.htm#igc.

53 Resolution on Parliament's opinion on the convening of the Intergovernmental Conference; and evaluation of the work of the Reflection Group and definition of the political priorities of the European Parliament with a view to the Intergovernmental Conference. Based on the DURY/MAIJ-WEGGEN report (A4-0068/96), 13 March, 1996. Accessed at: http://europa.eu.int/en/agenda/igc-home/eu-doc/parlment/opinion.html#1, 28 June 2005.

54 See its text at: http://europa.eu.int/eur-lex/lex/en/treaties/dat/11997E/htm/11997E.html#0001010001.

The Schengen Agreements were incorporated into the legal system of the EU, effectively abolishing border controls within the territory of the EU and coordinating external border controls. The position of a High Representative for EU Foreign Policy was established so that the external policy of the EU could be vested in one personality more easily and it was decided that most legislation would be adopted by the co-decision procedure, which involves a greater role for the European Parliament. The EU decided to create an area of freedom, security and justice for its citizens and with this objective it took the significant decision to give itself the competence to legislate on immigration, civil law and civil procedure as long as this is necessary for one of the internal market's basic freedoms: the free movement of persons within the EU. Member states were moreover encouraged to further coordinate their policies on the sensitive issue of police and criminal justice as the EU promoted intergovernmental cooperation in the relevant areas. Despite the decisive push for further deepening, promoted by the Treaty of Amsterdam, the lack of any significant institutional reform to prepare the EU for the enlargement to the East was notable. Therefore, the so-called 'Amsterdam left-overs' (basically all the institutional reforms that the Treaty failed to provide for) were to be included in a new constitutional document to be signed in 2000 in another Summit in Nice.

THE FIFTH ENLARGEMENT

The Treaty of Nice was a result of the Summit held in the idyllic city on the southern French coast. Despite the favourable surroundings, the Summit was characterised by high political tensions marked by intense negotiations on behalf of the leaders involved. The lively political debates that accompanied the Treaty's negotiations proved that spirits can sometimes be more easily stimulated when the subject of the ongoing talks is the distribution of power within the EU rather than when discussing new areas of European cooperation. The Treaty of Nice was the least ideological of the European Treaties in the sense that it did not – significantly at least – regulate any new field of European law or activities. It just dealt with what was in political and legal terminology known as the left-overs from the previous Treaty of Amsterdam; namely, the much-needed reforms to the function and composition of the European Union institutions on the way to the Union's big bang enlargement to the East. The focus of the reform was fundamental for the function of the Union institutions of the European Commission, the European Council and the European Parliament. More specifically the main political emphasis was placed on the structure of the particular institutions, since the EU would soon comprise many small and medium-sized countries which would upset the current composition of the aforementioned institutions and the issue of qualified majority, a shift from unanimity, which was perceived as a threat to the future smooth operation of a Union enlarged to 25 member states.

The Treaty of Nice came into force in 2003. The leaders decided to hold yet another IGC in 2004, which produced the unfortunate Constitutional Treaty. Since the latter was spectacularly rejected by the French and Dutch electorates on 29 May and 1 June 2005 respectively, the Treaty of Nice remained in force. Thus, its institutional provisions constitute the guiding regulating provisions for the EU at least until any new initiative is assumed.

For the European Council the Treaty introduced an important innovation: a new concept of qualified majority. In order for a decision to be passed by the European Council according to the Final Act annexed to the Treaty 'acts of the Council shall require for their adoption at least *258* votes in favour, cast by a *majority* of members, where this Treaty requires them to be adopted on a proposal from the Commission. In other cases, for their adoption acts of the Council shall require at least 258 votes in favour cast by at least two-thirds of the members. When a decision is to be adopted by the Council by a qualified majority, a member of the Council may request verification that the Member States constituting the qualified majority represent at least *62%* of the total population of the Union. If that condition is shown not to have been met, the decision in question shall not be adopted' (emphasis added).[55]

The distribution of votes was set as shown in Table 2.1.[56]

As far as the European Commission is concerned, it now consists of one Commissioner per member state as the bigger member states have given up their second commissioner. However, Article 4 of the Protocol on the Enlargement of the EU annexed to the Treaty provides that 'when the Union consists of 27 Member States . . . the number of Members of the Commission shall be less than the number of Member States . . . this amendment shall apply as from the date on which the first Commission following the date of accession of the 27th Member State of the Union takes up its duties'.[57]

Finally, the number of Members of the European Parliament has rocketed to new heights after the enlargement. Declaration 20 of the Final Act had to be modified by the Accession Treaty of Athens in 2003 in order to bring the Czech Republic and Hungary onto an equal footing with Greece, Belgium and

---

55 Access the Final Act at the European Union site at: http://europa.eu.int/eur-lex/lex/en/treaties/dat/12001C/htm/C_2001080EN.007001.html.

56 There would be further changes in the Accession Treaty of Bulgaria and Romania, 25 April 2005, Part II, Article 10.

57 Article 4 of the Protocol. Access at: http://www.europa.eu.int/eur-lex/en/treaties/dat/C_2002325EN.016301.html.

Table 2.1 Members of the Council: weighted votes

Members of the Council	Weighted votes
Germany	29
United Kingdom	29
France	29
Italy	29
Spain	27
Poland	27
Romania	14
Netherlands	13
Greece	12
Czech Republic	12
Belgium	12
Hungary	12
Portugal	12
Sweden	10
Bulgaria	10
Austria	10
Slovakia	7
Denmark	7
Finland	7
Ireland	7
Lithuania	7
Latvia	4
Slovenia	4
Estonia	4
Cyprus	4
Luxembourg	4
Malta	3
Total	345

Portugal.[58] The Accession Treaty of Bulgaria and Romania will bring new changes to the composition of the European Parliament to be introduced in 2009.[59] However, the total number of seats shall not exceed 736.

[58] The Treaty of Athens, 2003, Act of Accession, Part II Adjustment of the Treaties, Article 11 on the European Parliament.

[59] See the Accession Treaty of Bulgaria and Romania, 25 April 2005, Part II, Article 9.

Table 2.2 Composition of the European Parliament 2004–2009

Member State	European Parliament seats
Germany	99
United Kingdom	78
France	78
Italy	78
Spain	54
Poland	54
Netherlands	27
Greece	24
Czech Republic	24
Belgium	24
Hungary	24
Portugal	24
Sweden	19
Austria	18
Slovakia	14
Denmark	14
Finland	14
Ireland	13
Lithuania	13
Latvia	9
Slovenia	7
Estonia	6
Cyprus	6
Luxembourg	6
Malta	5
Total	732

EVOLUTION OF MEMBERSHIP CRITERIA

As noted before, the EC stated in the text of the founding Treaty that it did not intend to confine the common European project only to the small group of six founding members. The consecutive enlargements that raised the number of states in the Union from six to a staggering 25 and in the future to maybe 30 or even more depending on whether enlargement is to be viewed as an endless process or as a process with some reasonably defined limits, proved the adherence of the Community to that principle. The EC from the very beginning of its existence was based on some common principles, namely respect for democracy and free markets. As the Community grew in numbers but, even more significantly, as the scope of its competence and areas of activities were expanding, further exploration of principles became necessary. As the Community evolved from a purely economic entity to a political union, a rapidly growing body of laws, regulations and court rulings was assuming a place of central importance. Thus, respect for the legislative basis and regulative achievements of the EU, widely known as the *acquis communautaire*, gradually took its place as one of the fundamental requirements of membership.

Having requirements of membership in the first place was a conscious choice by the Union. The most obvious reason underlying this choice is the fact that almost all groups in the world tend to establish certain criteria for entry. This choice assures the existing members that newcomers will not bring radical changes to the existing organisation of the group but will respect its fundamentals as a prerequisite for their admission. Although changes are inevitable after the acceptance of new members in a group, guaranteeing from the initial stage that aspirant new members assume the constitutional obligation, through their respective Treaty of Accession, to fully adhere to the Union's fundamental values and system of operation is a necessary safeguard for the existing members of the group. Moreover, usually the criteria for membership tend to reflect the basic political values of a given group. Therefore, the EU through its membership criteria made a political declaration of the set of principles it considers absolutely fundamental. If a certain candidate does not embrace one of the Union's fundamentals, it cannot reasonably expect to be welcomed. In this way, although the EU can reasonably expect that political differences and cultural divergences will exist among its members, all members ascribe to a certain list of values that guarantee that its fundamentals will remain non-negotiable.

The shaping of a certain catalogue of membership criteria can offer the additional safeguard that the achievements of the EU will not be brought into question by the promotion of a divergent political agenda on the part of new members. The history of the Union reveals its radical change from a customs union and a purely European Economic Community in the 1960s to a European Union of member states cooperating within the framework of the Common Foreign and Security Policy and on areas as sensitive as Justice and Home Affairs in the 1990s. These achievements are crucially important and they were the result of constant and sometimes painful debate between existing members. Failing to provide certain guarantees for these achievements would have been a demonstration of political negligence on the part of the EU. Thus, the shaping of a catalogue with clearly stated requirements of entry can be viewed also within the context of the widening versus deepening interrelationship, discussed above. As the EU decided to enlarge, it promoted tougher requirements for entry as a safeguard for the supporters of deepening to reassure them that further widening is not going to undermine further integration. Integration is closely linked with other elements as well, however; the issue of conditionality can certainly be examined from this angle. This statement assumes a greater importance as the Union exercises its choice to expand to include countries which have not shared the same historical experiences as the initial participants and therefore can envisage their future role in the Union in a wholly different way. The membership criteria clarify the Union's demand upon all future aspirants that its historical evolution and the achievements therein are not a subject for bilateral negotiations. This statement of course does not exclude the always relevant claim for reform of regulations, policies or achievements, especially when they admittedly fail to produce the results envisaged when first introduced.

Finally, an important reason for setting an explicit set of criteria for new entrants is simply because, by incorporating its basic values into the list of criteria to be met by new entrants, the EU has from an early stage realised that it had a very powerful political tool in its hands. The criteria include political and economic requirements along with the obligation to implement the full body of EU law and regulations. Therefore, the EU acquires a decisive say in the transformation of the societies of its future members and more importantly in a legitimate manner since compliance with the criteria is not imposed by the Union as it absolutely falls within the discretion of a non-member state whether or not to apply for EU membership. Hence, the EU has created a powerful and simultaneously legitimate political tool which helps it to export its model to neighbouring countries. The latter are implementing economic, political and societal reforms to match the Community pattern. And when they do, they become full members of the Union.

The first form of membership conditionality, albeit in an embryonic form, can be traced to the founding Treaty: the Treaty of Rome. In Article 237 it provided that 'any European state may apply to become a member of the Community'. Thus, the element of 'Europeanness' was the only necessary precondition for membership eligibility. Unfortunately, there was no definition of the actual borders of Europe which would subsequently determine the limits placed upon future enlargements. This could have been due to the fact that the Treaty of Rome was signed in 1958 at a period when Europe was divided between West and East and applications from countries lying on its Eastern borders or from countries such as Turkey were simply inconceivable. Morocco's application, however, was rejected in 1987 on the grounds that the country was not European.[60] In the present context more questions might

---

[60] See the European Parliament: http://www.europarl.eu.int/factsheets/6_3_1_en.htm, accessed 23 June 2005.

emerge over possible applications on behalf of Ukraine or even Georgia and Armenia. The issue of Russia as a member of the EU remains in the sphere of wild political imagination right now, but it is commonly accepted that a large part of the Russian territory falls within the geographical scope of Europe. Could a potential Russian application be considered by the EU? And does the small part of Turkish landmass lying in Europe and comprising mainly Istanbul justify its status as a European country when the rest of the country lies in Anatolia bordering Syria, Iraq and Iran? Are the criteria geographical, cultural or historical? Obviously, the EU appears to grant more importance to arguments of a historical nature, nevertheless the issue of agreeing on a common definition of the borders of Europe remains up to the present and especially in the light of the Turkish application a political imperative for the leaders of the Union.[61]

Thus, the entry of the UK, Ireland and Denmark in 1973 took place mainly on the basis of the all-encompassing 'Europeaness' criterion. However, as analysed within the framework of the widening versus deepening debate, the objection of France as expressed by its President Charles de Gaulle over the British application was partly based on the initial refusal of the British government to abide by the Common Agriculture Policy.[62] Among other political reasons the French government founded its objections on the refusal of an applicant country to accept an important aspect of the existing policies of the EU, namely the CAP. Therefore, France based its argument on its 'insistence that accession for the new members could only be on the basis of acceptance

---

[61] However, Olli Rehn, the Commissioner for Enlargement, has stated in his speech to the Transatlantic Institute on 20 June 2005 that 'Since the enlargement agenda is already stretched to its limits, we must be very cautious about taking on new commitments. But the EU was founded on the principle of "pacta sunt servanda", whereby sticking to one's word is a basic value. This means that Bulgaria and Romania will join the Union in 2007, if they fulfill the conditions. It also means that accession negotiations will start with Croatia and Turkey once the two countries meet the strict criteria. And the Western Balkans countries have the perspective of eventual EU membership. The European Council confirmed these commitments by referring to its conclusions of the June and December 2004 summits on enlargement'. He therefore implied that the limits of future enlargements may rest with the engagements the EU has already assumed with certain countries. See the speech at: http://europa.eu.int/rapid/pressReleasesAction.do?reference=SPEECH/05/363&format=HTML&aged=0&language=EN&guiLanguage=en, accessed 29 June 2005. Calls for defining the limits of Europe have been made on behalf of influential and important political figures with leadership potential such as Angela Merkel of Germany and Nicolas Sarkozy of France. See: *The Times*, 'Eleventh Hour Call for EU to Halt its Talks with Turkey', Anthony Browne, 28 June 2005.

[62] President Charles de Gaulle at his fifteenth press conference on 16 May 1967. See footnote 137.

of the complete *acquis communautaire*'.[63] France with its status as a current member state of the Union argued that a future member state cannot opt out of important EC policies. Therefore, although the entry of the first enlargement of the EC was not subject to certain membership conditionality, it can be argued that the basic requirement of accepting the *acquis communautaire* involving the entirety of EC legislation and policies was inherent in the political disputes between France and the UK which followed the British application to the EC. Thus, the very first stages of the development of membership conditionality can be discerned in the first enlargement of the club.

After the initial enlargement of the six founding members to the North so as to include the UK, Ireland and Denmark, the EU was embarking on its second attempt to increase its membership by reaching to the South of the continent. Greece was first on the list followed by Spain and Portugal. Along with the weak economic structures of these states, the main concerns over the expansion to the South were related to their fragile democratic systems. All three Southern European countries were emerging from dictatorships, which in the case of Spain and Portugal had lasted for several decades, thus, there were considerable doubts over their ability to support a stable democratic system. Along with its concerns, however, the EC was very interested in contributing to the consolidation of democracy on its southern flank and therefore, viewed their application as a means to entrench democratic institutions and avert any danger of a potential slide back to authoritarian regimes.

It is interesting to note that although the enlargement to the South did not take place on the basis of any conditionality, an initial form of entry requirements can be deduced from the European Council's declarations. More specifically, on 7 and 8 April the European Council in Copenhagen had declared in its conclusions that 'the Heads of State confirm their will, as expressed on the Copenhagen Declaration on the European Identity, to ensure that the cherished values of their legal, political and moral order are respected and to safeguard the principles of representative democracy, of the rule of law, of social justice, and of respect for human rights . . . they solemnly declare that respect for and maintenance of representative democracy and human rights in each member state are essential elements of membership of the European communities'.[64] Thus, although we still don't have officially prescribed conditions for membership at this time, we do have the first 'essential elements' of membership,

63 Stephen George and Ian Bache, *Politics in the European Union*, Oxford University Press, Oxford, 2001, p. 408.

64 The European Council, Copenhagen, 7–8 April 1978, Bulletin of the European Communities, 3/1978. See also: Joint Declaration by the European Parliament, the Council and the Commission on Fundamental Rights of 5 April 1977, OJ C 103, 27.4.1977.

which might not be conditions that have to be met before accession but do constitute parameters that were seriously to be taken into account in the course of enlargement.[65] The EC, therefore, appeared more flexible for purely political reasons. It wanted to promote democratic values in the southern European societies and at the same time extend its membership to countries placed in strategic areas in the framework of the Cold War. The extension of membership to these countries would extend security and stability to the South of the continent with an obvious beneficial impact on the West and North as well. Thus, political considerations prevailed and the respective countries gained the ticket for admission to the Union by setting aside economic assessments of a more technical nature. This was more evident in the case of Greece, where, uniquely, the reservations stated by the European Commission in its opinion

---

[65] The EC, however, did focus extensively on the economic aspects of the Southern Enlargement, especially in relation to structural weaknesses of the relevant economies and the need for transitional periods. See: Opinion on Greek application for membership (transmitted to the Council by the Commission on 29 January 1976), COM (76) 30, 20 January 1976. Bulletin of the European Communities, Supplement 2/76.

The transitional period and the institutional implications of enlargement (Commission Communication to the Council further to the Communication sent on 20 April 1978). COM (78) 190, 24 April 1978. Bulletin of the European Communities. Supplement 2/78.

Opinion on Greek application for membership (transmitted to the Council by the Commission on 29 January 1976). COM (76) 30, 20 January 1976. Bulletin of the European Communities, Supplement 2/76.

General considerations on the problems of enlargement (Communication sent by the Commission to the Council on 20 April 1978). COM (78) 120.

Economic and Sectoral Aspects. Commission analyses supplementing its views on enlargement, COM (78) 200, 27 April 1978, Part II.

Economic and sectoral aspects. Commission analyses supplementing its views on enlargement (Communication from the Commission, sent to the Council on 20 April 1978), COM (78) 200, 27 April 1978. Part I. Bulletin of the European Communities, Supplement 3/78 .

Consultation on Migration Policies vis-à-vis Third Countries (Communication of the Commission to the Council). COM (79) 115, 23 March 1979.

Spain and the European Community [May 1978]. Europe Information. External Relations, 5/78.

Portugal and the European Community [May 1978]. Europe Information. External Relations, 7/78.

Opinion on Spain's application for membership (transmitted to the Council by the Commission on 29 November 1978), COM (78) 630, 30 November 1978. Bulletin of the European Communities, 9/78.

Opinion on Portuguese application for membership (transmitted to the Council by the Commission on 19 May 1978), COM (78) 220. Bulletin of the European Communities, Supplement, 5/78.

on the Greek application that referred to the structural weaknesses of the Greek economy, were effectively ignored by the Council, which chose to promote rapid entry of the country into the EC.

The situation radically changed with the collapse of the Berlin Wall in 1989. The map of Europe was changed for good. New countries emerged, old alliances collapsed and Europe assumed a new shape, which rendered a redesign of the EC enlargement policy necessary. The subsequent applications of Eastern European countries to become members of the EC, the very important recent integrational achievements in the form of the Single European Act (1987) and the Treaty on the European Union (1992) that had to be protected and the realisation that the EC was no longer a 'Western European club' but should embrace the new democracies of the East resulted in the shaping of the first clearly stated membership conditionality.

The end of the Cold War entailed an increasing number of applicants which exceeded all respective past initiatives. As the first applications from the new European democracies were in the course of submission, the EU moved towards further clarification of the procedure to be followed in the case of a membership application. Therefore, the new article O of the Treaty of Maastricht stated that 'Any European State may apply to become a Member of the Union. It shall address its application to the Council, which shall act unanimously after consulting the Commission and after receiving the assent of the European Parliament, which shall act by an absolute majority of its component members. The conditions of admission and the adjustments to the Treaties on which the Union is founded which such admission entails shall be the subject of an agreement between the Member States and the applicant State. This agreement shall be submitted for ratification by all the Contracting States in accordance with their respective constitutional requirements'.[66] In addition to this the EU assumed responsibility in accordance with Article B to 'to maintain in full the *acquis communautaire* and build on it with a view to considering, through the procedure referred to in Article N(2), to what extent the policies and forms of cooperation introduced by this Treaty may need to be revised with the aim of ensuring the effectiveness of the mechanisms and the institutions of the Community'.

Thus, maintaining the *acquis communautaire* was emerging as one of the fundamental principles of the EU, finding its constitutional basis in the body of the TEU. Moreover, in article F it was stated that 'the Union shall respect the national identities of its Member States, whose systems of government are founded on the principles of democracy. The Union shall respect fundamental rights, as guaranteed by the European Convention for the Protection of Human

---

66 Article O of the Treaty of Maastricht.

Rights and Fundamental Freedoms signed in Rome on 4 November 1950 and as they result from the constitutional traditions common to the Member States, as general principles of Community law'. In this context the Commission in its report to the Council after noting that 'the Community has never been a closed club and cannot now refuse the historic challenge to assume its continental responsibilities . . . a state which applies for membership must therefore satisfy the three basic conditions of European identity, democratic status and respect for human rights . . . another set of criteria relate to the applicant state's acceptance of the Community system and its capacity to implement it . . . the obligations presuppose a functioning and competitive market economy and an adequate legal and administrative framework in the public and private sector'.[67] The Commission managed to draft the criteria, which appeared in almost identical form in the famous list of 'Copenhagen Criteria' to be drafted in 1993 in the capital of Denmark. Thus, the rather obscure notion of European identity (which even the Commission admitted in its report cannot be defined precisely), democracy, the respect for human rights, free market economy and the *acquis communautaire* appear to be the criteria presented by the Commission as the requirements for future entry. The Commission noted that enlargement to the East should not undermine the achievements of the EU, whose deepening should not be placed in peril. For this reason, although the current member states were granted several opt-outs (the UK from the Social Chapter and the final stage of the Economic and Monetary Union and Denmark only from the latter), the EU clarified its objection to granting further opt-outs to newcomers. The new member states would have to accept the *acquis* in its entirety before entry.

In the European Council in Copenhagen the EU engaged in an intense debate over whether it should assume a further widening initiative or not. The supporters of deepening stated that the EU had recently promoted various ambitious projects such as the final stage of the Monetary Union, thus further enlargement should be avoided to give the Union the space to absorb the new changes. However, the deteriorating situation in the Balkans with the ongoing war in Bosnia and further instability not only in the Balkan peninsula but also in Russia, caused the European leaders to promote further enlargement as a means to solidify security in the most problematic areas of the continent. Of course the Balkan countries were far from even being considered for membership but the extension of stability in the whole of Eastern Europe would be, and indeed proved to be, an essential step in consolidating security in the whole of the continent. In this context, setting strict entrance criteria served as

[67] European Commission, Report to the Council, Europe and the Challenge of Enlargement, Brussels, 24 June 1992, p. 53.

the factor that balanced the two conflicting parties. When the EU moved to enlarge at least it would do so by setting tight requirements so that its deepening would not be undermined. The result of the compromise was the famous Copenhagen Criteria, which will be considered in Chapter 3. Here, it is useful to state that the Copenhagen Criteria consist of political criteria (democracy, the rule of law, human rights, respect of minorities), economic criteria (market economy, the capacity to cope with competitive pressures within the EU) and the acceptance of the *acquis communautaire*. Furthermore, the EU stated that an important consideration would be 'the Union's capacity to absorb new members while maintaining the momentum of European integration'[68] a further safeguard for the supporters of deepening who were always fearful of the impact of widening on further integration.

This safeguard was also included in the Presidency conclusions of the European Summit in Essen in 1994, where the EU leaders stated that 'respecting its internal cohesion and its fundamental principles is also an important consideration in the general interest of both the Union and the candidate countries'.[69] The leaders also took the decision at the same summit to hold an Intergovernmental Conference in 1996 to discuss the 'the institutional conditions for ensuring the proper functioning of the Union'.[70] The latter led to the Treaty of Amsterdam, which, however, failed to deal with issues of institutional reform. Therefore, the 'Amsterdam left-overs', as stated above, were the subject of the Treaty of Nice.

In 1995 the European leaders confirmed in Madrid 'the need to make sound preparation for enlargement on the basis of the criteria established in Copenhagen and in the context of the pre-accession strategy defined in Essen for the CCEE; that strategy will have to be intensified in order to create the conditions for the gradual, harmonious integration of those States, particularly through the development of the market economy, the adjustment of their administrative structures and the creation of a stable economic and monetary environment'.[71] Thus, the EU attached great importance to the smooth operation of its cornerstone project, the internal market.

The preparations of the new member states' economies and administrative structures were central in their efforts to join the internal market and assumed massive importance. However, it was the political criterion that seemed to

---

68 European Council, Copenhagen, 21–22 June 1993. Access at: http://www.europarl.eu.int/summits/copenhagen/co_en.pdf.

69 European Council, 9–10 December 1994, Presidency Conclusions, Annex.

70 Ibid.

71 Madrid European Council, 15 and 16 December 2005, Presidency Conclusions, III. A Europe Open to the World, Enjoying Stability, Security, Freedom and Solidarity, A. Enlargement.

appear as the most fundamental. This is not only due to the fact that it is closely linked with the fundamental ideals of the European Union related to its democratic values, but also because the new wars erupting in the Balkans and more specifically in Kosovo in 1999 served as a reminder of the value of respect for minorities, democracy and stability. 'One of the key lessons of the Kosovo crisis is the need to achieve peace and security, democracy and the rule of law, growth and the foundations of prosperity throughout Europe. Enlargement is the best way to do this'.[72] As an indication of this, the political criterion was inserted into the Treaty of Amsterdam and, thus, now enjoys a constitutional basis. Article 6(1) of the Treaty of Amsterdam states that 'The Union is founded on the principles of liberty, democracy, respect for human rights and fundamental freedoms, and the rule of law, principles which are common to the Member States'. This should be viewed in conjunction with Article 49, which reads 'Any European State which respects the principles set out in Article 6(1) may apply to become a member of the Union'. The two articles serve as a constitutional codification of the political criterion.

In an even more significant step the European Council in Helsinki in 1999 declared that: 'compliance with the political criteria laid down at the Copenhagen European Council is a prerequisite for the opening of accession negotiations and that compliance with all the Copenhagen criteria is the basis for accession to the Union'.[73] Thus, the political criterion is not only a prerequisite for accession but also for the opening of negotiations leading to accession. Moreover 'the European Council confirmed the importance of the enlargement . . . for the stability and prosperity for the entire European continent'.[74] More importantly the European Council 'stressed the principle of peaceful settlement of disputes in accordance with the United Nations Charter and urges candidate States to make every effort to resolve any outstanding border disputes and other related issues. Failing this they should within a reasonable time bring the dispute to the International Court of Justice'. Therefore, a further requirement of 'good neighbourliness' was effectively added.

In 2004 the membership criteria were to become even stricter as the EU was preparing for the potential entry of Turkey. The European Council in Brussels in December 2004 shaped the regime under which Turkey will run its

---

[72] European Commission, Composite Paper, Reports on Progress towards Accession by each of the candidate countries, 13 October 1999. DG Enlargement: http://europa.eu.int/comm/enlargement/report_10_99/pdf/en/composite_en.pdf accessed on 29 June 2005.

[73] Helsinki European Council, 10 and 11 December 1999. Presidency Conclusions. I Preparing for Enlargement.

[74] Ibid.

accession negotiations with the Union. The potential entry of such a large country with a problematic record of human rights[75] (which formed the basis of the Union's past refusal to open negotiations with Turkey), divergent political standards and a population that will equal Germany's by the time of possible accession provoked considerable debate in the EU framework.

The issue of the entry of Turkey into the EU still possesses certain controversial characteristics and forms part of the internal political debates in several EU countries including Germany, France, Austria and the Netherlands where significant political powers and personalities refuse to consent to such a prospect. Turkish entry was one of the most debated issues in the public discussions that preceded the two referendums over the European Constitutional Treaty in France and the Netherlands. Its impact on the results cannot be accurately evaluated but, admittedly, it is one of the most challenging issues the EU is going to face over the next decade. The problem is aggravated by the rejection of the Constitutional Treaty since the EU is currently functioning on the basis of the Treaty of Nice, which does not include Turkey in its institutional arrangements. The entry of the latter will bring vast changes to the design of common European policies, institutional arrangements and the balance of power within the EU. In any case even if negotiations are concluded, the entry of Turkey will still be subject to the approval of the French and Austrian electorates and possibly of still more nations. France promoted a reform of its Constitution in order to introduce approval on behalf of its public opinion on the future enlargements of the EU excluding the cases of Bulgaria, Romania and Croatia.[76] Turkey is also under an obligation to sign

---

[75] The EU still declared its intention to closely watch the trial of Orhan Pamuk, accused of insulting Turkish national identity after an interview about the Armenian genocide. The trial is viewed as a test of Turkey's European credentials at the very beginning of its negotitation process. A delegation on behalf of the European Parliament is to attend the hearing. The prosecution of Mr Pamuk came under Article 301 of the *new* Penal Code on 'denigrating Turkish Identity'. Olli Rehn, the Enlargement Commissioner stated that 'the Turkish Penal Code will have to be amended in such a way that freedom of expression . . . follows European standards'. See: Speech by Olli Rehn, 'Accesssion Negotiations with Turkey: The Journey is as Important as the Final Destination', European Parliament Plenary Session, Strasbourg, 28 September 2005. Speech/05/556.

[76] Other potential candidates might include Bosnia and Herzegovina, with which negotiations for a Stabilisation and Accession Agreement were opened in November 2005, Serbia and Montenegro whose respective negotiations were opened in October 2005 and Albania, which opened negotiations in January 2003. The signing of Stabilisation and Association Agreements was viewed as the most adequate way to align the Western Balkans countries with the EU. It was promoted as a part of the 'Thessaloniki Agenda for the Western Balkans' adopted by the European Council in June 2003 in Thessaloniki, Greece.

the protocol extending a customs agreement it has with the EU to the ten new member states, including Cyprus. This is an indication of the challenges to be faced since Turkey has not yet officially recognised Cyprus. On 29 July 2005 Turkey signed the relevant agreement while attaching a statement that its conclusion does not in any way mean recognition of the Republic of Cyprus. The European Council reacted by declaring this declaration unilateral and without legal effect. Turkey is now under the obligation to 'apply the Protocol fully to all EU member states and the EU will monitor this closely and evaluate full implementation in 2006'.[77] Naturally, the Council concluded that 'recognition of all member states is a necessary component of the accession process'.[78] To this end, on 29 September 2005 the European Parliament postponed the vote to approve the protocol extending Turkey's association agreement with the EU to the ten new member states. MEPs feared that the Turkish declaration would form part of the ratification process in the Turkish Parliament and thus gain legal force.[79]

The unique challenges[80] stemming from the Turkish case were reflected in the process chosen by the European leaders to facilitate the enlargement to include Turkey. The EU will examine each chapter of the *acquis* independently and will have to unanimously agree not only on the legislative alignment with it but, more importantly, on 'a satisfactory track record of implementation'.[81] An interesting detail is that in the case of Turkey the *acquis*

---

[77] Council of the European Union, Enlargement: Turkey, Declaration by the European Community and its Member States, Document 12541/05 (Presse 243), 21 September 2005.

[78] Ibid.

[79] See: http://www.europarl.eu.int/news/expert/infopress_page/027-670-271-9-39-903-20050921IPR00563-28-09-2005-2005—true/default_en.htm, accessed 30 September 2005.

[80] One of which appears to be the reactions of European public opinion itself, as was reflected by the poll conducted by the *Eurobarometer*. In *Eurobarometer*, 63, Publication July 2005, accessed at: http://europa.eu.int/comm/public_opinion/archives/eb/eb63/eb63.4_en_first.pdf an increased 38% of Europeans appeared to oppose any future enlargement of the EU (p. 26). In France only 32% favours further enlargement of the Union and in Germany only 33% (p. 27). Only 32% of the EU-15 support the entry of Turkey, a percentage that rises to 48% when the EU-25 is measured. In any case 52% of all European Union citizens according to the *Eurobarometer* reject the enlargement to include Turkey, with only 35% supporting it (p. 29).

In *Eurobarometer* 64 published in December 2005 support for enlargement dropped slightly to 49% (p. 29). In the most recent *Eurobarometer* public opinion over Turkish membership was even more adverse as only 31% of Europeans seemed to approve it while 55% clearly objected to it. Albania and Serbia came second and third on the public opinion disapproval list with 50% and 44% respectively.

[81] European Council, Brussels, 16 and 17 December 2004, Presidency Conclusions, paragraph 23.

is broken down into 35 chapters[82] in sharp contrast to the 31 chapters on the basis of which negotiations with all previous countries were run. Specific arrangements, permanent safeguard clauses or even derogations in areas such as free movement of persons, structural policies and agriculture may be considered. Significantly enough, the individual member states are guaranteed a 'maximum role'[83] in the introduction of such derogations or permanent safeguards. This can lead to individual member states introducing derogations from the free movement of persons with Turkey while others choose not to. Turkish entry before 2014 is effectively excluded since it is not allowed by the current Financial Framework. Furthermore, the negotiations are 'an open ended process the outcome of which can not be guaranteed beforehand'.[84] However, if Turkey for internal reasons is not able to fully assume the obligations stemming from membership, it must be 'ensured that it is fully anchored in the European structures through the strongest possible bond'.[85] This is a reference to the case of a special or privileged relationship, which many parties in the EU view as a more acceptable compromise on the issue of Turkey's European ambitions. Prominent supporters of this proposal are the Christian Democratic Party in Germany, the Federal Chancellor of Austria, Mr Wolfgang Schuessel and the ruling UMP Party of Mr Sarkozy, Internal Minister of France. In the event of a persistent breach of the political criterion the Commission can recommend the suspension of negotiations, to which the Council has to consent with a qualified majority. The EU is also going to promote cultural dialogue between the two parties and the strengthening of civil society in Turkey.

The interesting point about the aforementioned procedure envisaged in the Brussels European Council in 2004 was that no more conditions were added to the famous Copenhagen list, but Turkey has to comply with a much more demanding procedure. The rationale behind adoption of the latter is the unique characteristics of the Turkish case that establish it as one of the most risky decisions in the Union's history. It is impossible at this point to make any prediction on the outcome of the process, which is likely to last for more than ten years, but it can be justifiably supposed that the EU will need radical reform before it renders itself ready to accept a country with the characteristics of

---

82 See the European Commission's Press Release, Commission presents a rigorous draft framework for accession negotiations with Turkey, Reference: IP/05/807, Brussels, 29/06/2005. Available at: http://europa.eu.int/rapid/pressReleasesAction.do?reference=IP/05/807&format=HTML&aged=0&language=en&guiLanguage=en.

83 European Council, Brussels, 16 and 17 December 2004, Presidency Conclusions, paragraph 23.

84 Ibid.

85 Ibid.

Turkey. It is certain that Turkey will not be the same country after ten years of intense reforms and changes, but exactly the same principle applies to the European Union. After the entry of Turkey it will never be the same again.

It was exactly this realisation, along with enlargement fatigue that was clearly revealed by the outcome of the referendums in France and the Netherlands, that turned the opening of negotiations with Turkey on 3 October 2005, an otherwise standard process, into a political and diplomatic thriller. Austria insisted on changing the objective of the negotiations from 'full membership' to a 'privileged partnership' as an acceptable alternative to the former. It was clear from the beginning of negotiations that such a change would be unsuccessful since the European leaders had already committed the Union to granting Turkey full membership if it successfully met the relevant criteria.[86] However, the change in mood in several EU countries towards Turkey and the local elections taking place in Austria on exactly the same day as the EU was to take the relevant decision were significant factors in causing political turmoil. Austrian public opinion continued to overwhelmingly oppose potential Turkish entry and the government had to act accordingly.

However, although Austria was not successful in altering the objective of negotiations, it was successful in its bid to add or rather to emphasise further another parameter in the negotiating process for Turkey. The 'capacity of the EU to absorb' new member states assumed increased importance as an additional factor that the EU had to closely monitor before it took a decision on further enlargement. When the size of Turkey and the subsequent changes it will bring to EU structures and policy shaping is taken into account, the political importance of emphasising such a parameter can be easily understood.

Austria was also successful in confirming the opening of negotiations with Croatia, which were frozen earlier that year due to a failure on the part of Croatia to constructively cooperate with the International Criminal Tribunal for the former Yugoslavia in its bid to arrest general Ante Gotovina. During the Council and as the Presidency (the UK at the moment) was trying to convince Austria to lift its veto, it received the report from the Chief Prosecutor of the ICTY stating the 'clear commitment by the Croatian Prime Minister that full cooperation would be maintained until the last remaining indictee was in the Hague'. The Chief Prosecutor felt, therefore, 'confident that Ante Gotovina

---

[86] Although the European Parliament upheld the opening of negotiations in the text it adopted in the light of the meeting of the Foreign ministers to decide on the opening of negotiations with Turkey, it simultaneously added further conditions such as recognition of the Armenian genocide as 'a prerequisite for accession'. See paragraph 5, Texts Adopted by the Parliament, 28 September 2005, P6_TA-PROV(2005)0350. The latter is not accepted by the European Commission.

would be transferred to the Hague soon'.[87] The expressed confidence of Carla del Ponte was the basis on which the European leaders dropped their previous reservations and, adhering to the Austrian position, paved the way for the opening of negotiations. Therefore, Croatia was set on course for Brussels and Austria retreated from its initial position and lifted its veto against Turkish full membership. The President of the European Commission José Manuel Barroso stated that the 'road will be long and difficult' while accession would be 'neither guaranteed nor automatic'.[88]

[87] Council of the European Union, Document 12514/05 (Presse 241), Press Release, 2678th Council Meeting, General Affairs and External Relations, General Affairs, Luxembourg, 3 October 2005, p. 7.

[88] Declaration of the President of the European Commission José Manuel Barroso, on the opening of accession negotiations with Turkey, Brussels, 3 October 2005, IP/05/1219, accessed also at: http://www.europa.eu.int/comm/external_relations/news/barroso/sp05_1210.htm, accessed 3 October 2005.

3. The criteria for entry

In 1993, the European Council in Copenhagen came to the historic decision to allow the countries of Eastern Europe that so desired to become members of the European Union.

> The European Council today agreed that the associated countries in Eastern and Central Europe that so desire *shall become members* of the European Union. Accession will take place as soon as an associated country is able to assume the obligations of membership by satisfying the economic and political conditions required.
>
> Membership requires that the candidate country has achieved stability of institutions guaranteeing *democracy*, the rule of law, human rights and respect for and protection of minorities; (the political criterion)
>
> The existence of a functioning *market economy* as well as the capacity to cope with competitive pressure and market forces within the European Union; (the economic criterion)
>
> Membership presupposes the candidate's ability to take on the *obligations of membership* including adherence to the aims of political, economic and monetary union. (the *acquis communautaire*)
>
> The Union's *capacity to absorb* new members while maintaining the momentum of European integration is also an *important consideration* in the general interests of both the Union and the candidate countries
>
> The European Council will continue to follow closely progress in each associated country towards fulfilling the conditions for accession to the Union and draw the appropriate conclusions
>
> The European Council agreed that the future cooperation with the associated countries shall be geared to the objective membership which has now been established'.[1]

In addition to that the European Council in Madrid in 1995 stated that:

> Enlargement must serve to strengthen the building of Europe in observance of the *acquis communautaire* which includes the common policies . . . the European Council also confirms the need . . . [for the pre-accession] strategy [to be] intensified in order to create the conditions for the gradual, harmonious integration of those (the applicant) states, particularly through the development of the market

[1] European Council in Copenhagen, Presidency Conclusions, 21 and 22 June, Bulletin of the European Communities, No. 6/1993, paragraph I.13 (emphasis added).

economy, the *adjustment of their administrative structures* and the creation of a stable economic and monetary environment' (emphasis added).[2]

Finally, the European Council in Luxembourg in 1997 concluded that:

The European Council decided to set up a European Conference which will bring together the Member States of the European Union and the European States aspiring to accede to it and sharing its values and internal and external objectives. The members of the Conference must share a common commitment to peace, security and *good neighbourliness, respect for other countries' sovereignty*, the principles upon which the European Union is founded, the integrity and inviolability of external borders and the principles of international law and a commitment to *the settlement of territorial disputes by peaceful means*, in particular through the jurisdiction of the International Court of Justice in the Hague. Countries which endorse these principles and respect the right of any European country fulfilling the required criteria to accede to the European Union and sharing the Union's commitment to building a Europe free of the divisions and difficulties of the past will be invited to take part in the Conference' (emphasis as original).[3]

The relevant part of the Copenhagen Presidency Conclusions was hugely significant for future political developments on the continent as it was the first official declaration by the European leaders in a text that they intended to welcome as full members of the Union all associated countries of the East[4] which comply with the requirements of an economic and political nature set by the Council. This date is of particular importance because it removed all the obstacles to a new enlargement that was to change the character of the Union. The latter expressed its clear political will to embrace the Eastern part of the continent and on the basis of fixed criteria to extend the zone of stability already enjoyed in the West to the greatest part of Europe, effectively ending the repercussions of the Cold War and the divisions of the past. For the first time the European leaders shaped a clear process, which had to be followed by both the Union and the candidates, with full membership as the final prize.

---

[2] European Council in Madrid, 15 and 16 December 1995, Presidency Conclusions, Bulletin of the European Communities, No. 12/1995, paragraph I. 25.

[3] European Council in Luxembourg, 12 and 13 December 1997, Presidency Conclusions, Bulletin of the European Communities, No. 12/1997, paragraphs 4 and 5.

[4] The European Union was prompt in financially assisting the CEEC after the collapse of communism. The Phare Programme, which was set up in 1989, provided finance for the efforts of the CEEC to rebuild their economies and from the beginning of the previous decade the EU concluded Association Agreements, so-called Europe Agreements, with ten countries of Central and Eastern Europe. Those Agreements functioned as the legal basis for the bilateral relations between the EU on the one hand and the CEEC on the other. Those associated countries were guaranteed such an option when they applied for membership if they successfully met the Union's criteria.

Now, all interested parties involved were well aware of the reforms they had to implement and the initiatives they would have to take in order to achieve the clearly set objective: membership.

The establishment of membership as the absolutely guaranteed outcome of a successful effort to meet the Union's demands had a profound impact on Eastern European societies. It served as a highly desired safeguard that after painful political, economic and societal reforms the countries involved would definitely enjoy inclusion in the European family. The latter had committed itself to admitting all candidates that satisfied its criteria. However, there was criticism that 'none of these elements (criteria) is clear-cut; certainly there are no ready made entrance criteria against which the preparedness of an aspirant can be checked off'.[5]

But even if there was some lack of clarity in the Copenhagen Criteria, considered in detail below, they did not completely form a one size fits all approach. Although the candidate countries had to accept the whole body of EU law and regulations, implementation was always bound to differ according to the particular conditions in the country. 'Therefore, in some ways each country's detailed obligations were unique. Some may include creating or strengthening competition laws . . . others may concern the protection of environment'.[6] The scope of the *acquis* is so great that the focus in each country would differ according to its own characteristics, strengths and weaknesses, although the demands, the goal and the means to achieve it remain identical for all.

However, guaranteeing membership at an initial stage was vital as 'the EU membership criteria required many applicants to dismantle functioning legal and economic systems, as well as deconstruct long lasting political ideologies, tasks that do not come without a significant prize'.[7] Membership functioned exactly as that: the significant award that would be definitely granted to all candidates that submitted to in the process of far-reaching reform. The latter 'did not concern only the law on the books; it required developing a wide range of societal institutions and nurturing a market oriented legal culture'.[8]

---

5 Jozef M. van Brabant, *Remaking Europe, The European Union and Transition Economies*, Rowman and Littlefield Publishers Inc, New York and Oxford, 1999, p. 65.

6 Christine Juliet Sohar, 'The European Union's Legal Integration, A Case Study of Living up to the Denver Summit of Eight', *Denver Journal of International Law and Policy*, 27, 1999, p. 710.

7 Peter Katz, 'The Treaty of Nice and European Union Enlargement: The Political, Economic, and Social Consequences of Ratifying the Treaty of Nice', *Pennsylvania Journal of International Economic Law*, 24, 2003, p. 232.

8 Rilka O. Dragneva and Thomas N. Jersild, 'Perspectives on Company Law Reform in Central and Eastern Europe: An Introduction', *Review of Central and East European Law*, 27, 2001, No. 1, p. 1.

Therefore, the EU 'came to act as transmitter of transition related models and ideas . . . as the CEEC were exposed to various kinds of external influence during their post communist transition. Some of these influences involved the voluntary transfer of ideas'.[9]

'The return to Europe was to mean, in domestic terms, the establishment of "normal", understood as Western European style institutions; a pluralist liberal democratic political system and a market economy which could offer both consumer affluence and a developed welfare state'.[10] It was not a foregone conclusion that countries in the phase of transition would look to align their policies with Western European norms. 'In many African, Asian and Latin American countries with emerging economies or in transition from socialist to market economies, the Western legislative economic model has proved unattractive'.[11]

Hence, convergence with the EU norms was made appealing to the CEEC because it could lead to membership. Linking the fulfilment of the criteria to membership and forging a process based on the annual publication of reports highlighting the achievements or failures of the candidate countries was found to constitute 'the golden carrot, which played a key role in encouraging reforms'.[12] These reforms 'have exposed the societies of the candidate countries to enormous pressure. They have had to make the transition from Communist rule and centrally planned economies to democracy and market economy . . . and to adapt to the highly developed system of European integration . . . therefore people needed to see where they were going and what is waiting for them when they arrive'.[13] 'Conditionality subjects the development or deepening of relations (or sometimes even their continued existence) with a country or a group of countries to compliance with specified conditions

9 Marcin Zaborowski, 'Westernising the East: External Influences in the Post Comunist Transformation of Eastern and Central Europe', *The Journal of Communist Studies and Transition Politics*, 21, March 2005, No. 1, 'Special Issue on Policy Transfer and Programmic Change in the Communist Successor Parties of Eastern and Central Europe', edited by Dan Hough, William E. Paterson, James Sloam, Routledge, London and New York, p. 17.

10 Wade Jacoby, *The Enlargement of the European Union and NATO, Ordering from the Menu in Central Europe*, Cambridge University Press, 2004, p. 41.

11 Simon Helm, 'Intellectual Property in Transition Economies: Assessing the Latvian Experience', *Fordham Intellectual Property, Media and Entertainment Law Journal*, 14, 2003, p. 123.

12 Graham Avery in Fraser Cameron, *Europe Integration and Enlargement*, Routledge, London and New York, 2004, p. 38.

13 Eneko Landaburu, Director General of DG Enlargement, European Commission, European Union Law Essay: 'The Fifth Enlargement of the European Union: The Power of Example', *Fordham International Law Journal*, 26, 1, 2002, p. 10.

or meeting of targets'.[14] In this sense 'European enlargement is interpreted as the political process or as an extension of the operating procedures onto the newly incorporated parts of the entity'.[15] On the other hand, conditionality granted the EU the chance to shape 'a balance between giving support to reforming governments while not devaluing the status of EU membership by admitting countries that fail to meet its standards'.[16] It was also 'designed to minimise the risk of new entrants becoming politically unstable and economically burdensome to the existing Union . . . and reassure reluctant member states that disruption risks would be minimal'.[17]

Although the EU did set the parameter of full membership as the guaranteed prize, there was much criticism of the actual roles the participant parties were assigned to play. 'The sweeping obligation for the approximation of the laws (of the CEEC) to those of the EU does not carry with it any rights to participate in the process of making or modifying EC law. This everyday aspect of accession is particularly offensive in Central and Eastern Europe, where transition and enlargement are intimately tied to the promotion of democracy'.[18] Therefore, 'conditionality shaping the whole enlargement process reveals strong asymmetries between the parties involved'.[19] 'Because the EU has significantly more power than the applicant countries, it is in a position to set the rules . . . the applicant countries negotiating bilaterally have been in a much weaker position to bargain over their conditions for entry'.[20] The argument refers to the inability of the candidates to shape the bundle of regulations and obligations to which they have to adhere. Although this element might have further complicated their efforts to comply with the specified criteria, it was a direct consequence of their absence from EU structures.

Their inability to influence EU decision making underlined the importance of membership. As soon as they managed to pass the necessary reforms and

---

14 Marise Cremona, 'EU Enlargement: Solidarity and Conditionality', *European Law Review*, 30(1), 2005, p. 15.

15 Nanette Neuwahl, *European Union Enlargement, Law and Socio-Economic Changes*, Les éditions thémis, Chaire Jean Monnet, Montréal, 2004, p. 165.

16 Heather Grabbe and Kirsty Hughes, *Enlarging the EU Eastwards*, The Royal Institute of International Affairs, London, 1998, p. 40.

17 Heather Grabbe, 'European Union Conditionality and the Acquis Communautaire', *International Political Science Review*, 23(3), 2002, p. 251.

18 Helen E. Hartnell, 'Subregional coalescence in European Regional Integration', *Wisconsin International Law Journal*, 16, 1997, p. 173.

19 Cesare Pinelli, 'Conditionality and Enlargement in Light of EU Constitutional Developments', *European Law Journal*, 10(3), May 2004, p. 357.

20 Amy Verdun and Osvaldo Croci, *The European Union in the Wake of Eastern Enlargement, Institutional and Policy Making Challenges*, Manchester University Press, Manchester and New York, 2005, p. 13.

comply with the EU, they would become full members of the Union with the ability to participate actively in the decision-making structures and contribute to the future shaping of the European edifice. Their contributions would constitute part of the *acquis communautaire* to be fully adhered to by the candidates included in the following waves of enlargement. Therefore, this asymmetry between the EU on the one hand, which had all the power as the principal negotiator in its hands and the CEEC on the other, may have further encouraged their efforts to fulfil the criteria and join as soon as possible. The advantages of being a full member were instantly perceived and that served as an important stimulus to change and convergence with the EU.

THE POLITICAL CRITERION

The European Union, 'designed as a community of states and peoples sharing political ethos, principles of government, human values and aspirations',[21] placed the fulfilment of the political criterion at the forefront of candidates' efforts to prepare for membership. As explained in the framework of the analysis of the deepening versus widening debate, the political criterion appeared for the first time in 1978 as the EC was preparing for its enlargement to the South. The countries concerned, Greece, Spain and Portugal, were all dealing with the painful heritage left by their respective dictatorial regimes and were implementing reforms to consolidate a new democratic political life, which at that time remained fragile. In this context, the European Council, convening again in Copenhagen, stated that respect for and maintenance of democracy and human rights constituted what the leaders chose to call 'essential elements of membership'[22] for joining the Community. Thus, as explained, political conditionality appeared albeit in embryonic form, but in milder wording fifteen years before its official recognition at Copenhagen in 1993.

Despite its inclusion in the core of the conditionality catalogue and although the enlargement 'procedures have evolved over the course of successive previous enlargements and are now well established',[23] the political criterion was not thoroughly analysed at least at the relevant European Council. The lack of clarification might have been due to the fact that 'there is no single

21 Jirí Pribán, 'European Union Constitution Making, Political Identity and Central European Reflections', *European Law Journal*, 11(2), March 2005, p. 149.

22 See Chapter 2 note 46 and p. 57.

23 Michael J. Baun, *A Wider Europe, The Process and Politics of European Union Enlargement*, Rowman and Littlefield Publishers Inc., New York and Oxford, 2000, p. 12.

model of democracy and rights protection in the EU itself, much less in the West'.[24]

Although 'the ordering of society through the application of a framework of laws and regulations based on the will of the people, as expressed through the democratic process and implemented by an independent judiciary, has deep roots in Europe going back at least to Roman times',[25] different European countries have divergent sensitivities on human rights issues reflected in their respective legislation. Of course the European Union and other organisations encompassing European countries such as the Council of Europe have promoted legislation and practices that guarantee an advanced protection of human rights in all member states; however, legislative priorities in this field continue to exist. For example, continental countries have founded their human rights protection on a draft bill of rights, while in the UK, until recently, advanced human rights protection was the result of Court rulings enforcing traditional principles rather than the result of the application of any document consistent with the common law system. Different societal values between the more liberal Northern European countries and the more conservative South and divergent historical experiences between for example Sweden with its long history of democratic stability and Greece or Spain with relatively recent experiences of political anomaly are certainly reflected in their respective human rights' protection legislation. These differences are in addition to scepticism over the human rights agenda as a whole, an aspect discussed in Chapter 4.

The political criterion was 'constitutionalised'[26] in Articles 6(1) and 49 of the Treaty of Amsterdam. Article 6(1) states that the Union is indeed based on the principles of liberty, democracy, respect for human rights and fundamental freedoms, and the rule of law. These principles are so fundamental that according to Article 49 only the countries that respect them can become members of the EU. Therefore, the political criterion found in the Treaty of Amsterdam its constitutional codification: a constitutional basis, which reveals the significance that the EU, as a union of countries based on certain values, ascribes to a catalogue of principles to be adhered to by any country which shares the aspiration of joining. The European leaders decided at the

24 Wojciech Sadurski, 'Accession's Democracy Dividend: The Impact of the EU Enlargement upon Democracy in the New Member States of Central and Eastern Europe', *European Law Journal*, 10(4), July 2004, p. 377.

25 John Richardson, Head of the Delegation of the European Commission to the United Nations, European Union Law Essay: 'The European Union in the World, A Community of Values', *Fordham International Law Journal*, 26, 2003, p. 18.

26 Christophe Hillion, *EU Enlargement: A Legal Approach*, Hart Publishing, Oxford and Portland, Ore., 2004, p. 3.

European Council held in Cologne in 1999[27] to entrust the task of drafting a Charter of Fundamental Rights to a convention. The Charter was signed at Nice[28] in 2000 and later, in a spectacular gesture aimed at enhancing its status as part of the most fundamental constitutional document of the Union, it became an integral part of the Constitutional Treaty, whose eventual rejection however effectively deprived it of its constitutional status.

The clarification of the exact nature and scope of the political criterion came much later in the form of Agenda 2000,[29] the document that contained the Commissions avis (opinions) on the applications of the eight CEEC plus Cyprus and Malta. The text of Agenda 2000 and the particular fields on which the European Commission chose to focus its research and attention when investigating the compliance of the political criterion by the candidates, reveal the specific parameters of the criterion and its elements of concern, which were only implied in the text of Copenhagen. The European Commission was not only interested in concluding whether democracy in its wide sense exists in a certain candidate country, but its research was orientated towards discerning the particular 'legal and institutional frameworks, and attempting to evaluate how democracy actually works in practice'.[30] More specifically, according to Agenda 2000, the Commission 'examined how various rights and freedoms, such as the freedom of expression, are exercised, through, for example, the role of political parties, non-governmental organisations and the media'.[31] The Commission deemed of maximum importance that 'the applicant countries' constitutions guarantee democratic freedoms, including political pluralism, the freedom of expression and the freedom of religion. They have set up democratic institutions and independent judicial and constitutional authorities, which permit different state authorities to function normally, have held free and fair elections, permitting the alternation of different political parties in power and, in general, recognise the role of the opposition'.[32] Moreover, 'stability of institutions enabling the public authorities to function properly and democracy to be consolidated' along with 'suitably qualified

---

27 European Council in Cologne, 3 and 4 June 1999, Presidency Conclusions. Access at the European Council site at: http://europa.eu.int/council/off/conclu/june99/june99_en.htm.

28 European Council in Nice, 7 to 9 December 2000, Presidency Conclusions. Access at the site of the European Parliament at: http://www.europarl.eu.int/summits/nice1_en.htm.

29 European Commission, Agenda 2000 – Volume I – Communication: For a Stronger and Wider Union, DOC/97/6.

30 Peter Coffey, *Europe: Toward the Next Enlargement*, Kluwer Academic Publishers, London, Boston and Dordrecht, 2000, p. 40.

31 Agenda 2000, Chapter 2, note 88 at p. 51.

32 Ibid.

judges and guarantees of their independence'[33] are factors whose examination falls within the ambit of the political criterion. Furthermore, police forces should be adequately paid and receive suitable training and discipline, while the autonomy of local government should enjoy a firm legal basis. As an indication of the Commission's approach, Romania was found to have made progress in the direction of convergence with the EU standards as 'the reform of the secret police services and the judicial system has been completed very quickly'.[34] Slovakia, on the other hand, failed to meet the political criterion because 'this would require a greater openness to opposing views, the proper functioning of state institutions and the respect for their individual roles in the constitutional order. A democracy cannot be considered stable if the respective rights and obligations of institutions such as the presidency, the constitutional court or the central referendum commission can be put into question by the government itself and if the legitimate role of the opposition in parliamentary committees is not accepted. The failure of the May 1997 referendum on NATO membership and on the direct election of the president, unsuccessful attempts by the government to reform the penal code, with a view to limiting the freedom of expression, the efforts to block an enquiry into the activities of the secret services and various forms of pressure exerted by the government on officials and cultural bodies, are symptomatic of the instability of the country's institutions'.[35] Thus, failing to recognise the constitutional role of the opposition and to safeguard the independence of certain institutions is enough for a country to fall below the standards set by the European Union in the political field.

The EU naturally placed the protection of human rights at the forefront of its approach and demanded accession 'to the Council of Europe's Convention for the Protection of Human Rights and Fundamental Freedoms and the Protocol allowing citizens to take cases to the European Court of Human Rights'.[36] The 'freedom of expression and of association and the independence of radio and television' along with respect for minorities proved among other indicators by the adoption and ratification of the 'Framework Convention for the Protection of National Minorities of the Council of Europe and recommendation 1201 adopted by the Parliamentary Assembly of the Council of Europe in 1993'.[37] The Commission therefore concluded that 'minority problems, if unresolved, could affect democratic stability or lead to disputes with neighbouring countries. It is therefore in the interest of the

[33] Ibid.
[34] Agenda 2000, p. 52.
[35] Ibid.
[36] Ibid.
[37] Agenda 2000, p. 53.

Union and of the applicant countries that satisfactory progress in integrating minority populations be achieved before the accession process is completed, using all opportunities offered in this context'.[38]

In addition to that the European Parliament, in response to the Commission's communication, underlined the following factors as indicative of a country in a position to match the political requirements. These factors included 'the ratification and implementation of legal human rights standards, the legal accountability of police, military and secret services, respect for the rights of minorities, the right to free speech, and the freedom of the media, the abolition of capital punishment, where applicable, the eradication of torture and ill-treatment, the acceptance of the principle of conscientious objection to military service, the acceptance and encouragement of the non-profit-making sector as an important partner in the task of continually improving respect for human rights'.[39]

From the above, it is evident that not only had the EU set standards which are very hard to meet, especially in the usually short pre-accession preparation period but, in addition, 'the EU is to influence many policy areas beyond the reach of Community competence in the member states . . . as the political criteria take the EU into areas such as judicial reform and prison conditions'.[40] Nevertheless, the candidate countries did have to comply with the criteria shaped by the Commission's documents and were found to effectively meet the standards set by the Union's executive before their accession.

THE ECONOMIC CRITERION

The economic criterion assumed its status as one of the three fundamental requirements for accession at Copenhagen in 1993. However, as analysed within the framework of the deepening versus widening analysis, the Commission had expressed its concerns about the structural weaknesses inherent in the economies of the Southern European states before their accession. As analysed, economic considerations were taken into account[41] in the design of a pre- and post-accession strategy for the countries involved. Despite previous

---

[38] Agenda 2000, p. 54.

[39] Official position of the European Parliament, Resolution on the Communication from the Commission, 'Agenda 2000 – for a stronger and wider Union' (COM (97) 2000 – C4-0371/97), accessed at the European Parliament's site at: http://www.europarl.eu.int/enlargement/positionep/resolutions/041297a_en.htm.

[40] Heather Grabbe, in Kevin Featherstone and Claudio M. Radaelli, *The Politics of Europeanisation*, Oxford University Press, Oxford, 2003, p. 308.

[41] See Chapter 2, Note 47 and p. 57.

experience on economic concerns, the application of eight countries taking the first steps of their post-communist era, certainly posed new and considerably heavier challenges to the European Union. Consequently, the European Commission brought the principle of the free market into the core of its enlargement policy. Only countries fully adhering to the free market capitalist system could become members of the Union. Chapter 4 examines what this might mean. Such clarification was necessary in the light of applications from 'former communist countries, which had worked and developed under radically different economic principles and structures'.[42] The problem was that 'economic contacts between the communist states and the states of western Europe were limited during the Soviet era . . . as a result the communist states were isolated from international markets and capital flows, and had limited exposure to international technological innovation and new economic ideas'.[43] Isolation from international markets and limited economic interaction with the Western part of the continent raised many concerns over the possible inability of the CEEC to function in such a highly integrated market as the Common Market, shaped within the EU framework. The EU acknowledged at an early stage that 'to shift from plan to market system of organisation implies first of all a set of reforms of the formal rules – like the legal system, the banking system, capital markets, and the informal rules – which determine the system of incentives of the individuals who govern economic activity and behaviour'.[44] Therefore, since traditionally the 'integration of markets has gone hand in hand with a proliferation of efforts to harmonise key aspects of the law relating to finance and trade',[45] the EU set these objectives at the heart of its strategy. As with the political criterion, the content of the economic criterion remained vague. The drafting of the conditionality catalogue in Copenhagen did not include the individual elements inherent in the relevant concept. Therefore, the examination of Agenda 2000 communication is essential for the further understanding of the precise extent of the economic criterion.

The European Commission states as important parameters the 'transition to a market economy, including privatisation and liberalisation'.[46] The 'existence

---

42 Roland Kobia, 'Reflections on the Effects of Future Enlargements of the EU on Industrial Property: The Case of Trade Marks', *European Intellectual Property Review*, 20(5), 1998, p. 183.

43 Alan Smith in Julie Smith and Charles Jenkins, *Through the Paper Curtain, Insiders and Outsiders in the New Europe*, Blackwell Publishing, Oxford, 2003, p. 16.

44 Nicholas C. Kyriazis and Michel S. Zouboulakis, 'Modeling Institutional Change in Transition Economies', *Communist and Post-Communist Studies*, 38, 2005, p. 118.

45 Katharina Pistor, 'The Standardisation of Law and its Effect on Developing Economies', *American Journal of Comparative Law*, 50, 2002, p. 97.

46 Agenda 2000 Communication, supra Chapter 2, note 88, p. 54.

of a functioning market economy' from the Copenhagen text is interpreted on the basis of the following parameters:

- equilibrium between demand and supply is established by the free interplay of market forces; prices, as well as trade, are liberalised;
- absence of significant barriers to market entry (establishment of new firms) and exit (bankruptcies);
- the legal system, including the regulation of property rights, is in place; laws and contracts can be enforced;
- macroeconomic stability has been achieved including adequate price stability and sustainable public finances and external accounts;
- broad consensus about the essentials of economic policy;
- the financial sector is sufficiently well-developed to channel savings towards productive investment'.[47]

Equally importantly the second element of the Copenhagen economic criterion referring to the 'capacity to cope with competitive pressure and market forces within the European Union' is defined to include:

- the existence of a functioning market economy, with a sufficient degree of macroeconomic stability for economic agents to make decisions in a climate of stability and predictability;
- a sufficient amount, at an appropriate cost, of human and physical capital, including infrastructure (energy supply, telecommunication, transport, etc.), education and research, and future developments in this field;
- the extent to which government policy and legislation influence competitiveness through trade policy, competition policy, state aids, support for SMEs, etc.;
- the degree and the pace of trade integration a country achieves with the Union before enlargement. This applies both to the volume and the nature of goods already traded with member states;
- the proportion of small firms, partly because small firms tend to benefit more from improved market access, and partly because a dominance of large firms could indicate a greater reluctance to adjust.[48]

The European Commission also stressed the importance of achieving 'further progress in implementing the measures indicated in the 1995 White Paper[49] on the Single Market [which] will remain both an essential method of preparation and an approximate yardstick for the applicants' degree of preparedness'.[50]

---

47 Ibid. at p. 55.

48 Ibid. at p. 56.

49 Its main tasks entail the elimination of physical, technical, fiscal and tariff barriers between participating states, see Susan Senior Nello, Karen E. Smith, *The European Union and Central and Eastern Europe, The Implications of Enlargement in Stages*, Ashgate, Aldershot and Brookfield USA, 1998, p. 17.

50 Page 57 of the Agenda 2000 Communication.

The European Commission stated that 'most applicants still need to restructure large state-owned industries, which dominate local economies and are very hard to reform for both social and economic reasons'.[51] It is evident that the requirements imposed on new members were considerably hard to meet as issues such as the restructuring of state-owned enterprises still form a subject of debates in various existing member states, where reform is also needed but it has been proven increasingly challenging to introduce and implement. The Commission also noted that 'in general, structural reform still has a long way to go, particularly as regards the banking and financial systems, and as regards social security'.[52]

It is interesting that the EU chose to deal with the issue of social security in this context. 'This is an important concession to the north-western EU members, none of whom wish to put their welfare states at risk through excessive competition from the CEEC',[53] so the question that soon arose was 'how much social security is needed before the EU will consider that a CEEC meets its standards?'. This element can serve as an indication of the asymmetry characterising the whole accession process as the candidate countries have to meet pre-determined standards set by the existing members, which might seek to pursue other objectives through them as well. It also reveals the importance of a foreign policy tool such as conditionality as it has proved to be a very effective way to significantly influence fundamental elements in the shaping of a given society. Therefore, the EU has interpreted its economic criterion to include 'reform of pension and social security systems',[54] areas where existing member states have been reluctant to cooperate.

THE *ACQUIS COMMUNAUTAIRE* AND THE OBLIGATIONS OF MEMBERSHIP

The acceptance, before its accession, by a candidate country of the *acquis communautaire*, emerged as a principle as early as 1967. The British application was in the hands of the European leaders and France refused to accept the British entry before the UK assumed the political commitment to abide to the Common Agriculture Policy.[55] The French argued that when a country applies to the EC, it should align its policies with the objectives and the existing regu-

51 Page 55 of the Agenda 2000 Communication.

52 Ibid.

53 Price et al., supra Chapter 1, note 7, p. 47.

54 Heather Grabbe , supra note 40, p. 308.

55 See the analysis in the framework of the deepening v. widening debate. Chapter 2, footnotes 44 and 45 of relevance at this point at p. 56 and 57.

lations of the Community. This principle was vigorously supported by President Charles de Gaulle,[56] who did not hesitate to veto the first enlargement on that basis. This principle was confirmed in 1969, when the European leaders stated that 'in so far as the applicant states accept the Treaties and their political aims, the decisions taken since the entry into force of the Treaty and the options adopted in the sphere of development the Heads of State or Government have indicated their agreement to the opening of negotiations'.[57] Thus, as early as in 1969 the European leaders decided that negotiations could open after a candidate accepted the Treaty, its political aims and the decisions assumed at Community level since the Treaty came into force. The far-reaching implications of such a decision were to be felt in all future enlargements, especially the most recent.

As mentioned before, the Community included enlargement among its original aims.[58] Therefore, from its foundation the Community aimed to evolve in a non-static way, as it 'was conceived from its origin as a phenomenon of progressive development . . . a system, which never ceases evolving to construct a more and more complicated machine, must refer to some types of acquired characteristics, guarantees of its integrity'.[59] The Community is engaged in a dynamic process of extending the scope of its competence and it chose to pursue its evolution through constant widening of its membership; therefore, it needs an element to assure its continuity. 'The *acquis* is a construction of the organisation to ensure its continuity . . . the term evokes the hard unyielding core, transgression of which would lead to effects of blockage or disintegration'.[60] The *acquis* encompassing the entirety of the Union's legislation, case law and policy objectives embodies the nature and fundamentals of the Union, without acceptance of which accession is literally unimaginable. This is the rationale behind the Union's insistence on imposing compliance with the *acquis* on all future member states.

'This bedrock principle is derived from the strongly held belief that new members are joining a club with a rule book rather than entering into a free

---

[56] President Charles de Gaulle at his fifteenth press conference on 16 May 1967, see chapter 2, footnote 11.

[57] Meeting of the Heads of State or Government, The Hague, 1–2 December 1969, Bulletin of the European Communities No 1/1970, Final Communiqué of the Conference, 2 December 1969, paragraph 13.

[58] See the preamble to the Treaty of Rome, where the founding parties expressed their determination 'to lay the foundations of an ever closer union among the *peoples* of Europe'. See the analysis in the framework of the widening v deepening debate. See chapter 1, footnote 127 at p. 39.

[59] Loïc Azoulai, 'The Acquis of the European Union and International Organisations', *European Law Journal*, 11(2), March 2005, p. 196.

[60] Ibid. at p. 197.

collective bargain'.[61] The aspirant members are faced with the challenge of incorporating a growing number of EU policies and legislation in divergent fields into their internal legal order and political life before their actual accession. Although the EU does have to introduce some reforms in its decision-making and institutional arrangements to accommodate new members or even modify the structure of some of its current policies such as the CAP or the Structural Funds for example, it is 'the new member states rather than the European Union that had to change their policies in various areas'.[62]

Especially in the case of the CEEC, the effort to incorporate the almost 100,000 pages of the *acquis* involved the demonstration of considerable political persistence on the part of the political elites and support or at least tolerance on the part of public opinion in the respective countries, since the transfer of the EU economic, political and societal model demanded extensive reforms with sometimes painful repercussions at least in the short term. The dismantling of the existing economic and societal structures and the rapidly evolving convergence with the standards promoted by the EU as the link to membership brought the Eastern European nations into a historical phase marked by rapid change. 'The migration of legal concepts, practices and institutions has been a commonplace occurrence all around the world . . . the large scale transfer of Western legal know-how to the post socialist countries of Eastern Europe',[63] however, 'was virtually to try and make acceding states into EU prototypes before they became members of the club'.[64] 'The motivation for transfer of part or all of a legal system implicitly reflects some notion of catch-up . . . the impetus of change (is viewed) as being external to the system, in this case legal transfer would reflect some kind of standardisation relating to membership in international regimes'.[65] The Union with its conditionality and with the explicit requirement to adopt the *acquis* proved very effective in influencing radical reforms in accordance with its model. The diffusion of Union policies and laws was on such a great scale that arguments linked to so-called 'europeanisation' were raised. Historically, the relevant term had been used 'in rela-

---

[61] Christopher Preston, *Enlargement and Integration in the European Union*, Routledge, London and New York, 1997, p. 228.

[62] Stanimir Alexandrov and Latchezar Petkov, 'Paving the Way for Bulgaria's Accession to the European Union', *Fordham International Law Journal*, 21, 1998, p. 598.

[63] Inga Markovits, 'Exporting Law Reform, But Will it Travel?', *Cornell International Law Journal*, 37, 2004, p. 95.

[64] Neill Nugent, *European Union Enlargement*, Palgrave Macmillan, London, 2004, p. 47.

[65] Rachel Sabates Wheeler, 'Legal Transfer and the Legitimisation of Law: Implications of Farm Family Property Provisions in Albanian Legislation', *The Journal of East European Law*, 9(1), 2002, p. 71.

tion to the transfer of European norms, practices, beliefs and patterns to other nations especially through the process of colonisation, in which several European nations engaged in the previous centuries'.[66] Today, however, 'it is often associated with domestic adaptation to the pressures emanating directly or indirectly by EU membership'.[67] The relevant reforms were the subject of widely perceived political and societal consent in the CEEC, because they were viewed as absolutely necessary to lead the candidates to full membership. 'Law is a complex phenomenon: for some, a product of underlying social pressure; for others, a tool for changing society'.[68] The legislative reforms taking place in the CEEC with a view to imminent membership tend to fall rather into the second category as they constituted an effective means of introducing or at least accelerating reforms in societies that were however ready or willing to accept such initiatives on behalf of their ruling political elites. Therefore, the societal parameter of this legislative reform should not be neglected. The relationship between transplantation of legislation and drafting rather for transition is further explored in Chapter 4.[69]

The obligation to accept the *acquis* was inserted in the Copenhagen Criteria along with the obligation to achieve 'the ability to take on the obligations of membership, including adherence to the aims of political, economic and monetary union'. As with the political and economic criteria there was no further illumination of the relevant concept in the body of the text of the Copenhagen Presidency conclusions. Therefore, the Agenda 2000 documents served once again as the main source of precise information over the angle from which the Commission examined compliance with each important criterion. Agenda 2000 also provided us with useful clarifications over the exact scope and content of the *acquis*. The 'aims of political, economic and monetary union' are viewed in relation to the common foreign and security policy and the new members had convinced the Commission of 'their will to contribute to effective action by the Union'.[70] As far as economic and monetary union was concerned, the Commission concluded that 'it is unlikely that the applicants will be able to join the euro area immediately upon accession . . . as further progress in structural reform will be necessary before they will

---

[66] See Kevin Featherstone, supra chapter 3, note 40, p. 6.

[67] Ibid. at p. 7.

[68] Renaud Dehousse in Francis Snyder, *The Europeanisation of Law: The Legal Effects of European Integration*, Hart Publishing, Oxford and Portland, Ore., 2000, p. 15.

[69] See also J. Dine and F. Dahan, 'Transplantation for Transition – Discussion on a Concept around Russian Reform of the Law on Reorganisation', *Legal Studies*, 2003, 284–310.

[70] Agenda 2000 Communication, supra chapter 2, note 88, p. 58.

be able to maintain sufficient macroeconomic stability in the long run'.[71] The Commission was firm in insisting however that 'new member states will have to adopt the *acquis* of Stage 2 of EMU. This implies central bank independence, coordination of economic policies (national convergence programmes, multilateral surveillance, excessive deficit procedure), and adherence to the relevant provisions of the stability and growth pact. New member states will forego any direct central bank financing of public sector deficits as well as privileged access of public authorities to financial institutions. They shall have completed the liberalisation of capital movements. Also, they are expected to participate in an exchange rate mechanism and avoid excessive exchange rate changes'.[72]

When it comes to defining the exact areas of the *acquis* the Commission acknowledges the difficulty of the task as being 'far greater than in earlier enlargements . . . (because) . . . in the last enlargement, the new members, as participants in the EEA with highly developed economies, had already taken on large parts of the *acquis*; this is not the case with present applicants', which not only had to start from scratch but were additionally obliged to adopt an increasing body of law now extending to areas such as 'the Single Market, CFSP, EMU, and justice and home affairs'.[73] Although the Commission endorsed the principle that 'problems of integration can be gradually solved by transitional measures', it made absolutely clear that permanent opt-outs were not permitted.

A deviation from its stance towards existing members can be observed. The UK, Denmark and Sweden had managed to obtain an opt-out from the final phase of the monetary union, deciding not to adopt the common currency. Such an option for the new member states has already been ruled out. The Commission interestingly enough states that 'the capacity to take on the obligations of membership, which include the whole range of policies and measures that constitute the *acquis* of the Union, can be judged, to some extent, by the applicant countries' record in implementing existing commitments'.[74] Therefore, the focus has shifted from adoption to implementation. The implementation of the existing commitments was scrutinised in order for the Commission to form an opinion about the capacity of a given candidate to assume its obligations from membership and the adoption of the *acquis*. This was a significant stage at which the Commission clarified the three basic elements on which emphasis would be placed. The first was 'their perfor-

71 Ibid.
72 Ibid.
73 Ibid.
74 Agenda 2000 Communication, p. 59.

mance in carrying out obligations under the Europe agreement',[75] the second 'the 1995 White Paper on the Single Market'[76] and the final 'the *acquis* in areas not covered or only partly covered by the White Paper,[77] that includes many other important areas of the Union's activity such as agriculture, environment, energy, transport and social policy'.[78] Therefore, the effective implementation of the content of the Europe or Association Agreements signed previously by the CEEC, the adoption of the measures included in the White Paper for the approximation of laws in relation to the Internal Market and the reforms in the fields which are not related to the internal market functioned as the basic indicators of a country's successful or otherwise fulfilment of the third Copenhagen criterion. 'The progressive adoption of the *acquis* in these different areas in this three stage framework is a task which the applicant countries need to complete as far as possible *before* accession'.[79] Thus, far-reaching reforms are strongly encouraged, if not dictated, and the Commission finds itself with the duty 'to ensure that all economic agents in the EU are able to operate under the same conditions . . . including the obligations covering freedom of establishment, free trade and national treatment of all goods and services, the rules on competition, harmonisation of the rules on company law and accountancy, harmonisation of the rules on intellectual property, the opening up of public works, supply and services, tax measures, protection of personal data, implementation of legal proceedings and the recognition of judgements'.[80] The EU based the negotiations on the process of 'screening', whereby the Commission and the applicant country jointly evaluated the compatibility of the candidate's legislation with the EU norms. As a result, the EU could indicate on a sectoral basis the exact measures that needed to be implemented, altered or adopted so that the future member state could assume its Treaty obligations as soon as possible. The Commission established a highly transparent process based on the publication of 'Regular Reports'[81]

---

75 Particularly those relating to the right of establishment, national treatment, free circulation of goods, intellectual property and public procurement

76 Particularly key Single Market directives in areas such as taxation, public procurement and banking.

77 In this area, the situation varies considerably among applicant countries. For most of the countries, significant and far-reaching adaptations will be needed in the fields of environment, energy, agriculture, industry, telecommunications, transport, social affairs, customs administration and justice and home affairs.

78 Agenda 2000 Communication, p. 59.

79 Agenda 2000 Communication, p. 59.

80 Daniel Piazolo, *The Integration Process between Eastern and Western Europe*, Springer, Berlin and Heidelberg, 2001, p. 63.

81 They can be accessed at the site of the DG Enlargement of the European Commission at: http://europa.eu.int/comm/enlargement/report_10_99/#1.%20 Progress%20Reports and http://europa.eu.int/comm/enlargement/docs/.

stating the progress of the candidate countries and highlighting the areas where they lag behind and where special attention should be given or additional measures adopted. For the purposes of the negotiations the *acquis* was divided in 31 chapters. The relevant chapters were:

1. Free movement of goods
2. Free movement of persons
3. Freedom to provide services
4. Free movement of capital
5. Company law
6. Competition policy
7. Agriculture
8. Fisheries
9. Transport policy
10. Taxation
11. Economic and Monetary Union
12. Statistics
13. Social policy and employment
14. Energy
15. Industrial policy
16. Small and medium-sized enterprises
17. Science and research
18. Education and training
19. Telecommunication and information technologies
20. Culture and audio-visual policy
21. Regional policy and coordination of structural instruments
22. Environment
23. Consumers and health protection
24. Cooperation in the field of Justice and Home Affairs
25. Customs union
26. External relations
27. Common Foreign and Security Policy (CFSP)
28. Financial control
29. Financial and budgetary provisions
30. Institutions
31. Others

THE ADDITIONAL CONSIDERATIONS FOR MEMBERSHIP

As stated above, the three Copenhagen Criteria were supplemented by two new parameters which, although they do not strictly form part of the Copenhagen list of requirements, constitute dimensions which the European Council will take very seriously into account when deciding upon the accession of a potential candidate. There will be no further reference at this stage to the 'ability of the EU to absorb new members' as this aspect of membership was inserted in the text of the Copenhagen Criteria and therefore, constitutes a recognised parameter for the existing member states to focus upon. In 1995 in the Madrid European Council it was decided that applicant countries should introduce the necessary adjustments to their administrative and judicial structures in order to ensure effective compliance with the *acquis*.[82] This requirement touches upon an ever increasing number of reforming initiatives affecting the organisation and structure of the administration and judiciary, which admittedly constitute two of the most fundamental pillars of public life and functions in a country. They both have to become the subject of reform if this is deemed necessary for the implementation of the *acquis*. So the basic principle emanating from the approach of the Commission is that adoption of the *acquis* is not enough; assuming the obligations of membership entails the actual implementation of the *acquis* before accession. The Commission insists that 'it is equally important for the applicants' administrations to be modernised so that they can implement and enforce the *acquis*. This will often require new administrative structures as well as properly trained and remunerated administrators. The applicants' judicial systems must be capable of ensuring that the law is enforced. This requires the retraining and in some cases, the replacement of judges to ensure that courts are able to operate effectively in cases involving Community law'.[83] This is due to the fact that one of the primary obligations of membership inherent in the implementation of the *acquis* is 'to apply the principles of Community law, such as primacy over national law or the direct effect of some legislation. It is also essential for these courts to have a sufficient number of judges trained in Community law in order to make use of the preliminary ruling procedure in Article 177 and to ensure effective cooperation with the Court of Justice of the European Communities'.[84] There are also 'cases [where] the applicants still lack the structures needed to apply new regulations, for example on environmental and technical inspections, banking supervision, public accounts and statistics and widespread problems of corruption which are now being tackled by most governments of the applicant countries'.[85]

---

[82] European Council in Madrid, 15 and 16 December 1995, Presidency Conclusions, Bulletin of the European Communities, No. 12/1995, paragraph I 25.

[83] Agenda 2000 Communication, supra chapter 2, note 88, p. 61.

[84] Ibid.

[85] Ibid.

Moreover, the European Council in Luxembourg in 1997 added yet another criterion for membership in the form of 'good neighbourliness', respect for other countries' sovereignty and resolution of territorial disputes by peaceful means.[86] The Commission stated that 'enlargement should not mean importing border conflicts. The prospect of accession acts as a powerful incentive for the states concerned to settle any border disputes. The Stability Pact promoted by the Union between May 1994 and March 1995 has also been influential in this regard'.[87] 'A key objective of the 1994–1995 Stability Pact was to encourage the Central and East European applicant countries to reach bilateral good neighbour agreements on borders and the treatment of minorities'.[88] 'The Commission considers that, before accession, applicants should make every effort to resolve any outstanding border dispute among themselves or involving third countries. Failing this they should agree that the dispute be referred to the International Court of Justice . . . all candidate countries should therefore, before accession negotiations are completed, commit themselves to submit unconditionally to compulsory jurisdiction, including advance ruling of the International Court of Justice in any present or future disputes of this nature'.[89] The same statement was endorsed by the European Council in Helsinki, where the European leaders stated that 'in this respect the European Council stresses the principle of peaceful settlement of disputes in accordance with the United Nations Charter and urges candidate States to make every effort to resolve any outstanding border disputes and other related issues. Failing this they should within a reasonable time bring the dispute to the International Court of Justice. The European Council will review the situation relating to any outstanding disputes, in particular concerning the repercussions on the accession process and in order to promote their settlement through the International Court of Justice, at the latest by the end of 2004'.[90] Therefore, 'good neighbourliness' becomes the policy tool with which the EU hopes to avoid importing any of the existing disputes between future members states in its framework.

As noted above, all of the criteria have a degree of vagueness about them and the way in which they should be implemented. The following chapter

---

86 European Council in Luxembourg, 12 and 13 December 1997, Presidency Conclusions, Bulletin of the European Communities No. 12/1997, paragraphs 4 and 5.

87 Agenda 2000 Communication, supra chapter 2, note 88, p. 69.

88 Karen E. Smith, in Marise Cremona, *The Enlargement of the European Union*, Oxford University Press, Oxford, 2003, p. 118.

89 Agenda 2000 Communication, supra chapter 2, note 88, p. 69.

90 Helsinki European Council, 10th and 11th December 1999, Presidency Conclusions, paragraph 4, access at: http://www.europarl.eu.int/summits/hel1_en.htm#a.

therefore analyses the foundations of the political and economic understanding reached by the Western market economies and seeks to develop a methodology for drafing commercial law. In the final part of the book a company law drafted for transition economies using this method is presented and explained.

4. Political and economic conditions for drafting commercial and company law in transition and developing countries*

WHERE SHOULD TRANSITION AND DEVELOPMENT LEAD TO?

The concept of EU enlargement is tied closely to a concept of transition and raises the daunting question of transition to what? Likewise, development concepts are claiming to know what should be developed.

Gros and Steinherr point out that 'today, communism appears to many as a historic stupidity and, without a shadow of a doubt, capitalism has victoriously emerged as the dominant paradigm'.[1] However, they characterise that view as 'too short-sighted and conditioned by the recent demise of communism'.[2] For them such a simplistic view neglects 'at least two points. First, the realisation of any theory always differs from the theoretic model which, at any rate, captures only part of societal organisation. History and the distribution of social and political values interfere with the economic model. For example, only under very restrictive assumptions could it be claimed that, say, colonial capitalism was superior to Soviet communism. Second, because the working class suffered from unbearable misery during the take-off phase of the now successfully developed capitalist countries – a misery still prevalent throughout the developing world – the Marxist vision gave hope to large fractions of society of both developed and developing countries, a hope that capitalism was unable to provide.'[3]

In this quotation, the reference to post-colonialism does not occur by accident. It is indeed interesting to see the parallels between the mentioned vision of 'the end of communism' in Eastern European and the vision of the end of communism's importance for the post-colonial age entered by economically

* Some of the content of this chapter appeared first in the *Journal of Comparative Law*. The authors are grateful for permission to reproduce it here.

1 D. Gros and A. Steinherr, *Economic Transition in Central and Eastern Europe*, 2nd edn, Cambridge University Press, Cambridge, 2004, p. 1.

2 Gross and Steinherr, supra note 1 p. 2.

3 Ibid., 2.

less developed countries. In the immediate post-colonial phase during the 1970s, recognition of the validity of the communist discourse for the state of deprivation caused by centuries of colonial rule was still present even in the official EU development discourse as against ACP[4] countries. Its effect was a recognition of responsibility for the causes of 'under-development' and a paternalist attitude in providing development assistance as a 'gift' to be delivered without any expectations of return in the aftermath of the First Lomé Agreement. This discourse has 'transited' towards the definition of 'mutual debts' during the 1980s and passed definitively to a vision of 'mutual economic exchange between equals' which makes the 'less developed' countries' dependency on the mercy of the heirs of the colonialist regime and on the unquestioned conditions of global capitalism simply disappear.[5]

This shows that Gros and Steinherr's review of the neglected implementation problems of communist social theory and hopes for change connected to it, implies another neglected dimension, that is the definition of a (global) capitalist economy with its own theories and conditions for realisation. These three neglected points raise fundamental questions about the enlargement (and the development) process. Discussions about the drafting and implementation of economic laws meet complex problems of institution building, democracy and the organisation of society. Burchill argues that 'in addressing the "wider issues" of democracy, we are taken beyond the political sphere to engage with the social and economic organisation of society. Once we move in his direction, agreement about the nature, scope and content of democracy becomes very contentious. If the overall purpose of democracy is "to provide the conditions for the full and free development of the essential human capacities of all members of the society"[6] . . . democracy needs to be something more than the existence of a few basic political procedures'.[7] Joerges notes that 'markets are social institutions which cannot be governed through some objective mechanism and do not simply respond to some functional needs. They are in the last instance "polities". . . . The opening of our national economies (*Volkswirtschaften*) requires responses, on the one hand, to the erosion of the political powers of the nation state, and, on the other, to

---

4 African, Caribbean and Pacific nations.

5 For this description of the three main stages of the EU development discourse, see N. Karagiannis, *Avoiding Responsibility. The Politics and Discourse of European Development Policy*, Pluto Press, London and Ann Arbor, 2004.

6 As posited by M. Loughlin in 'Rights, Democracy and Law' in T. Campbell, K. Ewing and A. Tomkins (eds), *Sceptical Essays on Human Rights*, Oxford University Press, Oxford, 1992.

7 R. Burchill, 'The EU and Social Democracy or Democracy with a Social Dimension', *Canadian Journal of Law and Jurisprudence on Social Democracy*, 185 at 186.

the risks of unaccountable trans-national government'.[8] Joerges argues that responses to this challenge have been 'one-dimensionally restricted to an institutionalisation of economic rationality criteria at trans-national levels of governance. The post-national constellations in which we find ourselves require more complex and socially more sensitive responses to the tensions between the opening of formerly national economies and the pre-requisites of social solidarity. Such answers are not readily available'.[9]

It is particularly important to understand that the transition economies find themselves in transition from highly nationalised ideology into a *post-national* situation.[10] It is not the purpose of this book to provide a comprehensive constitutional theory of enlargement but the authors adopt the scepticism of Joerges towards the neo-liberal 'de-coupling of economic integration from the welfare state and its social policy'[11] by examining the purpose of commercial law in society, examining the foundations of the package that the transition states are being expected to buy into and offering a methodology of commercial law drafting which seeks to integrate the realities about the impact of markets on individuals into the design of commercial law, giving as an example a company law designed for transition economies.

In spite of evident differences, last but not least with respect to the lack of membership ambitions, the same reasoning applies in parallel also to the permanent post-colonial transition or development of 'less developed countries'.

THE ECONOMIC, POLITICAL AND LEGAL NETWORK OF MARKET-BASED SOCIETIES

Drafting law in European transition economies is heavily influenced by ambi-

---

[8] C. Joerges, 'What is Left of the European Economic Constitution', *European Law Review*, 30, 2005, 461 at 464.

[9] Ibid., pp. 464–5. Cf. on the way 'economic efficiency' has dominated the EU's development discourse and any concept of solidarity and responsibility, N. Karagiannis, supra note 5.

[10] At first glance, the post-colonial construction of national states may seem to be a 're-nationalisation' instead. However, such a view would not take into account, first, the mentioned dependency of these countries on the 'heirs' of the colonialist regime which find themselves all 'in transition' towards a post-national constellation. With respect to some countries, this linkage to the destiny of their former rulers was even institutionalised by the EC Treaty's recognition of special relations to 'overseas territories'. Secondly, one may not neglect the fact that the globalised economy strongly conditions political and social structures in *all* countries around the world. In our view, the 'post-national constellation' is therefore absolutely ubiquitous.

[11] Joerges, supra note 5, p. 469.

tions for membership of the EU and consequent compliance with EU norms. However, attempts to comply with European company law are severely hampered by fundamental differences in the way in which companies are viewed in the current member states, particularly regarding the role of shareholders. Due to the lack of any harmonising supranational structure in developing economies these differences transform into competition or even battles between social, economic and legal concepts and the development organisations which represent their home interests, that is, those of the Western developed world and its grip on globalisation.

It is necessary to dig below the surface of regulation and seek to identify exactly what role commercial law (and within it, company law) is supposed to play in a market economy and, deeper, what role a market economy should play in a democratic society. This exercise is important in understanding exactly what role the network of various mechanisms already in place in our own jurisdictions was devised to play; and it will deliver us a legal concept of the commercial rules to be drafted.

The Property Rhetoric

The role of commercial law in a market economy is to allocate risk. Controlled economies attempted to eliminate the risks of commercial transactions to individuals, transferring the risk of failure to the whole community. The move to a market economy from a controlled economy thus entails complex political questions about which market participants shall bear the risk of market transactions. Two very simple examples illustrate this fundamental role: one is the law of contract. At first sight agreement between two individuals to buy and sell might seem a politically neutral transaction and the decision by the state to provide enforcement mechanisms to back such a transaction (such as sanctions for non-performance) might similarly appear to be politically uncontroversial. However, immediately any disparity of bargaining power is taken into consideration, a state decision to provide enforcement mechanisms will clearly benefit the party who started in the more powerful position since that bargaining power will have been used to gain a more beneficial bargain. Only if safeguards such as Unfair Contract Terms legislation are enacted can the equation be re-balanced. This political-legal function shows that there has never been anything like 'neutrality' in the social network unless by political decision.

In transition (and developing) economies the fundamental political question that needs to be addressed in the drafting of legislation is which party do we consider should bear the risk of market transactions, on whom will we place these burdens, bearing in mind the pre-existing advantages of bargaining power which some actors will have. Methods of assessing risk and allocating it will be considered later.

More fundamentally, the allocation of risk depends on identifying the way in which a particular society wishes to understand property rights. Since commercial law, in particular, regulates the way in which people acquire and dispose of property, a society's understanding of property rights is fundamental to the way in which commercial risks are allocated. If property rights are seen to be a fundamental right for individuals, commercial law will be constructed to give nearly absolute protection to individual rights to property against any claims that might be made in favour of use of property 'for the common good'. Commercial law will therefore permit and encourage accumulations of property without imposing countervailing responsibilities to use that property in any particular way. In corporate terms we will have companies but no corporate social responsibility. If, on the other hand, property rights are understood as exercisable only subject to significant responsibilities, an opposing model of companies and commercial law will be constructed within which the accumulation of property brings responsibility.

In constructing a market economy, the population is effectively being asked to subscribe to the philosophical underpinnings of a construct of property rights and the consequent allocation of property and through that allocation, the distribution of power. In establishing a firm base for decision making about commercial law it is therefore necessary to go back to the foundations of market society to understand the 'package' that is being sold to transition economies and to understand more clearly the parameters of the foundation notions so that decisions will be made in a clear-sighted way. The reason for the fundamental importance of these decisions is that commercial law regulates the accumulation and disposal of property; by distributing risks it will 'rig' the ability of groups of people to benefit as against others. The decision on how to 'rig the risks' will depend on an understanding of property rights and property rights are equivalent to economic and political power.

In any discussion of property rights it is important to keep in mind the insight that property rights are, in essence, rights against other people. This means that all property rights govern power relations between people. If property rights are seen as a person having rights over a thing, this ignores the fact that the rights actually lie against other persons, most obviously a right to exclude others from claiming rights over that thing. This means that the role that property rights play in wealth distribution is often ignored because the person to person relationship is clouded by the person to thing discussion. Thus 'A theorist who supposes that ownership interests in objects may be justified, say, by a natural-rights argument, but then ignores questions of wealth-distribution, tells only half the story. The same is true, in the opposite direction of one who advocates a certain distribution of "resources" but who neglects the question whether person-thing ownership relations are to form part of a property-institutional design.'[12] It is because rights over things can never be absolute, but rather made up of a web of rights and responsibilities operating interpersonally that the debate resonates with issues of wealth distribution and power relations. If property ownership meant that I have absolute dominion over three beans and the right to use them as I wished and you have similar rights over five beans, the property distribution debates would exist but they would be a mere matter of counting. Do I deserve more beans than you? Because the reality of property relations is that I may exclude some (but not others) from use of an item and I may use that item only in non-harmful ways, the discussion of rights and duties becomes infinitely more complex and balanced. It is important, then, to understand what the nature of the bundle of rights called property rights actually consists of.

Harris argues that the Hohfeldian 'bundle of rights' concept which emphasises rights against other persons, rather than rights over things, can best be expressed on an 'ownership' spectrum which enables an individual to have more or less exclusivity over the use of the property and more or less power to use it in designated ways.[13] This understanding means that attempts to infuse more weight into a particular side of the balance of interests by claiming it is a 'property' right is mere rhetoric designed to appeal to the conceptions underlying a particular society's view of the standing of 'property'. Of considerable interest in this context is the examination by Harris of 'expansive' definitions of property.[14]

'Conventional' property is 'cashable rights' such as bank accounts, shares etc. 'because expropriation and appropriation rules apply to them – they pass into a bankrupt's estate and they can be inherited . . . Cashable rights are the subject of real markets'.[15] Such an understanding would exclude 'social rights' such as the right to use public spaces, which some have claimed as property rights. While Harris is not in principle opposed to this extended use of property, he nevertheless does not see it as an aid to clarity: 'By all means let rights of all kinds be analysed in these terms. Calling all rights "property rights" is, however, anything but an aid to clarity for the enterprises at hand since both the analyst and the reader must constantly remind themselves that they are not talking about "property" as ordinarily understood.' More important is perhaps the insight that the use of 'property rights' is a rhetoric which will resonate with the reader according to the 'meaning' of property in a particular society:

---

12 J.W. Harris, *Property and Justice,* Oxford University Press, Oxford, 2002, p. 141.

13 Ibid., p. 141.

14 Ibid., p. 146.

15 Ibid., p. 149.

The plausibility of rhetorical expedients of this sort is difficult to assess. They depend on the way you suppose 'property' will ring in the ears of an addressee and on his willingness to fall in line with the terminological shift. Imagine the following dialogue:

Egalitarian: 'For reasons of a, b and c, I maintain that everyone ought to have an enforceable right to work.'

Conservative: 'For reasons of X, Y and Z, I disagree with you.'

Egalitarian: 'But you believe that property ought to be protected, don't you?'

Conservative: 'I do.'

Egalitarian: 'Well the right to work is property.'

Conservative response 1: 'No it isn't.'

Conservative response 2: 'Why didn't you say that before? Of course, I now change my view to yours.'[16]

In Harris's dialogue the right to work is put forward as a 'property right' which can only be interfered with with care and probably with compensation following. This is likely to have the effect of a redistribution of wealth to poorer communities. As we shall see, a common understanding of companies is that they are 'owned' by shareholders. In this case the claim of shareholders-as-owners is making an expansive property claim about shareholder rights and is an attempt to persuade law-makers to 'rig the risks' in favour of shareholders, to the detriment of others on whose life the company may have an impact.[17] In this case the redistributive effect is likely to be reversed. In particular, strengthening the shareholders' rights excludes from consideration the interests of others and assumes that shareholders may profit at the expense of employees. This enhanced protection by representation of these rights as property rights is likely to have the effect of redistribution of wealth from employees to wealthy shareholders.

We need, therefore to examine very closely the results which might be achieved by the use of any expanded property rhetoric. As Harris notes, 'The concept-expanding arguments . . . concede, at least arguendo, that property as conventionally understood really deserves prestige and that the rights contended for have an importance which is merely parallel to conventional proprietary interests . . . [the arguments] make too much of property.'[18]

The Origins of the Liberal Market Discourse

In what way are property rights viewed in the liberal democratic market economies which we expect transition and developing economies to aspire to?

---

16 Ibid., p. 160.

17 Making a 'property claim' about intellectual property will have the same regressive effect.

18 Harris, supra note 12, p. 161.

In undertaking a study of the origins of market economies it is imperative to dispel the myth that 'the market is a universal social and even anthropological phenomenon that is found in the same form among all peoples and at all times'.[19] It is important to deny the determinist 'triumph of capitalism' which asserts that the collapse of the Soviet Union was inevitable because capitalism is the 'natural' basis of society. On the contrary, the 'market' was deliberately constructed as part of an economic and political package, using such philosophical concepts as equality, human rights and property rights. Nevertheless the modern appeal to the natural nature of market relations is particularly interesting in view of the work of one of the founders of the liberal democratic and market state, John Locke, as we shall see.

Although many factors had an effect on the transformation of feudal systems into a market economy,[20] enclosures played a significant part because 'Through enclosure, the village common land that the medieval peasants cultivated together became private land. Polaner gives an impressive description of how this changed all the traditional relations between people. The mutual assistance and common work of the peasants was supplanted by relations of contract and competition mediated by money'.[21] Once the land had been enclosed, the owners were free to deal with it as they pleased, regardless of any community considerations. 'Enclosure introduced a new concept of human relationships into European civilization that changed the basis of economic security and the perception of human life. Land was no longer something people belonged to, but rather a commodity people possessed. Land was reduced to a quantitative status and measured by its exchange value. So, too, with people. Relationships were reorganised. Neighbours became employees or contractors. Reciprocity was replaced with hourly wages. People sold their time and labour where they used to share their toil. Human beings began to view each other and everything around them in financial terms. Virtually everyone and everything became negotiable and could be purchased at an appropriate price.'[22]

This shift led to increased attention being paid by the courts to rights to property and the enforcement of contracts. Hobbes conceptualised the market conditions arising from this new society as made up of actors motivated by

---

[19] Duchrow and Hinkelammert, *Property for People not for Profit*, Zed Books, London, 2004, p. 29.

[20] Including climate change and the plague, Duchrow and Hinkeammert, supra note 19, p. 31.

[21] U. Duchrow and F. Hinkelammert, supra note 19, pp. 31–2, citing K. Polanyi, *Origins of our Time: The Great Transformation,* Gollancz, London, 1945.

[22] J. Rifkin, *The Biotech Century*, Putnam, New York, 1998, p. 40, cited by Duchrow and Hinkelammert, supra note 19, p. 32.

desire, especially desire of power over others which may be *natural* power (special physical or mental abilities) or *instrumental* power (riches, reputation and good friends). From this a power market develops in which all struggle to attain power over others.[23] Since property is power this creates a situation where property may be used to increase power over others, while simultaneously accumulating more property.[24] However, the very fact that all are pitted against all requires the establishment of a sovereign body to prevent wars over property; 'to do whatever is necessary to maintain the right of possession'.[25] This sovereign is necessary 'to appoint in what manner, all kinds of contract between subjects, (as buying, selling, exchanging, borrowing, lending, letting, and taking to hire) are to be made'.[26] In other words, to determine the parameters and content of commercial law. For Hobbes it was for the men of property to choose the sovereign.

It is very important that this insight should be recognised as a truism which holds good today. It means that every legislature should be aware of the likelihood that it will be composed to a greater or lesser extent of those with property. All rules should therefore be scrutinised on the understanding that the tendency of such bodies is always to allocate risk so that it falls on others, in other words all legislatures are likely to have the interests of the powerful at heart. This is nowhere more likely than in legislation governing commercial relations.

The Role of Human Rights Discourse

Is this the final word on the role of law in market-based societies? In modern times this tendency seems surely reversed by our understanding of human rights and the fundamental part they play in society. This comfortable belief has many consequences, not least the inclusion of human rights requirements in constitutions and the imposition of human rights conditionality in numerous situations, including as a condition for the discussion of the status of Kosovo. However, it might be less comfortably held if the origins of the human rights and property debate were fully understood.

Michael Freeman describes them as 'uncomfortably close'[27] but this may

---

[23] Thomas Hobbes, *The Leviathan* [1660], republished by University of Oregon, 1999, p. 151.

[24] Ibid., p. 54.

[25] Ibid., p. 94.

[26] Ibid., p. 299.

[27] M. Freeman, 'Beyond Capitalism and Socialism', in J. Dine and A. Fagan (eds), *Capitalism and Human Rights*, Edward Elgar, Cheltenham and Northampton, MA, 2005.

be an understatement. In discussing the relationship between capitalism and human rights, Freeman's particular emphasis is on the conceptual relationship between these subjects and he sees the strongest foundation of their conceptual relationship to be theories of property rights. The natural rights philosophy which formed the foundation of human rights discourse derived from theories of property. The commitment to 'rights' thus includes a strong commitment to private property 'and thus to complicity in the behaviour of capitalist organisations, even to acts which empirically can be seen as human rights violations'. Freeman unpacks the story of the property rights relationship which is revealed as more complex than it at first appears. Tracing natural rights discourse back to late medieval controversies and the struggle between the Franciscan's vows of poverty (including absence of power) with the opposing Catholic perspective and the relationship between man's understanding of his natural rights and his freedom to exercise them to the possible damage of fellow citizens, this debate reached the point at which the right to having, possessing, using, enjoying and disposing of things was understood as rooted in the divine creation of human freedom. Freeman thus pinpoints the close relationship between natural rights and property rights. Discussing Locke, Freeman believes that Locke clearly argued that the proper function of government was to secure natural rights (including property rights). Freeman sees in Locke a precursor of 'a society in which Christian constraints and mercantilist goals were displaced by a secular society with limited government and a capitalist economy'.

The query that must be pursued, therefore, is the extent to which societies based on the concepts of human rights, including democracy and market freedom, must adopt a regime of property rights which favours Hobbes' 'men of property'. To what extent must market risks be rigged in favour of the powerful or can human rights in some way divorce themselves from their roots in property rights and be used to mitigate or confront the tendency of capitalism to become extreme, favouring the few over the many? To discover this we must look especially carefully at Locke's interpretation of human rights. This is to be found in the *Second Treatise of Government* published in England in 1690. The timing of the publication was crucial as English imperial ambitions had lost the justification of the divine right of kings on the beheading of Charles I and the promulgation of habeas corpus (1679) and the Bill of Rights (1689), which reduced the king to the status of constitutional monarch. In particular, expansion into India and control of the slave trade were seen as desirable and, as Freeman noted, Locke found the excuse to carry out this expansion in the name of human rights.

> Habeas Corpus and the Bill of Rights had posited human rights that the bourgeoisie were not able or willing to forgo. It was their answer to the divine right of kings,

> and there could be no other response, these rights guaranteed the physical integrity of persons and property . . . Taking these rights literally, however, meant excluding forced labour through slavery and the violent appropriation of the indigenous territories in North America . . . There was therefore a contradiction between the declaration of the equality of all people before the law and the power positions of the expanding bourgeoisie. It was Locke who showed a way out of this situation . . . He says that 'all Men by Nature are equal'; this includes the 'equal Right that every Man hath, to his Natural Freedom, without being subjected to the Will or Authority of any other Man'.[28] Locke's theoretical feat consists in his drawing the following conclusion: therefore slavery is legitimate. And he adds: therefore the indigenous peoples of North America can be unconditionally expropriated. And also India can be colonised with the use of force.[29]

And all in the name of human rights. How?

Locke develops a concept of a state of nature quite different from that envisaged by Hobbes. It is not contradicted by the establishment of civil society (a political system) but such a system is a confirmation and perfection of the state of nature. The law prevailing in the state of nature implies respect for physical integrity and property. Locke uses the concept of equality to establish the right of all men to judge when this law has been broken. And violent consequences may ensue since such a contravention is 'a trespass against the whole species'.[30] Thus such a transgressor 'having renounced reason, the Common Rule and Measure, God hath given to Mankind, hath by the unjust Violence and Slaughter he hath committed upon one, declared War against all Mankind, and therefore may be destroyed as a Lyon or a Tiger, one of those wild Savage Beasts, with whom men can have no Society nor Security'.[31]

Thus, anyone has the right to decide when the law has been contravened and a decision carries the demotion of the violator to non-human status and the loss of all human rights. Further, anyone injured by the transgression of the law of nature may seek 'Reparation'; 'the damnified Person has this Power of appropriating to himself, the Goods or Service of the Offender'.[32]

'According to Locke, this state of nature is in reality not a state of peace but one of constant threat through potential offenders – wild beasts and monsters all. Locke declares war on them in the name of peace.'[33]

Where there is civil society the political authorities have been given the power to mediate disputes so that the offender is dealt with by those authori-

---

28 J. Locke, *Second Treatise of Government* [1690], republished by Prometheus Books, New York, 1986, paragraph 54.

29 Duchrow and Hinkelammert, supra note 19, p. 46.

30 Locke, supra note 28, paragraph 8.

31 Ibid., paragraph 11.

32 Ibid., paragraph 11.

33 Duchrow and Hinkelammert, supra note 19, 50.

ties and is therefore immune from the judgment of equals. So this regime can only apply to places where a state of nature still exists. And where the state of nature exists, everyone is entitled to settle. Resisting this is against the law of nature and consequently the resistance loses any claim to be human. Those who do so lose all human rights, including the right to property:

> But there is another sort of Servants, which By a peculiar Name we call Slaves, who, being captives taken in a just War, are by the Right of Nature subjected to the Absolute Dominion and Arbitrary Power of their Masters. These Men Having, as I say, forfeited their Liberties, and lost their Estates; and being in the State of Slavery, not capable of any Property, cannot in that state be considered as any part of Civil Society; the chief end of which is the preservation of Property.[34]

Thus Locke conveniently justifies the conquest of the Americas and India and the institution of slavery in the name of upholding the rights of mankind.

> Locke accuses the whole world of wanting to enslave the bourgeoisie so that the bourgeoisie can enslave everyone in a just war. He accuses the whole world of wanting to take the wealth of the bourgeoisie so that the bourgeoisie can justly appropriate the wealth of the whole world. And the whole world is nothing but wild animals which one can destroy if they are in the way. And that is a consequence of what Locke propounds as human rights.[35]

Although this may justifiably give rise to an inherent suspicion of human rights discourse, and the excesses to which expanded property rights claims are vulnerable, several vital aspects of the philosophy are notable for our purposes; the first is how fundamental property ownership is to the understanding of a person as truly human. Locke elevated property ownership into a fundamental dignity necessary for human beings. The second is the centrality of his ringing declaration of equality and the hollowness of that ring. We must therefore examine with great care the institutions which are erected on the basis of 'equality' and 'ownership of property', and it is these concepts that are at the very heart of commercial law in a market, capitalist economy.

Despite the fact that both the US and EU economies are market economies, the underlying Lockean concepts have nevertheless come to be somewhat differently interpreted. The difference in interpretation provides emerging economies with illustrations of the legal policy choices that can be made within the market framework and provide models for the understanding of property rights dialogue.

---

34 Locke, supra note 28, paragraph 85.

35 Duchrow and Hinkelammert, supra note 19, 54.

Euro-Atlantic Differences in Property Rights Perspectives

Hutton has analysed very different attitudes which may be discerned in the USA and Europe.[36] His thesis is that the attitude to the ownership of property in the US has been informed by a number of factors. One of these is the existence of the experience of the settlers who arrived at 'a wilderness pregnant with riches', had 'risked all crossing the Atlantic and who, as fervent Protestants, believed they had a direct relationship with God'. They believed that they were serving God's purpose by taking possession of the land and using it for their own individual purpose.[37] Hutton shows how the writings of John Locke encouraged the view that property both claimed by and created from the land belonged 'exclusively and completely' to the settler and, moreover that the 'purpose of society and Government' was to 'further the enjoyment of property, and political power was only legitimate if it served this end'.[38] Two passages cited by Hutton seem particularly apt: 'The only way whereby any one divests himself of his Natural Liberty and puts on the bonds of Civil Society is by agreeing with other Men to join and unite and into a Community, for their comfortable, safe and peaceable living one amongst another, in a secure Enjoyment of their Properties, and a greater Security against any that are not of it'.[39] An instructive viewpoint comes from competition law, which for many years has been struggling to identify the boundary between enjoyment of a right to property and an abusive use of the power that the right to property brings with it, and 'Every man has a property in his own person. There is no body has any right to it but himself. The labour of his body, and the work of his hands we may say are properly his. Whatsoever then he removes out of the state that nature has provided, and left it in, he hath mixed his labour with and joined to it something that is his own, and thereby makes his property.'[40] The war of independence and the writing of the constitution did nothing to dispel this mindset, the justification for revolution being the interference by King George III with the settler's rights to enjoy their property freely.[41] 'Any notion that property rights were a concession granted by the state in the name of the common interest – the European tradition . . . had been dispelled by the revolution'.[42]

---

36 W. Hutton, *The World We're In*, Little Brown, London, 2002.

37 Ibid., pp. 52–3.

38 Ibid.

39 John Locke, *Two Treatises of Government*, P. Laslett (ed.), Cambridge University Press, Cambridge, 1988, p. 331.

40 Ibid., p. 288.

41 Hutton, supra note 36, p. 56

42 Ibid., pp. 58–9.

The understanding of the nature of property rights then is founded in nature and religion, giving at once a mystical and religious significance to ownership. If a settler prospered it was evidence of a healthy relationship with God. The availability of vast stretches of land made any egalitarian notions realisable without the concept of redistribution becoming a problem, so that redistribution of property became contrary both to nature and religion. The role of the central government was thus reduced to protection of individual property. The constitution prevented states from doing anything that might impair obligations embodied in contracts. Once the right to own property and to contract had been granted to corporations as well as individuals[43] and companies holding shares in other companies were equated with individual shareholders, the stage was set for the giant groups of companies that we see today. Further the resistance to redistribution enshrined in the Fifth Amendment is a fertile ground for those seeking to resist regulation on the basis that it is a 'confiscation of property'. The Fifth Amendment prevents the government from depriving an individual of 'life, liberty and property without due process; nor shall property be taken for public use without just compensation'. Thus, although there was a long period between the 1930s and 1970 when property rights were regulated, the fundamental understanding of individual liberty as inextricably intertwined with ownership of property made it very much easier for the ultra conservatives to build their anti-regulatory policies and have them widely accepted. 'For the constitution remains explicit. Without powerful popular support and a clear sense of national crisis – as over slavery in the 1860s or unemployment in the 1930s – the American constitutional conception is that government at federal and state level is the custodian of private property rights; and the Supreme Court sees its task as policing that injunction.'[44] The old settler cast of mind provided fertile ground for Nozick's arguments that taxation to finance any minimum income for the poor is a form of forced labour and all forms of redistributive justice are coercive.[45] It also provided fertile soil for the concept that corporations are nothing but a 'nexus of contracts'[46] with the obvious result that government should not interfere in that 'contract'.

---

43 *Dartmouth College v Woodward* (1819) 17 US 518.

44 Hutton, supra note 36, p. 60.

45 R. Nozick, *Anarchy, State and Utopia*, Harvard University Press, Cambridge, MA, 1973. See also Hutton, supra note 36, p. 68.

46 R. Posner, *Economic Analysis of Law*, 4th edn, Little Brown, Boston, 1992; F. Easterbrook and D. Fischel, *The Economic Structure of Corporate Law*, Harvard University Press, Cambridge, MA, 1991. B. Cheffins, *Company Law, Theory, Structure and Operation*, Clarendon Press, Oxford, 1997; J. Dine, *The Governance of Corporate Groups*, Cambridge University Press, Cambridge, 2000.

All these influences can be seen at work in the anti-environmentalist movements chronicled by Rowell[47] with the use of dominion theology (God gave man 'dominion' over the earth[48]) to justify exploitation of natural resources ('you can't really hurt the planet because God wouldn't allow that. God wouldn't have given man chain saws if he didn't think they were benign'[49]); coupled with allegations that environmental regulation destroys jobs and interferes with private property rights.

One of the aims of Alliance for America is 'To restore and protect constitutional private property rights'. Part of the 'Wise Use' movement assisted in constructing Gingrich's now notorious 'contract with America' which the National Resources Defence Council explained 'threatens to undermine virtually every federal environmental law on the books, meaning dirtier air, dirtier water and more species pushed to the brink'.[50] No wonder, then, that the Government, in international trade negotiations, regards itself as acting to protect private property, in this case the interests of corporate America: 'One USTR [Office of the US Trade Representative] was remarkably frank in saying that the US has no intellectual plan about the long-term national interest, no consistent commitment to any principle. Rather the "client state" is the model of the USTR: "It's too socialist to plan . . . the businessman is the man who knows. So you respond to him".'[51] Given the underlying understanding of the moral value attached to property ownership coupled with the conceptualisation of corporations as individual property owners, there would seem no reason for the trade official not to be frank. He has every reason to be happy in his job of increasing the property ownership of US constituents.

What, then, of the 'European' conception of property ownership? Of course, it is not possible to reflect subtle and complex differences between the understanding of property across Europe. However, it may be possible to detect a general difference of view. Hutton cites Article 14 of the post-war German constitution as capturing some of the flavour of the difference:

---

47 A. Rowell, *Green Backlash*, Routledge, London, 1996.

48 Genesis 2:27–8: 'So God created man in his own image, in the image of God created he him; male and female created he them. And God blessed them, and God said to them, Be fruitful and multiply, and replenish the earth, and subdue it: and have dominion over the fish of the sea, and over the fowl of the air, and over every living thing that moveth on the earth'.

49 Rowell, supra note 47 p. 9, citing speech by Chip Berlet.

50 National Resources Defence Council, *Breach of Faith*, 1995, cited in Rowell, supra note 47, p. 32.

51 P. Drahos and J. Braithwaite, *Global Business Regulation*, Cambridge University Press, Cambridge, 2000.

> property is not seen in Europe as an absolute right, as it is by US conservatives. Rather, it is a privilege that confers reciprocal obligations – a notion captured by article 14 of the post-war German constitution, which specifies that 'property imposes duties. Its use should also serve the public weal.' Those who own and hold property are members of society, and society has a public dimension to which necessarily they must contribute as the quid pro quo for the privilege of exercising property rights.[52]

This legal conception of property ownership is coupled with a 'profound commitment to the notion that all citizens should have an equal right to participate in economic and social life, and that the state is more than a safety net of last resort: it is the fundamental vehicle for the delivery of this equality'.[53]

To some extent, this attitude was driven by the different experiences vis-à-vis land ownership when notions of equality became important. In Europe, any attempt at equality meant redistribution, and this redistribution was strongly and continuously reclaimed by society, from bourgeois to labour movements. In the US, 'When John Adams argued in 1776 that the acquisition of land should be made easy for every member of society in order to achieve equality and liberty, he could disregard European concerns with how the state had to intervene to construct a just society: a continent lay before him waiting to be claimed'.[54] Social evolution in Europe pushed the state to take over a real and vital role in constructing a fair society with regard of the various social interests involved, a far cry from a minimalist role in protecting individual property rights. However, as our description of the 'property bias' has shown, there is never 'neutrality' in the state's activities. Its oscillation between discipline and distribution has always depended on the way societal forces have put organised and institutional pressure on political thought. Likewise, legal risk allocation in transition and development countries will strongly depend on how the local 'civil society' contributes to shaping the definitions of social reciprocity to be institutionalised by state organisation.

LEGAL RISK ALLOCATION[55]

It is vital, when designing commercial law, that there be an attempt to arrive

---

52 Hutton, supra note 36, pp. 50–1.

53 Ibid., p. 51.

54 Ibid., p. 61.

55 The following part of the text was written by Janet Dine and Frederique Dahan and first appeared in 'Transplantation for Transition – Discussion on a Concept around Russian Reform of the Law on Reorganisation, *Legal Studies*, 2003, 284–310. We are grateful for permission to reproduce it here.

at an abstract evaluation of the interests at stake so that the regulatory systems can be understood as a framework which holds the balance between the competing interests. At the heart of making suitable choices for regulation is a series of options concerning the risks undertaken by participants in the reorganisation of corporations. This does not make choices simple as is evident in the light of the complexity and uncertainty surrounding the issue of risk, especially in the regulation of market economies.[56] Black[57] contrasts 'technical perceptions' of risk with psychological or social accounts of risk. Technical perceptions 'tend to the view that risks are ultimately measurable and controllable' whereas psychological or social accounts of risk 'emphasise that risk is a multi-dimensional concept that cannot be reduced to mere products of probability and consequences'.[58] Psychological perception of risk may vary according to the ability of those at risk to undertake it voluntarily rather than have it imposed upon them and the 'extent to which they are perceived to pose a threat to valued social and institutional arrangements'.[59] It is clear that in seeking to regulate risk addressing some extremely complex questions with significant political and cultural roots is necessary.[60]

A series of questions must be asked:

1. Who is at risk?
2. What is their moral claim to protection?
3. What is the degree and nature of the risk?
4. What are the mechanisms and institutions available to manage the risk?

Who?

In a market economy there are risks inherent in all commercial transactions; a simple sale of a car may end with the customer dissatisfied with the perfor-

---

56 See R. Baldwin, 'Introduction-Risk: The Legal Contribution', in R. Baldwin (ed.), *Law and Uncertainty:Risks and the Legal Processes*, Kluwer, Berlin, 1997; Julia Black, 'Perspectives on Derivatives Regulation', in A. Hudson (ed.), *Modern Financial Techniques, Derivatives and Law*, Kluwer, London, 2000.

57 Ibid., note 5.

58 Ibid., p. 178.

59 Ibid., p. 180.

60 The technical perception of risk as objective and measurable is losing ground: 'the view that a separation can be maintained between "objective" risk and "subjective" and perceived risk has come under increasing attack, to the extent that it is no longer a mainstream position . . . Assessments of risk, whether they are based upon individual attitudes, the wider beliefs within a culture, or on the models of mathematical risk assessment, necessarily depend on human judgment'. See Royal Society, *Risk: Analysis, Perception and Management*, Royal Society, London, 1992, p. 90.

mance of the vehicle and the seller dissatisfied with the payment. The role of the law is to provide some mechanism for balancing the competing claims against each other. The management of corporations is no exception to this rule. Indeed by introducing a legal person into the equation the management of risk becomes more complex, not least because the participating groups in corporations may not be a single interest group but may contain competing elements. Thus, for example, shareholders do not necessarily share exactly the same interests; a group of ordinary voting shareholders may have interests diametrically opposed to those of non-voting preference shareholders. Similarly a minority shareholder may be in peril of being outvoted and disadvantaged by those in the majority. Creditors have competing priority claims and employees may have different interests depending on their geographical place of work and their position in the company. In seeking to protect a particular interest group it is therefore vital to identify with precision the interest group or individual that is at risk when any change takes place.

The Moral Claim to Protection

Companies in a market economy exist to encourage risk-taking behaviour by spreading the risk amongst a number of participants who may only invest a small amount, and protecting them by allowing some companies to operate with limited liability. If we take shareholders as a homogeneous group we can see already that their moral claim to protection *as shareholders* depends on a complex evaluation of the degree to which entrepreneurial behaviour is to be encouraged in a particular society and the extent to which they are already protected by such mechanisms as limited liability. In assessing the answer to this question two levels must therefore be identified: the fundamental purpose of corporations in particular economies and the extent to which the law has already 'rigged the market' in favour or against a particular interest group. For example, while shareholders enjoy some protection by reason of the limited liability of companies, creditors undertake greater risks in contracting with limited liability corporations. Thus the very existence of limited liability corporate organisations has already interfered with the distribution of risk inherent in individual commercial contracts. Much has been written on the role which corporations do and should serve within society,[61] suffice it to say here

[61] See, for a small sample, J. Dine, *The Governance of Corporate Groups* Cambridge University Press, 2000; S. Bottomley, 'Taking Corporations Seriously: Some Considerations for Corporate Regulation', [1990] 19 *Federal Law Review*, 203; K. Greenfield, 'From Rights to Regulation', in F. Patfield (ed.), *Perspectives on Company Law 1*, Kluwer, London, 1997; J. Parkinson, *Corporate Power and Responsibility*, Clarendon, Oxford, 1995; D. Sugarman and G. Rubin, *Law, Economy*

that there is a fundamental tension between a goal of making as much money as possible and serving other goals,[62] for example providing employment, serving a local economy and protecting the environment.

The balance between these differing goals can be fundamentally affected by the way in which the law allocates risk between the various participants in companies. While US corporations have tended to espouse profit maximisation as a paramount goal,[63] thus minimising shareholder risk at the expense of other participants in the commercial venture, the countries of the European Union have, in general, espoused the view that a more balanced approach to the allocation of risk within commercial enterprises is proper and has therefore followed a more protective approach to creditors and employees.

Article 44[64] of the EC Treaty requires 'co-ordination to the necessary extent [of] the safeguards which, for the protection of the interests of members and others, are required by Member States of companies or firms'. The important words in this context are 'members and others'. As Edwards points out, the wording gives rise to 'obvious scope for debate as to what is necessary and why: the spectrum ranges from the view that only a minimum level throughout the Community is necessary to the view that all members, creditors and employees of companies established throughout the Community should benefit from uniform rights'.[65] As Gower points out the reference to 'others' 'has been taken to include at least creditors and employees'.[66] This has also tended to have the effect of protecting local communities as the protective measures militate against complete mobility of corporations. This is in contrast with, for example, the US where corporations are seen to serve the shareholders' interests exclusively. These considerations raise fundamental questions of how to strike the balance between permitting and encouraging entrepreneurial behav-

---

and Society, Professional Books, Abingdon, 1984; M. Stokes, 'Company Law and Legal Theory', in W. Twining (ed.), *Legal Theory and Common Law*, Blackwell, Oxford, 1986; R. Posner, *Economic Analysis of Law*, 4th edn, Little Brown, Boston, 1992.

62 D. Korten, *When Corporations Rule the World*, Kumarian Press, Connecticut, 1995; M. Chossudovsky, *The Globalisation of Poverty*, Pluto Press, Halifax, 1998; P. Harrison, *Inside the Third World*, 3rd edn, Penguin, Harmondsworth, 1993; J. Karliner, *The Corporate Planet*, Sierra Club, San Francisco, 1997.

63 See sources cited in footnote 61.

64 Previously Article 54(3)(g).

65 V. Edwards, *EC Company Law*, Oxford University Press, Oxford, 1999, p. 8. For an inclusive view of EC company law including creditor and employee protection see J. Dine and P. Hughes, *EC Company Law*, Jordans, Bristol, looseleaf, 1991. See also B. Bercusson, *European Labour Law*, Butterworths, London, 1996.

66 P. Davies, *Gower's Principles of Modern Company Law*, 6th edn, Sweet and Maxwell, London, 1997, p. 55.

iour aimed at profit maximisation and the protection of vulnerable participants.[67]

The Degree of Risk and its Nature

Again, side-stepping the complexities of perceived risk, it is necessary to have some understanding of what it is that each interest group has at risk. The risks differ even amongst particular interest groups. For example, it is important to understand that shareholders are not a homogeneous group; they may have different interests according to the rights attached to their shares. An ordinary shareholder whose dividend rights are subject to surplus being available after the payment of a set amount to a preference shareholder clearly has interests differing substantially from that preference shareholder. Similarly, a shareholder may be less interested in the economic risks of a reorganisation and more interested in the risk of loss of control over a particular enterprise. Creditors will have different interests dependent on how their debt is secured, what priority they can claim over others with a stake in the assets of the company. The categories of participants at risk must therefore be scrutinised with some subtlety. The nature of the risk is also an important consideration. Laws often take a very stringent view on protecting citizens from damage to their physical safety. The degree of protection which is given to financial risk may be much less. Similarly, some balance has to be struck between protecting employees against the risk of losing their livelihood and with it possibly their community and psychological well-being and protecting shareholders from the risk of less gain or perhaps even loss of a financial nature.

What Mechanisms and Institutions Are Available to Regulate?

The final part of the calculation is the way in which the allocation of risk

---

[67] For a wider perspective on this debate, see Bottomley, supra note 61, p. 204; R.M. Dworkin 'Is Wealth a Value?' (1980), *Journal of Legal Studies*, 9, 191, D. Campbell 'Ayres *versus* Coase: An Attempt to Recover the Issue of Equality in Law and Economics' (1994) *Journal of Law and Society*, 21, 434, R. Cooter, 'Law and Unified Social Theory' (1995) *Journal of Law and Society*, 22, 50. As well as the issues of psychological and cultural perception of risk, a further question relates to the issue of differential bargaining power. The extreme US model is based on the fiction that creditors and employees are in an equal bargaining position to even the biggest corporation. The European Union has rejected that fiction and enacted substantial legislation to protect employees and creditors. See B. Cheffins, *Company Law, Theory, Structure and Operation,* Clarendon, Oxford, 1997; A. Ogus, *Regulation, Legal Form and Economic Theory,* Clarendon, Oxford, 1994.

may be regulated. Central here is the tension between 'public' law regulation by law or decree and 'private' regulation which seeks to use agreement between the parties as a foundation for control. Most jurisdictions adopt a mixture of the two approaches[68] but the balance may be different depending on different cultural approaches. The calculation of regulatory mechanisms needs to take account of the institutional framework available in the host country.

Risk Allocation by the State: Some Company Law Examples

As we saw at the outset, even the upholding of a simple contract by the state favours the party in the most powerful bargaining position. It is treated as a 'neutral' act where both parties bargain on level terms. Neo-classical economics' attempt to 'deconstruct' companies into a 'nexus of contracts' and (inconsistently) to represent companies as 'individuals' creates a discourse in which the power of companies is concealed.[69] Upholding a contract (say an employment contract) between two individuals thus becomes a neutral act, although the bargaining power of the human individual and the legal individual is in fact grossly disparate.

And company law itself is a central player in commercial market law. Legislating to permit limited liability is a key element in risk allocation. Its purpose is to permit investment by those who are prepared only to take a limited risk, that of loss of the amount invested, as opposed to the risk (carried by those in general partnerships) of loss of all possessions. The risk is transferred from investors (shareholders) to creditors who will be unpaid in the event of insolvent liquidation. These creditors may include 'involuntary creditors', such as those injured by tortuous actions of the company (including those poisoned by violations of environmental regulation) or employees who are injured or whose wages go unpaid. At a more subtle level the way in which companies are structured and operated within societies reflects a statement of beliefs about the way in which power-through-property should be distributed by risk distribution. As we have seen, shareholders are protected by the legal device of limited liability but a number of other more subtle risk distribution devices, often appealing both to a 'property rights' and to an 'equality' concept for support operate to further tilt the balance of risk in favour of shareholders and away from others who may be affected by the operations of companies. One of these is the 'myth' that shareholders are 'owners' of a company, that is,

---

[68] Thus avoiding the extremes of the pure neo-classical approaches to the regulation of markets; see Posner, supra note 61; Easterbrook and Fischel, supra note 46, 1991.

[69] J. Dine, supra note 46.

entitled to property rights.[70] This leads to the conclusion that companies should operate in the interests of their 'owners'.[71]

Companies: An Expansionary Use of Property Rights?

In order to reach a proper understanding of what companies should be doing in a market-based democratic society and how they could improve their governance it is extremely important to explode the 'shareholder-owner' myth, to see the company as a free-standing structure and to create mechanisms to reflect the responsibilities which the company has towards those over whom it has power by reason of the exercise of its property rights by its managers.[72] Paddy Ireland has made it clear that companies fit with difficulty into the property rights discourse.[73] He exposes the falsity of the traditional 'take' on companies, which is that they are 'the property of the shareholders' or in the 'nexus of contracts' or 'agency' theory of the company, in what amounts to the same thing, that the shareholders own not 'the company' but 'the capital', the company itself having been spirited out of existence.[74] Ireland also shows that there is considerable convergence between the property rights of creditors and those of shareholders, since each can be seen as essentially 'outsiders' having contractual rights against the company, rather than 'insiders' with membership rights. The remaining 'insider' rights of shareholders are relics of the time when joint-stock companies were run by members and of an even earlier time when lending for interest was banned but partnership for profit was not. An investment as a 'sleeping partner' was a convenient way to circumvent this rule. What are the relics? One is the rule that the residue of capital on a winding-up belongs to shareholders. The other is that they should have a significant role in the way the company is run.

There are two aspects to the debate within the 'property' rhetoric: one is the shareholder-as-owner-therefore-profit-maximisation debate, the other is the shareholder-as-owner-therefore-state-should-protect-that-property-and-not-regulate. Both claims envisage the company as the 'creature' of the shareholders and deny decision-making platform to any other constituency who

---

70 P. Ireland, 'Company Law and the Myth of Shareholder Ownership' (1999) *Modern Law Review*, 62. See also J. Hill, 'Visions and Revisions of the Shareholder' (2000) *American Journal of Comparative Law*, 39.

71 This concept is more fully explored and debunked in J. Dine, *Companies, International Trade and Human Rights*, Cambridge University Press, Cambridge, 2005, especially chapter 6.

72 Although, as Paddy Ireland notes, this will be a difficult process; P. Ireland, 'Property and Contract in Contemporary Corporate Theory' (2004) *Legal Studies*, 451.

73 Ireland, supra note 70, See also J. Hill, supra note 70.

74 Ireland, supra note 70.

may be affected by the company's operations. Hence the concept of rules governing directors' duties which seek to align the interests of the managers with the interests of the shareholders. These are a direct reflection of the first debate. The second debate is essentially deregulatory, using the 'property' claim to fend off regulation of private 'property rights' by the state acting in the 'public good'.

However, the identification of the relationship between shareholders and companies as a property right does not in any way, as Harris points out, identify its parameters; it merely appeals to the importance of 'property'. The 'property concept' tells us nothing about the limitations to be imposed. Any recognition of property rights involves (i) a bestowal of the right on one or more persons; (ii) a corresponding limitation of the rights of others; (iii) limitations on the use of the right by its owner. Where the balance should be struck cannot be deduced from the 'nature' of the rights but needs to be considered as a distributional issue of social justice. If I make and patent a crossbow, and that gives me 'natural' rights in it, this does not mean I may use those rights to injure or bully others.

DESIGNING COMPANIES FOR TRANSITION AND DEVELOPING ECONOMIES

It follows from the discussion above that considerable care should be taken when societies design their companies. A conscious political choice must be taken about where market risks should fall and this entails understanding the nature of risk assessment.

Employees

The concept of shareholders as property owners has disguised the risk debate, particularly so far as employees are concerned. Employees are 'outsiders' in UK/US company law, only connected to the company by contracts negotiated between 'individuals', which are seen for the most part to be on equal bargaining terms. However the risks to shareholders and the risks to employees are significantly different if we look at the impact of a company failure. The shareholders are carefully protected by the state imposition of limited liability and if the company fails will lose only the amount which they have invested. They may therefore calculate in advance how much they are prepared to gamble in the hope of profit. And what they lose is *money*. In contrast an employee will lose the opportunity to earn a living, will undergo what has been shown to be one of the most psychologically damaging life experiences and will be in danger of having to relocate with significant disruption to support networks.

So the *degree and nature* of the risk is potentially much greater, more so because there will usually be no way in which the risk could be calculated in advance or, even if it were, avoided, particularly since any information regarding the financial well-being of the firm will be unavailable to employees. It is the understanding of the disparate nature of the type of risks run by shareholders and employees that has prompted the EU to put into company law safeguards which seek to tilt the relative risks away from employees. These initiatives have been obstructed by the UK 'property rights rhetoric' but their purpose is not just to be 'kind to employees' but was clearly articulated by a committee set up to try and resolve the difficulties being experienced in negotiating the proposal for a European Company (Societas Europa or SE). In 1996 a legal expert group working party was established under the chairmanship of Viscount Davignon to attempt to find a solution to the disagreements on the worker participation proposals for the SE. The report of the group was published in May 1997. The group took as a starting point the importance of the involvement of the workforce in company decision making:

> Globalisation of the economy and the special place of European industry raises fundamental questions regarding the power of social partners within the company. The type of labour needed by European companies – skilled, mobile, committed, responsible and capable of using technical innovations and of identifying with the objective of increasing competitiveness and quality – cannot be expected simply to obey the employer's instructions. Workers must be closely and permanently involved in decision making at all levels of the company.[75]

Further the group accepted that a concerted approach to work organisation within the company 'will improve industrial relations, increase worker participation in decisions, and is likely to lead to an improvement in product quality'.[76]

These are valuable standards for both transition and developing economies. As many transition economies will seek membership of the EU, it is for them even more sensible to design companies which reflect these aims, providing methods of worker involvement with company decision making.

Shareholder v. Shareholder risk

One further example of risk allocation is given here by way of example, particularly since it may be less well known than the shareholder-employee

---

[75] Final Report of the Group of Experts on European Systems of Workers Involvement headed by Viscount Davignon (Davignon Report), European Commission, May 1997, paragraph 19.

[76] Ibid., paragraph 20.

dichotomy. This is the example of minority shareholder protection. So far the protections for shareholders and the advantages of belonging to a corporation have been considered. But there is a downside. In UK law, however, this does not consist of any substantial legal duties or liabilities imposed on the shareholder for, although the court may sometimes interfere with the freedom to vote, imposition of duties are minimal. Shareholders have no obligation to read the documents provided by the company or to vote on any issue. They have no obligation to police the performance of the company or find out if it is creating pollution or employing slave labour. They can throw all the information in the bin and await the arrival of dividends. Many small investors do so.

However, becoming a shareholder has two potential disadvantages; one is that shareholders must cede power over their investment to the directors who are managing the company, the other is that they run the risk of becoming a minority shareholder likely to be oppressed by majority decisions. As we have seen, it can be considered an advantage to have someone else running the company, but when they fail to deliver dividends but still continue to pay themselves large salaries and bonuses, frustrations can set in. An example may illustrate this: in July 2001 Marconi announced results described by the financial press as 'disastrous'. Following an annual general meeting where shareholders had angry exchanges with the management, the situation for management was little changed. The meeting was attended by about 1,000 shareholders and employees 'furious with 8,000 job cuts and this month's shock profits warning that wiped £4 billion off the value of the telecoms equipment company'.[77] One shareholder called for the resignation of the whole board. However, the chief executive signed a new contract to continue although he is reported as saying that he will 'probably not' accept any offers of a rise in his £702,000 a year salary.[78] An executive widely blamed for the disastrous results had been sacked earlier in the year but was nevertheless due to receive a package worth approximately £830,000.

The two major problems experienced by shareholders could also be seen as two sides of the same problem as the furious individuals at Marconi are inevitably in a minority because of the power held by the institutional investors, the pension and insurance funds. Patience Wheatcroft, the financial commentator for *The Times* wrote:

> Lord Simpson of Dunkeld gave an admirable demonstration of how to do contrition at the Queen Elizabeth II Conference Centre yesterday . . . but he need hardly have bothered . . . the occasion provided an opportunity for private shareholders to vent

77 *The Times*, 18 July 2001.
78 Ibid.

their feelings but it was little more than a piece of play-acting. The real work had already been done behind the scenes with institutional shareholders who had, as usual, agreed not to make a fuss.

In UK law it can be seen that the contractual theorists have very much the upper hand, with the courts very reluctant to intervene in decisions taken according to the constitution even where there is evidence that those voting have a vested interest in maintaining their positions. It should be noted that even directors may vote in their own interests when they vote *as shareholders*. If, for example, a vote to dismiss a director was held and the director was a shareholder owning more than half the shares, his vote against his own dismissal would be valid pending the possible interference by the courts following a long, tortuous and expensive litigation process. Thus shareholders who have been disadvantaged by the use of majority power are left trying to pursue redress through the courts without the protection of a legal rule which requires that members should vote in the interests of the corporation and that where there is a conflict between interests of the corporation and personal interests, votes of shareholders should be disregarded. This concept of shareholder-as-owner, entitled to cast a vote in support of a selfish interest, is therefore in stark contrast to many European legal systems which provide for shareholder votes to be cast in the interests of the company as a whole, taking account of the interests of all participants in the corporate enterprise. This is a little known but fundamental contrast between two diametrically opposed systems.

The Danger of Becoming a Minority Shareholder in UK Law

If decisions are made by majority voting (as they almost always will be) then, because of the concept that shareholders may, on most occasions, vote in their own selfish interests, the minority shareholder is, by definition, in some danger. There are usually no safeguards against exploitation of minority shareholders built into the constitutions of companies (although some may contain an arbitration clause). Consequently an unscrupulous majority may take the opportunity to exploit a minority. There are an almost infinite number of ways in which such behaviour may manifest itself but two of the most common are:

- where management hold a majority of the shares they will commit a wrongful act (such as causing the company to purchase their personal property at an overvalue) and then vote to prevent the company from suing to redress that wrong;
- where a director holds a minority of shares, expelling that director from his post and refusing to pay any dividends on the shares. In that way the

> director no longer receives a salary as director and will get no return on his shareholding. Where the company is a private one it is forbidden to advertise the sale of shares or in any way sell them to the public so that the ex-director has capital locked up in the company from which he is receiving no return. Because of the division of powers (discussed above) the discretion to issue a dividend belongs to the directors; it is not a decision in which shareholders can interfere.

While the courts are reluctant to interfere in the internal affairs of companies, these and similar situations appear to them to be so inequitable that they cannot be tolerated. The courts invented a convoluted way of permitting redress by way of a *derivative action*. This common law route was later supplemented by a much more widely used statutory action for *unfair prejudice*. Although this latter action is the more widely used, it is the derivative action which most clearly illustrates the tensions between the 'public' concessionary view of companies and the private contractual one and we will turn to that first. Both actions show clearly the balancing of risk between participants that the courts have to contend with, but neither is satisfactory. A much better balancing of the risks between minority and majority shareholders should be achievable by insisting on a duty always to consider the interests of the enterprise when a vote is taken, thus defusing the confrontation between internal shareholder factions. It is certainly arguable that exclusion of selfish interests will also make for healthier decision making by the company.

CONCLUSION

In designing commercial laws for transition and developing economies it is necessary for all participants to be aware of the murky origins of liberal market economies and to be alive to the fact that dominant philosophies, including human rights discourse, have consistently had the tendency to be manipulated to benefit 'the men of property'. So far as possible a balanced legal assessment of the risks run by interested parties must be arrived at, free of the emotive rhetoric of property rights discourse, since it is too frequently used to unduly shelter powerful sectors of society from market risk. In turn the lessons learnt from the design for transition and developing economies should give us further insights into the way in which risk is distributed in established market economies.

PART II

A model company law for transition economies

Contents of Part II

A model company law for transition economies: introduction

The following draft sets out, with comments, a draft model for company law in transition (and developing) economies. The comments seek to identify the purpose underlying the provisions, identifying the way in which market risk is balanced between majority and minority shareholders, shareholders and employees, entrepreneurs and consumers etc.

The law is based on the Yugoslav Enterprise Law (YEL) of 1996, which itself was a text based on a simplified version of German Law. This is compatible with other civil law in the region which was heavily influenced by German law.[1] The text also takes account of a report by Professor Peter Behrens of the University of Hamburg which assessed the YEL and proposed amendments.[2] However, the draft also adopts solutions to legal problems directly from EU Directives in order to assure compliance with the EU *Acquis*. Other influences are French law, United Kingdom law, the High Level Expert Group's report on Company Law and the huge comparative study on global corporate governance codes and practices undertaken by Weil, Gotshal & Manges LLP in consultation with the European Association of Securities Dealers and the European Corporate Governance Network on behalf of the European Commission.

The derivation of the articles is indicated in brackets. The number refers to the equivalent article in the relevant law or, in the case of the Behrens Report, to the page number. *Alb* = Albanian, *Behrens* = Behrens Report, *Dir* = Directive, *French* = French, *GCC* = German Civil Code, *GSCL* = German Stock Company Law, *HLEGR* = High Level Expert Group Report, *Macedonia* = Macedonia, *SE* = Societas Europa or European Company Statute, *UK* = UK Companies Act 1985 or Partnership Act 1890. Other references are made in full and explained in the footnotes.

---

1 References will, for example, be made to Albanian, Macedonian and Slovenian Law.

2 P. Behrens, *The Yugoslav Enterprise Law: An Assessment in Light of EC Company Law*. Study Prepared for Deutsche Gesellschaft Fur Technische Zusammenarbeit, Sluzbeni list SRJ Nos. 29/96 and 29/97.

SECTION 1

LAW ON BUSINESS ENTERPRISES

1. Common provisions

SECTION 1 SCOPE OF LAW AND TYPES OF ENTERPRISE

Article 1 Scope of this law

(1) This law provides the legal forms for business enterprises. Business enterprises are continuous economic activities as organised by entrepreneurs, general partnerships, limited partnerships, limited liability companies or joint-stock companies. *(1, 2 YEL, 1 French/Albanian Comp. Law; 1 German Commercial Code = GCC, Behrens 5–6)*

(2) Business enterprises must register with the Enterprise Registry. Other applicable laws and regulations lay down the formalities of registration and publication required for enterprise foundation and for any subsequent legal act and defines public access to the Registry, the publication organs authorised to publish registered data and the legal effect of registration for the enterprise and third parties. *(5 French/Alb, Behrens 8)*

(3) Business enterprises shall keep books, compile and disclose annual accounts and performance reports including verification of authorised auditors in conformity with the *Accountancy Regulation in conformity with the EU Directives in the field. (57 YEL)*

(4) If not provided otherwise, the court referred to in this law is the commercial section of the court of first instance of the location where the enterprise has its registered office. *(12 French/Alb, 14 German Stock Company Law – GSCL)*

(5) As used in this Law, the singular includes the plural and the plural includes the singular, unless the context otherwise requires. The personal pronoun 'he' includes 'she' and 'it'; and the word 'him' includes 'her' and 'it' unless the context otherwise requires.

1. DEFINITION OF BUSINESS ENTERPRISES

The definition of business enterprises of paragraph 1 of Art. 1 includes all kinds of **organised economic activities** without reference to types of business which is still made by some laws in the region. In this respect, Art. 1 is in line with the EU's acquis. The words in principle show that the list is open to any other kind of economic activities of enterprises (self-employed entrepreneurs, partnerships and companies) one can think of.

Art. 1 **does not require** that the economic activity is **profit making**. By doing so, important activities like the simple management of assets (e.g. buildings), the holding of participations or any cooperation of enterprises which is not profitable in and of itself but rather reduces costs for its members (e.g. joint research and development) come into the range of the enterprise law without special enterprise forms being needed (e.g. provisions on 'business associations' and 'holdings' in the former Yugoslav Enterprise Law).

The mentioned activities are '**continuous**', i.e. they must have some duration. This criterion is linked to the expectation that the economic activities under the Enterprise Law are 'organised'. The Law presumes that the establishment of a registered 'organised business' referred to in Arts. 1, 2 and 3 can only be carried out in a period of some duration. If some persons, for example, agree to jointly carry out an exhibition which is supposed to last 5 days, such an agreement would not aim to create a form of business organisation.

Article 2 Entrepreneur
(1 YEL, 1 GCC, 1–7 Macedonia)

(1) An entrepreneur is a natural person whose independent economic activities require an ordinary business organisation.

(2) A natural person pursuing an independent profession (as lawyer, notary, accountant, physician, engineer, architect, artist, etc.) shall be regarded as an entrepreneur if so provided by special laws.

(3) A natural person conducting agricultural or forestry activities shall be regarded as an entrepreneur if he is mainly organising the processing and sale of agricultural or forestry products (agro-business).

(4) Economic activities, which, due to their volume, do not require an ordinary business organization (small scale business) are not subjected to this law.[1]

(5) Within 1 month from the date of starting his business, the entrepreneur must apply for registration by reporting the following information to the Registry:

1. Enterprise name;
2. Name, surname, date of birth and residence of the entrepreneur;
3. Business activity;
4. Registered office;
5. Date of starting business;
6. Any approval by public authorities if necessary. *(95, 96 YEL, 106 GCC, Behrens 8)*

If applicable, the permission of state authorities to conduct this type of business must be submitted together with the other data. The signature of the entrepreneur must be deposited at the Registry. He shall report any change of registered data occurring during the conduct of his business. In case he has created a website, all data reported to the Registry shall be placed on this website and be available to every interested person.

(6) Entrepreneurs are obliged to apply the standard of professional diligence that their business environment is entitled to expect. They are personally liable for the obligations deriving from their activities with all their assets, i.e. with any right regarding movables and immovables, intellectual and industrial property, claims, concessions, and any other position the value of which can be expressed in money. *(50, 53 YEL)*

(7) The entrepreneur will lose his status once he ceases or is obliged to cease his activities. In this case he will be deleted from the Registry. *(101 YEL)*

2. THE (PERSONAL) ENTREPRENEUR

Art. 2 builds on the definition of Art. 1. Like other laws in the region, it contains provisions on the role of the self-employed personal entrepreneur. The basic regulatory purpose regarding

[1] In transition countries, very often all individual entrepreneurs are registered by the Registry. This may be an obstacle once the local business environment develops further. In this case, it does not seem suitable to use types of business to distinguish small business from larger business to be registered. Thresholds to be defined by the Registry Court or Agency or the supervising Ministry are an option.

this 'classical' commercial actor (in German commercial law: 'the merchant') derives nowadays from the fact that an organised personal enterprise can have an important role in the market which should be disclosed to the interested public. Continental laws or jurisdictions have therefore given such 'important' entrepreneurs special privileges and obligations (reduction of contracting formalities, obligation of swift reaction in case of contractual proposals or defects of goods, special liability standards with respect to professional skills, etc.). Such obligations and privileges would basically be applicable to all enterprise forms unless otherwise provided by the special provisions concerning them.

In order to define when an entrepreneur is 'important' enough to be addressee of the above mentioned privileges and obligations, paragraph 4 of Art. 2 establishes that **the 'volume' of activities requires 'an ordinary business organization**'.The latter includes the keeping of books and accounts and the employment of auxiliary personnel as a business of this volume is usually too big to be managed by one person alone. The threshold establishing the volume of business from which the attribution of the role of the entrepreneur and registration are appropriate must either be defined by the law itself or by a court or Government agency. Art. 2 (4), second sentence.

As regards the legal consequences connected to the status of the entrepreneur, paragraph 6 of Art. 2 establishes a special objective(!) liability standard by declaring that entrepreneurs must comply with 'the standard of professional diligence that their business environment is entitled to expect'. It will be up to the courts to set this standard of expected professional know-how and care regarding the rights and property of other participants in the business context which the case in question is addressing. The courts will probably also develop other obligations and privileges. Up to now, the only special legal requirement connected to the role of the entrepreneur is the obligation of being registered

In addition to civil liability, entrepreneurs are also subject to the penal provisions of Art. 303 (wrongful statements) and 304 (false balance sheets), and of the administrative punishments of Art. 310.

Art. 2 (2) excludes the application of the entrepreneur status to so-called '**free professions**'. Due to their special social status, special laws usually establish that these professions have their own registry and professional association. Art. 2 (2) takes for granted that such laws will be created. These laws often do not allow the use of legal forms of business organisation, especially the company form. Only the simple partnership form may usually be used. This was, for example, the case for lawyers in Germany until recently. Due to his special professional role and skills, the single 'free professional' should only be forced to be treated as an entrepreneur if special legislation requires this.

Art. 2 (3) mentions the special case of **agricultural and forestry activities**. As long as they are focused on subsistence agriculture or forestry, they are usually small-scale activities and therefore excluded by Article 2 (4). However, Art. 1 (3) clarifies that these activities are not excluded as such from the Enterprise Law. Their legal treatment follows the same logistics of all entrepreneurs: processing and sale of agricultural or forestry products usually require a business organisation which exceeds small-scale business and requires registration. Therefore, a farmer doing agro-processing and agro-business will have to prove that his business does not reach the threshold established by the Ministry of Trade and Industry.

Article 3 Partnerships and companies
(2, 5, 53 YEL, 1 Alb, Behrens 19)

(1) Partnerships and companies are founded by two or more persons, who agree on achieving joint economic objectives through contributions defined by the statute. A company may also be formed by one person only (single member company).

(2) Partnerships and companies acquire legal personality on the date of their registration in the Registry. They are liable with all their assets for the obligations deriving from their activities.

3. LEGAL FORMS, LEGAL PERSONALITY AND REGISTRATION

The first sentence of Art. 3 provides the general definition for (general and limited) partnerships and companies. Their **purpose** must be an **economic** one. This aspect distinguishes the Enterprise Law partnerships from a simple partnership form which may be available in the relevant Civil Code. The difference between general and simple partnerships derives, however, from the context of Arts. 1 to 3 of the Enterprise Law. These provisions exclusively address 'continuous economic activities which require an ordinary business organisation'. With respect to the entrepreneur, the Law presumes that this stage of organisation is reached when the threshold of business volume defined by the Ministry of Trade and Industry is reached. We think that the same criterion must apply to simple partnerships as there is no reason to treat joint economic activities better than those of a single natural business person. Once the threshold is reached, the simple partnership must register its continuous economic activities as a general partnership. This interpretation also prevents simple partnerships from being used to avoid the formalities of general (or limited) partnerships.

Art. 3 (2) declares that partnerships and companies acquire **legal personality by registration**. In this respect, the new Law incorporates the solution of other laws in the region which treat all partnerships and companies as legal entities capable of acquiring rights and obligations, in particular through transactions governed by civil law, and capable of suing and being sued before the courts. Applying the concept of legal personality to all economic associations (partnerships as well as companies) avoids the creation of complex legal problems.

As regards **registration**, the Enterprise Law defines for every enterprise form the data which must be submitted to the Registry and disclosed with respect to every legal event which is important for the enterprise's business environment. As regards the functioning of the Registry, the formalities and the legal effects of registration and publication, Art. 1 (2) declares that 'other applicable laws and regulations lay down the formalities of registration and publication required for enterprise foundation and for any subsequent legal act and defines public access to the Registry, the publication organs authorized to publish registered data and the legal effect of registration for the enterprise and third parties'.

The creation of the new Law on Enterprises requires adaptation to new registration and disclosure requirements which reflect European standards. This relates, above all, the legal effects of registration and publication as envisaged by Art. 3 of the First Company Law Directive. Paragraphs 5 to 7 of Art. 3 establish a principle which we will continuously meet throughout the Enterprise Law, i.e. the protection of third parties acting in good faith as against the enterprise.[2]

[2] As Paragraphs 5 to 7 of Art. 3 of the First Directive are very important for the disclosure of data during the live cycle of an enterprise, we quote them entirely in the

SECTION 2 FORMATION

Article 4 Statute

(10, 11, 13 YEL, 2 First Dir)

(1) The statute of partnerships and companies shall be in writing. Signatures of founders shall be authenticated by the Registry. The statute must be submitted to the Registry together with the other data required by law. If any provision of the statute requires the permission of state authorities, the permission must be submitted together with the statute.

(2) The statute includes the following particulars:

1. Form of enterprise;
2. Duration, in case the enterprise is formed for a certain time period;
3. Name of founders; in case of enterprises, registered office and registry number;[3]
4. Enterprise name;
5. Registered office;
6. Objects of the enterprise;
7. Enterprise capital and amounts of founders' contributions including the value of non-cash contributions;
8. Rights and duties of the founders in relation to the enterprise.
9. Conditions for and modality of determining and distributing profits and sharing losses;
10. Number, appointment, scope, termination and particulars of persons in charge of management, representation and of supervision, where deviating from non-mandatory provisions;

---

following. The First Directive is only applicable to companies. However, the same rules have been established by Member States for all enterprise registrations.

(5) The company may rely on registered documents and particulars as against third parties only after they were published, unless the company proves that the third parties had knowledge thereof. However, with regard to transactions taking place before the sixteenth day following the publication, the documents and particulars shall not be relied on as against third parties who prove that it was impossible for them to have had knowledge thereof.

(6) In cases of discrepancy between what is disclosed by publication and what appears in the register, the text published may not be relied on as against third parties; the latter may nevertheless rely thereon, unless the company proves that they had knowledge of the texts deposited in the file or entered in the register.

(7) Third parties may, moreover, always rely on any documents and particulars in respect of which the disclosure formalities have not yet been completed, save where non-disclosure causes them not to have effect.'

3 The requirement of reporting the *address of founders* has been cancelled as the First Company Law Directive is supposed to change in this respect.

11. Anticipated estimated environmental impact of business planned;[4]
12. Other matters required by this law.

4. FORMATION DOCUMENT

The Draft introduces only one constitutional or formation document for partnerships and companies, a written '**statute**', Art. 4 (1). This simplification reacts to the experience that laws in the region and elsewhere requiring a foundation agreement and 'articles of association', 'by-laws' etc. result in an unnecessary overlapping of the contents of these documents. Duplication of documents containing at least partly the same provisions may give rise to the risk of confusion in case of differences between the two. This is particularly troublesome if third parties want to inform themselves of the contents of the documents, for instance, with regard to who is entitled to represent the enterprise. However, this solution certainly does not exclude an enterprise from establishing internal by-laws with respect to its governance, cf. Art. 155 (1). Founders must sign the statute; their signatures shall be authenticated by the Registry, Art. 4 (1).

Art. 4 lists the minimum requirements for all partnerships and companies. The special provisions concerning these enterprises contain more specific requirements in addition to those of Art. 4. This regards, above all, Art. 97 which aligns requirements for joint-stock companies with those established by Arts. 2 and 3 of the Second ('Capital') Company Directive. We will comment on certain of these requirements in the relevant context. At this point, we would like to mention paragraph 2, 10, which states that the statute must include 'particulars' on the 'anticipated estimated environmental impact of the planned business'. It will certainly not

4 In spite of Behrens's reasonable comments (pp. 6 and 9), the standard of corporate ecological responsibility reached by the YEL should be kept. It is, certainly, inadequately expressed by the vague reference of no. 8 of Article 11 YEL to 'environmental protection'. We propose to translate this expression into minimum procedural requirements. One is the awareness of the environmental impact of business during the foundation procedure as mentioned in the text above. The other refers to the general good governance duties in Article 180, as environmental sustainability is *nolens volens* part of the *enterprise* 'interest'. One could also attribute responsibilities of the kind specifically to one or more managers, but this should definitely be done by future environmental legislation.

be enough to do a kind of box-ticking here and simply write 'none'. The expected impact must be sufficiently substantiated in proportion to the planned activity. The riskier this activity is, the more a full-fledged assessment of environmental consequences and risk avoiding strategies will be expected unless environmental laws set up more precise requirements. Otherwise, an important constitutional aspect would be missing which may lead to enterprise dissolution by registry or court order by applying the standards on 'defective statute provisions' treated in the next chapter.

Article 5 Lawful objects
(16–21 YEL, Behrens 7)

An enterprise may engage in any activity that is not prohibited by law.

5. SCOPE OF ENTERPRISE ACTIVITIES AND THE AVOIDANCE OF ENTERPRISE NULLITY

Art. 5 declares that an enterprise may engage in **any activity that is not prohibited by law**. Limitations to enterprise objects established by some laws in the region have been excluded. Provisions from outside the Enterprise Law may obviously require the relevant public authorities to approve certain activities due to special concerns linked to these activities like safety or environmental protection. Such authorisations must be submitted together with the request of registration.[5]

In case the statutory object is lacking or unlawful, the Registry may dissolve the company also 'ex officio', if the company is not able to regularise the defect within 3 months, Arts. 210 and 276 (1), 6th case. In case a company is carrying out 'illegal activities', it has to be dissolved, Arts. 210 and 276 (1), at the end.

It is important to underline that dissolution for 'illegal activities' requires a court decision as of Arts. 210 and 276 (1), 5th case, even if this is not especially mentioned. This is necessary in order to be in line with the 'spirit' of Art. 11, no. 1, of the First Company Law Directive, which tries to avoid a situation where

5 See Art. 2 (5) no. 6, Art. 4 (1) 3, Art. 31 (1), Art. 96 (1), Art. 229 (1).

illegality of statute provisions or activities automatically leads to **nullity of the company**. This can have a detrimental effect on the market place as many transactions may be nullified with the demise of the company. Art. 11 requires a court decision which declares the company null and dissolved for the future ('ex nunc'). Dissolution referred to in the last case of Arts. 210 (1) and 276 (1) must be treated accordingly and be declared by the court as it has the **same legal effect**, i.e. to change the company purpose from an actively operating company into a company deemed to be liquidated.

However, the impact of Art. 11 of the First Directive goes even further. This provision tries to reduce the cases of nullity of companies in order to protect third parties interacting with them. This is the reason why the ECJ applies even the nullity cases envisaged by Art. 11 in a restrictive way. The ECJ established that 'unlawfulness of the company object' (Art. 11, no. 2 b) only refers to the object envisaged by the statute. A company may not be declared null just because it is de facto carrying out unlawful activities.[6] Arts. 210 (1) and 276 (1) must be interpreted accordingly as the legal effect of a declaration of nullity and a declaration of dissolution are the same: the company goes into liquidation. Therefore, when Art. 210 (1) and 276 (1) allows for dissolution in case the company is carrying out illegal activities, this leads to **dissolution by court decision only in case the statutory object and corresponding activities are illegal.** In other cases, the company is simply subject to administrative and penal sanctions envisaged for such activities. Art. 308 (1) 1 is an example.

The new Enterprise Law does not envisage any nullity case for companies at all and is therefore in line with the 'word and spirit' of Art. 11 of the First Company Law Directive.

The **nullity question** seems to be different for **partnerships** as there are no Enterprise Law provisions regarding defects of the statute or the achievement of illegal objects. However, the interests of third parties, including enterprise employees and the 'public', are the same: they should always be sure to interact with an existing partnership which may only be dissolved with legal effect for the future. This is why also an operating partnership, the foundation of which was defective or the objects of which are de

6 See Case 106/89, *Marleasing*.

facto illegal, should be fully valid as long as nobody claims it to be dissolved according to Arts. 56 and 53 (1). Once such a **'defective partnership'**[7] is registered and its existence publicly disclosed, it can only be dissolved by court or Registry decision for the future. In other words, in case of lack or unlawfulness of mandatory statutory requirements (Art. 4 – including the 'object'), the Registry may dissolve the partnership ex officio after regularisation attempts have failed. If illegal activities objects are carried out, any interested person may request dissolution by court decision: **Arts. 210 (1) and 276 (1) should apply accordingly to these cases as the situation does not differ from those of companies in this respect.**

As long as the defective partnership is not dissolved on such grounds, the statute is deemed fully effective.

Article 6 Registered office[8]

(22–4 YEL, 4 Alb/3 French)

(1) The registered office of an enterprise shall be the place in which an enterprise conducts its business. If business is conducted at several places, the place in which its head office is situated shall be the registered office.

(2) Enterprises the head office of which is located in the territory of *X-country* are subjected to the law of *X-country*.

6. APPLICABLE LAW: REGISTERED OFFICE OR ACTUAL BUSINESS LOCATION

Art. 6 (2) applies the Law of the place of registration to an enterprise. But which law applies if an enterprise is registered in one country and does all its business abroad? Must the enterprise be

[7] The arguments loosely follow the German 'defective enterprise doctrine'; cf. U. Eisenhardt, *Gesellschaftsrecht*, 9th edn, Munich, Beck, 2000, pp. 186–94; B. Nagel, *Deutsches und Europäisches Gesellschaftsrecht*, Munich, Vahlen, 2000, p. 75.

[8] This law is following the real seat doctrine. There is disagreement across the European Union as to whether this doctrine or the registered office doctrine is the proper basis for European harmonization. The registered office doctrine permits a company to elect its place of registration without regard to where the actual business is carried out. This debate should be monitored by the legislator in case future amendments are necessary.

dissolved and liquidated? And if an enterprise founded in accordance with foreign law wants to transfer its head office to another country, will it have to comply with the local foundation provisions?

Questions of this kind where the facts of a case involve a foreign element, deemed to be 'significant' by a domestic court, are resolved by the domestic rules of 'conflict of laws' or 'private international law'. As regards enterprise law, the rules of conflict are informed by two opposing underlying philosophies which originate in the above-mentioned contractual and concession theory.[9]

The **'registration' or 'incorporation' approach** regards a company as fully formed and constituted under national law if it has its registered office within that state. It does not matter where the actual central administration is located. The enterprise may freely choose where it wants to be registered and do its business elsewhere. In this case, it is often believed that it will choose the location with the laxest regulatory regime.[10]

Instead, the **'real seat' doctrine** recognises an enterprise only if it has a real connection with the legal system under which it operates. That means an enterprise will not be regarded as fully constituted in a state unless it has both its registered office and its central administration in the same jurisdiction. If such an enterprise splits the registered office and the place of central administration, the 'real seat' doctrine will view the enterprise as losing the nationality of the place of origin, and the new country will not recognise it until it has been reconstituted according to local laws so that it can have a local registered office. The question is whether this approach is acceptable from the point of view of alignment with EU Law as it might conflict with the adoption of the 'freedom of establishment'.

The two concepts do lead to a clash between two regulatory strategies. On the one hand stand the two principles of **freedom of establishment and non-discrimination** on national grounds which are also two main pillars of the EU Internal

[9] See for details, M. Habersack, *Europäisches Gesellschaftsrecht*, 2nd edn, Munich, Beck, 2003, pp. 8–17; J. Dine, *The Governance of Corporate Groups*, Cambridge University Press, Cambridge, 2000, pp. 67–105.

[10] This was called the 'Delaware-effect' due to the relatively lax foundation requirements of this state of the US; cf. C. Villiers, *European Company Law – Towards Democracy?*, Dartmouth, Aldershot, 1998, p. 17.

Market.[11] On the other hand stands **the right of the state where the enterprise's operations actually occur to regulate and control those activities and, above all, to subject it to national taxation**. No reconciliation of these views has ever been brokered. The ECJ has, in three important decisions,[12] established a pragmatic approach. The ECJ recognises, on the one hand, the reasons behind the 'real seat' doctrine, i.e. the right of the state to protect interests of creditors, minority shareholders, employees or taxation as 'compulsory reasons of the common good' which may legitimate a restriction of the freedom of establishment without being considered discriminatory. On the other hand, however, the refusal to recognise the legal personality of an enterprise as such is a restriction of the freedom of establishment which cannot be legitimated by 'compulsory reasons of the common good' as it de facto results in a complete negation of the right of establishment. That means that the 'real seat' doctrine is basically accepted by the ECJ. However, no state may apply its entire enterprise law without restrictions deriving from the freedom of establishment. **The application of protective mechanisms may never preclude the freedom of establishment as such.**

Countries may, therefore, well apply the 'real seat' doctrine if the 'spirit' of Art. 48 EC Treaty is taken into account. That means that **foreign enterprises are to be recognised in the country if they were legally founded abroad and if the real connection with the founding state continues.** Such an enterprise may, therefore, conclude contracts in the country, file court cases, create subsidiaries or branches and acquire shares in local enterprises.

Article 7 Branches

(7, 23 YEL)

The statute or decision of partners or members or the board of directors of a joint-stock company may provide for the establishment of branches of the enterprise. Branches are places of business without legal personality. They have a degree of permanence, a management and transact business with third

11 See Art. 43 EC Treaty.

12 Case 81/87, *Daily Mail*; Case 212/97, *Centros*; Case 208/00, *Überseering*.

parties in the name of the enterprise. Branches must be registered as required by the Registry Law.[13]

7. BRANCHES AND SUBSIDIARIES

Art. 7 of the new Enterprise Law explicitly mentions the possibility of creating **branches**. It defines branches as places of business without legal personality which have a degree of permanence, a management and transact business with third parties in the name of the enterprise. This is the main difference from '**subsidiaries**', which possess legal personality. Their autonomy is, however, to a greater or lesser extent 'influenced' by a 'parent enterprise' due to contract, significant shareholdings or the right to nominate board members of the subsidiary.

We will treat subsidiaries of this kind below in the chapter on 'groups of enterprises'. At this point we would, first of all, like to invite the 'users' of the law to avoid a misleading 'language mix' which often occurs with respect to the terms 'subsidiary' and 'branch'. This confusion derives from the fact that subsidiaries are often also called 'affiliations' and groups of enterprises 'affiliated enterprises'. On the other hand, branches are often called 'filiale', meaning 'branch' in German, Italian and other non-English languages. It is obvious that the similarity of the core of these words may become a cause of confusion. When applying the Law, the difference between branches and subsidiaries must certainly be kept in mind.

Branches must also be covered by the standard of registration of branches required by the Eleventh or Branch Directive. This directive has two protective purposes. On the one hand, it wants to **facilitate making use of the freedom of establishment:** an enterprise which wants to open a branch in another member state may expect formalities similar to those at home.

On the other hand, persons who get in touch with a foreign enterprise by transacting with its branch should be protected. As the branch, which has no legal personality, is subject to the law of the enterprise headquarters, **creation of branches by foreign enterprises means import of foreign enterprise law**. This is

[13] Obviously, the relevant Registry Law will have to be established or amended in accordance with the requirements set up by EU Law.

important above all for creditors, because they cannot make their claims against an enterprise founded according to domestic enterprise law, as would be the case with a subsidiary. This is why they need fast access to information regarding the branch and its enterprise. In fact, registration of branches means just a disclosure of facts. Branches do not acquire legal personality. Branches come into existence by simply opening their shops/offices. The registration of the branch is important to create a legal linkage to the 'main' enterprise as the legal person and attribute corresponding responsibilities. In other words, **the sense of registering branches is to inform the public**

- **who is the responsible legal person (enterprise) behind the branch,**
- **who represents this legal person in the offices of the branch, and**
- **if this legal person is permanent**.

Directive 89/666/EEC is 'concerning disclosure requirements in respect of branches opened in a Member State by certain types of company governed by the law of another State'. That means it only applies to companies carrying out business between at least two Member States; however, based on the Directive, a **standard for registration of branches of national and foreign enterprises** has been developed in the EU. Law-makers in the countries will have to follow this model when introducing the formalities for branch registration in the Registry Law.[14]

---

[14] In order to demonstrate respective registration requirements, we present in the following provisions on branch registration, which have been recently proposed in Albania. The Albanian branch provisions are considering also Enterprise **'representations'** which are 'less' than branches as they are not 'equipped to negotiate business'. The following provisions will show how this could be done as compared to branches.

At least for *national* enterprises, it does not make sense to request the same formalities for a branch as for the 'main' enterprise. This is even more true if there is actually only one Registry holding all the enterprise information. In this case it should be sufficient that the enterprises apply for branch registration making reference to the 'main' enterprise's registration number and stating who in the branch has the right to represent the enterprise and to what extent. The above-mentioned provisions may, then, be shaped as follows:

(1) Enterprises have to apply for registration of a branch at the Registry of Business Organizations.

Article 8 Restrictions on enterprise formation
(9, 168, 196, 341 YEL, Behrens 9–10, 19)

(1) Partnerships and companies may form limited liability and joint-stock companies and, only as limited partners, limited partnerships.

(2) Partnerships may not be partner in other general partnerships.

---

(2) An entrepreneur has to submit the application personally. It must enclose:

- enterprise name and registration number;
- name, address and object of the branch establishment;
- the persons authorised to represent the enterprise for the activities of the branch, with an indication of the extent of their powers;
- the closure of the branch.

In the case of companies, the same request has to be presented by the legal representatives of the company.
(3) In case the main office of an entrepreneur or seat of an enterprise is abroad, the single entrepreneur or the organ representing the enterprise submit the request together with their signatures. The following data have to be declared separately, if the statute of a foreign enterprise does not provide them:

- the name and the seat of the enterprise abroad;
- the legal form of the enterprise;
- the subject of the enterprise;
- the basic capital;
- the appointment, termination of office and particulars of the company organ authorised to represent the enterprise in dealing with third parties including the range of this authorisation.

(4) Enterprises as of paragraph 3 will deposit together with their application a certified copy of the statute and a certified copy of the annual statement of accounts and of the verification report.
(5) If the required data and documents are not available in the Albanian language, certified translations must be submitted additionally.
(6) In addition to data required by paragraphs 2 to 4, applicants of countries which are not EU Member States also declare which foreign commercial law they are subjected to. The Registry may ask them to specifically prove that their authorisation to represent the enterprise includes the competency to establish branches abroad, unless the statute or the law they are subjected to explicitly provide so. In case accountancy documents are not drawn up in the same form, the Registry may request separate accounting for the branch.
(7) The applicants have to announce any change of the data and documents submitted to the Registry, including the winding up of the enterprise, the appointment and powers of liquidators and the end of liquidation and insolvency procedures.
(8) Paragraphs 1, 2 and 5 apply for representations accordingly.
(9) When examining the applications of foreign enterprises, the Registry applies the formalities of the local registry provisions accordingly unless the application of foreign law requires a different treatment.

(3) A natural person may join only one enterprise as member with unlimited liability.

(4) A natural person who is partner in a general partnership or general partner in a limited partnership, or who conducts business as an entrepreneur, may not form a single member company.

(5) Single member companies may not form another single member company.

8. RESTRICTIONS OF ENTERPRISE FORMATION

The new Enterprise Law expressly **excludes the possibility that companies can become general partners of a general or limited partnership**, Art. 8 (1). The law thereby excludes the possibility of forming a partnership where no individual assumes personal liability for the partnership's debts. Investors who all want to limit their liability have to choose one of the company forms (e.g. a limited liability company) instead of a partnership. Art. 8 (2) and (3) **prevent partnerships from becoming personally liable members of other partnerships and individuals from becoming personally liable members of more than one partnership.** Paragraph 4 tries to **avoid entrepreneurs or unlimited partners using single member companies to externalize risky or loss-making activities or to subject these companies completely to their personal interests** while these (often undercapitalized) companies are only liable with their assets. The same legal policy concept stands behind paragraph 5 which **avoids the creation of 'pyramids' of single member companies** the interdependence of which often remains completely un-transparent for other market players.

The restrictions of paragraphs 4 and 5 are in line with Art. 2 of the Twelfth Company Law Directive, which accepted the single member company form Europe wide. In spite of other provisions which generally try to limit the abuse of the company form (Art. 24) and the negative influence of dominant shareholders (Art. 282, 284), the restrictions of Art. 8 still appear reasonable. Given the present transition situation of the economy and law, there are enough reasons to avoid the legal complexities inherent in the combinations of partnerships and companies. Even though Western European and regional legal systems do not impose similar restrictions on the formation of hybrid enterprise forms, it should be accepted that the new Enterprise Law tries as much as possible to enhance the transparency of legal forms available.[15]

Another 'restriction' should be noted though: **foundation and existence of partnerships always require at least 2 natural persons.** Art. 3 (1) 2 allows only companies to be formed with a single member; and if for any reason only one partner remains, he shall either take all the necessary measures to adapt the company within 6 months to the requirements of this law, i.e. above all, find a new partner, or continue the business as an entrepreneur, Art. 60 (1).

Article 9 Liability of founders

(Behrens 22)

(1) If, before a partnership or company being formed has acquired legal personality, action has been carried out in anticipation of its formation, the persons who acted shall, without limit, be jointly and severally liable therefor, unless otherwise agreed. Once a partnership or company has acquired legal personality, all rights and obligations resulting from that action shall become rights and obligations of the enterprise.

(2) Founders must make their contributions in cash or kind in time as required by the statute and respect the formation formalities required by this Law and the Registry Law. In case they fail to comply with these rules or they delay compliance, founders are jointly and severally liable to the company for any damage resulting from their failure.

(3) Claims based on Paragraph 2 may be brought by filing a case with the competent court or by similar action carried out by the legal representative of

---

15 Up to now, EU Company Law Directives have only referred to companies. Partnerships, including Civil Code 'simple partnerships', have not been targeted by European measures. Companies with limited liability of members and shareholders bear special risks and have the greater impact on European markets. This is why the EU has paid special attention to them. An exception is, however, certain hybrid forms which the text refers to. This is, above all, the 'Special Limited Partnership' ('GmbH & Co. KG'), a very common form of business organization in Germany and Luxembourg, where the unlimited partner of a limited partnership is a private limited liability company. The latter enters into a limited partnership agreement with the limited partners. Consequently, unlimited liability is avoided for the entire set of companies involved. This company form is legally accepted but still controversial as it exclusively tries to combine the advantages of both forms in question. As it has, above all, been used to build company pyramids, it was forced under the European regime of the Fourth and the Seventh Directive on Accounting and Consolidated Accounts.

the enterprise, or, in case of the latter's failure to do so within 90 days after being informed of the infringement, by the other partners, or by a quota of members or shareholders representing at least 5 percent of a joint-stock company's initial capital. Creditors have the same right if they fail to be satisfied by the enterprise and their claims amount to at least 5 percent of the enterprise's basic capital. The quota of members, shareholders and creditors must comply with the procedure of Article 163. Claims must be brought within 3 years after enterprise registration.

9. LIABILITY OF FOUNDERS AND FUTURE PARTNERS, MEMBERS OR SHAREHOLDERS

Art. 9 (1) establishes that, if action has been carried out in the anticipation of enterprise formation, the persons who acted shall be jointly and severally liable, unless otherwise agreed with creditors. Once a partnership or company has acquired legal personality, all rights and obligations resulting from that action become rights and obligations of the enterprise. These clear-cut provisions of the draft implement Article 7 of the First European Company Law Directive. They avoid the creation of legal concepts regarding a special enterprise form before registration which was developed by German jurisdiction and legal doctrine. Under the new Enterprise Law, **all persons involved in the founding process are liable if the foundation fails.** Otherwise the newly founded enterprise will automatically be the new creditor or debtor. However, the enterprise may charge the founder(s) 'internally' if the duty they breached during the foundation phase was also owed to the enterprise.

Art. 9 (2) establishes the principle that founders have to make their contributions in cash or kind in time as required by the statute and respect the formation formalities. In case they fail to comply with these rules or they are delaying compliance, founders are jointly and severally liable to the company for any damage resulting from their failure. **Partners, members or shareholders who enter an enterprise at a later stage bear the same liability regarding their contributions.** Art. 106 (5) and Art. 232 (6) state this explicitly for joint-stock and limited liability companies.

According to Art. 9 (3), claims of this kind may be made by the legal representative of the enterprise, or, in case of the latter's failure to do, by the other partners, or by a quota of members or shareholders representing at least 5 percent of a joint-stock company's initial capital. Creditors have the same right if they fail to be satisfied by the enterprise and their claims amount to at least 5 percent of the enterprise's basic capital. This right of the other partners, minorities or creditors is called **'derivative action'**[16] as it derives from the enterprise's right against founders which the other partners, minorities or creditors need to realise because the enterprise management does not do so whatever the reason is. However, as regards companies and their formalised decision-making competencies, the third sentence of Art. 9 (3) must be observed. It refers the minority or creditor quota to the procedural requirements of Art. 163 (1). The minority or creditor must first request the general meeting to file the court case against the founders. Only in case the general meeting does not do so within the time limit set by Art. 163 (1) may the minority or creditor quota file the case by themselves.

SECTION 3 REGISTERED NAME

(25–39 YEL,17–37a GCC, new 3a Alb, Behrens 8)

Article 10 Principles

(1) The registered name is the name to be used when conducting a business enterprise. It must be suitable to individualize the business enterprise and to distinguish it from others. *(25, 34 YEL)*

(2) The registered name may not contain any information designed to mislead or capable of misleading the public with respect to business circumstances of the enterprise which are relevant to them. *(29 YEL, 18 GCC)*

(3) The registered name of an entrepreneur shall contain the supplement 'registered entrepreneur' or the corresponding abbreviation '. . .'. The name of a general partnership shall contain the supplement 'general partnership' or the abbreviation '. . .'. The name of a limited partnership shall contain the supplement 'limited partnership' or the abbreviation '. . .'. The names of a limited liability company and of a joint-stock company shall include abbreviations denoting the limited liability company ('. . .') or joint-stock company ('. . .'). *(26 YEL)*

[16] That is, '*actio pro socio*' in German enterprise law; see U. Eisenhardt, Gesellschaftrechts, 10 August, Verlag CH Beck, Munich, 37, 314, 409, 2002.

(4) A branch shall act under the registered name of the enterprise concerned and its own name. *(34 YEL)*

Article 11 Restrictions
(30, 31 YEL)

(1) The symbols of a state or international organisation may be included in the registered name only with permission of these states or organisations.

(2) A registered name may not include product and service quality control and guarantee marks.

Article 12 Exclusiveness
(36 YEL, 30 GCC)

(1) Each name must be distinct from any other name existing and registered.

(2) If the entrepreneur, the partner of a general partnership or the general partner of a limited partnership uses the same personal name in his registered name as another enterprise, he must add a supplement to his registered name which clearly distinguishes it from the name of the previously registered enterprise.

(3) The enterprise which has first filed an application with the Registry, shall have the right to have its name entered first.

Article 13 Protection
(37 YEL, 37 GCC)

(1) The Registry will interdict the use of a registered name if it is used contrary to the provisions of this Chapter and announce coercive pecuniary measures as envisaged by the Registry Law in case of non-compliance.

(2) Anybody whose rights have been infringed by improper use of a registered name may request cessation of infringement and compensation of damages and file a case to the competent court respectively.

(3) The right to file a claim for the protection of a registered name shall expire 3 years from the date of registration of the enterprise against which protection is requested.

(4) The provisions of this Article shall not preclude the protection of a registered name based on other regulations.

Article 14 Transfer of registered name and liability
(39 YEL, 22, 25 GCC)

(1) He who acquires an enterprise may continue using the registered name

with or without a supplement indicating the succession, if the previous owner or his heirs agree.

(2) In case the registered name continues to be used, the acquirer shall be liable for all liabilities of the previous owner. Any different agreement may never be relied on as against third parties, even if it has been disclosed, unless the enterprise proves that the third party knew about the agreement or could, in view of evident circumstances, not have been unaware of it.

Article 15 Information on letters, order forms and other documents, signatures

(99 YEL, 4 First Directive)

(1) All letters, order forms and other documents issued by an enterprise either by use of paper or electronic means and addressed to third parties provide for the following information:

1. Registered name;
2. Registry Agency or Court and registry number;
3. The registered office;
4. In case the capital of a company is mentioned, the amount of the capital subscribed and paid up;
5. Names of legal representatives of the company and, where applicable, the name of the chairman of the board of directors or supervisory board.
6. If a company is in liquidation.

(2) Branches of local and foreign enterprises shall state, in addition to the information prescribed by Paragraph 1, the registration number of the branch.

(3) In case of non-compliance with the obligation to disclose the information of Paragraphs 1 and 2, the Registry will take coercive measures as provided by the Registry Law.

10. REGISTERED ENTERPRISE NAMES

Provisions on registered enterprise names have been significantly simplified by the Law following recent developments in the EU: **any name may be used** as long as it is suitable to **individualise** the business enterprise and to **distinguish** it from others, and as long as it does **not contain any information designed to or capable of misleading the public** with respect to business circumstances of the enterprise which are relevant to them, Art. 10 (1) and (2). This includes the legal form of the enterprise which must be added to the name either fully or in abbreviated form, Art. 10 (3). There are **restrictions** on using the names or symbols of states or international organisations, product and service quality control and guarantee marks and including religious or cultural references likely to prove offensive (Art. 11). The main protective claim against infringements of the registered name is supplied by Art. 13 (2).

Art. 14 (2) derives from Paragraph 25 of the German Commercial Code: where a registered name continues to be used, the acquirer shall be liable for all liabilities of the previous owner. Any different agreement may be used against third parties only where it has been registered and published by the Enterprise Registry or where the enterprise proves that the third party knew about the agreement or could, in view of evident circumstances, not have been unaware of it. That means that third parties may trust in the continuation of **liability for previous enterprise obligations by the successor**. Art. 14 (2) is therefore another example of the implementation of one of the main enterprise law concepts, i.e. the protection of third parties who interact with the enterprise and invest their property.

Art. 15 generalises the disclosure requirements regarding letters, order forms and other documents requested by Art. 4 of the First Directive for joint-stock and limited liability companies for all enterprises. It is important to note that this now also includes electronic means of communication.

SECTION 4 REPRESENTATION

Article 16 Legal representatives

(43 YEL, 9 First Directive)

(1) General partners and unlimited partners shall represent their enterprise according to this law and the statute. Companies shall be represented by one or more managing director according to this law and the statute. This legal representation comprises any kind of judicial and extra-judicial transaction.

(2) Legal representatives owe to the enterprise compliance with any restrictions of their powers of representation as established by the statute or decision of other competent enterprise organs. However, such limits may never be relied on as against third parties, even if they have been disclosed, unless the enterprise proves that the third party knew about those limits or could, in view of evident circumstances, not have been unaware of it.

(3) Likewise, acts done by legal representatives shall be binding upon the enterprise even if those acts are not within the objects of the company, unless such acts exceed the powers that the general law confers or allows to be conferred on them. The enterprise shall not be bound, if it proves that the third party knew that the act was outside those objects or could, in view of evident circumstances, not have been unaware of it; disclosure in the statutes shall not of itself be sufficient proof thereof.

11. REPRESENTATION, APPARENT REPRESENTATION AND ABUSE OF POWERS

The issue of the capacity to represent an enterprise has always been difficult to solve. Two solutions that have been adopted are: (1) to require registration of all details of representatives and expect third parties to inform themselves of these details. If the representative has not been properly appointed and the registration shows this, the contract will not be valid. The risk falls on the third party. (2) To protect third parties even in the event that the representative has not been properly appointed a contract will be valid and the risk falls on the enterprise. The EU has moved towards the second solution to try and protect the certainty of transactions with enterprises in order to increase economic activity. Paragraphs 2 and 3 of Art. 16 follow this second approach and implement Art. 9 of the First Company Law Directive: if a legal representative exceeds his powers of representation or the enterprise objects, this **'ultra vires' behaviour will not effect the relation to third parties and bind the enterprise unless it proves that the third party knew that the act was outside the authorisation or objects or could, in view of evident circumstances, not have been unaware of it**.

This **loss of third party protection in case the party knew or, due the circumstances, should have known about a defect of representation marks a general principle** throughout commercial law. Art. 91 (2) of the new Enterprise Law establishes that a limited partner who has concluded an agreement with a third party in the capacity of a procurator or authorised agent without indicating that he is acting in this authority, shall be liable for this transaction like a general partner, unless the partnership can prove that the third party knew of the absence of authority or could not have been unaware of it.

It is important to note that **paragraph 2 of Art. 16** applies this loss of third party protection contrary to **the wording of Art. 9 (2) of the First Directive.** The latter declares that the enterprise may never rely on limits of representation towards third parties even if they were published. That means the enterprise would be bound even if a third party positively knew about these restrictions or incited the representative to **abuse his authorisation**. It is hardly imaginable that the authors of the First Directive would have accepted such a result. The purpose of the Directive is not to protect third parties who are not in good faith. Therefore, the national legislation may well require that in case of an **evident abuse** the enterprise will not be bound. This evidence may certainly not be based alone on the publication of the restriction, Art. 9 (2) at the end. In this sense, paragraph 2 of Art. 16 aligns the definition of this evidence with the one the Directive applies in Art. 9 (1) to the representative who is acting outside the enterprise objects. The solution of Paragraph 2 of Art. 16 is therefore in line with the First Directive. The same concept of loss of third parties' rights in case of evident abuse also applies to the special forms of **abuse of legal form and position which may lead to 'piercing the corporate veil' of companies** as provided by Art. 24 (2).

The second part of the first sentence of Paragraph 3 in Art. 16 reflects the second half of the first paragraph of Art. 9 of the First Directive. Both provisions declare that the principle of **unlimited representation does not apply in case the acts of the representative 'exceed the powers that the general law confers or allows to be conferred on them'.** That means that the organ who represents the enterprise, say the managing director of a joint-stock company, may not interfere with the competency of another organ, say the supervisory board. In case this legal competency is breached, third parties' good faith is not protected; and as the legal competency structure provided by the Enterprise Law is generally not a matter which the same organs may change, any ex-post authorisation would only be possible if the law explicitly allowed it.

The ECJ extended this principle of Art. 9 (1) and established that even third parties with good faith may be affected if an **external rule** disables a decision-making organ.[17] The case in question regarded rules of **conflict of interest** which are also provided by Art. 21 (2) and (3) Enterprise Law which **require the approval**

---

[17] ECJ Case 104/96, Cooperative Rabobank.

of the other partners, members or by other company organs. Despite accepting that the purpose of the First Directive is, inter alia, the protection of third parties, the ECJ held that the provision disabling the representative where a conflict of interest arose, was valid, even if the third party were adversely affected. The rationale of this decision is that **in case an 'outside' legal rule changes the governance structure of the enterprise by adding decision-making structures, the latter prevail due to the recognition of other legal interests considered to take priority over those of enterprise organs and third parties involved (in this case: the transparency of economic interactions).**

We will come back to this formula for opening the governance structure of enterprises when treating fiduciary duties, the involvement of employees and the corporate governance structure of companies. However, this reasoning should also apply to the case of Art. 21 (1) which defines an **outside interest in the restriction of persons capable to represent an enterprise**: persons who have been convicted of crimes in the course of their duties in the enterprise or of crimes regarding abuse of public office may not, for up to three years after conviction, carry out the functions of legal representatives, members of the board of directors or the supervisory board, of procurators and of representatives of shareholders at the general meeting. Also in this case, the enterprise should not be bound as against third parties.

It is also important to provide rules for the situation where **apparent representatives** deal with third parties. This may, for example, occur where appointment procedures have not been correctly followed. In these circumstances, the EU solution is again to hold the enterprise liable in the absence of third party knowledge as Art. 8 of the First Directive shows.[18] Such rules are often found in the relevant Civil Code and should establish that a person who accepts somebody repeatedly acting as his representative in a way that lets third parties trust in the existence of the authorisation shall be treated as if he had authorised the apparent representative unless the third party knew or could have known of the lack of authorisation.

---

[18] Art. 8 of the First Directive reads as follows: 'Completion of the formalities of disclosure of the particulars concerning the persons who, as an organ of the company, are authorised to represent it shall constitute a bar to any irregularity in their appointment being relied upon as against third parties unless the company proves that such third parties had knowledge thereof'.

Article 17 Procuration

(45 YEL, 49–50 GCC)

(1) Procuration is a legal form of power of attorney which authorises to conduct any kind of legal transaction and judicial or extra-judicial arrangement in connection with the business of an enterprise.

(2) If it is not explicitly stated that the procuration is issued for a particular branch, procuration shall be deemed issued for the whole enterprise.

(3) Procuration shall not authorise the conclusion of contracts involving the transfer or charging of immovables, unless this authorisation was explicitly granted.

(4) Duties which the law has attributed to the board of directors as of Article 170 may not be delegated to procurator.

(5) Limitation of procuration does not have any legal effect against third parties, unless the enterprise proves that the third party knew about those limits or could not in view of evident circumstances have been unaware of it.

Article 18 Issuance and types of procuration

(43, 46 YEL, 48, 52 GCC)

(1) Procuration is explicitly issued by the entrepreneur, or by the legal representative of the enterprise, to one person, to several single persons or jointly to more than one person.

(2) If procuration is issued to several single persons, each procurator shall have all authorisations of the procuracy under this law.

(3) If procuration is issued jointly to more than one person, the legal validity of transactions shall be subject to a joint declaration of will. Declarations of third parties made to one of the procurators shall be deemed made to all procurators.

(4) Procuration is not transferable.

Article 19 Termination of procuration

(48 YEL, 52 GCC)

(1) Procuration may be revoked at any time.

(2) If procuration is revoked, the procurator may exercise towards the enterprise those rights which stem from the legal relationship on the basis of which procuration was issued.

(3) Procuration shall not be terminated by death or loss of capacity to act of the entrepreneur or the managing single company member.

Article 20 Registration of procuration
(44 YEL, 53 GCC)

The entrepreneur or the legal representative must report issuance or revocation of procuration to the Registry within 3 days. When applying for registration, the procurator shall deposit his signature and a document indicating his function with the Registry.

12. PROCURATION

With respect to 'procurators' one must be aware that, having a wide variety of enterprise representatives makes it increasingly likely that defects in their appointment will create legal difficulties. There are a number of jurisdictions where the concept of procuration is unknown. However, it is regarded as important in some countries. The draft maintains this special form of representation in line with the other laws of the region. Generally speaking, procuration embraces all kinds of activities which are necessary to carry out the enterprise's business with the exception of those concerning a substantial shift of assets. In these cases, the procurator needs special authorisation. It is important to note also with respect to procurators, that any limitation of their usual legal authorisation does not affect relations to third parties acting in good faith, Art. 17 (5).

Article 21 Non-eligibility and conflict of interests
(66, 93 YEL; 101, 102 French, 76 III GSCL, 69 HLEGR, Behrens 25–6)

(1) Persons who have been convicted of crimes committed in the course of their duties to the enterprise or of crimes regarding abuse of public office may not, for up to 5 years after conviction, carry out the functions of legal representatives, members of the board of directors or the supervisory board, of procurators and of representatives of shareholders at the general meeting.

(2) A person authorised to represent or to supervise the enterprise may not enter into contracts or into other relations with the company, unless they are agreed on:

- by the other partners in case of a partnership;
- by the members or other members in case of limited liability companies;
- by the board of directors or supervisory board in case of managing directors

of joint-stock companies or, where applicable, in case of managing directors of limited liability companies;
- by the board of directors or supervisory board in case of members of the board of directors or supervisory board in joint-stock companies or, where applicable, in limited liability companies.

Any generalised approval must be registered with the Registry.

(3) The approval referred to in Paragraph 2 shall also be required for any legal agreement on behalf of the enterprise with other persons whom the representative or supervisor is personally interested in.

(4) At the next general meeting, shareholders shall be notified of any approval as of Paragraphs 2 and 3.

(5) An individual managing his single member company may not enter into contracts with the company concerning loans, sureties, guarantees, or collateral.

SECTION 5 DUTIES OF MEMBERS AND FIDUCIARY DUTIES

Article 22 Principles[19]

(223, 268 YEL, 53a GSCL, Behrens 29–30)

(1) When exercising their membership rights, partners, members and shareholders are obliged to adequately take into consideration the interests of the enterprise and of the other partners, members or shareholders. The same duty applies to managing members and directors and the members of the board of directors and supervisory board.

(2) Unless otherwise provided by this law or the statute, partners, members and shareholders have the same rights and duties under the same circumstances and shall be treated equally.

Article 23 Rights to information

(86, 127 YEL)

(1) The managing partner, member or director will keep the other partners,

---

[19] This is an important provision which distinguishes this law from those of an Anglo-Saxon derivation where individuals engaged in enterprises are generally considered to be entitled to act in their own selfish interests, regardless of the interests of their fellow members. The provision therefore protects weaker parties such as minority shareholders from an abuse of the majority's powers. It also means that the enterprise is more likely to be run as a joint venture rather than simply as an investment opportunity for individual profit. See the discussion below after Art. 26.

members and the shareholders informed about the enterprise performance and make available, at their request, annual accounts, including consolidated accounts, reports regarding the performance status of the company, supervisory board reports and auditor's reports. This obligation may be fulfilled by placing information on an enterprise website and informing the persons making the request about this way of publication. Otherwise, the documents must be made available for inspection at the head office of the enterprise.

(2) The statute may not preclude or restrict the exercise of the rights referred to in Paragraph 1.

(3) If the managing partner, member or director fails to provide the information requested with respect to Paragraph 1, interested partners, members or shareholders may, within 30 days after the refusal, request the competent court to decide on the obligation to inform.

Article 24 Abuse of legal form and position

(54 YEL, German/ International doctrine/ jurisdiction)

(1) Company members and shareholders, managing directors and members of the board of directors shall be liable for enterprise commitments to the extent of their total assets:

1. If they abuse the company form for illegal purposes;
2. If, contrary to regulations, they treat company assets as if they were their own assets;
3. If they fail, with respect to the type of activities, to ensure that the company has sufficient capital at a time when they know or must have known that the company will not be able to meet its commitments as against third parties.

(2) Third parties cannot avail themselves of any claim with respect to Paragraph 1, if the company proves that the third party knew about the abuse or could not in view of evident circumstances have been unaware of it. The claims must be brought within 3 years after the violation.

Article 25 Prohibition of competition

(92 YEL, 112, 113 GCC etc.)

(1) No partner in a general partnership, general partner in a limited partnership, and no member or managing director or member of the board of directors of a company may have that status or be employed in, or be a procurator of any other enterprise pursuing the same or a competing business, nor may they be entrepreneurs engaging in that kind of business.

(2) The statute may provide that the prohibition referred to in Paragraph 1 may be abrogated by an extraordinary authorisation given by partners or general meetings of members or shareholders with a three-quarters majority.

(3) The statute may also provide that the prohibition referred to in Paragraph 1 is to remain in force after the loss of the status referred to in that paragraph, but for no longer than 2 years.

(4) Should any person referred to in Paragraph 1 be in breach of the competition clause, the enterprise concerned may:

1. Expel the person concerned from the enterprise;
2. Request cessation of the rival activity;
3. Claim damages.

(5) Instead of claiming damages, the enterprise may request the following of any person referred to in Paragraph 1 of this article:

1. To accept transactions made on its own account as being transactions made on account of the enterprise;
2. To transfer to the enterprise any benefits resulting from transactions made on somebody else's account;
3. To transfer to the enterprise any claims stemming from the transactions made on somebody else's account.

(6) Claims to enforce the rights of the enterprise must be brought within three years after the date of the realisation of the infringement. Paragraph 3 of Article 9 applies accordingly.

Article 26 Business secrets
(90, 91 YEL, 93, 404 GSCL, 85 German LLC, etc.)

(1) Business secrets are data and documents, which would significantly damage the business interests of the enterprise if they were disclosed to unauthorised persons.

(2) Information which is required to be disclosed by law or relates to violation of laws, good business practices and principles of business ethics, will not be regarded as business secrets. Disclosure may be legitimate if it is intended to protect the public interest.

(3) With respect to their present or former position in the enterprise, managing partners, members or directors are liable for damage caused to the enterprise by unlawful disclosure of business secrets.

(4) Claims must be brought within 3 years after the violation. Paragraph 3 of Article 9 applies accordingly.

13. FIDUCIARY DUTIES

Art. 22 (1) of the new Enterprise Law provides for fiduciary duties and adopts general European Law principles: When exercising their membership rights, **partners, members and shareholders are obliged to adequately take into consideration the interests of the enterprise and of the other partners, members or shareholders. The same duty applies to managing directors and the members of the board of directors or supervisory board.** These duties obviously also imply **fiduciary duties of majority shareholders as against minority shareholders**. If, for example, dividends are withheld from the shareholders for an extended period of time, this may amount to an oppression of the minority which needs to be controlled:

- Members and shareholders have the same rights and duties under the same circumstances and shall be **treated equally**, Art. 22 (2);
- Non-managing partners, members or shareholders have **information rights**, Art. 23;
- If the company form or a legal position in the company is abused, the **'corporate veil'** which guarantees 'limited liability' may be **'pierced'**, Art. 24. In these cases company members and shareholders, managing directors and members of the board of directors or supervisory board shall be liable for enterprise commitments with their total assets. This is an exception from the rule that only the company is liable for the action of its organs, Art. 224 (1) Draft Civil Code;
- **Prohibition of competition**, Art. 25, and
- Non-disclosure of **business secrets**, Art. 26.

The observation of special procedures for **self-dealing and conflict of interest** of Art. 21 which we mentioned in the context above in the context of limitations of representation, are in principle also an expression of a fiduciary duty.

The Law adds special requirements to these general fiduciary duties when it treats **fiduciary duties of managing directors and members of the board of directors or supervisory board in joint-stock and limited liability companies, Arts. 176, 180 (3), 257, 274.** In this respect, it is important to underline the

enlargement of management duties connected to the concept of the 'interest of the enterprise / company' in Arts. 22 (1), 176 (1) and 274 (1). This legal concept has become the main gateway for the 'internalisation of corporate social responsibility' into European enterprise law. In fact, no. 1 of Art. 176 (1) and Art. 274 (1) explicitly refer to **'environmental sustainability'** of operations as being part of the 'interest of the company'. The concept of 'environmental sustainability' certainly depends on the legislation on environmental protection which defines general protection rules, like rules on packaging, waste disposal and sewage water treatment, and special risk assessment and protection standards linked to specific enterprise activities like the emission of gases, treatment of hazardous waste, etc. Such standards are translated into internal information and consultation procedures as part of enterprise decision-making.

The example shows that the enterprise 'interest' can no longer be simply identified with the interest of company members or shareholders as it is in some jurisdictions, notably the UK. But 'environmental sustainability' is only one aspect of the general tendency to 'internalise' other interests. This ongoing process is reflected by a change in corporate communication policies which nowadays prefer to present **firms as institutions not as individuals.**[20] But why and how has the legal consideration of enterprises and management duties changed?

As **ownership and control of companies are separated** and structured by the role of the organs of an **enterprise constitution**, and as such companies play an important role in the production of social economic welfare, the question was raised how control of company management can be achieved and maintained. Based on spectacular company breakdowns caused by the short-sighted competitive pressure on managements to maximise profits, dividends and share prices and to gain and maintain shareholders' approbation herewith, important 'checks and balances' of corporate governance were shown to be inadequate. This is so, above all, in respect of the control which shareholders are supposed to exercise over management decisions in the classical ownership model. This is why the 'interests' which the management is supposed to be loyal to and to dedicate its

[20] See the special review on chief executives, 'Humbled – Pity the Poor, Post-Enron Company Boss', in the *Economist*, 20 December 2003, pp. 87–9.

skills and care to have legally been widened. If the **ongoing health of the company is to be management's continuous concern and if this defines the social expectation towards the company,** the interest of shareholders can only be one aspect in the formulation of adequate policies. The fiduciary duty is, first of all, also owed to creditors and employees whose participation has widely been accepted to add to the insufficient traditional control functions of shareholders.

The new Enterprise Law recognises this by introducing derivative action of creditors, employees' participation (Arts. 27–9) and **special organisational duties** which the management needs to observe if it wants to avoid liability. Such duties are contained in Arts. 166 (2), 171 (4), 271 (4) (convening the general meeting in case of substantial capital loss), Art. 171 (3) 5 (creation of an early warning system), the list of Art. 176 (4) and Art. 274 (4) (including the **'wrongful trading provision'** of continuation of business and failure to open an insolvency procedure in case the company is obviously not able to pay its debts, l6, Art. 177 (probity of financial statements and other key data).

However, the major step to legal recognition of 'outside' interests being part of the (internal) ongoing health of the company is to generally **extend 'fiduciary duties to cover the absence of proper control systems within the company.** The duty of loyalty to the company has as an essential component, the construction of proper systems of governance'.[21] 'If proper systems of management are not in place the company – whatever stakeholders are involved – will be damaged.'[22] This 'proper management' or 'good governance' concept has two aspects.

On the one hand, the system will be there to protect shareholders, but where **duties are imposed by non-company law regulations,** such as health, safety and environmental regulation, it is arguable that failure to provide proper systems of management for these other duties will be a breach of the fiduciary duty to the company because the direct addressee of the provision is the company even though the indirect beneficiaries are other stakeholders.

On the other hand, if interests which in former times were

---

[21] See J. Dine, *The Governance of Corporate Groups,* Cambridge University Press, Cambridge, 2000, 191.

[22] Ibid., p. 200.

considered 'outside' interests become legally a part of the company's internal decision-making process and therefore of the enterprise 'constitution' like employee participation, non-consideration of the relevant consultative procedures would be a breach of the same constitution and management duties. Management would be 'constitutionally disabled' to decide without following these procedures. The legal definition of '**constitutional disability** in the organs of a company will mean that acts taken in ignorance or in contravention of the disability are an abuse of the powers of the company and, as such, a breach of fiduciary duties **not susceptible to ratification by shareholders'**.[23] **Therefore, 'any exercise of powers that fails to follow proper decision-making mechanisms, imposed either by the company's constitution or by outside constraints, may be regarded as breach of a fiduciary duty''**.[24]

It is important to note at this point that the **personal liability standard of skills and care for directors** established by Art. 176 (1) 5) and 274 (1) 5 is 'objectivised' by the relation to 1 which links this standard to the 'best' interest of the company. While 'acting in the interest of the company' would give discretion to the directors, '**acting in the best interest of the company as a whole'** requires a review of business judgements and a widening of view in the aforementioned sense which can only be met by adequate organisational measures. The liability provided by Arts. 176 (2) and 274 (2) as breach of 'good faith', 'reasonable inquiry and information' and 'proper purpose' is to be linked to this objective definition of 'best practice'.

The legal definition of 'interest groups' which should have consultation or participation rights in enterprise decision-making procedures is certainly an open social process depending on the economic and political conditions of the country and corresponding expectations towards enterprises. It will be up to the law-makers in particular countries to develop the rules which define the (parts of) communities which should have an input into enterprise decision-making due to the significant impact that enterprise operations have on them. The direct applicability of international human rights standards in countries may play an important role in this legal development.

---

23 Ibid., p. 198.
24 Ibid., p. 201.

At this point it is important to note that economic actors cannot escape from **the above-mentioned legal parameters** by choosing an enterprise form which seems not to be subjected to the specific fiduciary duties established for company management. The latter are nothing else but specifications of the general fiduciary duties contained in Art. 21 (1). They **would also be applicable in case other enterprise forms are used to introduce company-like structures,** which due to the freedom of contract is always legally possible.[25]

Above all limited partnerships are suitable for being formed with joint-stock-company-style constitutions. This is even more the case, if the legal system of a country allows a company to be the unlimited partner. For such 'public limited partnerships' the German Federal Court has applied the rules of the joint-stock-company law accordingly, as regards both the protection of shareholders and creditors and the fiduciary duty standard mentioned in this chapter.

We will see below in the chapter on groups of enterprises how the legal responsibilities discussed in this section will also affect parent-subsidiary relations in enterprise networks.

SECTION 6 EMPLOYEE PARTICIPATION

Article 27 Employee participation on the board of directors or supervisory board

(65 I, 83IV YEL; HLEGR 113–16; Final Report of the Group of Experts on European Systems of Workers Involvement (Davignon Report); insufficient Behrens 37)

(1) In joint-stock companies with more than *50–100* employees, the assembly of enterprise employees shall elect a representative to the board of directors or to the supervisory board in secret ballot for the same term which the board members are elected for. The statute or special agreements between the company and the employee council may provide for stronger forms of participation.

(2) Limited liability companies with more than *50–100* employees will form either a board of directors or a supervisory board. The second sentence of Paragraph 1 applies accordingly.

---

[25] See Art. 32 of the Enterprise Law.

(3) Employee representatives as of Paragraphs 1 and 2 shall be elected at the expense of the number of representatives to be elected by the general meeting.

Article 28 Employee council
(84 YEL)

Employees of an enterprise having more than 50 employees shall set up an Employee Council for a maximum term of 5 years. In an enterprise having up to 50 employees, the functions of the employee council shall be covered by one employee representative elected by the assembly of enterprise employees through secret ballot. Additional council members shall be elected for each additional number of 50 employees up to a maximum of 30 council members. The council may establish by-laws to organise its procedures.

Article 29 Rights and obligations of the employee council
(85 YEL, European Works Council Rules of the Annex to Directive 94/45/EC; Standard Rules of the Annex 1 to the SE-Directive 2001/86)

(1) The Employee Council shall monitor the enforcement of laws, collective agreements and provisions of the statute and represent the interests of enterprise employees. It shall participate in the decision-making for the utilisation of special funds and other assets of the enterprise in conformity with collective agreements and the statute. Likewise, it shall take part in deciding on the distribution of profits, which by the decision of the general meeting belongs to the employees.

(2) The legal representative of the enterprise shall keep the Employee Council informed about the activities and performance of the enterprise with particular reference to the effects of enterprise policies regarding working conditions, wages, occupational safety, profit sharing, status changes, enterprise pension systems, enterprise restructuring and affiliation. On request of the Employee Council, the legal representative shall submit state of accounts, including consolidated accounts, progress reports, supervisory board reports and auditor's reports. These obligations may be fulfilled by placing information on an enterprise website and informing the employee council about this way of publication. Otherwise, answers may be requested to be in writing. Electronic message and transmission forms may be used.

(3) The Employee Council may also directly inform itself about enterprise performance and inspect books and documents. It will deliver opinions and suggestions to the managing organs with respect to the matters mentioned in Paragraph 2. The legal representative shall notify the Employee Council of the reasons for not accepting its opinions and suggestions.

(4) The statute may not preclude or restrict the exercise of the rights referred to in Paragraphs 2 and 3. If the legal representative refuses to provide the information as of Paragraphs 2 and 3, the Employee Council may, within 2 weeks after the refusal, request the competent court to decide on the obligation to inform.

(5) The Employee Council shall report about its activities to the assembly of enterprise employees at least twice yearly or if the majority of employees so requests.

(6) Costs of council election and operation are covered by the enterprise.

14. INVOLVEMENT OF EMPLOYEES

Present EU thinking on employee involvement can be learnt from the following quote of the report of an experts group established by the EU Commission in 1996: 'Globalization of the economy and the special place of European industry raises fundamental questions regarding the power of social partners within the company. The type of labour needed by European companies – skilled, mobile, committed, responsible, and capable of using technical innovations and of identifying with the objective of increasing competitiveness and quality – cannot be expected simply to obey the employers' instructions. Workers must be closely and permanently involved in decision making at all levels of the company'.[26] European legislation in force on employee involvement includes the European Works Council Directive 94/45/EC which requires the establishment of works councils in European-wide enterprises, and Directive 2002/14/EC on Informing and Consulting Employees. There are no European requirements for representation at board level. But Regulation 2157/2001 for the European Company anticipates the establishment of European companies which have this form of participation. These provisions are based on the law and practice of certain member states, like Germany and the Netherlands, where employee participation has a strong and successful tradition as part of the 'increase of enterprise control' mentioned in the previous chapter.

[26] Final Report of the Group of Experts on European Systems of Workers Involvement headed by Viscount Davignon (Davignon Report), European Commission, May 1997, paragraph 19.

For convergence with the EU standard, law makers in transition countries should consider establishing an **employees' council system with corresponding information and consultation rights (Arts. 28 and 29)** and introduce **employee representation at board level**. The rules on employee councils apply to all enterprises, employee participation on the board of directors or supervisory board only to companies, Art. 27 (1) and (2). It must be underlined also that limited liability companies the management of which does not usually require any board structure,[27] must introduce one of the board models if they have more than 50 employees, Art. 27 (2). Paragraph 6 of Art. 29 regarding the costs of Council election and operation must apply accordingly to the election of the board member envisaged by Art. 27. Non-compliance with the procedural requirements of Arts. 27–9 would result in 'constitutional disability' of management with the legal consequences described above.

27 See Art. 257.

2. General partnerships

(YEL almost identical to Slovenian Company Law, both based on German Law)

SECTION 1 GENERAL PROVISIONS

Article 30 Definition
(105 YEL, 105 GCC)

An enterprise, whose objective is to conduct business under a common name, is a general partnership if liability of partners towards creditors is unlimited.

Article 31 Registration
(108 YEL,106 GCC)

(1) In order to be registered, all partners have to submit the following information to the Registry:

- Legal form of enterprise;
- Duration, unless founded for an indefinite time;
- Enterprise name;
- Registered office;
- Type of business;
- Basic capital;
- Date the statute was established;
- Name, surname, date and place of birth as well as residence of each partner;
- Rules of the statute establishing representation authority;
- Any approval by public authorities if necessary.

Partners appointed to represent the partnership shall deposit their signatures with the Registry. They shall report any change of registered data occurring during the conduct of the partnership's business.

(2) Where the partnership has created a website, all data reported to the Registry shall be placed on this website and be available to every interested person.

SECTION 2 LEGAL RELATIONS BETWEEN PARTNERS

Article 32 Freedom of contract
(109 YEL, 109 GCC, Behrens 10)

Legal relations between partners shall be governed by the statute. Articles 33 to 48 only apply if the statute does not provide otherwise.

Article 33 Contributions
(110 YEL, 11 French/Alb, Behrens 13, 15)

(1) Initial contribution of partners may be in cash or in kind (property, rights, labour and services). Partners' contributions shall be equal.

(2) The partners in a general partnership shall appraise any contribution in kind by mutual agreement and express its value in money. If no agreement can be met, any partner may request the competent court to appoint by a binding decision a valuation expert. The partners' or the expert's report on the appraisal shall be submitted to the Registry together with the other data required.

Article 34 Internal liability
(111 YEL, 708 German Civil Code = GCivC)

During the fulfilment of their obligations, partners shall be liable to the general partnership for any damage caused deliberately or through gross negligence.

Article 35 Reimbursement for expenses
(112 YEL, 110 GCC)

Any partner shall have the right to claim from the general partnership reimbursement of expenses which he incurred in conducting the partnership's business and which he could consider necessary in view of the operating circumstances.

Article 36 Delay of payment of contributions
(113 YEL, 111 GCC)

Any partner who fails to pay his due contribution in cash or in kind within the term set in the statute, or who fails to transfer to the partnership any amount of cash he received on behalf of the partnership in good time, or who takes for himself money from the partnership without authorisation, shall pay interest starting from the day on which his contribution or the transfer were due, or from the day on which he took the money.

Article 37 Increase or reduction of contribution
(114, 115 YEL, 707 GCivC, 122 GCC)

(1) No partner is bound to increase his contribution above the agreed amount or to supplement it, if it is decreased by losses.

(2) No partner may reduce his contribution without the approval of the other partners.

Article 38 Disposing of the interest
(116, 117, 132 YEL, 717, 719 GCivC, Behrens 13)

(1) No partner may withdraw, transfer or pledge his interest without the approval of the other partners.

(2) The transfer of interests among partners shall be unrestricted, unless otherwise provided by the statute.

(3) A partner may request withdrawal only in case of dissolution of the general partnership or in case of termination of his relationship after distribution of profits and losses.

Article 39 Consequences of breach of competition clause
(118, 92 YEL, 112, 113 GCC)

(1) In case a partner is in breach of the competition clause, the other partners decide which action should be taken pursuant to Article 25.

(2) The provisions of Article 25 do not preclude the other partners' right to call for the dissolution of the partnership.

Article 40 Management
(119 YEL, 114 GCC, Behrens 10, 11)

(1) All partners shall have the right to manage the business of the partnership as managing directors.

(2) If the statute has assigned management to one or several partners, the other partners shall be excluded from management.

Article 41 Management by more than one partner
(121 YEL, 115 GCC)

(1) If all or several partners are vested with the management right, each of them shall have the right to act independently, unless the other managing directors contest the action, in which case it has to be abandoned.

(2) If the statute provides that managing directors may act only jointly, the approval of all managing directors shall be required for each transaction, except if deferment poses a hazard.

(3) If the statute provides that a managing director is bound to abide by instructions of another managing director and considers instructions given to be inappropriate, he shall notify the other managing directors for the purpose of deciding jointly on the transaction, unless deferment poses a hazard.

Article 42 Scope of management
(120 YEL, 116 GCC)

(1) The management right shall comprise all transactions carried out during the regular conduct of enterprise business.

(2) Transactions which are beyond the scope of authority referred by Paragraph 1 require approval of all partners.

Article 43 Transfer of management rights
(122 YEL)

No partner may transfer his management rights to a third party, unless all the other partners so approve.

Article 44 Notice and revocation of management rights
(124 YEL, 712 GCivC, 117 GCC, Behrens 11)

(1) A managing director may terminate his duties on reasonable grounds sending his notice in time to allow for continuation of undertaken transactions by other managing directors, unless an important reason legitimates untimely notice.

(2) Management authority may be revoked by decision of the competent court requested by the other partners, if legitimated on reasonable grounds like gross violation of duties or incapacity to perform managerial duties regularly.

Article 45 Decision making by partners
(125 YEL, 119 GCC)

(1) In the case of decisions which must be adopted by all partners, the consent of all those not limited by conflict of interest is required.

(2) In cases where the statute allows for decision-making by majority vote, the majority shall be determined with respect to the number of partners if not provided otherwise.

Article 46 Profit and loss
(128 YEL, 120 GCC, Behrens 14)

At the end of each business year, the annual statement of account is prepared, ascertaining profits or losses and each partner's share therein.

Article 47 Distribution of profits and losses
(129, 130 YEL, 121 GCC)

Each partner is entitled to an equal share of any profits and shall contribute equally to any losses resulting from the partnership

SECTION 3 LEGAL RELATIONS OF PARTNERS TOWARDS THIRD PARTIES

Article 48 Representation of the general partnership
(133 YEL, 125 GCC, Behrens 13)

(1) Each partner shall be entitled to represent the partnership, unless the statute otherwise provides.

(2) If partners represent the partnership jointly, declarations which are supposed to be received by the company may be addressed to one of the partners entitled to representation. Managing directors entitled to represent the company jointly may authorise some of them to carry out certain transactions or certain kinds of transactions.

(3) Any exclusion of a partner from representation or decision on joint representation as well as any change in a partner's entitlement to representation shall be reported for entry in the Registry.

Article 49 Notice and revocation of the right of representation
(134 YEL, 715 GCivC, 127 GCC, Behrens 13, 11)

(1) A representative may terminate his duties by reasonable notice taking into account the other representatives' ability to continue transactions.

(2) Authority for representation may be revoked by decision of the competent court requested by the other partners, in particular in the cases of gross violation of duties or incapacity to perform duties of representation regularly.

Article 50 Personal liability of partners
(135 YEL, 128, 135 GCC)

(1) Partners shall be personally, jointly and severally liable for the commitments of the partnership to the total extent of his assets. Agreements to the contrary are ineffective as against third parties.

(2) The claim of a personal creditor of the partner may also be settled from the partner's claims against the general partnership and from the partner's interest in the partnership.

Article 51 Objections
(136, 137 YEL, 129 GCC)

Should a creditor file a claim against a partner with respect to an obligation of the general partnership, the partner concerned may use defences available to him personally as well as those available to the partnership.

Article 52 Liability of a new partner
(138 YEL, 130 GCC)

Any person who becomes a partner in an existing general partnership assumes the liabilities of the partnership, including pre-existing liabilities, equally with all existing partners. Agreements to the contrary are ineffective as against third parties.

SECTION 4 DISSOLUTION OF GENERAL PARTNERSHIP AND EXIT OF PARTNERS

Article 53 Reasons for dissolution
(100, 139 YEL, 131 GCC, Behrens 14)

(1) The general partnership shall dissolve:

- By expiry of the period for which it was established;
- By decision of the partners;
- By opening of a bankruptcy procedure;
- By court decision;
- If it has not carried out any business activities for two years.

(2) The following events lead to exit of a partner unless the statute provides otherwise:

- Death of a partner;
- Opening of a bankruptcy procedure against a partner;
- Notice given by a partner;
- Notice given by a personal creditor of a partner in circumstances described by Article 55;
- Decision of partners;
- Other cases provided by the statute.

The partner will exit the general partnership once the event occurs; in the case of notice not before the end of the term envisaged for the notice.

Article 54 Partner's notice
(140 YEL, 132 GCC)

If a partnership has been established for an indefinite period of time, a partner may give written notice 6 months before the end of the business year unless the statute otherwise provides. A shorter period of notice may not be unreasonably excluded.

Article 55 Notice by a personal creditor
(135 YEL, 135 GCC)

If a personal creditor has failed to achieve satisfaction of a court order made against the partner he may give notice 6 months before the end of the business year.

Article 56 Dissolution by court decision
(141 YEL, 133 GCC)

Pursuant to a complaint filed by a partner, the partnership may be dissolved by court decision, in particular if another partner has failed deliberately or by gross negligence to perform any duty established by the statute or if the performance of such a duty has become impossible.

Article 57 Exclusion of a partner
(142 YEL, 140 GCC)

Under the circumstances set out in Article 56, the court may, pursuant to the complaint of the other partners, decide to exclude the partner concerned instead of dissolving the general partnership.

Article 58 Arrangement of accounts on exit of a partner
(145, 146 YEL, 738, 739 GCivC)

(1) The interest of each partner who leaves the general partnership will be distributed among remaining partners. The latter are obliged to pay him the amount he would have received if the general partnership were dissolved at the time of his exit without taking account of outstanding transactions.

(2) If the value of the assets of the general partnership is not sufficient to cover the partnership's commitments, the exiting partner shall accept a part of the missing amount proportionate to his share in bearing losses.

Article 59 Participation in the result of outstanding transactions
(147 YEL, 740 GCivC)

A partner leaving the general partnership shall have his share of profits and losses relating to pendent transactions valued at the time of his exit.

Article 60 Procedure in case of one remaining partner
(100 YEL, 116 Slovenian Company Law)

(1) If for any reason only one partner remains, he shall either take all the necessary measures to adapt the company within 6 months to the requirements of this law, or continue the business as an entrepreneur.

(2) If within the time limit referred to in the previous paragraph a partner fails to register the change with the Registry, the general partnership shall be deemed dissolved.

Article 61 Continuation of partnership with heirs
(143 YEL, 139 GCC)

(1) A general partnership shall continue with the heirs to a deceased partner, if so provided by the statute and accepted by the heirs.

(2) The heirs may exercise the right referred to in Paragraph 1 within 30 days from the date they came to know about the succession occurring or within 30 days from the appointment of the representative of an heir who has no legal capacity.

(3) If an heir opts for continuation as a limited partner, the enterprise will be transformed into a limited partnership with consent of the other partners.

Article 62 Entry in the enterprise registry
(148 YEL, 143 GCC)

All partners shall report the dissolution and the exit of a partner to the Registry for registration and publication. In case of dissolution by court decision, the court has to register the dissolution *ex officio*.

SECTION 5 LIQUIDATION OF GENERAL PARTNERSHIP

Article 63 Liquidation rule
(149 YEL, 145 GCC)

(1) After dissolution, liquidation will be carried out unless the partners decide to apply a different form of arrangement of accounts or a bankruptcy procedure has been opened with respect to the assets of the general partnership.

(2) Articles 64 to 76 provide the rules for regular liquidation. A summary procedure may be carried out according to Article 77.

Article 64 Appointment of liquidators
(150 YEL, 146 GCC)

(1) Liquidation shall be carried out by all partners, unless they decide otherwise. Where a partner has more than one heir, a joint representative should be appointed.

(2) Should the partners fail to appoint a liquidator within 15 days from the appearance of conditions for dissolution, any partner may request the competent court to appoint a liquidator.[1]

Article 65 Dismissal of a liquidator
(153 YEL, 147 GCC)

The persons mentioned in Paragraph 1 of the previous article may dismiss the liquidator by unanimous decision. At the request of one of these persons, dismissal can be carried out by the court.

Article 66 Entry in the enterprise registry
(151 YEL, 148 GCC)

(1) The partners shall report the appointment of a liquidator, change of liquidator and changes to his authorisations to the Registry.

---

[1] Liquidators' qualification must correspond to the standard established by the Eighth Company Law Directive 84/253/EEC on auditors' qualification; see in this respect Chapter 10, note 1 of the Draft.

(2) Registration of appointment and dismissal of liquidators appointed by the court are carried out *ex officio*.

Article 67 Rights and duties of liquidators
(152, 154 YEL, 149 GCC)

(1) Liquidators shall bring the current business transactions to a close, collect claims, sell remaining assets and pay creditors. Liquidators may conclude new business transactions for the purpose of bringing current transactions to a close. Within the limits of their assignment, liquidators shall represent the enterprise judicially and extra-judicially.

(2) Property loaned to the general partnership shall be returned to the partners concerned. Partners shall not be entitled to indemnification for unintentional destruction, damage or reduction of value of the objects.

Article 68 Joint representation and management
(155 YEL, 150 GCC)

(1) If there are several liquidators, they shall exercise their rights and duties jointly, unless it is provided that they may also act independently, which shall be entered in the Registry.

(2) The provision of Paragraph 1 shall not prevent the liquidators from authorising one of them to perform specified transactions.

Article 69 Unrestricted character of authorization
(156 YEL, 151 GCC)

Any restriction of the power of the liquidators shall have no effect as against third parties.

Article 70 Supplement to the registered name
(158 YEL, 153 GCC)

The words ‘in liquidation’ shall be added to the registered name of the general partnership.

Article 71 Balance sheets
(159 YEL, 154 GCC)

The liquidator shall prepare a balance sheet at the beginning and at the end of the liquidation. If the liquidation procedure is conducted for longer than a year, the liquidator shall also prepare the general partnership’s statements of account at the end of the business year.

Article 72 Distribution of assets
(160 YEL, 155 GCC)

(1) Having satisfied the creditors, the liquidator shall distribute the remaining assets among partners in proportion to their capital shares as declared in the final account.

(2) If a dispute over the distribution of assets arises between partners or in case of claims contested by creditors, liquidators shall postpone the distribution until the final settlement of the dispute.

Article 73 Meeting commitments towards creditors
(161 YEL, 735 GCivC)

If assets of the general partnership are not sufficient to meet its commitments towards creditors, the partners shall cover these commitments in proportion to their duty to bear losses. If a partner fails to pay his share, the other partners shall pay on his behalf in the above-mentioned proportions.

Article 74 Legal relationships between partners
(163 YEL, 156 GCC)

Until completion of liquidation, the provisions of Articles 32 to 52 of this Law shall apply accordingly to legal relationships between the partners and as against third parties, unless the articles on liquidation or its objective provide otherwise.

Article 75 Remuneration of third party liquidators
(163 YEL, 155 GCC, 265 GermJoint-StockCLaw)

(1) Third party liquidators shall be entitled to reimbursement of expenses and remuneration for their work. If liquidators and partners do not reach an agreement, the court will establish the amounts of reimbursement and remuneration.

(2) Reimbursement and remuneration shall be paid to the liquidator once commitments to the creditors have been met, but before the distribution of assets among the partners.

Article 76 Deletion of the partnership from the registry and deposit of documents
(164 YEL, 157 GCC)

(1) Once the liquidation procedure is completed, the liquidator shall request the deletion of the general partnership from the Registry.

(2) Books and documents of the liquidated general partnership shall be taken into deposit by one of the partners or a third party. In the event of the partners failing to reach an agreement, the competent court shall designate the partner or third party.

(3) The name of the person depositing the books and documents shall be entered into the Registry.

(4) The partners and their heirs maintain the right to inspect and use the books and documents.

Article 77 Summary procedure
(167 YEL)

(1) The partners may decide that the liquidation of the partnership be carried out by summary procedure, if they state before the competent court that they have settled all commitments of the partnership to the creditors and regulated all relationships with their employees.

(2) The court may request evidence concerning the truth of the statement referred to in Paragraph 1 and request security for the payments due to creditors.

(3) The decision on liquidating the general partnership by summary procedure must be reported to the Registry.

SECTION 6 TIME LIMITS

Article 78 Time limits of claims against a partner
(165, 166 YEL, 159 GCC)

(1) Claims against a partner for commitments of the general partnership must be brought within 3 years after the dissolution unless the claim towards the general partnership is subject to shorter prescription.

(2) Prescription starts from the day on which the dissolution was registered.

(3) If the claim against the general partnership will be mature after registration, prescription will start on the date of maturity.

(4) Any interruption of prescription towards the dissolved general partnership will also apply towards those who were partners at the moment of dissolution.

Article 79 Time limits in case of exit of a partner
(160 GCC)

A partner whose membership has terminated shall be liable for obligations of the general partnership which were incurred before termination if they mature earlier than 3 years after that date. The term starts on the day on which termination was registered.

15. GENERAL PARTNERSHIPS

Freedom of Contract

Freedom of contract is essential in partnership law, because the partners must be allowed to adjust the rules for their cooperation to the specific circumstances. The 'model partnership' which the Law envisages is very much a joint private activity, the relatively small social and economic impact of which does not require mandatory legal requirements. Therefore, Art. 32 declares that the provisions regarding the **internal relations** of partners (Arts. 33 to 47) only apply if the statute does not provide otherwise. Partnership law should be mandatory only to the extent that interests of third parties are involved (**external relations**). This is recognised by Arts. 48 to 52. And we have seen at the end of the section on fiduciary duties, that mandatory rules on companies may be applied accordingly to partnerships if contractual freedom is used to create company-like organisations with a comparable social economic impact.

Governance Structure

Management of the partnership is an important aspect of the internal relations between partners. The main legislative objective is to strike a proper balance between the practical requirements of operating a business firm, on the one hand, and of protecting each partner's legitimate interest in controlling the partnership's business, on the other hand.

The right to take management decisions normally lies with the partners
Art. 40, i.e. managing directors are not coming from outside, but this role is performed by one or more partners. However, Art. 43 allows for the transfer of a partner's right of management to a third party if all the other partners give their approval. Management of the partnership is not only conceived as a right, but also as a duty. This is necessarily so, because in the statute

partners legally oblige themselves to cooperate so as to pursue a common purpose jointly. Abandonment of duties is therefore strictly limited, Art. 44.

Since all partners are jointly and severally liable for the partnership's debts, it is only logical that Art. 40 provides that all partners participate in the management of the partnership (unless all the partners agree to the contrary). This is an indispensable safeguard against oppression of some partners by others. Art. 41 (1) provides for the partners' individual right to take management decisions. This is necessary for practical purposes. However, the same paragraph also gives each managing partner a right to object to management decisions taken by other partners.

The scope of the partners' authority to take management decisions is limited to the regular business objects, Art. 42 (1). Otherwise the approval of all partners is necessary, Art. 42 (2). Any decision that fundamentally affects the basis of the partners' cooperation is therefore to be taken by the partners collectively. Art. 45 (1) normally requires unanimity. The statute may derogate from this requirement by providing for decision-making by majority, Art. 45 (2). All these provisions reflect a proper balancing of partners' interests and the practical requirements of operating a business firm.

The right of representation is normally exercised by the partners individually, unless the partners provide for joint representation, Art. 48. In the latter case, each partner's right to represent the partnership is limited. However, third parties relying on the rule of partners' individual right of representation are protected by the rules expressed by Art. 16. That means that the partnership and the partners remain liable.

Financial Structure and Liability

As with every enterprise, partnerships have to fix their capital in the statute, Art. 4. This is in line with the practical requirements of partnerships doing business. The capital may be raised by partners' contributions in cash or in kind; labour or services may also be contributed, Art. 33 (1). Partners are free to evaluate contributions according to their mutual agreement. In case an agreement cannot be reached, the court may be requested to appoint an evaluation expert, Art. 33 (2).

Voluntary expenses which a partner incurred in conducting the partnership's business shall be reimbursed by the partnership, Art.

35. This includes also losses incurred including those deriving from the realisation of risks connected to the management activity. No partner may withdraw, transfer or pledge his interest without the approval of the other partners, Art. 38 (1). This rule is supposed to protect the partnership against asset stripping by the partners.

In absence of contrary agreements (Art. 32), each partner is entitled to an equal share of any profits and shall contribute equally to any losses resulting from the operation of the partnership, Art. 47. In this respect, the Draft has definitely abandoned the complicated 'German' solutions of the YEL and adopted the solution used in the UK for more than a century.

Partners are personally liable for the debts of the partnership Art. 50 (1). Their liability is joint and several as well as unlimited. Also new partners are liable for all existing liabilities of the partnership, Art. 52. It must be noted that these provisions are bound to serve the **protection of creditors in the external relations** of the partnership.

As regards the **internal relations**, there is no obligation to personally cover the partnership's debts. Therefore, if a partner voluntarily pays debts of the partnership to a creditor, he may request the payment from the partnership as 'expenses' according to Art. 35. If the partnership does not pay, the partner who has the claim against the partnership based on Art. 35 may not request payment from the other partners based on Art. 50 (1). He is no 'third party' as of Art. 48 seq. whose claims would need to be protected by personal liability of partners. His claim derives directly from the partnership relation, i.e. it corresponds as an individual claim to a 'collective ("social") obligation' of the partnership. Otherwise, the principle of Art. 37, which limits contributions to those agreed in the statute, would be overthrown by the creation of an additional obligation based on Arts. 35 and 50 (1). Therefore, Art. 50 (1) is not applicable in case of such internal 'collective partnership obligations'.

However, based on the internal relationship (and not on Art. 50 I), the unsatisfied payment against the partnership may be requested from the other partners proportionally with respect to their internal joint and several liability.

Membership

No partner may dispose of his interest without the approval of the other partners, Art. 38.

In case of a partner's death, the partnership may be continued with the heirs, if the partnership agreement so provides, Art. 61 (1).

A partner may unilaterally withdraw from the partnership, Art. 54. A partner whose membership is terminated, is entitled to receive from the partnership what he would have received had the partnership been dissolved, Art. 58. A leaving partner's financial interest is thereby properly protected and the other partners are prevented from expropriating the leaving partner.

If a partner fails deliberately or by gross negligence to perform any duty established by statute or if the performance of his duties has become impossible he may be expelled if the other partners unanimously agree, Art. 57. The expelled partner may file a complaint with the competent court within 90 days of the expulsion. The burden of proving the allegation against the expelled partner shall be on the partners which took the decision to expel. The exclusion of a partner does not prevent the continuation of the partnership. This is in line with the concept expressed by Art. 53 (2).

Dissolution and Liquidation

Partners are free to **dissolve** the partnership at their will. The partnership also dissolves, if it has been economically inactive for more than two years, Art. 53 (1). The termination of membership of one of the partners does not call the existence of the partnership's business firm into question. This would be in the interest neither of workers, nor of creditors. Western European partnership laws have therefore largely been changed so as to leave the partnership normally unaffected by the termination of the membership of one of the partners, unless the partners agree to the contrary.

After dissolution, the partnership goes into **liquidation**, Art. 63. The liquidation rules of the new Enterprise Law are in line with European standards. The partners may act as liquidators unless they decide the liquidator is to be nominated by the court, Art. 64. The authority of liquidators cannot be restricted in relation to third parties, Art. 69. In case the partnership turns out be unable to satisfy its creditors, partners are held jointly and severally liable, Art. 73. Consequently, each partner takes the risk that another partner's assets are insufficient to meet his liability. Once the liquidation procedure is completed, the partnership will be deleted from the Registry, Art. 76.

3. Limited partnerships

Article 80 Definition
(168, 169 YEL, 161 GCC, Behrens 15)

(1) A partnership is a limited partnership, if at least one partner's liability is limited to the amount of his interest (limited partner), while the liability of other partners is not limited (general partners). General partners have the status of partners in a general partnership.

(2) Unless this part of the law provides otherwise, provisions on general partnerships also apply to limited partnerships.

Article 81 Registration
(170 YEL, 162 GCC)

The application for registration must contain the information required by Article 31 plus the name, surname, date and place of birth and residence of each limited partner as well as the amount of contribution of each of them. The same information must be submitted in case of entry or exit of a limited partner.

Article 82 Contributions
(171 YEL, Behrens 15)

(1) The contribution of a limited partner may be in cash or in kind.

(2) A limited partner must transfer all his contributions to the limited partnership prior to the registration of the partnership, unless otherwise provided by the statute.

Article 83 Legal relationship between the partners
(163 GCC)

The relations between partners are governed by Articles 84 to 88, unless provided otherwise by the statute. The statute may also submit the limited partners to a competition clause in deviation from Article 27.

Article 84 Management
(172 YEL, 164 GCC)

(1) One or more general partners shall manage the business of the limited partnership as managing directors. Limited partners are excluded from management.

(2) A limited partner may not object to the management of the general partner, unless he is acting outside the normal conduct of the enterprise's business.

Article 85 Limited partner's supervision rights
(174 YEL, 166 GCC)

(1) A limited partner shall have the right to request a copy of the annual statement of accounts and to verify its correctness by inspecting the books and documents.

(2) The court may, on the reasonable request of a limited partner, at any time order the limited partnership to provide copies of balance sheets, annual statement of accounts or other explanations and to present books and documents for inspection.

Article 86 Profit and loss
(175, 128 YEL, 167 GCC)

(1) The provisions of Article 46 apply also to limited partners.

(2) The limited partner shall bear losses only up to the amount of his part of the capital and to the amount of any outstanding contribution.

Article 87 Distribution of profit and loss
(176 YEL, 168 GCC)

Distribution of profit and losses will be carried out according to Article 47.

Article 88 Representation
(178 YEL, 170 GCC)

A limited partner may not represent the limited partnership, except on the basis of an issued power of attorney or procuracy.

Article 89 Liability of limited partners
(179 YEL; 171, 172, 174 GCC; Behrens 15, 16)

(1) Up to the outstanding amount of his contribution, the limited partner shall

be personally liable to the creditors of the limited partnership. As far as the contribution has been paid, liability is excluded.

(2) In relation to creditors, the limited partner's contribution is defined by the amount which has been registered.

(3) An unregistered increase in the registered contribution only has effect as against creditors if the enterprise informed them about the increase or if it has been published in an ordinary way.

(4) Any agreement by the partners releasing a limited partner from paying his contribution or postponing the payment is ineffective as against creditors.

(5) The same is true for a reduction of contribution as long as it has not been registered, unless the creditor knew about it. Even if registered, the reduction is without effect as against creditors' claims which already existed at the moment of registration.

(6) If a limited partner's contribution is returned to him, it is considered unpaid in relation to creditors. The same applies if a limited partner is drawing a share of the profit and his part of the capital becomes lower than the stipulated contribution.

(7) A limited partner shall not be bound to return profits which he received in good faith based on a statement of accounts prepared in good faith.

Article 90 Entry of changes of contribution in the registry

(185 YEL, 175 GCC)

The partners must report any increase or reduction in the contribution of a limited partner to the Registry.

Article 91 Liability based on legal appearance

(180 YEL)

(1) A limited partner shall be liable like a general partner, if his name has been included in the registered name of the limited partnership with his consent.

(2) A limited partner who has concluded an agreement with a third party in the capacity of a procurator or authorised agent without indicating that he is acting in this authority shall be liable for this transaction like a general partner, if the third party is acting in good faith.

(3) A limited partner shall be liable like a general partner if he acts contrary to the second sentence of the first paragraph of Article 84.

Article 92 Liability prior to registration

(181 YEL, 176 GCC)

Should the founders of a limited partnership assume commitments in connection with the business of the partnership prior to its entry in the Register, a limited partner who agreed to assume such commitments shall be liable like a general partner, unless the creditor knew about his limited participation.

Article 93 Liability of a new limited partner
(182 YEL, 173 GCC)

A limited partner who joins a limited partnership after its formation shall be liable according to Article 89 for the partnership commitments entered into before his entry.

Article 94 Termination of partner status and transformation of legal form
(YEL 186)

(1) A limited partnership shall not dissolve in the event of the death of a limited partner or dissolution of one or more limited partners.

(2) If all general partners withdraw from a limited partnership, the partnership may be transformed into a limited liability company or joint-stock company.

(3) If all limited partners withdraw from a limited partnership, the enterprise may continue as a general partnership or as the business of an entrepreneur.

(4) The changes referred to in Paragraphs 1 through 3 must be reported to the Registry.

16. LIMITED PARTNERSHIPS

The limited partnership is a very useful legal form for small and medium-sized enterprises, especially family enterprises, because it allows the **participation of partners who merely want to make a limited investment without actively participating in the management of the firm**. There must, however, always be at least one person who is able and willing to personally manage the firm and assume the responsibility of a general partner. This person, on the other hand, may benefit from the greater flexibility of the limited partnership form as compared with a limited liability company.

The limited partnership differs from the general partnership mainly with regard to the limited liability of limited partners. Limited partners are personally liable towards the partnership's creditors only up to the outstanding portion of their contribution to the partnership's capital, Art. 80 (1). Therefore, by paying in their contributions, limited partners may avoid personal liability altogether. The idea is that, once the contributions are transferred into the partnership's assets, it is no longer necessary to hold the limited partners liable with their personal assets.

Where liability of investors is in this way limited, the question of creditors' protection against overvaluation or paying back of contributions arises. That is why a limited partner must transfer all his contributions to the limited partnership prior to the registration of the partnership, Art. 82. Only as far as the contribution has been paid, is liability excluded. Any agreement of the partners releasing a limited partner from paying his contribution or postponing the payment is ineffective as against creditors. The same is true for a reduction of contribution as long as it has not been registered, unless the creditor knew about it. Even if registered, the reduction is without effect as against creditors' claims which already existed at the moment of registration. If a limited partner's contribution is returned to him, it is considered unpaid in relation to creditors. The same applies if a limited partner is drawing profit shares while his part of the capital has become lower than the stipulated contribution, Art. 89. These rules show a structural alignment of the status of a limited partner with the position of members in a limited liability company.

A limited partner need not be totally excluded from the management and from the representation of the partnership. In the new Enterprise Law, the provisions which establish this – the second sentence of Art. 84 (1) and Art. 88 – are only default rules. That means the statute may provide otherwise, Art. 83. Even if he is excluded from management, the limited partner may object to decisions of the general partner if the latter is acting in breach of duty, with gross negligence or exceeding the regular conduct of the enterprise's business, Art. 84 (2).

There are some important rules which establish unlimited liability of the limited partner due to legal recognition of his 'appearance' to outsiders. These rules apply the same standard which we have already met when addressing the question of apparent representation: a person causing a certain legal appearance is treated as if this appearance was correct unless third parties were not in good faith. These are the cases addressed by Arts. 91 and 92:

- The limited partner allows his name to be part of the partnership name, Art. 91 (1);
- He acts for the partnership without mentioning his special representation status, Art. 91 (2);
- He is managing the partnership in spite of being excluded from management, Art. 91 (3);
- He agrees with the other founders to assume foundation commitments prior to registration, Art. 92.

4. Joint-stock companies

SECTION 1 GENERAL PROVISIONS AND FORMATION

Article 95 Definition
(187I YEL, Behrens 17)

A joint-stock company is a company the basic capital of which is set and divided into shares. Joint-stock companies are founded by natural or juridical persons, which are not liable for the company's commitments and which bear losses only to the extent of their shares in the basic capital.

Article 96 Application for registration
(201 YEL, HLEGR 49)

(1) In order to be registered, all managing directors and members of the board of directors or supervisory board have to submit the following information to the Registry:

- Legal form of enterprise;
- Duration, unless founded for an indefinite time;
- Enterprise name;
- Registered office;
- Type of business;
- Basic capital;
- Date the statute was established;
- Name, surname, date and place of birth as well as residence of the managing directors;
- Rules of the statute establishing representation authority;
- Any approval by public authorities if necessary.

The managing directors and the chairman of the board of directors or supervisory board shall deposit their signatures with the Registry. The managing directors shall report any change of registered data occurring during the conduct of the company's business.

(2) All data reported to the Registry shall be placed and be available on the company's website.[1]

Article 97 Statute

(188, 219 YEL; 2, 3 Second Directive, Behrens 19, 20)

In addition to the items referred to in Article 4, the statute of a joint-stock company shall also include the following:

1. The nominal value and number of shares subscribed;
2. The different classes of shares together with the information required by 1 above for each class;
3. Whether the shares are registered or bearer shares;
4. The amount of subscribed capital paid up;
5. Method of payment for shares;
6. Any penalties for untimely payment for shares;
7. The total amount, or at least an estimate, of all the costs payable by the company or chargeable to it by reason of its formation;
8. Any special advantages granted at the time of the company's formation to any person who took part in the formation.
9. Any special contracts relating to contributions in kind;
10. Any accessory agreement between the company and a shareholder beyond his contribution and any penalties requested for no or untimely fulfilment;
11. Any special conditions limiting the transfer of the shares;
12. Method of convening general assemblies and decision-making unless provided by the present law;
13. Reserves;
14. Procedure for making amendments to the statute;
15. Any authorisation and procedure for withdrawing shares;
16. Any authorisations to the managing directors to increase the basic capital;
17. Any limitation of the assignment of registered shares.
18. Any possibility and the method of turning shares of one type or class into another type or class.

Article 98 Basic capital

(190 YEL, problem of 6 Second Directive)

(1) The legal capital of a company formed simultaneously shall not be less

[1] Requiring a website should not be compulsory if it does not comply with local conditions.

than the equivalent of 10,000 Euro, calculated at the exchange rate on the day of payment.

(2) The legal capital of a company formed successively shall not be less than the equivalent of 20,000 Euro, calculated at the exchange rate on the day of payment.

Article 99 Types of contribution
(194 I YEL)

Shareholders' contributions may consist of cash or property and rights expressed in money. They may not consist of labour or services.

Article 100 Minimum single contribution in cash
(192 YEL)

(1) The minimum cash-contribution of each shareholder shall be the equivalent of 500 Euro, calculated at the exchange rate on the day of payment.

(2) If shareholders acquire shares under privileged terms pursuant to special regulations, the cash-contribution may be lower.

Article 101 Minimum par value of shares
(193 YEL, 8 German Stock Company Law – GSCL)

(1) The minimum par value of a share shall be the equivalent of 5.00 Euro, calculated at the exchange rate on the day of payment. Any shares of a lower par value shall be invalid. The issuers shall be jointly and severally liable to the owners for any damage caused by such issue.

(2) Higher par values of the shares shall be set at the corresponding equivalents divisible by 10.

(3) The provisions of Paragraphs 1 and 2 also apply to contribution certificates issued to shareholders before the shares are issued (interim shares).

Article 102 Value of issued shares
(187 II, 191, 193 III YEL)

(1) The overall amount of issued shares may not be less than the legal capital. Therefore, shares may not be issued or sold below their par value, except in cases referred to in the second paragraph of Article 100.

(2) Issuing for a higher amount is allowed.

Article 103 Formation costs
(195 YEL, 3i Second Directive, 26 GSCL)

(1) The founders may request the company to reimburse formation costs up to the highest amount set for formation costs by the statute.

(2) Formation costs are paid from profits generated by the company. Shareholders may decide to give them priority when profits are distributed, unless otherwise provided by the statute.

Article 104 Founders' report on the formation
(200 YEL, 32 GSCL, Behrens 21)

Before the company is registered, the founders shall file a written report on the formation procedure. It must contain the main reasons for the adequacy of the valuation of contributions in kind and for any special advantage granted to founders. The report shall be submitted to the Registry together with the application for registration.

Article 105 Contributions in kind
(194 II and III, 200, 201 YEL; 10, 11 Second Directive, Behrens 21)

(1) In case of contributions in kind, one or more independent experts appointed by the competent court shall draw up a report before the company is registered. Such experts may be natural persons as well as partnerships or companies authorised for auditing by special regulations.

(2) The experts' report shall contain a description of each of the assets comprising the contribution as well as of the methods of valuation used and shall state whether the values arrived at by the application of these methods correspond at least to the number and nominal value par and, where appropriate, to the premium on the shares to be issued for them.

(3) If an enterprise is being brought in as a contribution, the balance sheets for the preceding 2 business years of the enterprise concerned, as well as documents relating to the appraisal of its value, shall be submitted together with the report referred to in Paragraph 2.

(4) The report mentioned in the previous paragraphs shall be submitted to the Registry together with the application for registration.

(5) The provisions of the previous paragraphs also apply if the company is buying property or rights from a founder within 2 years from its formation.

Article 106 Payment and transfer of contributions before registration
(198, 205, 210 YEL, 9 Second Directive; 36a GSCL)

(1) 50 percent of each stipulated cash-contribution must be paid up before registration. However, the overall paid up amount may not be lower than 50 percent of the entire cash portion of the legal capital. The outstanding amounts are payable within 2 years from the company's registration.

(2) If the entire cash-contribution to the basic capital is higher than the

equivalent of 25,000 Euro or 50,000 Euro in the case of successively formed companies calculated at the exchange rate on the day of payment, at least 25 percent of that amount shall be paid in prior to the joint-stock company's registration. *(9 Second Directive)*

(3) Payments with respect to Paragraphs 1 and 2 shall be made into a suspense bank account as defined by the statute. A statement of the bank confirming the deposit of cash-contributions will be submitted to the Registry together with the application for registration. The funds may be managed by the managing directors only after registration. *(210 YEL)*

(4) Contributions in kind must be transferred wholly to the company assets before registration, in a manner which depends on their character or as provided by the statute or by the prospectus as of the first paragraph of Article 111.

(5) Shareholders who fail to pay or transfer their contributions in time shall be liable to the company with respect to Paragraphs 2 and 3 of Article 9, unless Article 133 provides otherwise.

Article 107 Special provisions for single member companies
(196, 202 YEL, 3 Twelfth Directive, Behrens 19)

(1) If, prior to registration, the single founder has not fully paid up his cash-contribution or has not brought in his contribution in kind, he must provide adequate security in this respect and present a corresponding certificate to the Registry together with the application for registration.

(2) When the number of shareholders decreases to one, the single shareholder shall report the decrease and his name to the Registry for registration and publication. If the single shareholder fails to do so, he shall be personally liable for the commitments the company assumes in the meantime.

Article 108 No issuance or transfer of shares before registration
(218 YEL, 41 IV GSCL)

(1) The rights connected with the shares cannot be transferred before registration.

(2) Shares or interim shares may not be issued before registration. Shares or interim shares issued earlier are invalid. The founders are jointly and severally liable as against the holders for any damage caused by such issuing.

SECTION 2 TYPES OF FORMATION

Article 109 Simultaneous and successive formation

(189 YEL, 76 Alb/72 French, HLEGR 35, deviating from Behrens's understanding)

(1) Joint-stock companies may be formed as follows:

(a) Founders shall subscribe and acquire all shares in the formation procedure without offering them to the public (simultaneous formation). Companies of this kind neither register their shares with the stock market nor trade shares on any other securities market. However, they may keep their shares freely transferable allowing for a dispersed ownership outside the securities market. Such companies shall be known as open joint-stock companies. Alternatively companies may exclude free transfer of shares avoiding dispersed ownership. Such companies shall be known as closed joint-stock companies.

(b) A subscription for shares means the first purchase of shares and subscription; subscribe, oversubscription and subscription form accordingly bear that meaning.

(c) Founders may invite the public by announcement or prospectus to subscribe for shares. This method of formation shall be known as successive formation. Companies of this kind either list their shares officially with the stock market or use financial intermediaries (banks, financial service enterprises, brokers) or other means of publication and advertisement to sell their shares (publicly held companies including listed companies).

(d) Successive formation of companies will not be available until a date to be determined by regulations made by the Ministry of Trade.

(2) A joint-stock company founded with respect to no. 1 of Paragraph 1 may choose to continue its activities as a company of no. 2 or vice versa, following a decision of the general meeting and in compliance with the minimum capital requirements and the disclosure requirements of the present Law, Registry Law and the legislation concerning regulated security markets.[2]

(3) Simultaneous formation is carried out with respect to Article 110; successive formation is carried out with respect to Articles 111 to 121.

---

[2] Cf. note 1.

Article 110 Simultaneous formation
(197 YEL; 2, 28, 29, 36 GSCL, Behrens 16, 19, sceptical towards general threshold for closed jsc)

(1) The founders adopt the statute and subscribe the shares. The statute shall determine the members of the first board of directors or supervisory board which will nominate the first managing directors. These nominations expire on the date on which the board members are elected by the first general meeting.

(2) All founders, managing directors and members of the board of directors or supervisory board shall apply for registration once the requirements of Articles 97 to 108 are fulfilled.

Article 111 Successive formation, publication of prospectus
(203 YEL; 59, 60 French Decree 67-236 'Sur les Sociétés Commerciales'; Prospectus Directive 2003/71/EC)

(1) In the case of publicly held companies, the founders shall publish an invitation for subscription of shares on their websites, in newspapers authorised for official publications in conformity with the Registry Law, or in the form of brochures. Any invitation to the public to subscribe for shares is deemed to be a prospectus and shall include the following particulars:

1. Registered name, registered office and type of business of the future company;
2. Amount of basic capital which has to be subscribed;
3. Duration unless founded for an indefinite time;
4. Location, which must include the company website, and date of the deposit of the draft statute;
5. Number and par value of shares or value at which they are issued, and – in the case of issuing different kinds and classes of shares – their designation and the rights stemming from them;
6. Location, time and deadline for subscription and payment, including a remark on the possibility of premature closure of the subscription if it was completed before the deadline;
7. Details of the bank where subscribed amounts can be paid;
8. Deadline for the restitution of amounts paid, in the event of unsuccessful formation;
9. Amount payable for the shares subscribed prior to registration of the company and consequences of untimely payment;
10. Special rights accorded to founders (priority in subscribing to new share issues, right to appoint members of the first board of directors, preference shares, etc.);

11. List of number, kind and class of shares subscribed by founders outside of the public offer;
12. Conditions for executing voting rights in the general meeting;
13. If applicable, conditions regarding any agreement on the sale of shares;
14. Rules on distribution of profits, creation of reserves and distribution of assets after liquidation;
15. Nature and value of contributions in kind, number of shares issuable for them, name or registered office and address or registered office of person making contributions in kind, and title of the organisation or person in charge of appraising the contribution;
16. Maximum formation costs to be borne by the company;
17. Procedure to be followed in the event of oversubscription of shares;
18. Manner of convening the formation meeting and location of the meeting;

(2) The founders have to declare in the prospectus that the information contained is in accordance with the facts and that it makes no omission likely to affect its import. The prospectus shall be signed by the founders who must add their name and surname and residence and the following information of their enterprise:

1. The Registry in which the enterprise file is kept, together with the registry number;
2. The legal form of the enterprise;
3. The location of its registered office;
4. In case of a capital company, the amount of the capital subscribed and paid up.

(3) Any misstatement made in the prospectus carries such liabilities which the Civil Code prescribes.

Article 112 Subscription form

(204 YEL, 61 French Decree 67-236 'Sur les Sociétés Commerciales')

(1) Shares shall be subscribed to by signing a subscription form. The subscriber may be represented by another person. The subscriber or his representative shall receive a copy of the subscription form.

(2) A subscription form shall include the following:

1. Date of the prospectus;
2. Registered name, registered office and type of business of the future company;
3. Amount of basic capital which has to be subscribed;

4. Location and date of the deposit of the draft statute;
5. If applicable, the part of the capital subscribed in cash and the part to be delivered in kind;
6. The manner of issuance of the shares subscribed in cash;
7. Coordinates of the bank where subscribed amounts can be paid;
8. Name, surname and residence of the subscriber;
9. Number, kind and class of the shares subscribed, their par value, issued value and the entire amount owed by the subscriber;
10. Date of expiration of the obligation if by that date all shares referred to in the prospectus are not subscribed;
11. Remark that the subscriber or his representative received a copy of the subscription form;
12. Subscriber's statement that he was aware of the contents of the information contained in the prospectus;

(3) Any subscription form not containing the particulars of Paragraph 2 shall be null and void. Any limitation of rights which is not laid down in the subscription form shall have no legal effect in relation to the company.

Article 113 Oversubscription of shares
(206 YEL)

(1) In the event of subscription to a larger number of shares than specified in the prospectus, the founders may either reject or accept the excessive subscriptions.

(2) Should the founders fail to decide on excessive subscriptions, the acceptance or rejection shall be decided on by the formation meeting in setting the final amount of basic capital.

(3) Should excessive subscriptions be rejected, the amounts paid in shall be returned to the subscribers within 8 days from the rejection date, without any deductions and increased by average interests. The founders shall be jointly and severally liable for the fulfilment of this obligation.

Article 114 Unsuccessful subscription and payment
(207, 209 YEL)

(1) The time-limits for subscription and payment shall not exceed 3 months from the opening date of the subscription.

(2) Should shares not be subscribed and duly paid up, the founders may subscribe to unsubscribed shares themselves, within 15 days from the expiration of the time-limit of Paragraph 1.

(3) Should shares not be subscribed and duly paid up by founders in

compliance with Paragraph 2, the formation shall be deemed unsuccessful, and the founders shall return to the subscribers the amounts paid and the contributions in kind, within 8 days from the expiration of the time-limit of Paragraph 1. The founders shall be jointly and severally liable for the fulfilment of this obligation. Claims under this article must be brought within 3 years.

(4) The provisions of Paragraphs 1 through 3 shall not apply if shareholders are buying shares under privileged conditions pursuant to law.

Article 115 Issue of receipt for subscription and payment
(208 YEL, 83 Alb, 78 French)

(1) In case of successful subscription and payment, the founders shall issue receipts to the subscribers within 15 days from the expiration of the deadline for subscription and payment specified in the prospectus, or from the subsequent takeover of the shares by the founders in accordance with Paragraph 2 of Article 114.

(2) The receipt shall contain the paid up amount and any outstanding amount as well as the elements and rules required for the subscription form by Paragraphs 2 and 3 of Article 112.

(3) The list of issued receipts shall be accessible to the subscribers in the bank in which the payments of subscribed shares are deposited.

Article 116 Formation meeting, applicable provisions
(216 YEL)

The provisions of this Law governing the proceedings of and decision-making by the general meeting (Articles 150 to 165) shall apply to the proceedings of and decision-making by the formation meeting if Articles 117 to 121 do not provide otherwise.

Article 117 Convening the formation meeting
(211 YEL)

(1) The founders are bound to convene the formation meeting within 60 days from the expiration of the time-limit for subscription and payment set in the public announcement or prospectus.

(2) Should the founders fail to convene the formation meeting within the time-limit of Paragraph 1, the formation shall be deemed unsuccessful. In this case, the provisions of the third Paragraph of Article 114 shall apply accordingly.

(3) The formation meeting shall be convened by an announcement which

shall be published in the same way as the invitation for subscription at least 15 days before the scheduled date of the meeting.

(4) The draft statute, experts' reports regarding contribution in kind, the list of distributed share certificates, as well as the list of the number, kind and class of the shares taken over by founders outside the public offer shall be made accessible to the subscribers within the terms of Paragraph 3. The documents must be available in any case on the company's website.[3]

Article 118 Quorum and reconvention
(212 YEL)

(1) The formation meeting may only make valid decisions if it is attended by the subscribers holding more than 40 percent of the subscribed voting shares. Subsequent meetings may only make valid decisions if attended by subscribers holding more than 30 percent of the subscribed voting shares.

(2) If the formation meeting is without the quorum of Paragraph 1, the founders may reconvene the meeting which must take place not less than 8 and not more than 15 days from the first one.

(3) If the founders fail to reconvene the formation meeting or if even the reconvened meeting is without quorum, the formation of the company shall be deemed unsuccessful. In this case, the provisions of the third paragraph of Article 114 shall apply accordingly.

Article 119 Proceedings of the formation meeting
(213 YEL)

(1) The formation meeting shall elect its chairman and a person taking minutes of meeting. The founders will read their formation report and the experts' report on contributions in kind as well as any supplements to these reports if so requested by shareholders covering at least 10 percent of the attending or represented shareholders.

(2) The minutes of meeting will be signed by the chairman, the record-taking person and the founders. A copy of the minutes has to be deposited with the Registry. The data shall also be placed on the company's website.

Article 120 Rights and duties of the formation meeting
(214 YEL)

The formation meeting shall:

---

[3] See note 33.

1. Establish whether basic capital has been paid up in conformity with this law;
2. Accept or reject oversubscription to shares;
3. Adopt the statute;
4. Elect the first members of the board of directors or supervisory board organs, unless the founders have reserved this right for themselves in the public announcement or prospectus;
5. Decide on special rights of the founders and approve special agreements with the founders or other parties (accessory obligations, etc.);
6. Accept the appraised value of contributions in kind;

Article 121 Decision-making
(215 YEL)

(1) The formation meeting shall decide by majority of votes based on the par value of the paid up voting shares.

(2) If the formation meeting unanimously decides to desist from issuing public announcements or a prospectus with respect to further subscriptions, the value of contributions in kind, special rights of founders, commitments towards founders or other persons as well as other formation costs to be borne by the company may not be changed from the original offer.

(3) When decisions are taken with respect to contributions in kind, special rights of founders and commitments towards founders or other persons as well as to other formation costs to be borne by the company, the interested founders or persons among subscribers shall have no right to vote.

Article 122 Application for registration
(217 YEL)

The company formed by public subscription shall be reported to the Registry for registration as required by Article 96 after

1. Contributions for successfully subscribed shares were paid up or transferred in compliance with Article 106;
2. The formation meeting was held in compliance with Articles 116 to 121;
3. The first managing directors were nominated by the first board of directors or supervisory board;
4. Any necessary approval by public authorities was achieved.

17. COMPANIES (1)

Basic Common Features and Distinctions

The Law distinguishes between **two company forms, the joint-stock company and the limited liability company, Arts. 95-227 and 228-280.** Whereas the joint-stock company is typically designed for large enterprises which satisfy their financial needs by offering shares to the public, the limited liability company is typically designed for small and medium-sized enterprises which are financed by a closed group of shareholders. Whereas joint-stock companies, due to their size and importance for the economic system, are subjected to rather rigid rules of governance and the protection of investors and creditors, limited liability companies usually require a less rigid regime of internal relations while the protection of creditors is quite similarly designed.

All company forms share important common features. They acquire legal personality by registration, and their assets are separated from their members' (shareholders') private assets, Art. 3 (2). In addition to that – and contrary to partnerships – companies are liable for their debts with their own assets only. They are therefore characterised by the absence of personal liability of the members or shareholders vis-à-vis the company's creditors. This is what 'limited liability' means – as is explicitly stated in Arts. 95 and 228 (1).

Art. 109 (1) introduces further **distinctions of joint-stock companies**. There are, on the one hand, joint-stock companies which sell their shares only outside of an organized security market **(open companies)** or do not permit transfer of shares at all **(closely held companies),** Art. 109 (1) 1. These companies undergo an easier ('simultaneous') foundation procedure as compared to another group of joint-stock companies, which are 'successively' formed by publishing an announcement (prospectus) on the organized security market inviting the public to subscribe for their shares **(publicly held joint-stock companies including those 'listed' on the stock exchange)**, Art. 109 (1), 3. These distinctions are not only reflected by different foundation rules[4] but also by those concerning the capital[5] and the transparency of the governance structure.[6]

If there is no authority such as a financial regulator or a stock exchange to oversee the issue of shares to the public a listed joint-stock company cannot usually be formed until the stock exchange is up and running. However, 'open companies' may also issue shares to the public without the safeguard of a regulator. On the one hand, these models of joint-stock companies put the public at significant risk from fraudulent promotions. On the other hand, the possibility of raising money from the public for large infrastructure projects is a necessary feature of countries the economy of which is 'in transition'. The 'compromise' which is set out here to cope with this transition problem is to allow for the creation of open joint-stock companies which may freely transfer their shares to raise financial support, while **publicly held and listed companies will not be available to economic actors until a date to be determined by regulations made by the Ministry of Trade (or similar)**, Art. 109 (1) 4. This means to say that Enterprise Law provisions regarding these companies will not be applicable until a security market including stock exchange structures and the corresponding legislation have been created.

Even though the Law normally leaves the choice between joint stock and limited liability companies to the founders, it nevertheless imposes limits in terms of maximum numbers of shareholders: **limited liability companies may not have more than 50 members, Art. 228 (4).** By defining this maximum number, the law attempts to limit the access to the less rigidly regulated limited liability company to small and medium-sized enterprises whose capital is raised by a limited group of investors. This is acceptable, because the freedom of choice between company forms is not restricted, since access to the joint-stock company form remains open even for smaller groups of shareholders as the introduction of closely held joint-stock companies shows.

Another important question is whether enterprise law allows for the formation of **single-member companies.** This is particularly relevant for parent companies who want to set up wholly owned

4 See Arts. 110 and 97 to 108 for simultaneous formation, on the one hand, plus the special provisions of Arts. 111 to 122 for successive formation, on the other hand.

5 See Arts. 98 and 106 (2).

6 See Art. 149 (2).

subsidiaries as a device for limiting certain business risks to certain assets. The new Enterprise Law allows for the creation of single member companies in Art. 3 (1). Besides certain foundation restrictions mentioned above,[7] it establishes special rules in this regard which apply to both single joint-stock and limited liability companies[8] and which are in line with the Twelfth Company Law Directive (Single-Member Company Directive).

If, prior to registration, the single founder has not fully paid up his cash-contribution or has not brought in his contribution in kind, he must stand **adequate security** in this respect and present a corresponding certificate to the Registry together with the application for registration, Art. 107 (1).

Where a single-shareholder company comes into existence after the company has initially been formed by several shareholders, this occurrence must be **disclosed by a special entry in the Register**; otherwise the privilege of limited liability will be lost, Art. 107 (2).

On the other hand, a single-member company may use the instrument of an increase of capital to change its status and become a multi-member company by issuing shares to new shareholders. Also this change must obviously be reported to the Registry, Arts. 200 and 275.

The rights and duties of the general meeting in a single-member company are performed by the single member. However, this requires that all decisions taken in this function shall be entered into a **decision register** the data of which may not be altered nor deleted, Art. 150 (4). It is important to note that any decision not registered in this register is null and void towards the company while, due to the general principle mentioned above, third parties (acting in good faith!) will be protected.

There is also a **special anti-self-dealing clause for single-member companies** in Art. 21 (5): an individual managing his single-member company may not enter into contracts with the company concerning loans, sureties, guarantees, or collateral. Questions regarding management in single-member companies will be discussed below.

---

[7] See Arts. 4–6.
[8] See Arts. 107, 234 and 258 (3).

Raising of Minimum Capital

According to the European legal systems, the 'price' for limited liability (i.e. absence of personal liability of the shareholders) consists of the protection of shareholders and creditors by minimum capital requirements, i.e. companies must have a fixed capital the minimum amount of which is set by law. The Law follows this concept. It differentiates though between publicly held and not publicly held joint-stock companies. In both cases, the Ministry of Trade and Industry is supposed to define the minimum capital amount by regulation, Art. 98. Due to the large number of subscribers, the minimum capital of publicly held companies can be expected to be higher than that of the other company types. The Ministry will also define the minimum amount for limited liability companies, Art. 231 (1). If the EU Law was fully effective, joint-stock companies would require a capital of 25,000 Euro, Art. 6 (1) Second Company ('Capital') Directive.[9]

The Law makes sure that, in the interest of potential creditors, the company's capital is raised according to the provisions of the law before a company can be registered and thereby come into existence as an independent legal entity. The legal concepts applied are in line with the Second Directive:

First, the Law makes sure that the **full amount of the company's initial capital is represented by shares**, Arts. 95

[9] It is easily understood that the business world in some countries in transition would not appreciate such an immediate alignment with European standards and might refuse it as contrary to economic development and the need to attract foreign direct investment. Moreover, there are good reasons to expect the minimum capital requirement to be altered by future European legislation as recommended by the report of the 'High Level Group of Company Law Experts' (available at: http:/europa.eu.int/comm/internal_market/en/company/company/modern/index.htm). The control functions of the minimum guarantee capital and its function to protect creditors and investors have become highly controversial among European business lawyers, scholars and law-makers. The minimum capital is, above all, only 'safe' when the company is founded. If it is consumed by the losses of everyday business, the protection is gone. In spite of the protection mechanisms discussed in the text below, this consumption of guaranteee capital has become quite normal as the amount established at the beginning is very often not enough to achieve the company's statutory purposes, above all with respect to new technologies. An alternative could, for example, be the introduction of a kind of 'basic capital' established as a certain percentage of the company's turnover. Consequently, the 'basic capital' would have to grow while the company was expanding. Under these circumstances, countries in transition have good reasons to postpone the alignment with the present EU standard.

and 228 (1), which are subscribed and acquired either by the founders themselves during the 'simultaneous formation' according to Art. 109 (1) 1, 110 (1) and Art. 228 (2), 232 (1), or, in case of a successively formed joint-stock company, by the public according to Art. 109 (1) 3, 111 (1). In the latter case, the public offering of the shares must be based on a prospectus which contains certain minimum information about the company to be formed as defined in Art. 111 (1) and (2). The share subscriptions must meet certain formal requirements, Art. 112. The Law also takes care of potential oversubscriptions (Art. 113) or insufficient subscriptions (Art. 114).

Second, the Law **prohibits** the issuing of shares to and the acquisition of shares by the initial shareholders **below their par value**, Art. 102 and 228 (2), 231 (1) and (2).

Third, the **contributions of shareholders must represent an economic value**. This is important in order to make sure that contributions can be properly valued and that the initial assets really meet the capital requirements. Therefore, the Law provides that they must consist of assets the value of which may be 'expressed in money', Arts. 99 and 232 (2). The same provisions state that contributions may not consist of labour or services. This is reasonable, because performance of an obligation to work or render services is not sufficiently certain and cannot legally be guaranteed.

Fourth, a problem may be caused by the **overvaluation of non-cash contributions (contributions in kind).** Overvaluation of such contributions not only violates the principle that shares must not be issued below their par value, but also leads to discriminatory treatment of shareholders. Shareholders contributing overvalued assets get their shares at a cheaper price than others. In line with Art. 10 of the Second Directive, Art. 105 of the new Enterprise Law declares that one or more independent experts appointed by the competent court shall draw up a report before the company is registered.

Fifth, the Law requires that shareholders' **contributions are effectively paid** in: contributions in kind must be fully paid up, Art. 106 (4) and 232 (2), contributions in cash must be paid in 50 percent before registration, the other 50 percent being due within 2 years after registration of the company, Arts. 106 (1) and 232 (3). An exception is made in favour of companies whose capital made up by cash contributions is equivalent to an amount set by the Ministry of Trade and Industry; then only 25 per cent must be paid in before registration, Arts. 106 (2) and 232 (4). Also, cash contributions must be paid into a suspense bank account with an authorised bank where they are frozen until registration, Arts. 106 (3) and 232 (5). Only after registration may the competent organs of companies manage the funds paid in. Companies may not release shareholders from their obligations to pay in their contributions, Arts. 134 and 243. Furthermore, the founders may not simply benefit from the company's initial capital by incurring formation costs; the total amount of such costs or at least an estimate must be established by the statute and shall be reimbursed only out of the company's future profits, Arts. 97, 7, 195 and 233. The founders must also report on any advantage they received in accordance with the statute, Arts. 97, 8, and 104.

Sixth, in case of 'successive formation' of a publicly held joint-stock company, a formation meeting of the subscribers to the company's shares is required, Arts. 116–21. The validity of the meeting depends on the presence of more than half of the subscribers having a right to vote, Art. 118. Certain information must be submitted to the meeting; in particular the subscribers must be informed of the shares taken over by the founders themselves, Art. 117 (4). The agenda of the meeting includes, in particular, the adoption of the company's statute and the election of the first members of the company's management and supervisory bodies, Art. 120, 3 and 4. As potential abuses by founders are a major concern of successively formed companies, the Law contains certain safeguards in this respect. It requires the formation meeting to decide on the maximum formation costs to be borne by the company, on the evaluation of contributions in kind made by the founders, on special rights granted to the founders and on special contracts with the founders, Art. 120, 5 and 6). The founders' voting rights are suspended in this respect, Art. 121 (3).[10]

Finally, shares may not be issued to the shareholders before registration of the company, Art. 108.

[10] See also Arts. 117 and 160 on exclusion of voting in case of conflict of interest.

SECTION 3 SHARES

Article 123 Types and classes of shares

(220 YEL; 11, 139 GSCL, unsatisfactory Behrens 30)

(1) Shares are either registered in the register of shareholders in the shareholder's name (registered shares) or they are bearer shares.

(2) Shares issued before the nominal or higher amount has been paid must be registered shares. The same applies to shares the subscription to which is supplemented by an accessory contractual obligation.

(3) According to the sequence of issue, shares may be designated as founders' (first issued) shares and subsequently issued shares.

(4) With respect to profit-sharing rights, shares may be ordinary or preferential. Ordinary shares entitle their holders to exercise their rights in the general meeting and to receive a proportional share of profits and of liquidated assets. Preferential shares entitle their holders to have a certain amount or percentage of the par value of their shares paid from profits prior to ordinary shareholders if a dividend is declared, priority in the distribution of liquidated assets, and other rights set by law or the statute.

(5) Preferential shares are participative, if they allow for preferential treatment with respect to present profit-sharing. They are cumulative if they entitle the holder to being paid all outstanding dividends, including those for past years when no dividends were issued, before holders of ordinary shares receive their dividend. They are cumulative and participating if, in addition to the outstanding dividends, they participate with priority in the present profit-sharing.

(6) Shares carrying the same rights shall make up one class (ordinary shares, preferential shares, voting shares and non-voting shares).

Article 124 Voting rights

(221 YEL, 12, 134 GSCL)

(1) Each share carries voting rights in proportion to its par value.

(2) Preferential shares may be issued without voting rights, in which case their par value may not be greater than 49 percent of the company's basic capital.

(3) Shares which, at the same par value, give multiple voting rights are prohibited.

(4) The statute may establish the maximum number of votes to which a shareholder is entitled irrespective of the number of his shares, if this rule is applicable to all shareholders.

Article 125 Issuance of share certificates

(222 YEL, 10 V, 41 IV GSCL, Behrens 30)

(1) The company shall issue share certificates at the expense of any shareholder requesting it.

(2) The decision to issue the certificates is taken by the founders or the general meeting in conformity with the elements required by the law on negotiable instruments.

Article 126 Entry in the register of shareholders

(232 YEL, 67 GSCL, Behrens 30 ambiguous)

(1) Shares issued on the name of the shareholder shall be entered into the register of shareholders.

(2) Shareholders entered in the register on subscription or transfer are presumed entitled as shareholders as against the company.

(3) Every shareholder has the right to inspect the register of shareholders.

(4) The provisions of Paragraphs 1 to 3 also apply to interim shares.

Article 127 Limited transfer of registered shares

(233 YEL; 41 IV 1, 68 GSCL)

(1) In a simultaneously formed company, the statute may provide that the transfer of registered shares requires the consent of the management and that the shareholders of the company have a pre-emption right.

(2) The provisions of Paragraph 2 also applies to interim shares.

Article 128 Co-owned shares

(234 YEL, 69 GSCL)

(1) Several persons may own one share. They shall exercise their shareholders' rights through a joint representative.

(2) They are jointly and severally liable for the commitments linked to the share.

(3) The shares referred to in Paragraph 1 and the name of the representative shall be entered in the register of shareholders.

Article 129 Replacement of lost or destroyed shares

(235 YEL, 72 GSCL)

(1) In the event of a share or interim share certificate being lost or destroyed,

it may be publicly declared invalid and replaced by a new one, in conformity with corresponding procedures of the law on negotiable instruments.

(2) If dividend coupons have been issued to the bearer and the claim of the coupon is not yet due, the claim will become invalid with the announcement of invalidity of the share or interim share.

Article 130 Treatment of incorrect shares
(236 YEL, 73 GSCL)

(1) If the contents of a share certificate have become incorrect because of changes of the legal status of the company or for other reasons, the company may, with permission of the competent court, publicly invite shareholders concerned to submit these certificates for correction or exchange and declare that, in case of non-compliance with the invitation, the shares will be invalidated.

(2) The company shall publish the announcement twice, with a 30-days interval, in an authorised newspaper as referred to in Paragraph 1 of Article 111 and on the company's website.

(3) New certificates shall be issued in lieu of the invalidated ones and handed out to the shareholder against return of the existing ones.

Article 131 Replacement of shares
(237 YEL, 74 GSCL)

If a share certificate or an interim share certificate is so damaged that it is no longer fit for circulation, but its contents are still readable, its holder may request the company to replace it by a new share certificate at his own expense, against return of the old share certificate. Shares and interim shares may be united in one or several shares, or be divided into several shares at the request and expense of the holder, provided that the par value of the newly issued shares is not smaller than the par value of a specified series of shares. The shares to be united or divided shall be returned to the company for annulment.

SECTION 4 LEGAL RELATIONS BETWEEN THE COMPANY AND THE SHAREHOLDERS

Article 132 Obligation of payment of contribution
(224 YEL, 54 GSCL)

(1) Shareholders shall pay the nominal or higher price of their shares to the

company's account, and transfer their contributions in kind to the company in a manner which depends on the character of contributions in kind or as provided by the statute.

(2) Unless Article 133 provides otherwise, Paragraph 3 of Article 9 applies accordingly to shareholder liability as against the company if a shareholder fails to pay or transfer his contributions.

Article 133 Consequences of untimely payment
(198 VII, 225, 226 II YEL, 63–4 GSCL)

(1) In case of untimely payment of cash-contributions, the shareholder concerned will be obliged to pay 4 percent interest from the moment the payment was due. The company may ask for further compensation in damages. The statute may envisage penalties for untimely payment.

(2) A 30-days deadline for payment may be announced to shareholders who have not paid the amount in time. If the shareholder does not respond by the deadline, the company may declare that the shares and any payment carried out earlier are delinquent and the shareholder thereupon expelled. A delinquent shareholder shall be liable to the company for the unpaid amount including interest.

(3) If any outstanding payment is not made within the deadline referred to in Paragraph 2, the company may, instead of following the procedure of Paragraphs 2 to 4, reduce its basic capital by the amount not paid up for the share and terminate the latter in conformity with Article 208.

Article 134 No release from obligation to bring in contributions
(199, 224 IV,V, 226 I YEL, 66 GSCL)

(1) The company may neither release shareholders from their obligation to pay nor from their obligation to bring in a contribution in kind, nor from any liability resulting from non-fulfilment of these obligations.

(2) Shareholders may not offset the claims they have against the company against the payment for shares, nor may they pledge their contributions in kind.

(3) Shareholders may be released from their obligation to make contributions only by ordinary capital reduction in conformity with Articles 201 to 207, or by capital reduction through withdrawal of shares in conformity with Article 208.

Article 135 Prohibition of return of contributions
(227 YEL, 57I GSCL)

Contributions may not be returned to the shareholders, except in cases set out in this law.

Article 136 Declaration of dividends
(229 YEL, Behrens 30)

(1) Each shareholder shall have the right to his share in the distribution of annual profits (dividends) as determined by the general meeting.

(2) Profits shall be distributed proportionately to the par value of shares except in the case that the statute provides otherwise for preference shareholders.

(3) Respecting the principles established by Article 22, the general meeting may decide that profit is not to be distributed or that it is not to be paid to shareholders owning a specified class of shares, and that it is to be used for other purposes instead.

Article 137 Mandatory and other reserves
(51, 52, 56 YEL, 150 GSCL)

(1) The company shall allocate at least 5 percent of the annual profits as mandatory reserve until 10 percent of the basic capital or a higher ratio established by the statute has been reached.

(2) The statute may envisage other reserves being allocated from annual profits.

(3) Dividends shall be defined only after the amounts earmarked for reserves referred to in Paragraphs 1 and 2 have been deducted from the profit.

Article 138 Refunding prohibited payments
(230 YEL, 62 GSCL, Behrens 33)

(1) Shareholders shall return to the company any advantage received contrary to the provisions of this Law. This includes dividends received, if shareholders knew or ought to have known that these dividends or other advantages were received contrary to this law.

(2) The company's claims referred to in Paragraph 1 may be realised according to Paragraph 3 of Article 9. The prescription term shall start on the date of unlawful payment.

Article 139 Adequate remuneration for transactions between company and shareholders
(231 YEL, 61 GSCL, Behrens 33)

Remuneration for any legal transactions undertaken by the company and a shareholder beyond his contribution may not exceed the market value of such transactions.

Article 140 No repayment of inadequate credit
(245 YEL, 32a German Limited Liability Company Law – GLLCL, Behrens 33)

(1) If a shareholder has extended credit to a company on terms which are less favourable than those usually applied on the market, he may not request the company to repay the credit in the event of insolvency or composition where such repayment would reduce the capital of the company to below its basic capital.

(2) If a third party has extended the credit referred to by Paragraph 1 instead of the shareholder and the shareholder has provided surety for the repayment of the credit, the third party may, in the case of insolvency or composition, only claim the amount which it has not been able to realise from the surety.

(3) The provisions of Paragraphs 1 and 2 also apply to other legal transactions by a shareholder or third party, if these transactions economically correspond to a credit as of Paragraphs 1 and 2.

Article 141 Liability for repaid credits
(246 YEL, 32b GLLCL, Behrens 33)

(1) If, in cases referred to in Article 140, the company has repaid a credit in the year preceding the opening of insolvency proceedings, the shareholder to whom the credit has been repaid or who has given surety, shall refund the company the amount of repaid credit. The shareholder concerned shall be liable only up to the value of the surety at the time of credit repayment. The liability shall cease if the items which served as surety have been placed at the disposal of the company.

(2) The provisions of Paragraph 1 shall also apply to other legal transactions by a shareholder or third party, if these transactions economically correspond to a credit as of Paragraph 1.

Article 142 Other obligations of shareholders
(228 YEL)

(1) The statute may establish special obligations for shareholders, where the transfer of shares is subject to the company's consent. The same applies in a company the shares of which are not publicly traded, if shareholders have a pre-emption right in relation to the purchase of shares, in proportion to the par value of the shares possessed by them. Such obligations of the shareholders shall be written on their share certificates or interim share certificates.

(2) The statute may bind shareholders, who invest contributions in kind, to deposit their shares with the company for the duration of the liability linked to this contribution in kind (bound shares).

(3) The statute may bind the members of the company management to own a specified number of the company's shares and to deposit them with the company for the duration of their function (guarantee shares).

18. COMPANIES (2)

Membership in Joint-Stock Companies

Joint-stock companies and limited liability companies differ in all countries with regard to the legal characteristics of the membership of shareholders. This is also true for the new Enterprise Law.

Membership in a joint-stock company is represented by shares in the company's capital which may be **bearer shares or shares issued in the name of the shareholder (registered shares)**, Art. 123 (1). Shares issued in the name of the shareholder are entered in the **register of shareholders** which is subject to inspection by shareholders only, Art. 126 (1) and (3). The identity of the shareholders may therefore not be verified by third parties. This is in line with the generally accepted 'anonymous' character of joint-stock companies. This registration gives rise to a legal presumption in favour of the registered shareholder's entitlement, Art. 126 (2). The membership of shareholders in a joint-stock company may be represented by printed certificates (also called 'shares'), if shareholders so request and the founders or the general meeting allowed to do so in conformity with the rules relating to negotiable instruments, Art. 125. The Law takes for granted that the **rules on negotiable instruments would also apply to the transfer of share certificates.**

Shares may be freely transferred. Art. 127 (1) provides, however, for the possibility of subjecting the **transfer** of registered shares to the consent of the management or to a right of pre-emption by the other shareholders. This possibility is reasonably limited to simultaneously formed companies which do not trade their shares on the organised security market and become 'closely held companies' through this limitation, cf. Art. 109 (1) 1.

The obligations inherent in a share mainly relate to the **payment of the shareholder's contributions**, Art. 132 (1). In a case of non-performance of this duty, the shareholder may be expelled from the company. He remains nevertheless liable for the unpaid part of his contribution and for any damage caused to the company, Arts. 133, 134. Where the transfer of shares is restricted and subjected to the consent of the company or to shareholders' pre-emption right, other special obligations of shareholders may be established by the statute, Art. 142 (1).

The rights inherent in a share relate, first, to the **distribution of profits (dividends).** Such distribution is, however, subject to a resolution by the general meeting, Art. 136 (1). The general meeting is free to refuse any distribution of profits, Art. 136 (3). Although this rule is totally legitimate, it may give rise to abuse by controlling shareholders at the expense of minority shareholders. If dividends are withheld from the shareholders for an extended period of time, this may amount to an oppression of the minority which may only be controlled on the basis of general legal principles. However, Art. 136 (3) subjects the decision of the general meeting to the fiduciary duties of Art. 22 which not only provides for the principle of equal treatment of all shareholders under the same circumstances, Paragraph 2, but also to the duty of shareholders to take the interests of other shareholders adequately into consideration; this obviously also includes the relation of controlling shareholders towards minority shareholders.[11]

Shareholders are, second, entitled to **participate in general meetings** and to exercise their voting rights personally or through an authorised agent, Arts. 150 (2), 159 (1). This right is generally suspended, however, in case of a conflict of interests, Art. 160.

The Law also provides for **non-voting shares** which necessarily carry with them **preference rights** with regard to the distribution of profits, Arts. 123 (3) and (4), 161. The Law quite reasonably limits the issuing of such shares to 49 percent of the company's capital in order to eliminate the possibility that investors holding less than 51 percent of the company's capital may control the company, Art. 124 (2). Shares granting multiple voting rights are prohibited, Art. 124 (3), whereas a maximum of votes may be set for every single shareholder in the statute, provided all shareholders are treated equally, Art. 124 (4).

According to Arts. 209, 256 and 275, the statute may provide for the withdrawal and annulment of shares under certain circumstances. This necessarily implies a reduction of the company's capital, and therefore the general rules relating to the reduction of capital are applicable as long as Art. 209 (3) to (7) do not provide special legal consequences. Since shareholders whose shares

---

11 See above Box 13.

are withdrawn will normally be paid back their investments, these provisions practically amount to a redemption of shares. However, such redemption cannot surprise the shareholders, because its possibility must be provided in the statute before the subscription of shares. If it is later introduced by the general meeting, the approval of the shareholders concerned is necessary, Art. 209 (2).

SECTION 5 ACQUISITION AND TREATMENT OF COMPANY'S OWN SHARES[12]

Article 143 Prohibition of the company subscribing for its own shares
(239 YEL, 56 GSCL)

(1) The company may not subscribe for its own shares.

(2) A subsidiary company may not subscribe for the shares of its parent company and vice versa.

(3) If, during the formation or increase of basic capital, somebody has taken over the shares on behalf of one of the companies referred to in Paragraphs 1 and 2, he shall be deemed to be subscribing for them on his own account. He is fully liable for the contribution without regard to agreements with the companies mentioned in Paragraphs 1 and 2. However, he will not be able to exercise shareholder's rights, unless he takes over the shares for his own account.

Article 144 Direct acquisition of the company's own shares
(240 YEL, 71, 71e GSCL, 19 Second Directive)

(1) The company may acquire its own shares only:

1. If the acquisition of shares is necessary to prevent serious and imminent damage to the company;
2. If shares are to be offered for sale to employees of the company or group of companies;
3. If acquisition is free;

[12] The following articles are intended to prevent companies from falsifying the price of their shares. The EU is currently bringing in a new framework regulating insider dealing, money laundering and market abuse generally. Before the final draft, the articles of Section 5 of this Law will need to be coordinated with the European provisions covering these matters.

4. On the basis of legal succession;
5. Based on the decision of the general meeting on withdrawal of shares in conformity with the provisions of capital reduction;

(2) The total par value of shares which may be acquired in the cases of nos. 1 and 2 of Paragraph 1 may not be higher than 10 percent of the basic capital.

(3) A company may acquire its own shares only if their par value or higher issue value has been paid.

(4) In the case of no. 1 of Paragraph 1, the next general meeting must be informed by the managing director of the reasons for and nature of the acquisitions effected, of the number and nominal value of the shares acquired, of the proportion of the subscribed capital which they represent, and of the contribution for these shares. In case of no. 2 of Paragraph 1, shares must be offered for sale to employees within one year from the date of acquisition.

(5) Shares acquired in conformity with Paragraph 1 and still possessed by the company, shall be transferred within 3 years from the date of acquisition.

(6) If the company fails to dispose of its own shares in conformity with Paragraphs 4 and 5, it shall withdraw and annul them in conformity with Article 208.

(7) The company cannot avail itself of any rights attached to its own shares.

Article 145 Acquisition of company's own shares by a third party
(241 YEL, 71d GSCL)

(1) Persons acting in their own name but on account of the company may acquire the company's shares only under the same conditions as envisaged by Paragraph 1 of Article 144.

(2) Paragraph 1 also applies if the shares of a parent company are to be acquired by the subsidiary company or a company in which the other company has a majority share, or if such shares are acquired by persons acting in their own name but on account of the subsidiary company or the company in which the other company has a majority share.

(3) The persons mentioned in Paragraphs 1 and 2 shall transfer the shares to the company against full remuneration.

Article 146 Accepting a company's own shares as pledge
(242 YEL, 71e GSCL)

(1) Provisions of Articles 144 and 145 apply correspondingly to accepting the company's own shares as pledge.

(2) Any acceptance of pledge contrary to Paragraph 1 of this Article shall be null and void.

Article 147 Invalid arrangements
(244 YEL, 71a GSCL)

(1) Any legal transaction the subject of which is the granting of a cash-advance or credit or the securing of a cash-advance or credit by the company for the purpose of acquiring shares of the company shall be null and void.

(2) Paragraph 1 applies neither to the usual conduct of business of financial enterprises, nor to the facilitation of acquisition of the company's shares by employees of the company or its group of companies, if the company's financial situation allows such expenses.

(3) A legal agreement between the company and another person which will grant the latter the right and obligation to acquire the company's shares on account of the company or its subsidiary or a company in which it has a majority share, shall be null and void if the acquisition would breach the requirements of Article 144.

Article 148 Special rules for single member companies
(243 YEL)

(1) A single-member company may neither buy its own shares nor withdraw them or accept them as pledge.

(2) A single-member company may neither acquire its own shares for free nor based on legal succession.

SECTION 6 COMPANY ORGANS

Article 149 Kinds and disclosure
(60, 248 YEL; 38 SE-Regulation;13,18 German SE Law Draft – GSE; HLGR 45–7, 63; Behrens 23)

(1) Company organs of joint-stock companies are the general meeting and, depending on the provisions of the statute:

1. Either a board of directors as single administrative organ combining management and supervision (one-tier system),
2. Or supervisory board and managing directors distributing administrative functions between these 2 organs (two-tier system).[13]

[13] At this point, a 'special treatment' of 'simultaneously' formed or small joint-stock companies (cf. no. 1 of the first paragraph of Article 109) could be inserted

(2) Publicly held companies as of no. 2 of the first paragraph of Article 109 shall include in their annual report and accounts a coherent and descriptive statement covering the key elements of the corporate governance rules and practices they apply in reference to the present Law with which the company complies or in relation to which it explains deviations. The statement shall contain a profile of managing directors and board members and explain why individual directors or supervisors are qualified to serve in the light of this profile. The statement shall also be posted on the company's website.[14]

Title 1 General Meeting

Article 150 Rights and duties

(60, 61, 248 III–V, 249 YEL; 4 Twelfth Directive, Behrens 28)

(1) The shareholders exercise their rights regarding company matters in the general meeting unless the present regulation provides otherwise, in particular in Article 160.

(2) The general meeting shall decide on the following company matters:

1. Setting the business policies;
2. Amendments to the statute;
3. Election and dismissal of the members of the board of directors and the supervisory board, unless they are elected by the company's employees with respect to Article 29.
4. Election and dismissal of independent auditors and liquidators;

(maybe with regard to a certain size, e.g. the 50 shareholders limitation of the YEL). This could be done either by allowing the statute to avoid both tiers' board systems and by applying the new governance structure of the limited liability company which delegates supervising functions to the general meeting, or by applying the solution which the German SE Law Draft offers; i.e. the choice to appoint less than 3 board members. However, both solutions would have to face the threshold of number of employees of Article 27: The YEL established a threshold of 100 employees and in this case obliged small joint-stock companies and limited liability companies to have 'both boards' (cf. 65 I YEL).

We prefer a clear-cut regulation with one of the board models to be chosen by each joint-stock company. Smaller companies may choose the managing director to be part of the board of directors avoiding herewith exceeding the 3-board-member obligation. We think this is acceptable. We think, however, that this company law set-up only makes sense, if the limited liability company follows the 'private company' model and is exempted from any board solution. Certainly, the employee threshold which the legislator will establish for Article 27 and the related board requirements shall apply.

[14] See note 1.

5. Establishment of remuneration and incentive schemes regarding the persons mentioned under nos. 1 and 2;
6. Adoption of the annual statement of accounts and performance reports;
7. Distribution of annual profits;
8. Possible by-laws and their amendment;
9. Increase or decrease of the basic capital;
10. Changes in the rights associated with individual classes and kinds of shares;
11. Realisation, through other company organs or special representatives, of the company's claims against managing directors, members of the board of directors or supervisory board or shareholders concerning indemnity for damage or other obligations resulting from company formation or ongoing business;
12. Changes in the company status, company restructuring and dissolution;
13. Adoption of its own rules of procedure;
14. Other matters set by regulation or the statute.

(3) The general meeting shall decide on Items 6 and 7 after having obtained the relevant documents together with the report of the board of directors or supervisory board and the report of the auditor.

(4) The rights and duties of the general meeting in a single-member company shall be performed by the single member. All decisions taken in this capacity shall be entered into a decision register the data of which may not be altered nor deleted. In particular, the following decisions must be registered:

1. Adoption of annual statements of accounts and performance reports;
2. Distribution of profits and coverage of losses;
3. Increase or reduction of basic capital;
4. Investment decisions;
5. Status changes, transformation and dissolution.

Any decision not registered in the decision register is deemed null and void.

Article 151 Convening the general meeting
(250 YEL, 121 GSCL Behrens 28)

(1) The general meeting shall be convened in cases established by this law, other Regulations or by the statute and if it is necessary to safeguard the company's interests. The ordinary general meeting shall be convened at least once a year.

(2) The general meeting shall be convened by the managing directors or, in cases set by the present law, by the board of directors, the supervisory board or by shareholders.

(3) The general meeting must be convened, if annual or interim accounts show or if it is clear that losses amount to 50 percent of the basic capital. The same applies, if the company is becoming insolvent.

(4) The general meeting shall be convened at least 21 days before the scheduled date by an announcement to be placed on the company's website and published in a newspaper as referred to by Paragraph 1 of Article 111. For pre-meeting communication required by this law to be in writing electronic message and transmission forms may also be applied.

(5) The announcement must contain the company name, the registered office, place and time of the general meeting and the conditions for participating and voting.

(6) Shareholders who own registered shares and those who have deposited their shares with the company shall be called to attend the general meeting by special invitation.

(7) The statute may provide that attendance at the general meeting and exercise of voting rights shall depend on giving notice of attendance at least 3 days before the scheduled date of the general meeting and on deposit of shares.

Article 152 Convening on request of a minority of shareholders
(251 YEL, 122 GSCL, Behrens 29)

(1) Shareholders representing at least 5 percent of the basic capital or a smaller portion established by the statute may request in writing the managing directors to convene a general meeting. The request must contain the reasons and objectives and the matters the general meeting should decide on.

(2) Shareholders referred to in Paragraph 1 may request certain issues be put on the agenda for decision-making at a convened general meeting.

(3) Shareholders referred to in Paragraphs 1 and 2 are entitled to convene a general meeting in conformity with Paragraphs 4 to 7 of Article 151 or put the issue in question on the agenda, if their request has not been accepted.

(4) Should the general meeting not be held in spite of the provision of Paragraph 2, the shareholders concerned may request the company to buy their shares in conformity with this law.

Article 153 Agenda
(252 YEL; 121 VI, 124, 126 GSCL)

(1) The agenda of the general meeting shall be published together with the invitation as referred to in Paragraph 4 of Article 151. The publication will also include decision proposals for each item of the agenda which the general meeting is to decide on.

(2) If the general meeting is to decide on amendments to the statute, the text of draft amendments shall accompany the publication of the agenda.

(3) Any question concerning the agenda asked by a shareholder in writing not later than 8 days before the general meeting shall be answered in writing by the managing directors.

(4) Not later than 8 days before the general meeting, shareholders representing at least 5 percent of the basic capital or a smaller portion established by the statute may in writing and stating their reasons request the managing directors to put a specified subject on the agenda.

(5) Should the managing directors fail to comply with a request as of Paragraph 4 within 8 days from receipt of the request, the general meeting, when convening, is obliged to put that request on the agenda.

(6) A general meeting may be held without complying with the formalities of this Article and Article 151, if it is attended by all the shareholders and if no shareholder has any objections to its being held.

(7) Shareholders may make any decision they are entitled to make under this law or the statute by unanimous agreement provided that agreement is evidenced in writing

Article 154 Special notifications and entitlements

(253 YEL, 125,128 GSCL)

(1) Within 8 days after the announcement of Paragraph 4 of Article 151, the managing director shall transmit the announcement to financial service providers (banks, financial service enterprises, professional brokers or similar) and to shareholder associations which exercised shareholders' voting rights at the previous general meeting or which requested to be informed of the convening of the general meeting, as well as to the members of the board of directors or supervisory board.

(2) Financial service providers holding shares of company shareholders in deposit and shareholder associations having company shareholders among their members, shall transmit the announcement as of Paragraph 1 immediately to the shareholders concerned informing them about their plans to vote for these shareholders and submitting proposals on how they would like to vote on the subjects listed on the agenda during the announced general meeting. These proposals must always take shareholders' interests into account. The shareholders concerned must be invited to give instructions on how the voting should be exercised.

(3) Persons who will represent shareholders shall inform the managing director on their participation without delay.

Article 155 By-laws, list of participants

(254 YEL, 129 GSCL)

(1) The statute or the general meeting can establish by-laws concerning its

procedure. The decision in this regard requires a three-quarters majority of the basic capital represented during the general meeting. Unless otherwise established by the statute or the by-laws, the general meeting shall elect a chairman.

(2) During the general meeting, a list of participating and represented shareholders as well as their representatives shall be drawn up, all with their names and residence and with the nominal value and class of shares and the number of votes carried by them. The list must be put at the disposal of the attending shareholders and representatives prior to the first voting.

(3) The statute may provide that absentee shareholders are allowed to participate in the general meeting via electronic means, if identification of the shareholder is guaranteed.

Article 156 Minutes of meeting
(255 YEL, 130 GSCL)

(1) Each decision of the general meeting must be recorded in the minutes. The same is true of any request brought forward by minority shareholders with respect to provisions of this Law.

(2) The minutes must contain the following: place and date of the meeting, agenda, name of the record-keeping person, voting results, statement of the chairman regarding the decision-making and any dissenting opinions of shareholders.

(3) The list of participants shall be attached to the minutes as well as the documentation concerning the convening of the general meeting.

(4) The minutes must be signed by the chairman and the record-keeping person.

(5) Immediately after the general meeting, the managing director has to deposit a copy of the minutes and its attachments with the Registry. The data shall also be placed on the company's website.

Article 157 Quorum and decision-making
(256 YEL, Behrens 28, 29)

(1) The general meeting shall take decisions by simple majority of shareholders present and voting except in circumstances set out in Paragraph 2. In case of ordinary decisions, the general meeting may only make valid decisions if attended by subscribers holding more than 30 percent of the subscribed voting shares. In case of matters requiring qualified majorities, the general meeting may only make valid decisions if the members having more than half of the total number of votes are present, unless the statute requires another qualified majority for the proceedings of the general meeting.

(2) The general meeting shall decide by three-quarters majority of votes of

attending shareholders on the amendment of the statute, the increase or reduction of basic capital; election and dismissal of members of the board of directors or the supervisory board, of auditors and liquidators; adoption of annual accounts and performance reports, profit distribution, changes in the company status, company restructuring and dissolution, unless the statute requires a higher majority for these decisions.

(3) The validity of any decision assigning additional duties to or reducing the rights of the shareholders as provided by this Law, the statute or an issuing decision, is subject to the consent of the shareholders concerned, unless otherwise provided by this Law.

(4) The provision of Paragraph 3 shall also apply to any decision limiting the transfer of registered or interim shares, if such limitation was not provided by the statute or the issuing decision.

Article 158 Method of voting

(257 YEL, 134 I GSCL, Behrens 28)

(1) The general meeting shall take decisions by open ballot if not otherwise provided by this law or the statute.

(2) As regards election and dismissal of the members of the board of directors or supervisory board, the general meeting shall take decisions by secret ballot if shareholders representing at least 5 percent of the company's basic capital so request.

Article 159 Voting right

(258 YEL, 135 GSCL)

(1) Shareholders shall exercise their voting rights personally or through authorised agents. The authorised agent may be neither a managing director nor a member of the board of directors or supervisory board.

(2) The letter of authorisation shall be issued for one general meeting including the reconvened meeting.

(3) In case of shares given on a usufruct basis, pledged or transferred for deposit, the shareholder exercises the voting rights, whereas the usufructuary, secured creditor or depositor may exercise such rights only with special authorisation from the shareholder.

(4) In case the shareholder concerned did not instruct the financial service provider as of Paragraph 2 of Article 154, the financial service provider shall exercise the vote with respect to the proposals sent to the shareholder unless he could expect the shareholder to consent to deviation from the proposals if he had been aware of the circumstances.

(5) A shareholder may vote in absentia either by letter or by electronic

means as envisaged by the fourth paragraph of Article 151, if the authenticity of the vote is guaranteed.

(6) Other requirements for the exercising of voting rights shall be established by the statute or by the general meeting's by-laws.

Article 160 Exclusion from voting
(259 YEL)

A shareholder may not vote if the general meeting is deciding:

1. If his performance is acceptable;
2. If he will be released from obligations;
3. If the company will realise any claim against him;
4. If he will be granted any new benefit.

Article 161 Preferential shares without voting rights
(260 YEL, 140 GSCL)

(1) In case of preferential shares without voting rights all the other rights connected to the share are guaranteed.

(2) A decision of the general meeting on cancelling, limiting or prejudicing the preference requires the consent of the shareholder concerned.

(3) Shareholders representing more than a half of the par value of the preferential shares shall decide on the consent referred to in Paragraph 2 during a special meeting. The special decision requires at least a three-quarters majority of the preferential shareholders attending the special meeting. The statute may neither change this majority requirement nor request other requirements to be observed.

(4) If the preference is cancelled, the shares concerned shall be granted voting rights.

Article 162 Special investigation
(81 YEL, 142 GSCL, 61 HLEGR)

(1) In accordance with item no. 11 of the second paragraph of Article 150, the general meeting may decide to initiate a special investigation to be carried out by an auditing expert with respect to irregularities of certain events and decisions of formation or of the conduct of ongoing business. Shareholders representing at least 5 percent of the basic capital or a smaller amount envisaged by the statute and/or company creditors whose unsatisfied claims against the company amount to at least 5 percent of the basic capital, may request the general meeting to nominate a special auditor on the grounds that there has

been a serious suspicion of breach of law or statute. If the general meeting fails to render a decision within 60 days from the date of the request, or 30 days after a negative decision, the shareholders or creditors mentioned may ask the court to nominate a special auditor. The claimants must state sufficient reasons for their request.

(2) If the general meeting has nominated a special auditor, shareholders or creditors referred to in Paragraph 1 may request to the court to nominate another auditor on the grounds that there are sufficient reasons to believe that the auditor nominated by the general meeting may interfere with an ordinary execution of the special investigation.

(3) If the court confirms the requests of Paragraphs 1 and 2, the company will bear the costs of the nomination and the remuneration of the special auditor.

(4) The right to request the special investigation as of Paragraph 1 must be exercised within 3 years from the date of registration of the company as regards irregularities of the formation process, and within 3 years from the date of the event or decision in question as regards events or decisions regarding the conduct of ongoing business.

Article163 Annulment of illegal decisions and compensation

(75, 79, 80 YEL, 147 GSCL)

(1) In accordance with item no. 11 of the second paragraph of Article 150, the general meeting may request the competent court to annul a decision of a managing director, the board of directors or the supervisory board which it considers to be seriously in breach of the law or the statute. Shareholders representing at least 5 percent of the basic capital or a smaller amount envisaged by the statute or company creditors whose unsatisfied claims against the company amount to at least 5 percent of the basic capital, may file the request to the court, if the general meeting fails to render a decision within 60 days from the date of their request to initiate the court proceedings or within 30 days from the date of a negative decision.

(2) Depending on which organ referred to in Paragraph 1 took the decision considered to be unlawful, the general meeting shall be represented by the managing director or by the board of directors or the supervisory board. The general meeting may also authorise a special representative.

(3) The minority or creditor quota referred to in Paragraph 1 may ask the court to nominate a representative who is not among those mentioned in Paragraph 2 if they present sufficient reasons for this to be necessary for a proper assertion of the claim. If the court confirms the request, the company will bear the costs of the nomination and the remuneration of the representative.

(4) The court may order an adequate deadline for the regularisation of the nullity. It will declare the nullity, if regularisation is not possible.

(5) The second sentence of Paragraph 1 and Paragraphs 2 and 3 apply correspondingly to the minority or creditor quota concerned, if the general meeting does not decide or refuses to decide on their request for the realisation of claims on compensation of damages and other claims which this Law or the statute envisage against managing directors, members of the board of directors or the supervisory board.

Article 164 Rights attached to share
(Companies Act 1985, UK, s14)

In the event of a shareholder being prevented from exercising the rights attached to his shares he may request the court to enforce these rights or grant compensation. A claim must be brought within 3 years of the denial of the right.

Article 165 Exclusion of restrictions
(74, 75 YEL)

(1) Any provision of the statute which limits or excludes the rights of shareholders or creditors referred to in Articles 162 to 164 or which provides a general waiver with respect to the action envisaged by these Articles is null and void.

(2) No decision of the general meeting may interfere with the shareholders' or creditors' right to take action as envisaged by Articles 162 to 164.

19. COMPANIES (3)

Governance Structure

Another important concern is the organisational structure of the company and the distribution of competencies between company organs. Transparency and legal certainty are crucial in this respect. Those who are in charge of managing the company must always be accountable for their business conduct as against the company, its investors, creditors and employees and as against other social interests recognised by law. A major concern in transition economies is self-dealing of managers and mistreatment of minority shareholders by dominant shareholders. Where this is likely to occur, investors will either ask for an excessive risk premium which is reflected in extremely low share prices that make equity capital excessively expensive for the company, or investors will shy away from investing in shares altogether. In any case, insufficient protection against self-dealing by managers or oppression of minority shareholders will have a disastrous effect on economic reconstruction. Adequate supervision of the company's management as well as minority protection is therefore absolutely essential for a viable law of companies. In order to avoid mismanagement, enterprise law should provide for supervisory bodies and put restrictions on transactions by managers involving conflicts of interest, and provide for accounting and disclosure rules which are also essential for the proper functioning of enterprises. Furthermore, enterprise law should impose certain restrictions on the powers of dominant shareholders in order to make sure that they cannot exploit the company at the expense of the minority.

While the aspects of 'fiduciary duties', 'conflict of interest' and 'minority protection' have already been mentioned, the creation of clear-cut management and supervisory structures remains to be discussed.

General Meeting (General Assembly)

The new Enterprise Law does away with a 'hierarchical' company constitution and introduces a flexible 'balance of power' between the company organs, i.e. between the general meeting, the board of directors or supervisory board and the managing directors. This is much more realistic as the real distribution of power in a company depends on the distribution of shares and on the persons which represent them.

The general meeting should be **'setting the business policies',** Art. 150 (3), 1, Art. 258 (1) 1. This is a strong general competence, but it requires enough cooperation with and information from the management which Art. 150 (4), 166 (1) 3, 6, 7 and 13, 271 (3) 4 and 11 try to provide. However, this does not mean that the law generally envisages the general meeting to be directly involved in management decisions of the company. The general policy will be set during the ordinary meetings which normally take place only once a year, Art. 151 (1), 259 (1). After the business policy is set by the meeting, the board of directors gives concrete instructions to the managing directors to implement these policies throughout the year, Art. 166 (1), 1, and the managing directors are actually carrying out the company's business, Art. 171 (3) 1, 271 (3) 1.

However, this is a default model as **the law allows the role of the meeting to be stronger** if company founders, shareholders or members so wish. While the last sentence of Art. 171 (3) declares that competencies of the board of directors may not be delegated to the managing directors, there is no such clause with respect to the relation between the board, managing directors and the general meeting. The statute can provide for a different distribution of competencies as long as the law allows this. This is the sense of Art. 150 (2) 14 and 258 (1) 18. Another case where the law explicitly allows the statute to enlarge the competence of a company organ can be found in the last sentence of Art. 180 (1): the statute may define which management decisions require the approval of the supervisory board.

In limited liability companies, the general meeting usually has a stronger role than in joint-stock companies. On the one hand, it has all the supervisory functions which the board of directors or supervisory board usually have in joint stock companies, Art. 258 (1) 7. On the other hand, investors in a limited liability company normally have a stronger personal interest in the way the company is managed. They may therefore use the statute to design their involvement into company management by attributing to the general meeting a role of management and control with respect to their needs.

According to Art. 150 (3) or 258 (1), **the general meeting is specifically competent to decide on important matters** like amendments of the statute (2), adoption of annual accounts and performance reports (6 and 8), distribution of profits (7 and 9), changes of the company's capital (8 and 12), and fundamental changes of the status or form of the company, including its dissolution (12).

In joint-stock companies, **the general meeting appoints the members of the board of directors and of the supervisory board and decides on their receipts and fees**, Art. 150 (3) 3 and 5. Since it is the board of directors or supervisory board who appoint the managing director, Art. 166 (1) 9, 180 (1), the general meeting is not competent to do so. In limited liability companies without board structure,[15] the general meeting determines the

[15] Cf. Art. 25.

appointment of managing directors and their remuneration, Art. 258 (1) 4 and 6.

As with all important decisions (amendment of the statute; increase or reduction in basic capital; adoption of annual accounts and performance reports, profit distribution, changes in the company status, company restructuring and dissolution, Arts. 157 (2), 263 (2), the appointment and removal of members of the board of directors and of the supervisory board in a joint-stock company and of managing directors in a limited liability company normally require a **three-quarters majority of votes of attending shareholders**. The statute may only provide for a higher majority. This rule gives both board members in joint-stock companies and managing directors in limited liability companies a rather strong position as they are supported by large majorities.

The general meeting is also competent to **represent the company in court proceedings against the members of the company's administration**, Art. 150 (3) 14, and 258 (1) I4. It shall enforce the liability of directors, of members of the supervisory board, or of shareholders for damages caused to the company Art. 150 (1), 11, 258 (1) I5. Minority shareholders or groups of creditors may urge the meeting to do so, Art. 163 (5).

The Law properly sets out the details relating to the **procedural aspects** of general meetings, Arts. 151–61 and 259–69.

The **competence to convene** the general meeting normally lies with the managing directors, unless the law provides otherwise, Arts. 151 (2), 259 (2). **Electronic means** may be used for pre-assembly communications, Arts. 151 (4), 260 (1).[16]

The general meeting may vote on a resolution only if a **quorum of more than one half of total shareholders' votes** are present (or represented) in case the meeting votes **on a matter requiring a qualified majority**, Art. 157 (1) 2, Art. 262 (1) 1. In case of **ordinary resolutions which must be taken by simple majority** as referred to in Art. 157 (1) 1 and Art. 263 (3),

[16] The new Paragraph 8 of the 2003 revision of the First Directive which allows for the use of electronic means when filing registration requests, defines 'electronic means' as follows: 'For the purposes of this article, "by electronic means" shall mean that the information is sent initially and received at its destination by means of electronic equipment for the processing (including digital compression) and storage of data, and entirely transmitted, conveyed and received in a manner to be determined by Member States by wire, by radio, by optical means or by other electromagnetic means'.

at least 30 percent of the voting stock must be present, Art. 157 (1) 3, 262 (1) 2.[17]

Shareholders normally vote by **open ballot**; only exceptionally may resolutions be taken by secret ballot, Arts. 158 (1), 266. Shareholders may exercise their voting rights by letter or by electronic means, Arts. 159 (5) and 265.

In case of a joint-stock company, voting may be exercised also through **authorised agents**, Art. 159 (1) 1. Any letter of authorization shall be issued only for one general meeting including the reconvened meeting, Art. 159 (2). The authorised agent may be neither a managing director nor a member of the board of directors or supervisory board. So-called **'proxy-voting' is therewith excluded,** Art. 159 (1) 2.

Title 2 Board of Directors (One-Tier System)

Article 166 Rights and duties

(62,78 YEL, 98 French, 21 GSE, 17 Second Directive, Behrens 34)

(1) The board of directors has the following rights and duties:

1. Giving directives to the managing directors with respect to the implementation of business policies;
2. Monitoring and supervising the implementation of business policies by managing directors;
3. On request of the general meeting, preparation of measures which fall into the competencies of the latter, recommendation of decisions to be adopted by the general meeting and execution of the latter's decisions;
4. Convening a general meeting if it is necessary for the company's interests;
5. Ensuring that the company observes the applicable law and accounting standards;
6. Examination of the company's books, documents and assets;
7. Ensuring that the annual statement of accounts is prepared by the managing directors as well as their report regarding the performance status of the company and any other disclosures that may be required by law or

---

[17] Note that the *foundation meeting of successively founded joint stock companies* requires *only 40 percent* of subscribed voting shares to be present during the first meeting and 30 percent for any reconvened meeting, Art. 118 (1).

statute; these documents must be approved and signed by all directors to be presented to the general meeting together with a report by the board regarding the reasons for the approval and a description of the way the management has been monitored throughout the business year;
8. Ensuring that the audit of the books and records is performed at least annually by the independent auditor, with the auditor's report addressed to the general meeting of shareholders and made available to each director and managing director; the board report mentioned under no. 7 has also to comment on the auditor's report;
9. Hiring and discharging managing directors;
10. Determining the benefits for managing directors;
11. Causing the corporation to purchase its own shares;
12. Causing the company to incur substantial debt through loans or the issuance of bonds or convertible debt instruments;
13. Establishing lasting business cooperations and proposing policies regarding the formation of new companies or groups;
14. Other duties as set by law or statute.

(2) If annual or interim accounts show or if it is clear that losses amounting to 50 percent of the basic capital occur, the board must immediately convene a general meeting in order to consider whether the company should be wound up or if any other measure should be taken. The same applies, if the company is becoming insolvent.

Article 167 Number, election and composition of the board of directors

(61, 69, 261 YEL, 101 II GSCL)

(1) The Board of Directors shall consist of at least three members, who are natural persons, and of not more than 21.

(2) The members of the board of directors are elected by the general meeting with the majority required by Paragraph 2 of Article 157 for a term established by the statute not exceeding 5 years, with the possibility of re-election.

(3) The statute may provide that shareholders holding together a minority of at least 5 percent or less of basic capital may elect a member of the board of directors by special decision.

(4) The member of the board of directors elected with respect to Paragraph 3 shall count among the number to be elected by the general meeting.

(5) The application for registration referred to in Article 96 will enclose a list with the name, surname, date and place of birth as well as the residence of the board members.

Article 168 Deputies and interim directors
(262 YEL, 101 III GSCL)

(1) The statute may provide for the election of deputy members of the board of directors. The deputies have the rights of the members only in case the latter are hindered in the conduct of their activities.

(2) If the statute does not provide for deputies, in the event of vacancies amounting of more than one-third of the total number of members of the board of directors, a general meeting shall be held.

(3) The provisions relating to rights and duties of ordinary members of the board of directors shall also apply correspondingly to the deputy or interim members.

Article 169 Restricted eligibility
(68, 70, 261 YEL, 22 GSE)

(1) Members may be elected from the ranks of the company's shareholders and employees, as well as from the ranks of other persons outside the company.

(2) A person may not be elected as a member of the board of directors

1. If he is already a member of the board of directors or supervisory board of 2 other companies registered in the country;
2. If he is the managing director of a parent or subsidiary of that company;
3. If he is the legal representative of another company where a managing director or member of the board of directors of the first company is member of the board of directors or supervisory board.

(3) Any election made contrary to the provisions of Paragraph 2 is null and void.

(4) Membership of the board of directors or supervisory boards of other enterprises in a group shall be regarded as membership of only one board.

(5) The persons referred to in Paragraph 2 shall inform the company about their multiple election in time.

Article 170 Dismissal
(263 YEL, 103 GSCL)

(1) The general meeting may dismiss a member of the board of directors in accordance with Paragraph 2 of Article 157. The statute may determine additional requirements.

(2) A member of the board of directors who was elected to the board in

accordance with Paragraph 3 of Article 167 may be dismissed by decision of the minority. In the case that the conditions of the statute for the special assignment do not apply anymore, the general meeting may dismiss the member concerned by simple majority.

(3) The board of directors, by simple majority, may request the competent court to dismiss a board member if he has violated his duties as of Paragraph 3 of Article 177.

Article 171 Managing directors
(60, 63, 68, 265, no 266, 267 YEL, 24 GSE)

(1) The board of directors shall nominate one or more natural persons as managing directors for a term established by the statute not exceeding 5 years, with the possibility of re-election. Members of the board may be nominated managing directors as long as the majority of the board continues to be composed of non-managing directors. The nomination has legal effect once it is registered in the Registry. The statute may establish rules regarding the nomination.

(2) The managing director of a parent enterprise may not be elected managing director of a subsidiary and vice versa. The managing director of a parent enterprise may not be the chairman of the board of directors of a subsidiary, and the managing director of a subsidiary may not be the chairman of the board of directors of a parent enterprise. Any elections made contrary to these provisions are null and void.

(3) The managing directors shall:

1. Manage the company's business;
2. Represent the company;
3. Ensure that the necessary accountancy books and documents are kept;
4. Provide for and sign the annual statement of accounts and consolidated accounts and the performance report and present it to the board for approval together with the proposals for the distribution of profits which the managing director will make in the general meeting;
5. Create an early warning system with respect to developments threatening the existence of the company;
6. Submit company data to be registered to the Registry, if not otherwise provided by this law;
7. Report to the board of directors with respect to the implementation of business policies and to the realisation of transactions of particular importance for company performance;
8. Perform other duties set by law or the statute.

Duties which the law has attributed to the board of directors may not be delegated to managing directors.

(4) If annual or interim accounts show or if it is clear that losses amounting to 50 percent of the basic capital occur, the managing directors must immediately inform the chairman of the board of directors. The same applies, if the company is becoming insolvent.

(5) In case more than one managing director has been nominated, they manage the company jointly. The statute or the by-laws established by the board of directors may provide otherwise.

(6) The board may discharge the managing directors at any time, unless the statute provides otherwise. General civil law rules apply for claims deriving from the employment contract.

Article 172 Representation

(25 GSE)

(1) Managing directors' authority cannot be limited in respect of third parties. Paragraphs 2 and 3 of Article 16 apply.

(2) Managing directors entitled to represent the company jointly may authorise some of them to carry out certain transactions or certain kinds of transactions. Declarations which are supposed to be received by the company may be addressed to one of the managing directors.

(3) A managing director's entitlement to representation and any change thereof shall be reported for entry to the Registry.

Article 173 Remuneration

(269–71, 273 YEL, HLEGR 61–7; 87 GSCL, Behrens 25)

(1) Board members may be granted remuneration or incentives (parts of the company profit, share options or similar) for their work. The salary of managing directors may be supplemented by incentives. The scheme for these benefits shall be prepared by the board and approved by decision of the general meeting.

(2) Individual benefits shall be established by the board and must adequately reflect the duties of non-managing board members and the managing directors with respect to the scheme referred to in Paragraph 1 and to the financial situation of the company.

(3) In case the company's financial standing is seriously deteriorating, the benefits granted as of the second paragraph may be adequately reduced if so determined by the general meeting in accordance with Article 163.

(4) The scheme for benefits referred to in Paragraph 1, the individual benefits attributed to each non-managing board member and the managing director

as well as the annual impact of the incentive schemes on the company's cost structure shall be disclosed together with the annual financial statement as of no. 7 of the first paragraph of Article 166.

Article 174 By-laws, chairman and committees of the board

(38 GSE)

(1) The statute or the board may establish by-laws concerning its procedures. Decisions of the board regarding these by-laws must be taken unanimously.

(2) The board must elect its chairman and vice-chairman in accordance with the statute. The vice-chairman has the rights of the chairman only in case the latter is unable to conduct his activities. If the board consists of only one person, he will also carry out the functions of the chairman.

(3) Each board meeting must be recorded by minutes of meeting which the chairman shall sign. The minutes must contain the place and date of the meeting, participants, agenda, outline of the contents of the meeting and decisions taken. Formal defects in respect of the minutes do not invalidate the decision. Each board member may request a copy of the minutes. Sentences 1 to 4 do not apply in case the board consists of one person only.

(4) The board may create committees composed by its members to prepare its meetings and decisions or to supervise the implementation of its decisions, in particular, the nomination of managing directors, the remuneration of directors and the audit of the accounting of the company's performance.[18]

Article 175 Decision-making

(264 YEL)

(1) The board of directors may make decisions if more than half of its members are present. It shall take its decisions by majority vote of the attending members, unless otherwise provided by the statute. In case of an equal number of votes, the chairman shall have the casting vote, unless otherwise provided by the statute.

(2) Decisions of the board of directors may be made by letter, phone or electronic transmission forms as envisaged by the statute or the board's by-laws unless a board member objects.

(3) The provisions of Article 160 shall apply correspondingly to the exclusion from decision-making of a member of the board of directors.

---

[18] At this point, mandatory committees in the 3 special areas mentioned in the text (and by the HLEGR) could be inserted with respect to publicly held companies. Members of these committees should be non-managing or even 'independent' directors. It seems, however, that this would require a minimum number of directors higher than 3 for those companies.

Article 176 Fiduciary duties and liability
(72 III, 75, 268, 272 YEL, 93 GSCL; HLEGR 68–9;Behrens 25)

(1) In addition to the general fiduciary duties expressed by Articles 22 to 26, directors must

1. Perform their duties established by law or statute in good faith to the best interest of the company as a whole, which includes environmental sustainability of its operations;
2. Exercise powers granted to them by law or statute only for the purposes established therein;
3. Give adequate consideration to matters to be decided;
4. Avoid actual and potential conflicts between personal interests and those of the corporation;
5. Exercise reasonable care and skill in the performance of their functions.

(2) Directors may be held liable for any action or failure to act unless the action or omission was made in good faith, based upon reasonable inquiry and information, and rationally related to the purposes of the company.

(3) In case of violation of duties and the standard of diligence referred to in Paragraphs 1 and 2, directors shall compensate the company for any damage which occurred due to the violation. Directors bear the burden of proving compliance with their duties and standards.

(4) In particular, directors are obliged to compensate the company in damages, if they are, contrary to this law, carrying out the following transactions or if they were aware or could have been aware of such transactions carried out by other directors without notifying the general meeting in this respect:

1. Returning contributions to shareholders;
2. Paying interests or dividends to shareholders;
3. Subscribing, acquiring, accepting as pledge or withdrawing the company's own shares or shares of another company;
4. Issuing shares prior to full payment of their par value or a higher issue price;
5. Distributing the company's assets;
6. Letting the company continue to do business when it should be foreseen that it will not be able to pay its debts;
7. Making payments after the company has become insolvent;
8. In case of conditional increase of capital, issuing shares contrary to the set purpose or before they have been fully paid for;
9. Making payments to board members or managing directors;
10. Granting loans.

(5) Paragraph 5 of Article 163 applies to the realization of claims deriving from Paragraphs 3 and 4. These claims must be brought within 3 years from the damage being caused.

Article 177 Collective liability of the board of directors and managing directors

(67–8 HLEGR)

Members of the board of directors and the managing directors are jointly and severally liable for the probity of all financial statements and of statements on other key data, such as information on the company's risk management system, its business prospects, investment plans, technical, organisational and human resources and corporate governance structures and practices. Paragraphs 3 and 5 of Article 176 apply accordingly.

Article 178 Request to the board of directors to perform supervisory duties in special cases

(277, 278 YEL, Behrens 29)

(1) Shareholders representing at least 5 percent of the basic capital or a smaller amount envisaged by the statute or company creditors whose unsatisfied claims against the company amount to at least 5 percent of the basic capital, may request the board to perform its supervisory duties with respect to special cases, in particular, when they consider the lawfulness of the work of the managing director as being questioned.

(2) Should the board fail to comply with the request referred to in Paragraph 1 within 30 days, shareholders and creditors concerned may initiate the procedure established by Article 162.

Title 3 Managing Directors and Supervisory Board (Two-Tier System)

Article 179 General rule

(1) In the two-tier system of administration, the managing directors lead the company and decide on the manner of implementation of the business policy while the supervisory board assesses the policy implementation and controls its compliance with the law and the statute.

(2) Based on the general rule for the distribution of functions expressed by Paragraph 1, Articles 166 to 178 apply to the legal position and relations between managing directors and supervisory board, with the functions of the supervisory board corresponding to the supervisory functions of the board of directors as defined by the following provisions.

Article 180 Composition, rights, duties and liabilities of the supervisory board and the managing directors
(64, 67, 76, 274–6, 278, 280 YEL, Behrens 27)

(1) The supervisory board is responsible for all functions listed in nos. 2 to 10 and 14 of the first paragraph and for those of the second paragraph of Article 166. The managing director, beyond the functions established by Paragraphs 3 and 4 of Article 171, is in charge of the functions listed in nos. 1, and 11 to 13 of the first paragraph of Article 166. Approval by the supervisory board of decisions of the managing director in other cases than the one mentioned in no. 7 of the first paragraph of Article 166 can only be required if established by the statute.

(2) Neither managing directors nor procurators of the company and of companies in a group and employees as determined by the statute, nor the relatives of such persons may be elected as members of the supervisory board.

(3) Supervisory board members are liable for damage caused by violation of their duties and the standard of diligence expressed by Paragraphs 1 to 3 of Article 176. As regards violations by managing directors with respect to Paragraph 4 of Article 176, supervisory board members are liable if they were aware or could have been aware of a violation of duties without notifying the general meeting in this respect.

20. COMPANIES (4)

Boards and Managing Directors

The new Enterprise Law takes the latest developments of European enterprise law into account, especially the European Company Regulation 2157/2001, and leaves it to the founders of the joint-stock company to decide if they want to introduce the **'one-tier system'** of administration, Arts. 166–78, providing a board of directors which usually includes the managing directors; or if they want to introduce the **'two-tier system'** where supervisory functions are clearly distinct from the management function by creating a supervisory board. In this case, the management function is exclusively carried out by the managing directors, Arts. 179 and 180.

In the one-tier system, all power is concentrated in the hands of one single board. This board unites managing and supervisory functions as Art. 166 (1) shows: 1 and 11–13 describe managing functions, 2 to 10 supervisory functions.[19] If there are no additional **(executive) managing directors** appointed, board members may act as such managing directors. In this case it is important to assure that a sufficient number of **non-executive directors** are appointed to the board to oversee the managers' powers as required by the supervisory functions of Art. 166. The Law therefore provides that, **if board members are nominated (executive) managing directors, it must be guaranteed that the majority of the board is composed of non-managing (non-executive) directors,** Art. 171 (1).

For **single member companies** which are allowed by Art. 167 (1) to have less than 3 board members, application of the rule Art. 171 (1) means that they need these 3 board members in case one of them, for example a natural person being the single member, is also managing the company. If the natural single member is managing director without being on the board, only one board member is necessary.

In the two-tier system, the managing directors lead the company and decide on the manner of implementation of the business policy while the supervisory board assesses the policy implementation and controls its compliance with the law and the statute (Art. 179 I). The statute may extend the functions of the supervisory board by binding certain important management decisions to the approval of the supervisory board, Art. 180 (1) 3.[20]

Company practice has shown that distinction of and compliance with the supervisory functions is a major difficulty in the single board. Therefore, often not only a majority of non-executive directors but also their **independence** has been requested in the worldwide reform debate; these directors would probably have to come from outside of the company and not have any links to managing directors or majority shareholders who dominate the

[19] See Art. 180 (1) which lists the managing and supervisory functions of the board of directors in the one-tier system in order to define attribution of the different functions to the managing directors and to the supervisory board in the two-tier-system.

[20] In the German system, such approval requirements may also be introduced by the supervisory board itself, Art. 111 (4) of the German Stock Company Law. In spite of the rule that the supervisory board should not generally participate in management, the Federal Court has been in favour of the extension of these 'approvals' as they have proved to be an adequate device for corporate control, not least because employee representatives are part of the supervisory board and enlarge the interests reflected by corporate decision-making.

general meeting (nor to employee representatives). Other voices proposed a **special supervisory role for the chairman of the board** who would be required to be non-executive and 'work alongside' the chief executive, notably on the preparation of the board's agenda.

The new Enterprise Law has not adopted any general provision that the board should always have a majority of independent directors, nor can any definition of independence be found. The chairman of the board must be elected, Art. 174 (2). He has a casting vote in case of an equal number of votes in the board, Art. 175 (1). But the law leaves it to the statute or the board's by-laws to adequately shape the role of the chairman as compared to the role of executive managers, Arts. 171 (5), 174 (1), 175 (1). According to Art. 174 (4), the board may also create committees composed by its members to prepare its meetings and decisions or to supervise the implementation of its decisions, in particular, the nomination of managing directors, the remuneration of directors and the audit of the accounts. Separation of these central board functions in the form of committees has been recommended by the High Level Group of Company Law Experts[21] to be an organisational device to increase transparency of decision-making. Finally, in order to connect the personal interest of members of the management (i.e. board members and managing directors) to the ongoing health of the company, the statute may bind them to own a specified number of the company's shares and to deposit them with the company for the duration of their function or even until their retirement, Art. 142 (3).

However, the Law has not opted for mandatory provisions in this context. It places more reliance on the **flexible definition of liability** of company organs, in their **mutual cooperation and control** and in **the transparency of governance structures**.

Three aspects of this concept have already been mentioned: first, the liability for the fiduciary duties of Art. 176; second, the **cooperation and information requirements of the board in relation to the general assembly** (Arts. 150 (4), 166 (1), 3, 7, 8 and 13; and, third, the broad possibility of **shareholders' and creditors' derivative actions** (Art. 9 (3), 162–5).

Fourth, to avoid involvement of board members in too many companies and possible conflicts of interest, Art. 169 (2) strongly

21 See note 9.

restricts their eligibility. Also managing directors' eligibility is restricted, Art. 171 (2).

Fifth, as regards the important and often abused aspect of **remuneration of directors,** the **scheme of benefits** granted to board members and managing directors (remuneration or incentives including a share in the company's profit and share options) **must be approved by decision of the general meeting.** The individual benefits must adequately reflect the duties of non-managing board members and the managing directors with respect to this scheme and to the financial situation of the company. In case the company's financial standing is seriously deteriorating, the benefits granted may be adequately reduced if so determined by the general meeting. The scheme for benefits, the individual benefits attributed to each non-managing board member and the managing director as well as the annual impact of the incentive scheme on the company's cost structure shall be disclosed together with the annual financial statement, Art. 173.

Sixth, members of the board of directors (or supervisory board) and managing directors are jointly and severally liable for the **probity of all financial statements and of statements on other key-data**, such as information on the company's risk management system, its business prospects, investment plans, technical, organisational and human resources and corporate governance structures and practices, Art. 177.

Seventh, as regards publicly held joint-stock companies where the separation of ownership and control has reached its peak, Art. 149 (2) provides that these companies shall include in their annual report and accounts **a coherent and descriptive statement covering the key elements of the corporate governance rules and practices they apply in reference to the present law with which the company complies or in relation to which it explains deviations.** The statement shall contain details of any **Code of Conduct** developed by the company and **details of how the independence of non-managing directors is assured.** The statement shall contain a profile of managing directors and board members and explain why individual directors or supervisors are qualified to serve in the light of this profile. In other words, the Law's 'comply-or-explain' concept leaves it to the company to show to the public that it abides by the structure of the Law or of other reasonable governance models/codes of conduct. This concept brings us back to the 'fiduciary duty for proper enterprise organisation' discussed above, which translates the 'comply-or-explain' concept into the liability standard of the new Law.

Eighth, the civil liability of board members and managing directors as of Art. 176 (and 274) is accompanied by penal provisions for wrongful statements, Art. 303, false balance sheets, Art. 304, breach of duty in case of losses and bankruptcy, Art. 305, and breach of business secrets, Art. 306. The same replies to administrative fines for major and minor offences according to Arts. 308 (2) and 309 (2).

SECTION 7 INCREASE OF CAPITAL

Title 1 Increase of Capital by Issuing New Shares

Article 181 Conditions
(281 YEL, 182, 183 GSCL)

(1) Basic capital may be increased by issuing new shares against new contributions.

(2) In case the increase interferes with the rights of a certain class of shares, the validity of the general meeting's decision taken in accordance with Paragraph 2 of Article 157 is subject to the consent of the shareholders concerned, which has to comply with the formal requirements of Paragraph 3 of Article 161.

(3) Basic capital may not be increased as long as outstanding payments on previously subscribed shares have not been made, except if the outstanding capital does not exceed 1 percent of the paid up capital, in case of a company merger and in other cases provided by law.

Article 182 Registration of decision
(282 YEL, 184 GSCL)

(1) The decision to increase the basic capital shall be submitted to the Registry by the managing director and the chairman of the board of directors or supervisory board. It shall be published on the company's website and in conformity with provisions of the Registry Law.

(2) The report of an authorised expert verifying the value of any contribution in kind shall be attached to the application for registration of the decision referred to in Paragraph 1.

Article 183 Applicable provisions on capital raising
(283 YEL)

Provisions of this Law on the invitation for subscription, payment and transfer of contributions, on subscribers, on appraisal of contributions in kind, on subscription forms and lists, oversubscription to shares, failed subscription, management of the amounts paid in, forfeiture of rights stemming from shares, prohibition of exemption from payment, prohibition to return contributions and on liabilities shall apply correspondingly to the increase of basic capital.

Article 184 Pre-emption right
(284 YEL, 186 GSCL, 29 IV Second Directive, Behrens 33)

(1) All shareholders shall have a pre-emption right as against the newly issued shares in proportion to the par value of their previous capital contribution.

(2) The owners of convertible bonds carrying the pre-emption right in relation to shares may exercise such right prior to the shareholders referred to in Paragraph 1.

(3) The rights referred to in Paragraphs 1 and 2 may be restricted or withdrawn by the decision of the general meeting on the increase of basic capital. The managing director shall be required to present to such a meeting a written report indicating the reasons for restriction or withdrawal and justifying the proposed issue price. The decision may only be taken if the restriction or withdrawal was announced on the company's website and published in a newspaper as referred to by Paragraph 1 of Article 111.

Article 185 Registration and publication of accomplishment and start of effectiveness
(285 YEL; 188–90 GSCL)

(1) The accomplishment of the capital increase shall be submitted for registration to the Registry by the managing director and the chairman of the board of directors or supervisory board. Information supplied must include the list of the subscribers signed by the managing director, copies of the subscription forms, reports on amounts paid up and on the estimated costs of the capital increase and, in case the capital increase was subject to approval by competent authorities, this approval.

(2) The capital increase shall be effective from the date of its entry in the Registry.

(3) The registration of the accomplishment of the capital increase shall be published on the company's website and in conformity with the provisions of the Registry Law. The publication must include the issued value of the new

shares as well as the subject, the subscriber and the value of contributions in kind indicating the expert report deposited with the Registry.

Article 186 Prohibition on the issue of shares and interim shares
(286 YEL, 191 GSCL)

Before the accomplishment of the capital increase has been registered, rights connected to the new shares cannot be transferred, and shares and interim shares may not be issued. Shares or interim shares issued earlier are invalid. The issuers are jointly and severally liable as against the holders for any damage caused by such issuing.

Title 2 Conditional Capital Increase

Article 187 Conditions
(287 YEL, 192 GSCL, 41 Second Directive)

(1) The general meeting may decide to increase the capital only to the extent that interested persons will make use of pre-emption or conversion rights which the company is granting for the new shares (conditional capital increase).

(2) Conditional capital increase may only be carried out for the purpose of:

1. Granting pre-emption or conversion rights to holders of convertible bonds;
2. Granting a conversion right to shareholders against their claims on profit shares;
3. Granting a conversion right to creditors against their claims against the company;
4. Preparing an enterprise merger;
5. Granting stock options to employees and members of the management of the company or an associated company;

(3) The nominal increase may not be greater than half of the basic capital amount at the time when the conditional increase was decided. In case of no. 5 of the second paragraph the increase may not exceed 10 percent of that basic capital amount.

Article 188 Registration and publication of decision
(288 YEL, 195 GSCL)

(1) The decision on the conditional capital increase shall be submitted to the

Registry by the managing director and the chairman of the board of directors or supervisory board. If applicable, it shall include the subject, the subscriber and the value of contributions in kind, the report of an authorised expert verifying the value of the contribution in kind, the estimated costs of the capital increase and, in case the capital increase was subject to approval by competent authorities, this approval.

(2) The publication of the registration referred to in Paragraph 1 must include the subject, the subscriber and the value of contributions in kind indicating the expert report deposited with the Registry. Publication will be carried out through the company's website and in conformity with the provisions of Administrative Direction 2002/22.

Article 189 Prohibited share issue

(289 YEL, 197 GSCL)

The provisions of Article 186 shall apply to any issue of shares or interim shares before the decision on conditional capital increase was registered.

Article 190 Registration of share issuing

(290 YEL, 201 GSCL)

(1) Within 15 days from the adoption of the annual statement of accounts the managing director shall submit to the Registry the volume of shares issued on the occasion of the conditional capital increase during the past business year.

(2) In his application, the managing director must declare that the shares have been exclusively issued for the purposes set out in the decision on the conditional capital increase and not before full payment of the value set in the decision.

Title 3 Authorised Capital

Article 191 Authorised capital

(291 YEL, 202, 203 GSCL)

(1) The statute or a statute amending the decision of the general meeting may entitle the managing director for a maximum of 5 years after company registration to increase the basic capital up to a specified par value by issuing new shares (authorised capital). The par value of authorised capital may not exceed half of the basic capital as existing on the date of such authorisation.

(2) The statute may establish further conditions. In particular, it may provide that, if the managing director implements his authorisation, all or parts of the shares issued may or must be granted to company employees or to those of associated companies.

(3) Articles 186 to 190 apply accordingly.

Title 4 Capital Increase from Company Assets

Article 192 Conditions
(292, 293 YEL, 207, 208 GSCL)

(1) After the adoption of the statement of accounts for the previous year, the general meeting may decide to increase the capital by converting the available reserves and undistributed profits into basic capital.

(2) The portion of the reserves which exceeds one-tenth of the basic capital or such a greater amount as is set in the statute, as well as undistributed profits, may be converted into initial capital.

(3) Reserves and undistributed profits may not be converted into basic capital if the statement of accounts for the previous year has revealed losses.

Article 193 Registration and start of effectiveness
(294 YEL, 210, 211 GSCL)

(1) The balance sheet on the basis of which the basic capital was increased, the auditor's confirmation and the last profit-and-loss statement shall be attached to the application for registration of the capital increase decision. The application shall also include the managing directors' declaration that, to their knowledge, no reduction of assets has been carried out in the period between the adoption of the balance sheet and the application for registration which would impede the capital increase if it would have been adopted on the date of registration.

(2) The Registry may register the decision only if the declaration referred to in the second sentence of Paragraph 1 has been submitted and if not more than 6 months have elapsed from the date the balance sheet which the capital increase was based on was adopted.

(3) The registration must mention that the capital increase has been carried out from company reserves or undistributed profits.

(4) The capital is increased on the date of registration.

(5) The increase of basic capital and the amendments to registered data shall be published on the company's website and in conformity with provisions of the Registry Law.

Article 194 Proportional distribution
(295 YEL, 212 GSCL)

Shareholders are entitled to own the new shares in proportion to their shares in the capital prior to the increase. Any decision of the general meeting contrary to this provision shall be null and void.

Article 195 Announcement for shareholders
(296 YEL, 214 GSCL)

(1) After registration of the decision on capital increase, managing directors shall publish an announcement on the company's website and in an authorised newspaper as of the first paragraph of Article 111 inviting shareholders to collect the new shares. The announcement shall include:

1. The amount by which the basic capital has been increased;
2. The ratio of new shares to the old ones;
3. A reminder that the company has the right to sell shares at the shareholders' expense if they have not been collected within 1 year from the public announcement and after having repeated the invitation 3 times at an interval of at least 3 months.

(2) After the expiration of 1 year from the publication of the last reminder referred to in Paragraph 1, the company shall sell the uncollected shares at the shareholders' expense at the official stock-exchange price or, if there is no stock-exchange price, at the price realised during a public auction.

Article 196 Prohibited share issuing
(297 YEL, 219 GSCL)

Before the decision on capital increase has been registered, shares or interim shares may not be issued.

Article 197 Partially paid shares
(298 YEL, 215, 216 II GSCL)

(1) Partially paid shares participate in the capital increase according to their basic capital share. However, the increase cannot be carried out by issuing new shares. Instead, the par value of the partially paid shares is increased. If there are both partially and fully paid shares, capital increase for fully paid shares may be carried out either by increase of their par value or by issuing new shares. The decision on capital increase must mention which type of increase has been chosen for the fully paid shares.

(2) The capital increase referred to in Paragraph 1 increases the voting and profit-sharing rights of holders of partially paid shares accordingly. However, these rights exist only with respect to the partial amount paid in and the proportional increase.

Article 198 Start of profit-sharing
(299 YEL, 217 GSCL)

(1) New shares participate in the profits of the entire business year in which the decision on capital increase was made, unless otherwise provided by that decision.

(2) The decision on capital increase may provide that the new shares will already participate in the profits of the business year preceding the year in which the decision on capital increase was made.

Article 199 Protection of shareholders' rights
(302 YEL, 216 GSCL)

The rights connected to the shares are not changed by the capital increase.

Article 200 Capital increase and change of a single-member company status
(301 YEL)

A single-member company may use the capital increase to change its status and become a multi-member company by issuing shares to new shareholders. The change must be reported to the Registry.

Title 5 Convertible and Profit Sharing Bonds

Article 201 Convertible and profit sharing bonds
(247 YEL, 221 GSCL)

(1) Bonds the holders of which are guaranteed the right to conversion into shares or the pre-emption right in relation to shares (convertible bonds) and bonds connecting the rights of their holders to a shareholder's profit share (profit sharing bonds), may only be issued by decision of the general meeting.

(2) The general meeting may authorise the management to issue shares referred to in Paragraph 1 for a period not exceeding 5 years. The management shall report the decision referred to in Paragraph 1 to the Registry for registration and publication.

(3) Profit sharing bonds may award priority in profit sharing in the same way as participating preferential shares do as of Paragraph 5 of Article 123.

(4) With respect to the issue of convertible and profit sharing bonds, shareholders have a pre-emption right corresponding to a shareholder's pre-emption right during the emission of new shares.

SECTION 8 REDUCTION OF CAPITAL

Title 1 Ordinary Capital Reduction

Article 202 Conditions

(304 YEL, 222 GSCL)

(1) The basic capital of the company may be reduced by decision of the general meeting taken according to Paragraph 2 of Article 157.

(2) In the case that the decrease will interfere with the rights of a certain class of shares, the validity of the general meeting's decision is subject to the consent of the shareholders concerned which has to comply with the formal requirements of Paragraph 3 of Article 161.

(3) Capital reduction requires decreasing the shares' par value or, in case the par value should fall beneath the minimum value of Paragraph 1 of Article 101, the consolidation of shares.

Article 203 Registration and effectiveness of decision

(305 YEL; 223, 224 GSCL)

(1) The decision to reduce the basic capital shall be submitted to the Registry by the managing director and the chairman of the board of directors or the supervisory board. It shall be published on the company's website and in conformity with the provisions of the Registry Law.

(2) The basic capital is reduced from the time the decision has been registered.

Article 204 Protection of creditors' rights

(306 YEL, 225 GSCL, 32 Second Capital Directive)

(1) Creditors whose claims antedate the publication of the decision to make the reduction shall be entitled to obtain security for claims which have not fallen due by that date of publication. The right referred to in the first sentence can only be exercised if it was claimed by creditors within 90 days after publication.

(2) Payments to shareholders or release from their obligation to pay contributions based on the capital reduction may not be carried out prior to the expiration of the time-limit referred to in Paragraph 1 and not before creditors concerned have been paid or received security.

Article 205 Amortisation of shares

(307 YEL, 226 GSCL)

(1) When the company, in order to carry out a capital reduction, wants to

consolidate shares by conversion or similar procedure, it may publicly invite shareholders concerned to present these shares to the company. The announcement shall contain the declaration that, in case of non-compliance with the invitation, the shares will be invalidated.

(2) The company shall publish the announcement twice, with a 30-days interval, in an authorised newspaper as referred to in Paragraph 1 of Article 111 and on the company's website.

(3) New shares which have replaced invalidated ones shall be sold immediately through a stock broker for the stock exchange price or, in case such a price lacking, through public auction.

Article 206 Registration of accomplishment

(308 YEL, 227 GSCL)

(1) The managing director shall submit the accomplishment of the capital reduction to the Registry for registration.

(2) Application and registration of the accomplishment of the capital reduction and application and registration of the decision on the reduction may be united.

Article 207 Reduction below the minimum par value

(228 GSCL, 34 Second Directive)

The basic capital may only be reduced below the minimum amounts established in Article 98, if these amounts are regained by an increase of capital which was decided simultaneously with the reduction.

Title 2 Simplified Capital Reduction

Article 208 Conditions

(311 YEL, 229 GSCL)

(1) Capital reduction for the purposes of covering losses or transferring funds to reserves shall be carried out by simplified procedure.

(2) Simplified reduction may only be carried out, if amounts exceeding the mandatory reserves and profit reserves have been used up.

(3) Provisions of Articles 202, 203, and 205 to 207 apply accordingly.

Title 3 Capital Reduction by Withdrawal of Shares

Article 209 Conditions

(238, 312 YEL; 237 GSCL, 36 Second Directive, Behrens 31)

(1) Shares may be withdrawn in a compulsory way or after acquisition by the company.

(2) Compulsory withdrawal of shares is only allowed if it had been authorised by the statute or an amendment of the statute before the shares to be withdrawn were subscribed for. In case shareholders concerned agree on the withdrawal, no prior statutory provision is required.

(3) Any kind of withdrawal has to comply with the provisions of an ordinary capital reduction. Details of compulsory withdrawal shall be established by the statute or in the decision of the general meeting. Payment to shareholders pursuant to the withdrawal has to comply with the requirements of the second paragraph of Article 204.

(4) Provisions on ordinary capital reduction do not need to be complied with, if shares which are fully paid up are given to the company gratuitously. The decision of the general meeting is necessary also in this case. However, it may be taken by simple majority, if the statute does not provide otherwise. The managing director and the chairman of the board of directors or the supervisory board must submit the decision for registration to the Registry.

(5) In case of compulsory withdrawal ordered by the statute, the decision of the general meeting required for ordinary capital increase is replaced by the decision of the managing director.

(6) The capital is reduced when the decision has been registered or once the withdrawal comprising the annulment of rights deriving from the shares concerned has been carried out.

(7) Article 206 applies accordingly.

21. COMPANIES (5)

Preservation and Changes of Companies' Capital

During the lifetime of a company, the value of the company's assets will necessarily vary according to the company's economic development. It cannot therefore be excluded that the value of the assets may be reduced so as to be no longer sufficient to cover the company's capital. Since shareholders are usually not personally liable to the company's creditors, **preservation of the company's capital** is an essential concern. In this respect the Law again applies legal concepts that are in line with the Second Directive.

First, the Law normally **prohibits any return of investments** to the shareholders, Arts. 135 and 248. **Only profits** declared in the annual accounts of the company may be distributed out of the company's assets to the shareholders, Arts. 136 and 249. Such dividends may however only be defined after at least 5 percent of the annual profits have been set aside as a **mandatory reserve** until 10 percent of the basic capital or a higher ratio established by the statute have been reached, Art. 137 (1) and (3).

Prohibited payments must be refunded to the company, Arts. 138 and 251. **In case of limited liability companies, if collection from a member of the sum to be refunded is impossible, the other members are proportionately liable,** Art. 251 (3). This special obligation shows the more 'personal' relationship between members in a limited liability company the capital of which usually depends on the contributions of a limited number of members. The German Law on Limited Liability Companies even generalises the concept inherent to Art. 251 (3) and declares the other members proportionally liable in all cases where (parts of) contributions cannot be obtained from a member. Courts might consider applying this approach, too.

Second, the Law addresses the **problem of hidden dividends**. A transaction between the company and its shareholders may be used as a disguised transfer of wealth from the company to the shareholders. Therefore, it is **prohibited for the company to pay any amount exceeding the market value of a transaction** to shareholders, Arts. 139 and 252.

Arts. 140 (1) and 253 particularly provide that a shareholder who granted **debt financing** to the company on terms less favourable than usual are excluded, in case of bankruptcy, from asking for repayment, where such repayment would reduce the capital of the company to below its basic capital. If repayment has already occurred during the year preceding the bankruptcy of the company, shareholders are obliged to refund the payment, Arts. 141 and 254. The same rules apply to loans granted by third parties for which shareholders have provided guarantee, Arts. 140 (2) and 141 (2). Art. 141 (3) extends the effect of Art. 141 (1) and (2) to similar transactions.

For limited liability companies which depend usually on a restricted number of members, the German Federal Court went even further and generalised the debt financing concept of Arts. 140 and 141 in order to prevent any hidden return of investments in breach of Arts. 135 and 248: in a situation where a responsible member would have invested additional capital, any loan granted to the company to compensate capital losses shall be treated as a contribution which may not be returned to the member in question.

Third, Arts. 143 and 255 **prohibit the subscription** by the company or by one of its subsidiaries to **the company's own shares**. The reason for this lies in the fact that the company does not gain any new investment; it reduces its assets without any compensation.

Likewise, **acquisition** of own shares endangers the company property. Economically it corresponds to a return of contributions. This is not in line with the principal of capital raising and maintenance and the interest of creditors. There is also the risk that management artificially keeps share prices high by buying up shares of the company with company assets. Therefore, acquisition or mortgaging by the company or by one of its subsidiaries of such shares **are limited to certain legitimate circumstances**, Arts. 144–7 and 255. Even then, the shares to be acquired must have been fully paid up and they must not represent more than 10 percent of the company's capital, Art. 144 (2). The company must dispose of the shares within 3 years, otherwise they must be annulled, Art. 144 (5). According to Art. 144 (7), the voting rights relating to the company's own shares are suspended. Companies are furthermore prevented from extending advances or loans to third parties and from securing any advance or credit for the purpose of acquiring their own shares, Art. 147. Single-member companies are totally precluded from acquiring or mortgaging their own shares, Art. 148.

Fourth, a **reduction of the company's capital** (Arts. 202–9, 275) which may lead to a return of investments to shareholders is subject to safeguards in favour of the company's creditors who are entitled to collect their claims or to ask for securities before the reduction of the company's capital may become effective, Art. 204. Capital reduction is usually carried out to compensate for losses, to increase legal reserves or to reorganise the company. It requires a decision of three-quarters of the general meeting as well as the increase of capital, Art. 157 (2).

Capital reduction for reorganisation usually combines a reduction with an increase of capital. The reason for this is to adapt the statutory capital to the real capital status of the company. This is to avoid capital losses requiring to be compensated over many years without the company being able to pay any dividends, a situation which is not attractive for new investors. The reduction of capital has the effect that only the old shareholders are bearing the losses. The simultaneous increase of capital by emission of new shares brings in the necessary new investments, and the new shareholders have the chance to immediately benefit from dividends. This procedure is mandatory in case the capital is reduced below the legal minimum capital level. In this case a simultaneous increase must at least regain the legal minimum capital, Art. 207.

Fifth, as far as an increase of the company's capital is concerned, creditors' as well as shareholders' interests require protection. Besides being an adequate instrument for reorganisation, capital increase is mainly an instrument to finance the company's expansion. This is, for example, an important instrument if acquisition of financial capital from outside sources is too expensive because interest rates are very high.

In such a situation, creditors are appropriately protected by applying the rules relating to the raising of the company's capital during the formation of the company accordingly, Arts. 183 and 275. Shareholders are protected by a **right of pre-emption for new shares**, Arts. 184 and 275, or, in case of an increase of capital out of company reserves, by the right to receive new shares, Arts. 194 and 275. Often the increase is carried out with the help of banks which subscribe to the shares while agreeing to offer them to shareholders to honour their pre-emption right.

The right of **pre-emption may be excluded** by a decision of the general meeting on the increase of the company's capital, Arts. 184 (3) and 275. Since this may give rise to abuses by majority shareholders, the managing director must present a written report to the meeting indicating the reasons for restriction or withdrawal and justifying the proposed issue price. It is important to note that **only a real interest** of the company should legitimate the intrusion into shareholders' pre-emption rights. The measure is only justified if an adequate balance between means and aims is maintained.

The Law also incorporates the concept of a conditional increase of capital, Arts. 187, 201 and 275, and of authorised capital, Arts. 191 and 275.

Sixth, whenever the assets no longer cover the company's capital, the company is no longer doing business at the risk of the shareholders – whose investment is lost in this case – but at the risk of the company's creditors. The legal solution of this problem lies in **insolvency law**: A company, but also other enterprises, which have lost their capital must be compelled to exit the market. Insolvency law is therefore an indispensable element of a viable system of enterprise law. Arts. 53, 210 and 276 make sure that any enterprise is dissolved in case of insolvency.

In this context we recall the **special organisational duties of management** which we mentioned in the comments on 'Fiduciary Duties'. As regards the context **of capital maintenance**, the duties listed by Arts. 176 (4) and 274 (4) provide that management is specifically prevented from engaging in any transaction which may lead to the depletion of the company's capital. The general meeting has to be convened, if annual or interim accounts show or if it is clear that losses are amounting to 50 percent of the basic capital. The same applies, if the company is becoming insolvent or over-indebted, Arts. 151 (3), 166 (2), 171 (4), 259 (3), 271 (4), or in the case that the company is proposing to dispose of a substantial proportion of its assets, Art. 166 (2). Responsibility for the creation of an early warning system (Art. 171 (3) 5), and for the probity of financial statements and other key data (Art. 177), are other indirect legal capital protection devices.

Finally, Art. 24 provides for directors' **personal liability for the company's debts in case of misuse** of the company for illegal purposes, in case of mingling of the company's assets with their own private assets, or in case of a decrease in the company's assets in spite of financial difficulties of the company.

SECTION 9 DISSOLUTION AND LIQUIDATION

Article 210 Dissolution
(100 YEL, 262 GSCL, Behrens 34)

(1) The joint-stock company is dissolved

- By expiry of the period for which it was established;
- By decision of the general meeting;
- By opening of an insolvency procedure;
- If it has not carried out any business activities for two years;
- By court decision;
- By Registry decision taken *ex officio*, due to lack or unlawfulness of the following statute provisions not regularised within 3 months as ordered by the Registry: enterprise name, registered office, object, legal capital, nominal value and number of shares subscribed, classes of shares and their number, qualification of registered or bearer shares; number of managing directors.

(2) Reduction of number of shareholders to one does not lead to company dissolution. The second paragraph of Article 107 applies.

Article 211 Registration of dissolution
(315 YEL, 263 GSCL)

The managing director has to submit the dissolution of the company to the Registry for registration. In case of dissolution by court decision, the court has to register the dissolution *ex officio*.

Title 1 Ordinary Liquidation

Article 212 Appointment of liquidators
(314 YEL, 264, 265 GSCL, Behrens 34)

(1) After dissolution, liquidation will be carried out unless a bankruptcy procedure has been opened with respect to the company's assets. Unless otherwise established in this Title, provisions regarding undissolved companies apply to the company under liquidation.

(2) Liquidation shall be carried out by liquidators appointed by the general meeting. If the general meeting fails to appoint liquidators within 30 days after the dissolution, shareholders representing at least 5 percent of the basic capital or a smaller amount provided by the statute or company creditors whose unsatisfied claims against the company amount to at least 5 percent of the basic capital may request the court to appoint the liquidators. These shareholders and creditors have the same right if they show sufficient reasons that the liquidation objective might be impaired by the liquidators appointed by the general meeting. The request to the court must be filed within 30 days of the appointment by the general meeting.

Article 213 Dismissal of liquidators
(318 YEL)

(1) Liquidators who have not been appointed by the court may be dismissed by the general meeting at any time. General civil and labour law rules apply for claims deriving from employment contracts.

(2) The court shall dismiss the liquidators whom it appointed. Shareholders and creditors as referred to in Paragraph 2 of Article 212 may request the liquidators to be discharged for the reasons provided in the third sentence of that paragraph.

Article 214 Registration of liquidators
(315, 316, no. 317 YEL; 266, 267 GSCL)

(1) The managing director will submit the name of the first liquidators and their authority to represent the company together with corresponding documents to the Registry. Liquidators shall deposit their signature. They shall report each change with respect to their identity or power of attorney. Appointment of liquidators by the court shall be registered *ex officio*.

(2) The words 'in liquidation' shall be added to the company's registered name.

Article 215 Invitation to creditors
(314 YEL, 267 GSCL)

Liquidators must invite the company's creditors to file their claims with respect to the dissolution of the company. The company shall publish the announcement twice, with a 30-days interval, in an authorised newspaper as referred to in Paragraph 1 of Article 111 and on the company's website. The announcement must declare that claims must be filed within 30 days from the last announcement.

Article 216 Rights and duties of liquidators
(319, 320 YEL, 268 GSCL)

(1) Liquidators shall bring the current business transactions to a close, collect claims, sell remaining assets and pay creditors. Liquidators may conclude new business transactions for the purpose of bringing current transactions to a close. Within the limits of their assignment, liquidators have the same rights as managing directors. They are subjected to the supervisory function of the board of directors or the supervisory board. Article 25 does not apply to them. Any restriction of their power shall have no effect as against third parties.

(2) If, based on claims filed by creditors as referred to in Article 215, liquidators find that company assets are not sufficient to settle these claims including interest, they shall suspend the liquidation proceedings and file a request to the competent court to open insolvency proceedings.

Article 217 Balance sheets
(321 YEL, 270 GSCL)

The liquidator shall prepare a balance sheet at the beginning and at the end of the liquidation. If the liquidation procedure is conducted for longer than a year, the liquidator shall also prepare the general partnership's statements of account at the end of the business year.

Article 218 Liquidator's report and recommended decision
(322 YEL)

Once the claims of the company's creditors have been settled, liquidators shall prepare a report on the liquidation proceedings and recommend a decision on distribution of remaining assets to the general meeting. The general meeting shall decide on the adoption of the report and recommendation.

Article 219 Distribution of assets
(323, 325 YEL, 271 GSCL)

Once the company's obligations have been settled, remaining assets shall be distributed among the shareholders in proportion to the par value of their shares unless preferences are granted by the statute. If assets are not enough to repay contributions, the shareholders bear this loss with respect to their share in the basic capital. If necessary, outstanding contributions shall be collected for this purpose from the shareholders concerned.

Article 220 Protection of creditors
(323 II, 325, 326 YEL, 272 GSCL)

(1) The liquidator may not distribute the remaining assets among shareholders prior to the expiration of 6 months from the publication of the second call to the creditors to file their claims.

(2) In case a creditor known to the liquidator does not claim his rights, the amount due shall be deposited with the court and goods shall be deposited in a public warehouse. The general rules on deposit apply.

(3) If, for the time being, an obligation cannot be settled or if it is controversial, the assets may only be distributed if the creditor has obtained security.

Article 221 Remuneration of liquidators
(327 YEL)

(1) Liquidators' expenses shall be reimbursed and remuneration paid for their work from the assets of the company as established by decision of the general meeting or of the court which appointed them.

(2) Liquidators' remuneration and expenses shall be paid once creditors' claims have been settled, and before the distribution of assets among shareholders.

Article 222 End of liquidation
(323III, 328 YEL, 273 I GSCL)

Once the assets have been distributed, the liquidator shall report the end of liquidation to the Registry including the declaration that all assets have been distributed in accordance with the decision on distribution. The company shall be deleted from the Register.

Article 223 Preservation of books and documents
(328 YEL, 273 II and III GSCL)

(1) The books and documents of the liquidated company shall be deposited at a safe location as determined by the Registry.

(2) Shareholders and creditors have the right to inspect the books and documents.

Article 224 Liquidator's liability
(324 YEL)

(1) Once the company has been deleted from the Register, liquidators' actions shall not be the subject of an appeal.

(2) Paragraphs 1 to 4 of Article 176 apply accordingly to the liquidator's liability to creditors for any damage caused during the liquidation proceedings. If there are several liquidators, they shall be jointly and severally liable. Besides the liquidators, the shareholders shall be jointly and severally liable up to the amounts of the eventual liquidation value. Creditors who did not file their claims in time as referred to in Article 215 or who were not and could not have been known to the liquidator, shall not be entitled to claim damages as referred to in the first and second sentences.

(3) Claims referred to in Paragraph 2 must be brought within 1 year after the company's deletion from the Register.

Title 2 Summary Liquidation

Article 225 Conditions and procedure
(329 YEL, Behrens 34)

(1) The company may be liquidated by summary procedure, if, after the decision to apply this procedure, all shareholders make court-authenticated statements that all commitments of the company concerning its creditors and employees have been settled.

(2) The shareholders shall be jointly and severally liable for the company's

commitments for 3 years after the date of the company's deletion from the Register.

(3) The court may request evidence concerning the truth of the statement referred to in Paragraph 1 and request security for the payments due to creditors.

(4) The managing director has to report the decision on liquidating the company by summary procedure to the Registry.

Article 226 Appealing the decision on summary procedure
(330 YEL)

(1) Shareholders, creditors or other parties with legal interests may appeal the decision to liquidate the company through summary procedure at the competent court within 15 days from the date of its announcement.

(2) The court shall annul the decision of summary procedure, if it considers that shareholders and creditors risk incurring damage through this procedure. In this case, the court will appoint one or more liquidators to conduct the liquidation by ordinary procedure.

(3) If the decision on summary procedure has been annulled, shareholders' statements on settlement of the company's commitments shall have no legal effect.

(4) The annulment of the decision on summary procedure has to be reported to the Registry.

Article 227 Joint and several liability of shareholders
(331 YEL)

At the end of the summary procedure, the company shall be deleted from the Register. Names and addresses or registered names and offices of shareholders shall be registered indicating their joint and several liability for the company's commitments for up to 3 years after the deletion.

22. COMPANIES (6)

Dissolution and Liquidation (other than Insolvency)

The dissolution of the company normally depends upon a resolution of the general meeting, Arts. 210, 276. On the one hand, this rule recognises the right of the shareholders as 'owners' of the company. On the other hand, there are certain instances where the company may be dissolved by decision of the court or the

Registry even against the will of the shareholders. The Registry may dissolve the company ex officio due to lack or unlawfulness of certain statute provisions which are not regularised within 3 months as ordered by the Registry (for joint-stock companies: enterprise name, registered office, objects, legal capital, nominal value and number of shares subscribed, classes of shares and their number, qualification of registered or bearer shares; number of managing directors). Once dissolved, the company must be liquidated. Arts. 212–27 and 280 of the Draft set out the procedure for liquidation and the safeguards for creditors and shareholders.

5. Limited liability companies

SECTION 1 GENERAL PROVISIONS AND FORMATION

Article 228 Definition

(332, 333 YEL, Behrens 16, 17)

(1) A limited liability company is an enterprise founded by natural or juridical persons which are not liable for the company's commitments and which personally bear losses only to the extent of any unpaid parts of stipulated contributions. Members' contributions constitute the company's initial capital.

(2) Each member shall acquire his share in the company in proportion to his contribution. Each member of the company may have only one share which may bear several voting rights.

(3) Shares may not be represented by negotiable share certificates.

(4) A limited liability company may not have more than *50* members, except if members are company employees acquiring interests under privileged conditions according to special laws.

Article 229 Application for registration

(342 YEL)

(1) In order to be registered, all managing directors and, if applicable, members of the board of directors or supervisory board have to submit the following information to the Registry:

- Legal form of enterprise;
- Duration, unless founded for an indefinite time;
- Enterprise name;
- Registered office;
- Type of business;
- Basic capital;
- Date the statute was established;
- Name, surname, date and place of birth as well as residence of the managing directors;
- Rules of the statute establishing representation authority;
- Any approval by public authorities if necessary.

The managing directors and, if applicable, the chairman of the board of directors or supervisory board shall deposit their signatures with the Registry. The managing directors shall report any change of registered data occurring during the conduct of the company's business.

(2) All data reported to the Registry shall be placed and be available on the company's website.

Article 230 Statute
(YEL 334, Behrens 19, 20)

In addition to the items referred to in Article 4, the statute of a limited liability company shall also include the following:

1. The number of company members;
2. The total amount, or at least an estimate, of all the costs payable by the company or chargeable to it by reason of its formation;
3. Any special advantages granted at the time of the company's formation to any person who took part in the formation.
4. Any accessory agreement between the company and a member beyond his contribution and any penalties requested for failed or untimely fulfilment;
5. Any authorisation of the general meeting to prescribe additional payments;
6. The decision-making procedure to be followed in case of equal number of votes.

Article 231 Basic capital and minimum single contribution
(336 YEL, Behrens 17)

(1) The basic capital shall not be less than 5,000 Euro calculated at the exchange rate valid on the day of payment.

(2) Member's contribution in cash may not be less than 500 Euro, calculated at the exchange rate valid on the day of payment.

(3) If members acquire shares under privileged terms pursuant to special regulations, the cash-contribution may be lower.

Article 232 Payment and transfer of contributions
(337, 339 YEL, Behrens 20, 21)

(1) Contributions shall be wholly subscribed prior to entry in the Registry.

(2) Contributions may consist of cash or property and rights expressed in money. They may not consist of labour or services. The provisions of Article 106 apply accordingly with respect to contributions in kind. Contributions in

kind must be transferred wholly to the company assets before registration, in a manner which depends on their character or as provided by the statute.

(3) 50 percent of each stipulated cash-contribution must be paid up before registration. However, the overall paid up amount may not be lower than 50 percent of the entire cash portion of the legal capital. The outstanding amounts are payable within 2 years from the company's registration.

(4) If the entire cash-contribution to the basic capital is higher than the equivalent of 15,000 Euro calculated at the exchange rate on the day of payment, at least 25 percent of that amount shall be paid in prior to the company's registration.

(5) Payments with respect to Paragraphs 1 to 3 shall be made into a suspense bank account as defined by the statute. A statement of the bank confirming the deposit of cash-contributions will be submitted to the Registry together with the application for registration. The funds may be managed by company organs only after registration.

(6) Shareholders who fail to pay or transfer their contributions in time, shall be liable to the company with respect to Paragraphs 2 and 3 of Article 9. Article 133 applies accordingly to the delay of payments.

Article 233 Formation costs and founders' report on formation

(339, 340 YEL, Behrens 21)

The provisions of Articles 103 and 104 apply accordingly to the company's formation costs and founders' report regarding the formation procedure.

Article 234 Special rules for single-member companies

(341 YEL, Behrens 19)

Article 107 also applies to limited liability companies.

SECTION 2 SHARES AND TRANSFER OF SHARES

Article 235 Acquisition of share and co-ownership

(344 III to VII YEL, 18 GLLC, Behrens 31)

(1) The share acquired on the basis of a contribution may belong to one or several persons.

(2) If a share belongs to several persons, these persons shall be regarded as one member in relation to the company and they shall exercise their rights through a common representative. They are, however, jointly and severally liable for the commitments encumbering membership.

(3) Several members owning one share may agree that they own this share in equal or different parts.

(4) Company's actions in relation to the share will have effect as against all owners even if it was addressed to only one of them.

(5) The company may issue a certificate in order to prove the ownership of the share. Such certificate shall not have the character of a security. The certificate shall be issued in the name of the members concerned.

Article 236 Preferential shares
(364 YEL, Behrens 32)

(1) Provisions of Articles 123, 124 and 161 regarding preferential shares in joint-stock companies apply accordingly to preferential shares in limited liability companies.

(2) The statute may determine members' rights arising from preferential shares.

Article 237 Book of company members
(343 YEL, Behrens 31)

(1) Each company shall keep a book of company members. The book shall include the following particulars:

1. Name and address or registered name and registered office of each member;
2. Contribution of each member and the amount paid in;
3. Any changes regarding membership data registered before.

(2) Members may inspect the book as well as the documents on the basis of which the particulars were entered. Other interested persons may do so subject to the company's approval.

Article 238 Transfer of shares
(349 YEL, 15 GLLCL, Behrens 31)

(1) A share may be transferred without restrictions among members of the limited liability company. The statute may require the transfer of shares to fulfil specific conditions. The company's consent shall be needed for a share transfer if a member has not performed all his obligations.

(2) If a member acquires several shares these shares shall be united in one share if contributions on all shares concerned have been fully paid up and, if applicable, additional payments made.

(3) A share may be transferred to a third party. In this case the other members and the company have a pre-emptive right as determined by the statute. If members and the company have not expressed their wish to purchase the share within 30 days from the date on which it was offered for sale, the share may be transferred to a third party under terms which may not be more favourable for the buyer.

(4) If several members of a limited liability company express their wish to buy a share and no agreement is reached between the transferor and these members, the stock shall be divided among them in proportion to their shares, unless otherwise provided by the statute.

Article 239 Transfer by execution procedure
(350 YEL)

(1) If the share of a member is sold by execution procedure, the court shall notify the company members and the company of the permission to sell and an appraisal of the share.

(2) If the members and the company itself fail to express their wish to buy the share within 15 days from the receipt of the notification, the share shall be sold in accordance with the execution procedure rules.

Article 240 Transfer of share in case of a member's death or exit
(351 YEL)

(1) In case of death or exit of a member of a limited liability company, his share shall be transferred to his heir or legal successor, unless otherwise provided by the statute.

(2) If the statute excludes the transfer of a share in these circumstances, it shall provide that the share has to be bought by members or the company itself.

(3) If the members or the company itself do not buy the share, it shall be withdrawn against full payment therefore, in conformity with the provisions on capital reduction.

Article 241 Consequences of transfer
(352 YEL)

(1) If a share is being transferred, the transferor and transferee shall be jointly and severally liable to the company for obligations associated with the membership.

(2) The share must be transferred by written agreement.

(3) The transferor of the share shall notify the company of the change of

owner and of the date of such change for the purpose of the change being registered in the book of company members.

(4) The transfer of the share shall have legal effect in relation to the company from the moment that the transfer is registered in the book of members.

Article 242 Parts of shares and transfer of parts

(353 YEL, 17 GLLCL)

(1) A share may be divided into parts in case of inheritance and legal succession.

(2) The statute may exclude division into parts, except in the case of the transfer of shares among company members.

(3) The provisions relating to the transfer of shares apply accordingly to the transfer of parts of shares.

SECTION 3 LEGAL RELATIONSHIPS BETWEEN COMPANY AND MEMBERS

Article 243 No release from obligation to bring in contributions

(338, 344 I, II YEL, Behrens 31)

(1) Articles 132 to 135 apply accordingly with respect to members' obligations to bring in their contributions, the rules in case of payment delay, the prohibition of releasing company members from their obligation or from offsetting from their contributions claims they have against the company.

Article 244 Accessory obligations

(345 YEL)

The statute may establish further obligations of members as against the company beyond the membership obligations in this law.

Article 245 Additional payments

(346 YEL, Behrens 31)

(1) The general meeting of a limited liability company may decide that members have to make additional payments and fix the amount payable, if so provided by the statute.

(2) Additional payments shall not increase members' shares or the basic capital.

(3) Additional payments shall be set in proportion to the shares.

(4) Members may not offset any claims against the obligation of additional payments.

Article 246 Delay of additional payment
(347 YEL, Behrens 31)

The provision of Article 133 regarding the delay of payment of contributions in a joint-stock company shall apply accordingly to the delay of additional payment, unless otherwise provided by the statute.

Article 247 Refunding additional payments
(348 YEL, 30 II GLLCL)

(1) Additional payments which are not serving to cover losses of the basic capital, may be refunded to members, but not sooner than 30 days after the refunding decision has been announced to the members.

(2) Additional payments may not be refunded before contributions have been paid up.

Article 248 Prohibition of return of contributions
(356 YEL, 30 I GLLCL, Behrens 32)

Contributions on shares may not be returned to the members, except in cases set by this law.

Article 249 Profit distribution
(354 YEL, 29 GLLCL, Behrens 33)

(1) Members are entitled to a share in the profit declared in the annual profit and loss account, unless otherwise provided by the statute.

(2) The profit shall be distributed among the members in proportion to their shares, unless otherwise provided by the statute.

(3) The provisions of Article 136 apply accordingly to the distribution of profits in a limited liability companies.

Article 250 Mandatory and other reserves
(51, 52, 56 YEL)

(1) Article 137 on mandatory and other reserves applies accordingly to limited liability companies.

Article 251 Refunding prohibited payments
(357 YEL, 31 I, III GLLCL, Behrens 33)

(1) Shareholders shall return to the company any advantage including dividends received contrary to the provisions of this law.

(2) The company's claims referred to in Paragraph 1 may be brought according to Paragraph 3 of Article 9.

(3) If a refund cannot be recovered from the member who received the unlawful payment, the other members are liable for the payment in proportion to their shares. Any amount which cannot be collected from one or more of these members shall be borne by the other ones in proportion to their shares.

(4) The prescription term for claims deriving from Paragraphs 1 to 3 shall start on the date of illegal payment.

Article 252 Adequate remuneration for transactions between company and shareholders
(355 YEL, Behrens 33)

Article 139 applies accordingly on remuneration for legal transactions between the limited liability company and a member.

Article 253 No repayment of inadequate credit
(359 YEL, 32a GLLCL, Behrens 33)

The provisions of Article 140 shall apply accordingly to inadequate credits granted to the company by a member.

Article 254 Liablity for repayed credits
(360 YEL, 32b GLLCL, Behrens 33)

The provisions of Article 141 shall apply accordingly to the liability for the repayment of inadequate credits by the company to members prior to bankruptcy proceedings.

Article 255 Acquisition and treatment of company's own shares
(358, 361 YEL, 33 GLLCL, Behrens 33)

The provisions of Articles 143 through 148 shall apply accordingly to the subscription to company's own shares, acquisition of its own shares, directly or by third parties, on accepting its own shares as pledge, credits to others to buy its own shares and to the exclusion of single-member companies from acquiring their own shares.

Article 256 Withdrawal of shares
(362 YEL, 34 GLLCL, Behrens 32)

(1) A share may be withdrawn if the statute allows. In this case, the statute shall determine the grounds and procedures for the withdrawal.

(2) A share may always be withdrawn, if the members concerned agree, unless otherwise provided by the statute.

(3) The member whose share has been withdrawn shall forfeit his rights and duties based on the share.

(4) The withdrawal has to comply with provisions on capital maintenance and capital reduction.

SECTION 4 COMPANY ORGANS

Article 257 Kinds
(60, 365 YEL, Behrens 23)

(1) The organs of a limited liability company shall be the general meeting and the managing directors, unless a board of directors or supervisory board is required by Paragraph 2 of Article 27. In that case, the company has the choice between a one-tier or two-tier solution. Articles 166 to 177 and 178 to 180 apply accordingly with respect to functions and liabilities concerned.

Title 1 General Meeting

Article 258 Rights and duties
(366 YEL, Behrens 27, 28)

(1) The general meeting shall decide on the following company matters:

1. Setting the business policies;
2. Amendments to the statute;
3. Creating of by-laws and their amendments;
4. Election and dismissal of the managing directors and, if applicable, of the members of the board of directors and the supervisory board, unless they are elected by the company's employees with respect to Article 27;
5. Election and dismissal of independent auditors and liquidators;
6. Establishment of remunerations to persons mentioned under no.s 4 and 5;
7. Monitoring and supervising the implementation of business policies by managing directors, including preparation of the annual statement of accounts and the performance report;
8. Adoption of the annual statement of accounts and performance reports;
9. Distribution of annual profits;

10. Additional payments;
11. Refunding additional payments;
12. Increase or decrease of the basic capital;
13. Dividing shares into parts and withdrawal of shares;
14. Representation of the company in court and in other proceedings against managing directors or, if applicable, against members of the board of directors or supervisory board;
15. Realising, either through other company organs or special representatives, the company's claims against managing directors, members of the board of directors or supervisory board or shareholders concerning indemnity for damage or other obligations resulting from company formation or ongoing business;
16. Changes in the company status, company restructuring and dissolution;
17. Adoption of its own rules of procedure;
18. Other matters set by law or the statute.

(2) The general meeting shall decide on Items 7 and 8 after having obtained the relevant documents together with the report of the auditor, and, if applicable, the report of the board of directors or supervisory board.

(3) Paragraph 4 of Article 150 applies accordingly to the rights and duties of the general meeting in a single-member liability company as being performed by the single member.

23. COMPANIES (7)

Governance of Limited Liability Companies

Limited liability companies are basically exempted from any 'board structures'. In order to respond to the smaller size and the more 'personal' character of relations between members, the Law requires just the general meeting and managing directors, Art. 257, with the general meeting having quite a strong position as we have seen above: besides defining the business policies, the general meeting is also in charge of monitoring and supervising the implementation by managing directors, Art. 258, and its functions may be extended by the statute (including decisions amending the statute). Board structures must be introduced by limited liability companies, too, in case their number of employees exceeds 50, Art. 27. This solution is perfectly acceptable from the European law point of view.

Article 259 Convening the general meeting
(367 YEL, Behrens 28)

(1) The general meeting shall be convened in cases established by this Law, other laws or by the statute and if it is necessary to safeguard the company's interests. The ordinary general meeting shall be convened at least once a year.

(2) The general meeting shall be convened by the managing directors or, if applicable, in cases requested by the present law, by the board of directors, the supervisory board or by shareholders.

(3) The general meeting has to be convened, if annual or interim accounts show or if it is clear that losses amounting to 50 percent of the basic capital occur. The same applies, if the company is becoming insolvent.

Article 260 Method of convening
(368 YEL)

(1) The general meeting shall be convened by letter or, if so provided by the statute, by electronic mail. The letter or mail and the agenda for the meeting must be delivered to all members not later than 7 days before the scheduled date of the meeting.

(2) In case the general meeting has not been convened in conformity with Paragraph 1, the general meeting may adopt decisions only if all members agree.

(3) The provision of Paragraph 2 shall also apply to decision-making on matters which are not included in the proposed agenda, provided that the proposed addition to the agenda has been presented to the company members not later than 3 days before the scheduled date of the meeting.

Article 261 Representation of members
(369 YEL)

(1) A member may be represented at the general meeting by another member authorised by him or another authorised person.

(2) Managing directors or, if applicable, members of the board of directors or supervisory board may not represent other members at the general meeting.

Article 262 Quorum
(370 YEL)

(1) In case of ordinary decisions, the general meeting may only make valid decisions if attended by subscribers holding more than 30 percent of the subscribed voting shares. In case of matters requiring qualified majorities, the

general meeting may only make valid decisions if the members having more than half of the total number of votes are present, unless the statute requires another qualified majority for the proceedings of the general meeting.

(2) If the general meeting could not be held due to lack of the quorum referred to in Paragraph 1, the meeting shall be reconvened with the same proposed agenda, in conformity with the statute.

Article 263 Decision-making
(371, 381 YEL, Behrens 28, 29)

(1) The statute may be amended by a three-quarters majority of votes of attending members unless a higher majority is provided by the statute. If the amendment is increasing the duties of company members, approval of those members concerned is mandatory.

(2) The general meeting shall make also the following decisions by three-quarters majority of votes of the attending members, unless the statute requires a higher majority for these decisions: appointment and removal of managing directors or, if applicable, the members of the board of directors or the supervisory board, increase and reduction of basic capital, changes of status, company restructuring, dissolution and profit distribution.

(3) On other matters listed in Article 258, the general meeting shall decide by majority of votes of the attending members, unless otherwise provided by this Law or the statute.

(4) The validity of any decision imposing additional commitments onto members or reducing their rights as provided by this Law or the statute, is subjected to the consent of all members concerned, unless otherwise provided by this Law.

Article 264 Right to vote
(372 YEL)

(1) Any member has the voting right in proportion to his contribution, unless holding a preference share without voting rights as of Article 236. The statute shall determine the amount of share granting one vote.

(2) The statute may not provide that a member may have more votes than relates to his share in the company.

Article 265 Voting in writing
(373 YEL)

A member may vote in absentia either by letter or by electronic mail, if the authenticity of the member is guaranteed. Details on the manner of absentia voting may be set by the statute.

Article 266 Method of voting
(374 YEL)

The provisions of Article 158 shall apply accordingly to the method of voting in the general meetings of limited liability companies.

Article 267 Exclusion of voting right
(375 YEL, Behrens 32)

The provisions of Article 160 shall apply accordingly to the exclusion of a member from voting at the general meeting.

Article 268 Convention on request of a minority of members
(376 YEL)

(1) Members representing at least 5 percent of the company's basic capital or a smaller portion set by the statute, may request the managing director in writing including electronic mail to convene a general meeting. The request must contain the reasons and objectives and the matters the general meeting should decide on.

(2) Members referred to in Paragraph 1 may request certain issues be put on the agenda for decision-making at a convened general meeting.

(3) Members referred to in Paragraphs 1 and 2 are entitled to convene a general meeting in conformity with Paragraph 1 of Article 260 or put the issue in question on the agenda, if their request has not been accepted.

(4) Should, contrary to Paragraph 3, the general meeting not be held or the issue in question not be put on the agenda, the members concerned may request the company to buy up their shares in conformity with this Law.

Article 269 Minutes of meeting
(377 YEL)

The provisions of Article 156 apply accordingly to the minutes of the general meeting of a limited liability company.

Article 270 Special investigation, annulment of unlawful decision and compensation
(73, 74, 79, 80, 81 YEL)

Articles 162 to 165 apply accordingly for special investigation into irregularities of formation and ongoing business, for the annulment of unlawful decisions of company organs and for the realisation of claims concerning compensation of damages against members, managing directors or, if applicable, against members of the board of directors or supervisory board.

Title 2 Managing Directors

Article 271 Appointment, rights and duties

(60, 63, 68, 378 YEL)

(1) The general meeting shall nominate one or more natural persons as managing directors for a term established by the statute not exceeding 5 years, with the possibility of re-election. The nomination has legal effect once it is registered in the Registry. The statute may establish rules regarding the nomination.

(2) The managing director of a parent enterprise may not be elected managing director of a subsidiary and vice versa. The managing directors of a parent enterprise may not be the chairman of the board of directors of a subsidiary, and the managing director of a subsidiary may not be the chairman of the board of directors of a parent enterprise. Any election made contrary to these provisions is null and void.

(3) The managing directors shall:

1. Manage the company's business by implementing the policies defined by the general meeting;
2. Represent the company;
3. Ensure that the necessary accountancy books and documents are kept;
4. Provide for and sign the annual statement of accounts and consolidated accounts and the performance report and present it to the board for approval together with the proposals for the distribution of profits which the managing director will make in the general meeting;
5. Create an early warning system with respect to developments threatening the existence of the company;
6. Submit company data to be registered to the Registry, if not otherwise provided by this Law;
7. Cause the corporation to purchase its own shares;
8. Cause the company to incur substantial debt through loans or other instruments;
9. Establish lasting business cooperations and propose policies regarding the formation of new companies or groups
10. Report to the general meeting with respect to the implementation of business policies and to the realisation of transactions of particular importance for company performance;
11. Perform other duties set by law or the statute.

(4) If annual or interim accounts show or if it is clear that losses amounting to 50 per cent of the basic capital occur, the managing director has to immediately convene a general meeting in order to consider whether the company should be wound up or if any other measure should be taken. The same applies, if the company is becoming insolvent.

(5) In case more than one managing directors are nominated, they manage the company jointly. The statute or by-laws established by the general meeting may provide otherwise.

(6) The general meeting may discharge the managing directors at any time, unless the statute provides otherwise. General civil law rules apply for claims deriving from any employment contract.

Article 272 Representation
(35 GLLCL)

(1) Managing directors' authority to represent the company cannot be limited. Paragraphs 2 and 3 of article 16 apply.

(2) Managing directors entitled to represent the company jointly may authorise some of them to carry out certain transactions or certain kinds of transactions. Declarations which are supposed to be received by the company may be addressed to one of the managing directors.

(3) A managing director's entitlement to representation and any change therof shall be reported for entry to the Registry.

Article 273 Remuneration
(269–71, 273 YEL, Behrens 25)

(1) The salary of managing directors may be supplemented by incentives (profit shares or similar). This remuneration must adequately reflect the duties of the managing director and the financial situation of the company.

(2) In case the company's financial standing is seriously deteriorating, the benefits granted as of the second paragraph may be adequately reduced if so determined by the general meeting in accordance with Article 173.

(3) Criteria for remuneration, the individual remuneration and the annual impact of the remuneration on the company's cost structure shall be disclosed together with the annual financial statement as of no. 8 of the first paragraph of Article 258.

Article 274 Fiduciary duties and liability
(43 GLLCL, Behrens 25)

(1) In addition to the general and fiduciary duties expressed by Articles 22 to 26, managing directors must

1. perform their duties established by law or statute in good faith in the best interests of the company as a whole which includes the environmental sustainability of its operations;
2. exercise powers granted to them by law or statute only for the purposes established therein;
3. give adequate consideration to matters to be decided;
4. avoid actual and potential conflicts between personal interests and those of the corporation;
5. exercise reasonable care and skill in the performance of their functions.

(2) A managing director may be held liable for any action or failure to act unless the action or omission was made in good faith, based upon reasonable inquiry and information, and rationally related to the purposes of the company.

(3) In case of violation of duties and the standard of diligence referred to in Paragraphs 1 and 2, a managing director has to compensate the company for any damage which occurred due to the violation. He has the burden of proving compliance with the duties and standards. In case the violation has been committed by more than one managing director, all directors in question are jointly and severally liable.

(4) In particular, managing directors are obliged to compensate the company in damages, if they are, contrary to this law, carrying out the following transactions:

1. Returning contributions to shareholders;
2. Paying interests or dividends to shareholders;
3. Subscribing, acquiring, accepting as pledge or withdrawing the company's own shares or shares of another company;
4. Distributing the company's assets;
5. Letting the company continue to do business when it should be foreseen that it will not be able to pay its debts;
6. Making payments after the company has become insolvent or over-indebted;
7. In case of conditional increase of capital, attributing a share contrary to the set purpose or before it has been fully paid for;
8. Granting loans.

(5) Article 270 applies for the realisation of claims deriving from previous paragraphs. These claims must be brought within 3 years.

24. COMPANIES (8)

Minority Protection

Company law must be particularly concerned with the protection of minority shareholders. The protection of minority shareholders against oppression by the majority or by the company's administration is a major concern of enterprise law. The administration may either be dependent upon a majority shareholder or itself hold the majority of shares. Minority protection is essential for the willingness of outside investors to invest in the company. Above all, experience in some transformation countries like Russia has shown that share prices of companies without minority protection are remarkably low and this in turn makes the raising of capital extremely expensive, because investors will ask for an excessive risk premium.

Minority protection is particularly important for joint-stock companies whose shares may be sold to the public. Joint-stock companies are explicitly designed to raise investment capital on the capital market so as to allow even the very small investors to invest their savings directly or indirectly in shares. This type of company is therefore crucial for the private funding of large investment projects: many small investments may be pooled so as to finance a large enterprise. Investors therefore need special protection against abusive behaviour by those who are in control of a joint-stock company. This is a matter not only for enterprise law but also for capital market law and stock exchange regulations which are, therefore, a crucial element of a viable system for such companies in any transition country.

Limited liability companies are designed to meet the needs of small and medium-sized enterprises. They are typically financed by a limited group of shareholders who are willing to raise the company's capital without calling on the public, because they themselves want to be exclusively in control of their enterprise. Therefore, the transfer of shares is also typically subject to legal requirements which prevent an easy transfer of shares to third parties. In the absence of capital market rules or stock exchange regulations, the protection of minority members depends here exclusively on enterprise law.

In the model Enterprise Law, protection of the position of

investors is very much the contents of management's **fiduciary duties** as against shareholders and among shareholders which we discussed above. Moreover, the Law provides the **minimum rules for groups of enterprises** including minority shareholders' rights, Arts. 282 to 284.

The **conflict of interest** clause of Art. 160 would also apply to a controlling shareholder: he would not be allowed to vote in a situation where he would be released from obligations, if company claims against him are voted or if he would be granted any new benefit.

Besides the **general information right** established by Arts. 23, Art. 9, 162, 163, and 270 allow a 5 percent minority (as well as creditors whose claims amount to 5 percent of the basic capital) to always request the court to order a **special investigation**, **annulment of illegal decisions of the company administration or compensation of damages in favour of the company**, if the competent enterprise organs do not become active in this respect. In the event of a shareholder being prevented from exercising the **rights attached to his shares** he may request the court to enforce these rights or grant compensation, Arts. 164, 165 and 270.

The 5 percent minority may also request the managing directors in writing to **convene a general meeting** and convene the meeting themselves if their request was not accepted. In this case they may even request the company to buy their shares, Arts. 152 and 268.

According to the statute, minority shareholders of joint-stock companies may be entitled to **appoint a member of the board of directors or supervisory board**, Arts. 167 (3), 179 (2). The same applies to limited liability companies in case a board structure is required, Art. 257.

The same minority (and quota of creditors) may **require the board to perform its supervisory duties** and, in particular, may ask to check the lawfulness of the administration's work, Art. 178 (Art. 257, in case a board structure is required for a limited liability company).

In the interest of shareholders, **directors' salaries and incentives are subject to control by the general meeting of shareholders.** Payments may be adequately reduced in case of financial deterioration of the company, Arts. 173 and 273.

SECTION 5 INCREASE AND REDUCTION OF BASIC CAPITAL

Article 275 Applicable provisions
(382, 383 YEL, Behrens 33)

(1) The provisions of Articles 181 to 201 and 202 to 209 regarding increase and reduction of basic capital apply accordingly to limited liability companies.

(2) The pre-emption right as of Article 184 may not be excluded or restricted for members of a limited liability company for up to 30 days after the decision on capital increase.

SECTION 6 DISSOLUTION, EXIT OF MEMBERS AND LIQUIDATION

Article 276 Dissolution
(386 YEL, Behrens 34)

(1) The limited liability company is dissolved

- By expiry of the period for which it was established;
- By decision of the general meeting;
- By opening of a bankruptcy procedure;
- If it has not carried out any business activities for 2 years;
- By court decision;
- By Registry decision taken *ex officio*, due to lack or unlawfulness of the following statute provisions not regularised within 3 months as ordered by the Registry: enterprise name, registered office, object, legal capital, number of managing directors;
- For other reasons provided by the statute.

(2) Reduction of number of shareholders to one does not lead to company dissolution. The Second Paragraph of Article 107 applies accordingly.

(3) Article 211 applies accordingly to the registration of dissolution of limited liability companies.

Article 277 Withdrawal of a member
(387 YEL, Behrens 32)

(1) A member may withdraw from the company on reasonable grounds which make the continuation of the membership unacceptable.

Article 278 Expulsion of a member
(388 YEL, Behrens 32)

(1) In case a member is failing to meet his commitments established by the statute in a manner that makes continuation of the company with that member unacceptable, the general meeting may request the court to expel the member concerned.

(2) The company member referred to in Paragraph 1 may not vote on his expulsion.

(3) The company may claim compensation for damage resulting from the infringement and the expulsion of the member. Claims must be brought within 3 years from the realisation of the important reason referred to in Paragraph 1. Paragraph 3 of Article 9 applies accordingly.

Article 279 Legal effects of withdrawal and expulsion
(389 YEL, Behrens 32)

(1) A member of a limited liability company who has withdrawn or has been expelled from the company has the right to compensation for the appraised value of his share.

(2) The legal effect of termination of membership occurs on the date of the withdrawal or on the final court decision regarding the withdrawal or expulsion.

(3) A member's right to withdraw from the company and the company's right to expel a member may not be restricted by the statute.

Article 280 Liquidation
(390, 391 YEL)

(1) Articles 212 to 227 apply accordingly to the liquidation of limited liability companies.

(2) As regards distribution of assets, the additional payments shall be refunded from the company assets immediately after creditors' claims have been settled. The remainder shall be distributed among members in proportion to their shares. The second sentence of Article 219 applies accordingly to restitution of additional payments and contributions.

25. COMPANIES (9)

Special Features of Limited Liability Companies

Each member of a limited liability company holds **one 'share' (or 'interest');** the value of the shares may, however, differ according to each member's investment, Art. 228 (2). Members are entered in a **book of company members** which is subject to inspection not only by members but also by other interested persons with permission of the company, Art. 237. The identity of the members may therefore always be verified by third parties. As opposed to the shareholders of joint-stock companies, members of limited liability companies are never anonymous. Shares in a limited liability company may be represented by share certificates which are not negotiable instruments, however, but merely proof of the membership, Arts. 228 (3), 235 (5).

Shares in a limited liability company may be freely transferred to other members. **Transfers** to third parties are subject to a right of pre-emption of the shareholders and the company, Art. 238 (3). The transfer of a share must be in writing and must be entered in the book of company members, Art. 241 (3) and (4). These rules deliberately prevent the establishment of a market for shares in limited liability companies.

The obligations inherent in a share relate to the **payment of the contributions**, Arts. 232, 243. Obligations to make additional payments in excess of the ordinary contributions, Arts. 245, as well as accessory obligations, Art. 244, may also be provided. In case of non-performance of these obligations, the member may be excluded from the company, Art. 246. He remains nevertheless liable for the unpaid part of the contributions and for any damage caused to the company, Arts. 232 (6) and 243.

The rights inherent in a share relate, first, to the **distribution of profits (dividends).** Such distribution is, however, subject to a resolution by the general meeting, Art. 249. As regards the right of the general meeting to refuse any distribution of profits, the application rules regarding Art. 136 for joint-stock companies apply. The same is true with respect to participation in general meetings and voting rights, Arts. 261, 264, suspension of voting rights in case of conflict of interests, Art. 267, non-voting preference shares, Art. 236, and the exclusion of multiple voting rights, Art. 264.

Members have the right to **withdraw from the company** on reasonable grounds, Art. 277. On the other hand, they may also be expelled from the company on reasonable grounds by court decision requested by the general meeting, Art. 278 (1). In case of withdrawal or **expulsion**, the member concerned is entitled to compensation for the appraised value of his share, Art. 279 (1). Finally, the share in a limited liability company may be terminated under certain conditions; members are sufficiently protected, however, since the Law requires that the possibility of terminating a share must be provided in the statute or the member concerned must agree to the termination, Arts. 256, 275, 209.

6. Groups of enterprises[1]

(15–22, 291–328 GSCL, Behrens 34–6)

Article 281 Parent and subsidiary enterprise
(406 YEL; 15, 16 GSCL, Behrens 35)

(1) If an enterprise has a majority or significant capital share in another enterprise or if, based on an agreement with that enterprise, it has the right to appoint the majority or at least 25 percent of members of the board of directors or supervisory board or of the managing directors of that enterprise, and if it has at least 25 percent of votes at the general meeting, it shall be regarded as the parent enterprise and the other as its subsidiary.

[1] Any provisions on *socially owned enterprises* (Articles 392 to 400 YEL) and *enterprises for the employment of the disabled* (Articles 403 and 404 YEL) are omitted. The 'special' nature of these companies derives either from a specific type of shareholders ('only socially held capital'/'the employee representatives') and/or their object ('professional rehabilitation') or employees ('at least 40 percent disabled'). We think these 'specialties' can be covered by the 'classical' company types referred to in the previous parts of the Draft. This is explicitly declared by Article 404 YEL for enterprises for the employment of the disabled. But socially owned enterprises could also easily adapt their statute to their special needs.

Also the provisions on *'business associations'* (Article 419 YEL) were not adopted by this Draft. This enterprise form resembles the French 'groupement d'intérêt économique' which was the 'model' for Regulation EEC/2137/85 on European Economic Interest Groupings (EEIG). Both may not have the purpose of making profits. However, contrary to the EEIG Regulation, the 'business association' allows for limited liability of members (Paragraph 4: 'status of a company'; cf. Article 24 of the EEIG Regulation). On the other hand, this quality contradicts Paragraphs 7 and 8 of Article 419 YEL which allow the statute to define the liability of members. It seems that these provisions have not been sufficiently thought through from the beginning. As all the evidence shows that they were in any case of marginal importance, we decided to omit them. Likewise, the introduction of a local form of EEIG would not fit into the system as the EEIG is designed for cooperation of economic actors from at least two Member States.

Provisions on *takeovers* have also been omitted from the current Draft. It is envisaged that, at the time of establishment of a stock exchange and/or a financial service regulator, a separate regulation should be drafted in the light of circumstances at that time. The EU has recently adopted a Directive on takeovers which should be followed when drafting these rules.

(2) A parent enterprise with majority capital share is an enterprise whose share in the capital of another enterprise is greater than 50 percent, on the basis of which it has, directly or through another enterprise, at least 25 percent of votes at the meeting or the right to appoint more than half of the members of the board of directors or supervisory board or of the managing directors of the subsidiary.

(3) A parent enterprise with a significant share is an enterprise whose share in the capital of another enterprise is at least 25 percent, on the basis of which it has, directly or through another enterprise, at least 25 percent of votes at the meeting or the right to appoint at least 25 percent of members of the board of directors, supervisory board or managing directors of the subsidiary.

(4) The capital share of the parent enterprise shall be determined on the basis of the ratio of the nominal value of such share to the total capital of the subsidiary enterprise.

(5) In determining the share referred to in Paragraph 4, the subsidiary's own shares and the shares and contributions held on account of the subsidiary by a third party, shall be deducted from the subsidiary's total capital.

(6) Part of the capital share of the parent enterprise shall also be the shares held by other subsidiaries or shares held by persons acting on account of the parent enterprise or by their subsidiaries.

(7) The parent enterprise shall immediately inform the subsidiary of the acquisition of a major or significant share and report the acquisition to the Registry for registration and publication. The registration requirement applies likewise to contracts allowing the parent to appoint members of the subsidiary's administration or subjecting the subsidiary to the management decisions of the parent enterprise.

Article 282 Treatment of parent enterprises managing subsidiaries in a unified manner

(414, 415, 416, 418 YEL, 18, 291–318 GSCL, Behrens 35)

(1) As long as the subsidiary has subjected itself by contract to the management decisions of the parent enterprise, or as long as, based on his capital share in the subsidiary, the parent enterprise is continuously and comprehensively subjecting the managing directors of the subsidiary to its instructions, the parent enterprise has to compensate the subsidiary for its annual losses.

(2) Shareholders of a subsidiary subjected to the parent enterprise as referred to in Paragraph 1, have at any time the rights to require

1. The parent enterprise to buy his securities against the parent enterprise's shares, or
2. The general meeting to guarantee him the dividend accruing to a shareholder owning participating shares.

(3) Creditors of a subsidiary subjected to the parent enterprise as referred to in Paragraph 1, have at any time the right to require the parent company to stand security for their immature claims.

Article 283 Sell-out right
If the parent enterprise holds 90 percent or more of the subsidiary's shares, the holders of the remaining shares have the right to require the parent enterprise within 6 months to buy his securities at the market price.

Article 284 Liability for damage
(412 YEL, 311, 317 GSCL, Behrens 35)

(1) If a parent enterprise causes a subsidiary to perform acts or omissions which are disadvantageous to the subsidiary, the parent enterprise shall indemnify the subsidiary enterprise for the damage caused on such grounds.

(2) In addition to the parent enterprise, joint and several liability shall be borne by members of the parent enterprise's administration who influenced the subsidiary as referred to in Paragraph 1.

(3) Together with persons mentioned in Paragraph 3, joint and several liability shall be borne by members of the subsidiary's administration for violation of their duties, unless they were acting on instructions from the parent enterprise's administration.

(4) If, within 90 days after the damage referred to in Paragraph 1 became evident, no competent company organ has taken action for compensation of the damage, the subsidiary's claim may be filed with the competent court by shareholders or members representing at least 5 percent of the basic capital or a smaller portion determined by the statute, or by the subsidiary's creditors whose claims amount to at least 5 percent of the subsidiary company's basic capital.

(5) Claims provided by this Article must be brought within 3 years after the damage has become evident.

26. GROUPS OF ENTERPRISES

The Enterprise Law introduces some provisions (Arts. 281–4) which are considered basic instruments and which, together with other legal mechanisms of the Law, should be able to cope with the legal problems which groups of enterprises raise.

Enterprises are normally managed in their own economic interest. We noted that the Law expressly obliges the administration to exercise their powers 'in the best interest of the company as a whole', Arts. 176 (1) 1, 274 (1) 1. We have seen that the ongoing health of the company is to be management's continuous concern and defines the social and legal expectation towards the company. Maximising the company's own assets and compliance with legal expectations is not only in the interest of all the investors (shareholders), but at the same time in the interest of creditors, employees and the economic system as such. The understanding that the 'interest' of the company is defined as recognising the social embeddedness of the company does not exclude the necessity of legal safeguards against the administration's use of the company's assets in favour of one specific investor or third party. The coincidence of shareholders', creditors', employees' and 'public' interests in the economic success of the individual company may be destroyed, if the company is integrated into a larger group of enterprises which may no longer pursue the interest of the individual company, but rather the economic and 'institutional' success of the whole group, potentially at the expense of an individual company belonging to the group.

On the other hand, the existence of groups of companies shows that 'the market' itself is pushing economic actors to strengthen their competitive role and use the instrument of 'grouping' to do so. Affiliated corporate entities owe their strength to their structure as a group and their wide range of interconnected relationships. These groups apply a system of decision making permitting coherent policies and a common strategy through one or more decision-making centres.[2] In transnational corporations, this decision-making structure 'has the "world" as its focus'.[3] Such entities may become very powerful social 'institutions', more powerful than many nation-states,[4] and lead to a restriction or even exclusion of competition. In this sense, groups are an exam-

2 UN Commission of Trans-national Corporations or 'Group of Eminent Persons', The Impact of Multinational Corporations on Development and on International Relations (UN pub E74 IIA 5), 25; as quoted by J. Dine, *Governance of Corporate Groups*, Cambridge University Press, 2000, p. 42.

3 Ibid., p. 42.

4 For example, the combined revenues of just General Motors and Ford exceed the combined 'gross domestic product' (GDP) for all of sub-Saharan Africa, and 51 of the largest 100 economies are corporations. The number of transnational corporations jumped from 7,000 in 1970 to 40,000 in 1995. These corporations and their more or less 250,000 foreign affiliates account for most of the world's industrial capacity, technological knowledge and international financial transactions. Ibid., pp. 151, 152.

ple for the **'imperfection' or 'paradoxes' of the idea of the market**. In a society which accepts the structures of market economy, it would, therefore, be useless to try to abolish them as they are an intrinsic part of the system.

However, there is obviously the necessity to cope with the undesired political, social and economic effects, or 'externalities', which such groups produce and to subject them to adequate national and international regulatory frameworks. While human rights, labour and environmental law may become instruments to cope with the political and social problems of such entities,[5] anti-trust regulation including merger control and measures against restrictions of competition and unfair competition try to protect the market functions from 'monopolising tendencies' inherent in groups of companies. Enterprise law is supposed to confront another set of legal problems which may be summed up as follows:[6]

- The fraudulent or immoral use of the corporate veil to shift resources between companies in order to defeat outside interests;
- Group decision-making, including the capacity for oppression of minority interests;
- Above all for tax and accounting legislation: the difficulties of definition of a single economic unit in an ever changing group environment.

Many efforts have been made to define parameters of the 'group' in order to challenge wrongful decisions in any place where the group has significant operations. Due to these difficulties, the EU has not pursued the finalisation of its proposal of a Ninth Directive on Enterprise Groups.[7] The EU's legal attitude has become 'pragmatic' by addressing single problem areas of corporate groups like annual accounting in a group and the acquisition of major shareholdings in publicly held companies by takeover bids. The Fourth Directive on companies' annual accounts and the Seventh

---

5 See ibid., pp. 151–75.

6 Ibid, p. 43.

7 Ibid, pp. 57–59. The Proposal was strongly influenced by German 'Konzernrecht' which tries to favour dominance agreements and to discriminate against *de-facto* groups. In spite of its reference to both cases of group building, the new Enterprise Law has not adopted this valuation.

Directive on consolidated (i.e. group) accounts[8] use a concept of dominance which the new Enterprise Law loosely follows. This concept of dominance is not a free-standing test of a parent-subsidiary relationship; the Law requires that group relationships are based on **majority or significant share ownership** or on a **contract** which permits the **parent enterprise** to have at least 25 percent of votes at the general meeting of the **subsidiary enterprise** and to appoint the majority or at least 25 percent of members of its board of directors or supervisory board or of the managing directors, Art. 281.

It is important to note, however, that application of the rules on groups does not depend upon the specific legal form of the enterprise. According to the definition of the term 'business enterprise' in Art. 1, **single entrepreneurs may also be regarded as a parent or subsidiary enterprise.**

The legal definitions of Art. 281 show, first, that **the Enterprise Law permits the formation of enterprise affiliations** which give rise to control relationships. However, it does not provide any rules for the formation process of enterprise groups. This means, second, that the Law will accept a certain relaxation of the principle that enterprises must be managed in their own interest: it must at least be accepted to some extent that the parent enterprise **may give instructions on the administration of the subsidiary** in order to integrate it into the group and to subject its interest to the interest of the whole group. In this respect, Art. 283 (1) takes for granted that managing directors of the subsidiary are subjected to instructions of the parent. Art. 284 (3) provides for an exemption from personal liability of the administration of a subsidiary enterprise in case of violation of its duty, if it was 'acting on instructions from the parent enterprise's administration'. This means that the administration of the subsidiary does not act unlawfully, if it follows instructions from the parent enterprise.

The third question that arises relates to the **protection of minority shareholders and creditors** of the subsidiaries. Obviously, the entire set of minority and creditors' protection discussed in previous chapters, including the extensive rules of the new Law regarding fiduciary duties (of majority shareholders)

[8] See Fourth Council Directive of 25 July 1978, 78/660/EEC (OJ 1978 L 222); Seventh Council Directive of 13 June 1983, 83/349/EEC (OJ 1983 L 193), especially Art. 1 of the latter.

and conflict of interests, also apply to the context of groups. However, the provisions on groups add on some specific guarantees and sanctions for typical cases of an existing enterprise affiliation. The cases in question regard the complete integration of the subsidiary into the governance structure of the group based on contract or continuous and comprehensive influence, on the one hand, and compensation for damages for single measures without 'unified management', on the other hand:

- If, based on a 'domination contract' or on its capital share, the parent enterprise is continuously and comprehensively subjecting the managing directors of the subsidiary to its instructions, the parent enterprise must compensate the subsidiary for its annual losses, Art. 282 (1). If the **subsidiary is governed in this unified manner**, its shareholders have at any time the rights to require either the parent to buy their securities at market price, or the general meeting to guarantee them the dividend accruing to a shareholder owning participating shares, Art. 282 (2). Creditors have in such a case at any time the right to require the parent company to stand security for their claims, Art. 282 (3).
- Shareholders as well as creditors of the subsidiary are protected by the parent's liability for any damage caused to the subsidiary by harmful transactions, Art. 284 (1). This is a safeguard for the integrity of the subsidiary's assets the effectiveness of which heavily depends on the ability of courts to identify the harm done to the subsidiary by specific transactions. In addition, according to Art. 284 (2), the members of the parent enterprise's administration may be held personally liable towards the subsidiary for such harmful transactions; likewise the administration of the subsidiary, Art. 284 (3), 'unless they were acting on instructions from the parent enterprise's administration' (see above).
- Finally, if the parent enterprise holds 90 percent or more of the subsidiary's shares, the holders of the remaining shares have the right to require the parent enterprise within 6 months to buy his securities at the market price, Art. 283. Even without being subjected to the parent's instructions, the possible 'totality of outside influence' represented by a specific majority share may be reason enough for a shareholder to request the sell-out.

As regards the 'ongoing health' of the subsidiary enterprise itself, the afore-mentioned comments show that **the reason behind the rules on enterprise groups is to promote groups which guarantee a kind of balance between the interest of the network and the interest of a single enterprise in this network by maintaining considerable independence in their subsidiaries without subjecting them to total instructions or exercising harmful influence in a single case.** As this is the underlying regulatory concept of a 'lawful dominance in groups', it cannot be excluded that courts will apply Arts. 282 to 284 accordingly in case economic practice tries to base dominance over a subsidiary on means other than on those envisaged by these rules. If we accept that one of the most important factors defining the existence of a significant relationship between enterprises is the flow of money rather than the share structure, it would be possible to formulate a test based on the dominance concept without referring to significant ownership and voting powers.[9] If the sole test was one of economic dominance in decision-making, this application could include relationships such as franchising or other kinds of supply or distribution, outsourcing of certain enterprise functions or quality-assurance systems which 'on the surface' are using the contractual instrument, but 'in reality' build organisations which may be treated according to different legal parameters. Application of the 'word and spirit' of Arts. 282–4 would probably be more adequate in such cases than contractual parameters which treat partners' powers as 'equal'.

Moreover, courts may want to align these arguments with those on fiduciary duties regarding the proper governance and decision-making structures in enterprises, and come to a concept of 'good governance of the group' which would apply organisation and liability standards of the single enterprise accordingly to group management. Then, liability could be attributed with respect to the major responsibility either to the subsidiary (or a group of subsidiaries) or to the group as such. **The group may be considered a liable single economic entity** not because of the degree of the integration of its business – the group which complies with the above-mentioned 'model' of the Law will probably want to avoid this 'unified management'; the attribution to the 'network' represented by the parent may instead be based on 'organisa-

[9] See Dine, supra note 2, p. 181.

tional mismanagement' because in setting the group up the directors of the parent had failed to consider properly the 'whole of the interests' (Art. 176 I, 1 concerned. Failure to address those interests, for example failure to consult employees concerning group restructuring, would thus be a reason to challenge the existence of the subsidiaries as separate and lead to an application of the abuse and piercing-the-veil provisions of Art. 24 (besides the application of Art. 29 IV in the above-mentioned case).[10]

[10] Ibid., p. 55.

7. Public enterprises

Article 285 Applicable provisions
(401, 402 YEL)

A public enterprise is a company conducting business of general economic interest where either all shares are directly or indirectly held by a central, regional or local authority, or where this authority has the role of a parent company as referred to in Article 281. Formation and operation of public enterprises are subjected to the provisions of the present Law.

27. PUBLIC ENTERPRISES

The definition of public enterprises of Art. 285 aligns with Article 2 of Directive 723/80/EEC 'On the Transparency of Financial Relations between Member States and Public Undertakings'. It should be no problem for the mentioned 'central authorities' to become an economic actor using enterprise forms if this is done within the framework of their special '**public concern**'. Some public enterprises in transition states already have similar management structures as foreseen by the Law.

This **limitation to 'general economic interests'** may become controversial, as it is in some member states. The European rules and debates are important in this respect; above all the limits of Arts. 31, 56, 86 and 87 of the EC Treaty (reorganisation of state monopolies with commercial character, no restrictions on the free movement of capital, no special rights for public enterprises, no restrictions on competition, strict limitation of subsidies). The EU pressure on many member states to privatise large parts of 'classical' public enterprises in the postal, telecom, transport and energy sector is well-known. The different grades of involvement of member states in these services is considered an obstacle to creating similar conditions everywhere in the Internal Market. Moreover, it is supposed that the public interest in these services can better and more cheaply be achieved if they are run as private enterprises. However, this has proved to be true only if deregulation, on the one side, is accompanied by re-regulation on the other, meaning the establishment of functioning public monitoring and supervising agencies which have the right to interfere in case of failures and distortions. In this respect, above all re-monopolisation on the private level is a risk to be faced by legal intervention.

Moreover, **state participation** giving public authorities special rights in enterprises with a particular public interest (so-called 'golden shares' etc.) has recently become the subject of decisions of the ECJ, which sets the limits of such special rights in the light of the freedom of capital movement, Art. 56 of the EC Treaty.

However, these questions are not a problem for Enterprise Law, which provides the forms of organisation to be used when doing business. Art. 285 just reflects the general 'openness' of enterprise law towards state participation in the economy and makes it possible that public authorities may not only create wholly owned enterprises but find themselves also with other shareholders which can be natural or juridical persons.

During the last phase of the drafting process, restrictions on the company form of public enterprises were amended. **Public enterprises may use any partnership or company form.** This does not mean that the restrictions of Art. 8 (1) would not apply. Art. 8 (1) only excludes companies and partnership from becoming general or unlimited partners. This would not exclude a juridical person like the relevant public authority from founding an enterprise as general or unlimited partner as the reason behind the restrictions would hardly apply: the public entity is unlikely to become insolvent and it is liable with all its assets!

Other limitations or specialties for public enterprises have to be set by rules regarding economic administration which will have to comply with the above-mentioned European rules. Also member states are under pressure in this regard. An example is the German case of the 'Volkswagen Law' of the late 1950s which has recently come under attack by the EU Commission for its special rules regarding voting right limits which try to prevent capital concentrations from realising their interest against the 'socially owned (employees') capital' of the Volkswagen AG.

8. Restructuring of enterprises

Article 286 General provisions
(421 YEL, 1 German Transformation Law – GTL, Third and Sixth Directive, Behrens 36, 37)

(1) An enterprise may be restructured by merging with another enterprise (merger), dividing into two or more enterprises (division) and changing its form (transformation).

(2) Enterprises of the same or different forms may only be restructured, if they have been registered for at least one year.

(3) Enterprises may not be merged contrary to monopoly regulations.

SECTION 1 MERGERS

Article 287 Definition
(422 YEL, 2 GTL)

Two or more enterprises may be merged on the basis of:

1. Transfer of the whole assets of one or more enterprises (the enterprise to be acquired) to another enterprise (the acquiring enterprise) in exchange for the interests of that enterprise (merger by acquisition);
2. Formation of a new enterprise to which the whole assets of the merging enterprises are transferred, in exchange for the interests of the new enterprise (merger by formation of a new enterprise).

Title 1 Merger by Acquisition

Article 288 Merger agreement and merger report
(423 YEL, 5, 8 GTL, 5, 9 Third Directive)

(1) The legal representatives of the enterprise which take part in the merger shall draw up an agreement in writing. The agreement shall specify at least:

1. Enterprise names and registered office of merging enterprises;
2. Agreement on the transfer of the assets of each of the enterprises to be acquired in exchange for the interests of the acquiring enterprise;
3. The share exchange ratio and the amount of any cash payment;
4. The terms relating to the allotment of interests in the acquiring enterprise;
5. The rights stemming from the interests of the acquiring enterprise;
6. The rights conferred by the acquiring enterprise on the holders of interests and on holders of special rights, or the measures proposed concerning them;
7. Any special advantage granted to managing directors, members of the board of directors or supervisory board and auditing experts;
8. The consequences of the merger for employees and their representatives and the measures proposed concerning them.

(2) The legal representatives of each of the merging enterprises shall draw up a detailed written report explaining the merger agreement and setting out the legal and economic grounds for it, in particular the interest exchange ratio. The report shall also describe any special valuation difficulties which have arisen.

(3) In case of joint-stock companies involved in the merger, the merger agreement shall be submitted to the Registry for registration and publication and be placed on companies' websites at least one month before the date fixed for the general meeting which is to decide thereon as referred to in Article 290.

Article 289 Examination

(424 YEL, 9, 12 GTL,10 Third Directive)

(1) The legal representatives of the enterprises involved in the merger shall appoint duly authorised experts to examine the merger agreement. The experts may be appointed for each enterprise involved or jointly for all of them. They shall be appointed by the competent court if so requested by the legal representatives.

(2) The experts shall draw up a written report. The report must state whether in their opinion the share exchange ratio is fair and reasonable. The statement must:

1. Indicate the method or methods used to arrive at the share exchange ratio proposed;
2. State whether such method or methods are adequate in the case in question, indicate the values arrived at using each such method and give an opinion on the relative importance attributed to such methods in arriving at the value decided on;
3. Describe any special valuation difficulties which have arisen.

(3) Each expert shall be entitled to obtain from the merging enterprises all relevant information and documents and to carry out all necessary investigations.

Article 290 Approval of the merger agreement
(425 YEL, 13, 49, 50, 63–5 GTL, 7, 11 Third Directive)

(1) In order to have legal effect, the merger agreement requires approval by decision of the interest holders of all the merging enterprises. Paragraph 2 of Article 157 and Paragraph 2 of Article 267 apply for the approval of the general meeting of companies involved in the merger.

(2) Where rights of single holders of interests or certain classes of shares are affected by the transaction, the decision concerning the merger shall be subject to a separate vote with a majority of three-quarters of each class of interest – or shareholders – concerned.

(3) Each interest holder of the merging enterprises has the right to inspect the documents based on which the merger is carried out. Article 23 applies. In case of companies, the merger agreement, the annual statements and performance reports of the last 3 business years, the reports mentioned in Paragraph 2 of Article 288 and experts' reports shall be placed on companies' websites before the general meeting and be easily accessible in the premises of the head office before and during the general meeting. Shareholders may require any information regarding the merger during the general meeting.

Article 291 Increase of basic capital
(426 YEL, 55, 69 GTL)

An increase of the acquiring company's basic capital in connection with the merger shall be exempt from provisions on capital increase regarding:

1. The prohibition of the increase until outstanding payments on previously subscribed shares have been made;
2. The conditions for subscription to new shares;
3. The pre-emption rights of shareholders and members in the purchase of new shares.

Article 292 Restrictions on an increase of capital
(427 YEL, 54, 68 GTL)

(1) The acquiring company may not increase its basic capital in connection with the merger as long as

1. It is holding interests of an enterprise to be acquired;
2. The enterprise to be acquired is holding own shares;
3. The enterprise to be acquired is holding shares of the acquiring company which have not been fully paid up.

(2) The acquiring company is not obliged to increase its capital, as long as

1. It has own shares;
2. The enterprise to be acquired is holding shares of the acquiring company which have been fully paid up.

Article 293 Registration, publication and legal effect
(430 YEL, 16–20 GTL, 18, 19 Third Directive)

(1) The legal representatives of the merging enterprises shall submit the merger to the Registry together with the merger agreement, the minutes regarding the merger decisions, the approval of single interest holders, the merger report and the examination report. Enterprises to be acquired shall also submit their final balance sheets to their Registry. Where applicable, the information mentioned shall also be placed on the enterprises' websites.

(2) If the basic capital of the acquiring company is to be increased in connection with the merger, the amount of the increase shall be submitted together with the merger.

(3) The merger shall have the following consequences *ipso jure* and simultaneously:

1. The transfer, both as between the merging enterprises and as regards third parties, to the acquiring enterprise of all the assets and liabilities of the enterprise being acquired;
2. The interest holders of the enterprise to be acquired become interest holders of the acquiring enterprise;
3. The enterprise to be acquired ceases to exist.

Article 294 Protection of creditors
(428 YEL, 22 GTL, 13, 22 Third Directive)

(1) If creditors of an enterprise participating in the merger, within 6 months from the publication of the merger agreement regarding this enterprise, report the cause and amount of their claims in writing, they shall obtain adequate safeguards for these claims from the enterprise. A written statement given by the legal representatives of the merging enterprises that the assets of these enterprises will be managed separately until the claim of each individual creditor is

settled, shall be regarded as a sufficient safeguard for the creditors. In case no safeguard has been obtained, the creditors may request the court to order the safeguard or otherwise to annul the merger decision.

(2) Creditors having priority rights in case of bankruptcy are not entitled to request the security referred to in Paragraph 1.

Article 295 Protection of the holders of special rights
(429 YEL, 23 GTL, 15 Third Directive)

The acquiring enterprise shall secure holders of convertible bonds and participating shares the same rights they possessed in the enterprise being acquired.

Article 296 Protection of the rights of interest holders
(431 YEL, 29–34 GTL)

(1) Interest holders of merging enterprises opposed to the merger may require their interests being bought by the acquiring company at market price or, in case of dispute, at the price set by an independent expert appointed by the court on their request. Alternatively, they may request the acquiring company to exchange their voting shares against preference shares without voting rights.

(2) Interest holders mentioned in Paragraph 1 may file a court case against the merger decision claiming that the exchange ratio has not been set at proper proportions.

(3) The rights referred to in Paragraphs 1 and 2 must be exercised within 60 days from the date of publication of the merger regarding the acquiring enterprise.

Article 297 Liability of administration and supervisory organs and experts
(432 YEL, 25 GTL, 21, 22 Third Directive)

(1) Legal representatives and members of the board of directors or supervisory board of the acquiring enterprise shall be jointly and severally liable together with the latter for any damage caused to interest holders and creditors of the enterprises participating in the merger, unless they prove they complied with their duties when examining the assets of the enterprise and concluding the merger agreement.

(2) Legal representatives and members of the board of directors or supervisory board of the enterprise being acquired as well as independent experts involved in the examination of the merger bear the same liability referred to in Paragraph 1. In both cases, claims must be brought within 3 years after the registration of the merger regarding the enterprise concerned.

Article 298 Merger by acquisition in special cases
(433 YEL, 62 GTL, 24–9 Third Directive)

(1) If at least 90 percent of the basic capital of a subsidiary company is owned by the parent company, the merger by acquisition may be carried out without the approval of the general meeting of the parent company, unless the shareholders or members of the latter representing at least 5 percent of the company's basic capital, request a meeting to be convened for the purpose of approving the merger. The subsidiary's own shares and the shares belonging to a third party acting on account of the subsidiary shall be deducted from the amount mentioned in the first sentence.

(2) If all shares of a subsidiary belong to the parent company, the acquiring company does not need to comply with the obligations of Art. 288 (1) letters b), c) and d); Art. 288 (2), Art. 289 and Art. 297.

Title 2 Merger by Formation of a New Enterprise

Article 299 Applicable provisions
(434 YEL)

(1) The provisions of Articles 288 to 298 shall apply accordingly to mergers by formation of new enterprises. The newly formed enterprise shall be regarded as the acquiring enterprise.

(2) Provisions of this law regarding enterprise formation shall apply accordingly to the formation of the new enterprise caused by merger.

28. RESTRUCTURING OF ENTERPRISES (1)

Flexible economic management of enterprise structures and the creation of enterprise networks often result in **merging** of enterprises, **transformation** of companies into partnerships (and the other way round) or in enterprises being **divided** and parts 'outsourced' and integrated into independent enterprises which, for example, may be managed as 'joint ventures' together with other interested enterprises. If special provisions on restructuring were missing, fulfilment of a contract establishing, for example, the transformation of a general partnership into a limited liability company would require the transfer of each single piece of property including real estate from the old enterprise to the new. The reserves of the old enterprise would need to be transformed into cash and taxed; not to mention other transfer costs for land registration, notaries, etc.

This Law introduces provisions (Arts. 286–302) which loosely follow the 'word and spirit' of the German Restructuring Law of 1994 and which are in line with the Third and Sixth European Company Law Directives.

Art. 286 (1) envisages a complete set of procedures for the restructuring of enterprises by merger, Art. 287–99, division, Art. 300, or transformation, Art. 301. **Restructuring mainly creates three legal problems** that the law should adequately solve:

- **The protection of interest holders of enterprises involved** in the restructuring. Interest holders of the enterprise to be acquired or divided have to accept an exchange of shares. Therefore an adequate share exchange ratio must be guaranteed. The exchange, however, has also effects on the old interest holders of the acquiring or recipient enterprise: if compensation by shares of the acquiring or recipient enterprise is too high, this results de facto in a 'subsidy' which the old interest holders 'grant' the new ones. Interest holders who are opposed to the restructuring, must get the chance to have the offered exchange rate controlled by the courts and/or to have their shares bought up if they do not want to participate in the restructuring.
- **The protection of the creditors** whose claims have come into existence before the restructuring. Creditors do not participate in the restructuring and may find themselves confronted with a less solvent debtor and a variety of competing creditors.
- **Protection of employees** of the restructuring enterprises.
- **The ipso jure transfer of the assets** of the existing enterprises to the newly formed legal entities.

Art. 286 (2) defines a precondition for any restructuring: **Enterprises may only be restructured, if they have been registered for at least one year**.

As regards the **protection of the rights of the employees of each of the restructuring enterprises**, Art. 302 establishes that this protection shall be regulated 'in accordance with Directive 2001/23/EC'.[1] This Directive concerns the safeguards

[1] Council Directive 2001/23/EC of 12 March 2001 on the approximation of the laws of the member states relating to the safeguarding of employees' rights in the event of transfers of undertakings, businesses or parts of undertakings or businesses.

of employees' rights in case of transfer of enterprises or their parts. Its most important provisions are

- Art. 3 (1): The 'transferor's' rights and obligations arising from an employment relationship existing on the date of a transfer shall, by reason of such transfer, be transferred to the 'transferee'. Both are jointly and severally liable for these obligations. This also applies to collective agreements (Paragraph 3);
- Art. 4 (1): The transfer as such may not constitute grounds for dismissal;
- Art. 6 (2): Continuation of employee representation must be guaranteed;
- Art. 7 (1): Information and consultation procedures must be respected. The new Enterprise Law contains such procedures in Art. 29 (2) regarding the rights of the employees' council.

Mergers

Any merger must, first of all, comply with another precondition contained in Art. 286 (3), **compliance with anti-monopoly laws and regulations**. This means that a merger is invalidated on these grounds even if it fully complies with all the other merger provisions of the Enterprise Law. Compliance with anti-monopoly law provisions becomes an Enterprise Law precondition for the legal validity of the merger.

Mergers may be effected either 'by acquisition' or 'by formation of a new enterprise', Art. 287. Provisions on mergers by acquisition are applicable accordingly to mergers by formation of a new enterprise, Art. 299 (1). The merger provisions cover all forms of enterprises involved unless they specify rules for a certain enterprise form.

The **merger agreement** must be drawn up in writing, Art. 288 (1) 1. It must, among other things, describe the share exchange ratio and any additional cash payment (3) and the rights stemming from the interest in the acquiring enterprise (4 and 5). The agreement must also list the rights which the acquiring enterprise confers upon single interest-holders, in particular the holders of special rights like interests without voting rights, preferential interests, convertible and profit sharing bonds or the measures which are proposed for these persons (6). Also the consequences of the merger for employees and their representatives as well as any measures concerning them must be part of the agreement (8). This is done in compliance with the above-mentioned Directive 2001/23.

Art. 288 (2) requires the merging enterprises to draw up a written **report explaining the merger** agreement and setting out the legal and economic grounds for it, in particular the interest exchange ratio and any special valuation difficulties which had arisen.

The merger agreement must be **examined by authorised experts**, Art. 289.

In case the acquiring company is **increasing its capital** on the occasion of the merger, certain procedural requirements for the usual capital increase do not apply due to the 'logistics' of the merger where shares of the interest holders of the acquired company are exchanged with those of the acquiring company, Art. 291. On the other hand, increase of capital is excluded as long as the existing capital connections between the merging enterprises have not been cleared, Art. 292.

In order to have legal effect, the merger agreement requires **approval by decision of the interest holders of all the merging enterprises**, Art. 290 (1). For companies this requires approval by three-quarters of votes in the general meeting. As sufficient information for the interest holders is crucial, Art. 290 (3) explicitly guarantees interest holders' right of access to all relevant documents and reports.

With the registration of the merger and its publication, the acquired enterprises cease to exist. All assets (including rights and obligations) are transferred ipso jure to the acquiring enterprise, and interest holders of the acquired enterprise(s) become interest holders of the acquiring enterprise, Art. 293 (3).

Creditors of the enterprises involved in the merger are protected. They may request that their claims are settled or secured and request the court to decide in case sufficient safeguard has not been obtained, Art. 294 (1). **Interest holders opposed to the merger** are granted the right to sell their shares or investments at the prevailing market price to the acquiring enterprise. Alternatively, they may request the acquiring company to exchange their voting shares against preference shares without voting rights, Art. 296 (1). They may request the court to decide on the adequacy of the exchange ratio and therewith the legality of the merger, Art. 296 (2).

The **management and supervisory organs and authorised experts of all enterprises taking part in the merger are jointly and severally liable for any damage** caused to interest holders and creditors by the merger, Art. 297. It is important to note that this liability is established **'as against the interest holders'**. This is an exception from the usual liability rule, for example of Arts. 176 (3) and 274 (3), which establishes liability of the management as against the enterprise'. Art. 297 aims, above all, at the situation where the share exchange ratio has been wrongly computed to the disadvantage of the interest holders of the acquired enterprise. In this case, there is indeed no damage to the acquired enterprise itself but only to its interest holders.

Art. 298 provides for **special rules in case of mergers taking place inside a group of enterprises**. If the acquiring company holds at least 90 percent, but not all, of the shares of the company to be acquired, a general meeting of the acquiring company is only necessary if at least 5 percent of the remaining shareholders so request.

SECTION 2 DIVISION

Article 300 Definition, applicable provisions

(435 YEL, 123–46 GTL, Sixth Directive)

(1) An enterprise may be divided by transferring its assets to two or more existing or new enterprises by decision of the interest holders or the general meeting, in which case the enterprise being divided shall cease to exist.

(2) The provisions of Articles 288 to 298 apply accordingly to enterprise divisions.

(3) The recipient enterprises shall be jointly and severally liable together with the enterprise being divided for the latter's commitments.

(4) The registration of the division shall have the following consequences *ipso jure* and simultaneously:

1. The transfer, both as between the enterprise being divided and the recipient enterprises and as regards third parties, to each of the recipient enterprises of all the assets and liabilities of the enterprise being divided in accordance with the allocation laid down in the division agreement;

2. The interest holders of the enterprise being divided become interest holders of one or more of the recipient enterprises in accordance with the allocation laid down in the division agreement;
3. The enterprise being divided ceases to exist.

29. RESTRUCTURING OF ENTERPRISES (2)

Divisions

At first sight, division of enterprises seems to be the opposite of mergers. While mergers unite assets, division is splitting property. Therefore, division is the adequate legal instrument to split up huge enterprises. On the other hand, the similitude to mergers cannot be denied, as also in the case of divisions, the entire assets of the enterprise being divided are transferred, shares exchanged and the enterprise being divided ceases to exist.

The difference from mergers lies only in the fact that the **assets of the enterprise in question are divided according to a division agreement and received by at least 2 existing or newly founded enterprises**; in other words, an undivided transfer uno actu to another enterprise is not possible. For interest holders, creditors, and employees, this difference is certainly irrelevant: their interests are affected by the division in the same way as by merging. Therefore, Art. 300 (2) declares provisions on mergers also applicable for divisions.

The only case of division which the Law provides is an enterprise being divided by transferring its assets to 2 or more existing or new enterprises by decision of the interest holders or the general meeting, in which case the enterprise being divided shall cease to exist, Art. 300 (1).[2]

The **legal effects of the division are the same as in the merger case**, Art. 300 (4) (ipso jure transfer of assets, share exchange, end of the divided enterprise). However, as the assets of the divided enterprise are received by at least 2 enterprises, several modalities of share exchange are thinkable and must be

[2] There are no provisions on divisions where the enterprise being divided keeps part of its assets and its interest holders and therefore continues to exist. In this case, these interest holders do not exchange their shares; instead, they receive in addition shares from the recipient enterprise.

allowed to be chosen in the division agreement with respect to the Sixth Directive:

- **The division maintains previous share proportions**. In this case, envisaged by Art. 17 (1) of the Sixth Directive, shareholders of the divided enterprise receive shares from all receiving enterprises and their proportion in the receiving enterprises corresponds to the proportion they had in the divided enterprise.
- **The division does not maintain previous share proportions**. In this case, envisaged by Art. 5 (2) of the Sixth Directive, the share proportions do not mirror those held in the individual enterprise.
- **A shareholder of the divided enterprise gets shares only from one of the receiving enterprises**. This case, envisaged by Art. 17 (1) (b) of the Sixth Directive, allows for the division of groups of interest holders.

Art. 300 (4) does not exclude any of these modalities and is therefore in line with the Directive. Independent of these modalities, interest holders of the divided enterprise must receive adequate compensation: the value of shares and of additional cash payments attributed to them must correspond to the value of the shares they held in the divided enterprise.

The **protection of creditors of the divided enterprises is particularly important**. As the creditors may not oppose the division of their debtor, they would need to raise their claims against the recipient enterprise to which their obligation has been transferred according to the division agreement. In this case, not only would they compete with the creditors of this recipient enterprise, but they might have to accept that the recipient enterprise in question has not been equipped with sufficient property. Also the old creditors of the recipient enterprise require protection as they run the risk that their debtor receives additional obligations without being sufficiently equipped with assets for all creditors involved. They may, like all the other creditors concerned by the division, request adequate safeguards from their enterprise according to Arts. 300 (2), 294 (1). Moreover, Art. 300 (3) establishes for the creditors of the divided enterprise that **also the recipient enterprises are jointly and severally liable together with the divided enterprise for the latter's commitments.**

SECTION 3 TRANSFORMATION

Article 301 Definition, applicable provisions
(436 YEL, 190–250 GTL)

(1) An enterprise may change its legal form by transformation. Formation formalities required by this Law for the new enterprise apply unless the following provisions determine otherwise.

(2) The transformation does not change rights and duties assumed by the enterprise.

(3) The decision to change the enterprise form must be taken by all interest holders or the general meeting with a three-quarters majority. If the transformation results in a change of the established rights and duties of the interest holders, the validity of the transformation decision shall depend on the approval of such interest holders. Paragraph 2 of Article 290 applies accordingly.

(4) By public announcement, which shall be published twice at an interval of not less than 15 and not more than 30 days including any enterprise website, the meeting of interest holders shall call on all interest holders who did not attend or were not represented at the meeting, to state in writing whether they accept the change of enterprise form pursuant to decision of the meeting, within 60 days from the date of the latest announcement.

(5) The publication of the public announcement referred to in Paragraph 4 shall not be necessary if all members and shareholders attended or were represented at the meeting, or if they were called on individually, in which case the 60-day term shall run from the date of receipt of the call. Should interest holders fail to declare their position in writing within the set term, their approval shall be deemed given.

(6) Articles 294 to 296 apply accordingly to the protection of creditors, holders of special rights and interest holders opposed to the transformation.

(7) Article 297 applies accordingly to the liability of legal representatives and members of the board of directors or supervisory board of the transforming enterprise for damages caused by their breach of duty during the conduct of the transformation to interest holders or creditors.

(8) The transformation shall be submitted to the Registry for registration and publication together with the transformation decision, the minutes regarding the transformation decision, the approval of single interest holders and of those absent during the meeting, any approval of public authorities if necessary for the transformation. Where applicable, the information mentioned shall also be placed on the enterprises' websites.

(9) The registration of the transformation shall have the following legal consequences *ipso jure* and simultaneously:

1. The transforming enterprise continues to exist in the legal form established by the transformation decision;
2. The interest holders of the transforming enterprise participate in the enterprise in conformity with the formalities required by this law for the new enterprise form;
3. The rights of third persons regarding the shares of the transforming enterprise continue to apply to the shares of the transformed enterprise.

30. RESTRUCTURING OF ENTERPRISES (3)

Transformation

Change of legal form is an important way of restructuring. For example, a successful limited liability company in the communications sector may want 'to go public' and list on the stock exchange as a publicly held joint-stock company. Such an enterprise receives a **new legal form without changing its legal identity as debtor or creditor**: The transformation does not change rights and duties assumed by the enterprise, Art. 301 (2).

Transformation requires a **decision by three-quarters of all interest holders at a company's general meeting,** Art. 301 (3). Interest holders who did not attend are publicly called to state their approval or disapproval in writing within 60 days, Art 301 (4). If they do not react, their approval is deemed given.

Those opposing the transformation may request their shares to be bought by the enterprise at market price or, if applicable, change their shares into preference shares without voting rights, Art. 301 (6), 296 (1). Also the other merger protection mechanisms for interest holders and creditors apply, Art. 301 (6), 294–6.

Art. 301 (7) provides for applicability of Art. 297, i.e. the **liability of managing and supervisory organs** of the acquiring and the acquired enterprise for damages caused by their breach of duties in case of a merger. This can only mean that in the transformation case also old and new management and supervisory organs are liable if the transformation has resulted in a change of management or supervisory personnel.

The **registration of the transformation** (Art. 301 (9)) shall have the following legal consequences ipso jure and simultaneously, Art. 301 (9):

- The transforming enterprise exists in the legal form established by the transformation decision;
- The interest holders of the transforming enterprise participate in the enterprise in conformity with the formalities required by this law for the new enterprise form;
- The rights of third persons regarding the shares of the transforming enterprise apply to the shares of the transformed enterprise.

SECTION 4 EMPLOYEE'S RIGHTS[3]

Article 302 Applicable provisions
(12 Third Directive, 11 Sixth Directive)

Protection of the rights of the employees of each of the restructuring companies shall be regulated in accordance with Directive 2001/23/EC.

[3] Cf. note 1.

9. Penal provisions[1]

SECTION 1 CRIMINAL OFFENCES

Article 303 Wrongful statements

(82 GLLCL, 399, 400 GSCL)

An entrepreneur, founder, managing director, member of the board of directors or supervisory board or liquidator shall be punished by up to 3 years of imprisonment or pecuniary punishment, if he is giving statements required by this Law wrongly or if he is omitting essential circumstances.

Article 304 False balance sheets

(437 YEL)

A person who prepares false balance sheets or profit-and-loss accounts or who wrongly establishes the profit and loss share of an interest holder in order to obtain benefits for himself or another person or to cause damage to another person, shall be punished by up to 3 years imprisonment or pecuniary punishment.

Article 305 Breach of duty in case of losses and bankruptcy

(84 GLLCL, 401 GSCL)

A managing director shall be punished by up to 3 years imprisonment or pecuniary punishment, if he

[1] The drafting of this part of the law must be coordinated with penal law provisions and concepts. Administrative ('economic') offence provisions should not confuse the external responsibility of 'the enterprise' with internal responsibilities of the organs of a company which may give rise to a claim against them. There is no public entity controlling all enterprises continuously. Being private law in the first place, measures against breaches of duties depend on the enterprise or partners/members/shareholders in the first place. Offences punished by fines should only be created for cases involving public trust in the company as a market player, as is for example the case with illegal issue or use of share certificates. As regards registration requirements, the Registry Law should provide the possibility of coercive pecuniary measures.

1. Does not convene the general meeting in the case of Paragraph 4 of Article 162;
2. Lets the company continue to do business when it should be foreseen that it will not be able to pay its debts;
3. Does not request opening of bankruptcy procedures after the company has become insolvent or over-indebted.

Article 306 Abuse of audit

(438 YEL)

Should an authorised expert wrongly report on enterprise assets and by doing so obtain any benefit for himself or some other person or cause damage to some other person, he shall be punished by up to 3 years imprisonment, or pecuniary punishment.

Article 307 Breach of duty to keep a business secret

(85 GLLCL, 404 GSCL)

If managing directors, members of the board of directors or supervisory board, liquidators or auditors are disclosing a business secret under breach of the provisions of Article 28, they shall be punished by up to 1 year imprisonment or by pecuniary punishment.

SECTION 2 ADMINISTRATIVE OFFENCES

Article 308 Fines for major offences

(439 YEL)

(1) A partnership or company shall be fined by to Euro for the following offences:

1. If its objects are illegal;
2. If, while conducting its business, it does not use the name entered in the Register;
3. If it does not allocate funds to the mandatory reserves or reduces the latter contrary to the provisions of this Law;
4. If, as a member or shareholder, it abuses the company form with the purpose of reaching an illegal objective, if it is treating the assets of another company as if they were its own assets, if it fails, with respect to the type of activities, to sufficiently equip the capital of another company while it knows or must know that the other company will not be able to meet its commitments as against third parties;

5. If it does not keep books and does not compile and publish statements of accounts in the manner set by federal law;
6. If it violates a competition clause;
7. If it prepares a false annual statement of accounts wrongly establishing the share of each company member of profits or losses;
8. If it fails to dissolve the company in cases set by this Law or if fails to meet its commitments to creditors prior to the distribution of assets;
9. If it issues shares whose value is less than the minimum amount of basic capital;
10. If it relieves a shareholder or member of the duty to pay up his share or of any liability, or if it postpones the fulfilment of the latter's commitments contrary to this Law;
11. If it does not keep a register of shareholders or a book of company members or the single member's book of decisions;
12. If it, contrary to this Law or the statute, pays dividends, refunds contributions, pays special benefits and remunerations, acquires its own shares, concludes or repays unreasonable credits.

(2) Managing directors, members of the board of directors or supervisory board and liquidators who carried out the actions mentioned in Paragraph 1, shall be fined by to Euro.

Article 309 Fines for minor offences
(440 YEL)

(1) A partnership or company shall be fined by to Euro for the following offences:

1. If it has no written statute or if the statute is lacking any information required by this Law;
2. If it fails to apply timely for the registration of any particulars or their changes as prescribed by this Law;
3. If it fails to elect its administration and supervisory organs;
4. If it accepts as members of its board of directors or supervisory board any person having this function in more than 3 companies;
5. If it is not represented as required by this Law;
6. If it fails to report the nomination of a procurator to the Registry;
7. If it refuses to give any information or answers requested pursuant to this Law or the statute to a member or shareholder or employee of the enterprise or if it gives false information, or prevents the mentioned persons from exercising their right to information;
8. If it allows that its legal representatives are making legal transactions

with the enterprise without prior approval of other partners, members or competent bodies;

9. If it does not make public announcements required by this Law, or if it makes a false public announcement;
10. If it becomes a single shareholder and fails to report that fact to the Registry;
11. If in the event of a failed subscription to shares, it fails as a founder to refund to the subscribers the amounts paid in within the term set;
12. If it fails in the capacity of a founder to convene the formation meeting timely;
13. If as a person operating in its own name and on account of a joint-stock company, it fails to transfer shares to the joint-stock company on whose account it has acquired them;
14. If it fails to convene the general meeting when it is bound to do so under this Law or it convenes it contrary to the provisions of this Law or statute;
15. If it makes a public announcement or emits a prospectus for subscription to and payment for shares which includes false particulars or does not include the particulars required and conditions set by this Law;
16. If it fails to issue share certificates within the statutory term;
17. If as director to whom the board of directors has delegated duties, he fails to present to the latter a report on the performance of such duties;
18. If it allows the statute to be changed without the approval of the quorum necessary for making amendments;
19. If it fails to file for bankruptcy proceedings;
20. If a majority or significant capital share is not acquired by the procedure for public offers;
21. If it fails, in conjunction with another enterprise, to reduce the capital to the amount set under this Law;
22. If it fails to notify the other enterprise of acquired shares to be reported by law;
23. If it fails to reorganise itself with respect to the entry into force of the present Law.

(2) Managing directors, members of the board of directors or supervisory board and liquidators who carried out the actions mentioned in paragraph 1, shall be fined to Euro.

Article 310 Offences committed by an entrepreneur
(441 YEL)

(1) Where applicable, an entrepreneur responsible for an act referred to in Paragraph 1 of Article 308 shall be fined by to Euro.

(2) Where applicable, an entrepreneur responsible for an act referred to in paragraph 1 of Article 309 shall be fined by to Euro.

31. PENAL PROVISIONS

The Law introduces penal provisions in Arts. 303–310. Penal Provisions are divided in acts classified as:

Criminal offences, Arts. 303–7;
Major administrative offences, Art. 308, and,
Minor administrative offences, Art. 309.

While, due to the rule of law, courts are in charge of sanctioning criminal offences, fines as envisaged by Arts. 308–10 will be issued by the economic policy section of public administration.

It is interesting to see that the main social value which Arts. 303, 304, and 306 protect through the requirements of correctness and transparency of statements and documents is the trust in economic transactions with the enterprise. The same value has already come up at times in this regulatory context (fiduciary duties, nullity, real seat doctrine, representation). The penal clause of Art. 305 is a confirmation of the tendency mentioned in the discussion on fiduciary duties to sanction the proper use of decision-making procedures to avoid wrongful trading. It may seem strange to find a penal sanction of wrongful auditing by authorised experts (Art. 306) in this context. However, in spite of the fact that accounting and monitoring rules will have to be established elsewhere together with the accreditation of auditors in alignment with the Eighth Directive,[2] trust in the judgment of an authorised expert is an important part of the general policy of transparency of the Law. This penal provision is therefore in the right place.

If the enterprise has good reasons to protect its business secrets and competitive position as of Art. 26, a breach of this ('internal') trust may potentially damage the enterprise's market position which is another important 'system value' to be protected by both civil and penal liability, Art. 307.

---

[2] Eighth Directive 84/253/EEC of 10 April 1984 on the Authorization of Persons in charge of Auditing Mandatory Accounting Documents.

10. Transitional and final provisions[1]

Article 311 Continuation of enterprise operation and the duty to adjust to this law
(442 YEL)

(1) When the present Law enters into force, existing enterprises shall continue to operate in the manner and under the conditions which were valid at the time of their registration.

(2) Within 2 years after this Law entered into force, enterprises shall bring their organisation and operation in line with the provisions of this Law.

(3) Should existing enterprises organise themselves as companies, they shall present evidence to the Registry that they have fulfilled the provisions of this law regarding the raising and maintenance of basic capital.

(4) Enterprises which fail to act in conformity with Paragraph 2 shall be dissolved, and the Registry shall delete them from the Register upon completion of liquidation proceedings, if applicable.

Article 312 Procedures in progress
(445 YEL)

If the procedure of formation or of change of a founder, shareholder or member of a company, as well as the election of organs, adoption of by-laws and other organisation procedures were under way on the day this Law is

[1] In accordance with commentaries throughout this draft, it should be noticed that other regulations are necessary in order to ensure comprehensive coverage of related issues. These include: adaptation of the current registration provisions in the Registry Law, regulations on the use of electronic information by companies, formulation of standard statutes to apply if not displaced by companies; accountancy and audit regulations and regulations on the qualification of auditors; valuation of shares provisions; financial services legislation including the establishment of a financial service regulator and/or a stock exchange; takeover rules; insolvency procedures; implementation of transfer of undertaking provisions in accordance with Directive 2001/23/EC; formulation of penal provisions including especially regulation of money laundering, insider dealing and market abuse; formulation of corporate governance codes and codes of corporate social responsibility; competition regulations.

entering into force, these procedures shall be completed in conformity with the present Law.

Article 313 Implementation
The Ministry of . . . may issue administrative regulations and directions for the implementation of the present law.

Article 314 Applicable law
The present Law shall supersede any provision in the applicable law which is inconsistent with it.

Article 315 Entry into force
(450 YEL)

The present Law shall enter into force on the eighth day after its publication in the Official Gazette.

32. TRANSITIONAL AND FINAL PROVISIONS

The transitional and final provisions foresee the following:
Harmonisation of existing enterprises with provisions of this Law in the first year after entry into force, Art. 311;
Finalisation of procedures in progress according to the provisions of the new Law, Art. 312;
The definition of the Government organ which has the general competency to issue implementing regulations, Art. 313;
Derogative effect of the new Law, Art. 314;
Procedure to regulate entry into force, Art. 315.

Bibliography

BOOKS

A Wider Europe, The Process and Politics of European Union Enlargement, Michael J. Baun, Rowman and Littlefield Publishers Inc., Lanham, Boulder, New York and Oxford, 2000.

Avoiding Responsibility. The Politics and Discourse of European Development Policy, N. Karagiannis, Pluto Press, London and Ann Arbor, 2004.

Building a New Europe, The Challenge of System Transformation and Systemic Reform, Reinicke H. Wolfgang, The Brookings Institution, Washington, DC, 1992.

Changing Borders: Legal and Economic Aspects of European Enlargement, Renate Kicker, Joseph Marko, Michael Steiner and Peter Lang: Frankfurt am Main, Berlin, Bern, New York, Paris and Wien, 1998.

Changing Europe, Identities, Nations and Citizens, David Dunkerley, Lesley Hodgson, Stanislaw Konopacki, Tony Spybey and Andrew Thompson, Routledge, London and New York, 2002.

Desperately Seeking Europe, Susan Stern and Elisabeth Seligmann, Archetype Publications, London, 2003.

Democracy and Enlargement in Post-Communist Europe, The Democratisation of the General Public in Fifteen Central and Eastern European Countries, 1991–1998, Christian W. Haerpfer, Routledge, London and New York, 2002.

Developments in the European Union, Maria Green Cowles and Desmond Dinan, Palgrave, New York, 2004.

Driven to Change, The European Union's Enlargement viewed from the East, Antoaneta L. Dimitrova, Manchester University Press, Manchester and New York, 2004.

East European Transition and EU Enlargement, A Quantitative Approach, Wojciech W. Charemza and Krystyna Strzala, Physica-Verlag, Heidelberg and New York, 2002.

Eastward Enlargement of the European Union, Heather Grabbe and Kirsty Hughes, The Royal Institute of International Affairs, London, 1997.

Economic Transition in Central and Eastern Europe, D. Gros and A. Steinherr, Cambridge University Press, second edition, 2004.

Enlargement and Integration in the European Union, Christopher Preston, Routledge, London and New York, 1997.

Enlarging the European Union, Relations between the EU and Central and Eastern Europe, Marc Maresceau, Longman, London and New York, 1997.

Enlarging the EU Eastwards, Heather Grabbe and Kirsty Hughes, The Royal Institute of International Affairs, London, 1998.

Europe, A Nietzschean Perspective, Stefan Elbe, Routledge, London and New York, 2003.

Europe Integration and Enlargement, Fraser Cameron, Routledge, London and New York, 2004.

Europe: Toward the Next Enlargement, International Handbooks on Economic Integration, Peter Coffey, Kluwer Academic Publishers, Boston, Dordrecht and London, 2000.

European Politics, A Comparative Introduction, Tim Bale, Palgrave Macmillan, London, 2005.

European Politics Today, Hogwood Patricia and Roberts K. Geoffrey, Manchester University Press, second Edition, Manchester, 2003.

European Union Enlargement, Neill Nugent, Palgrave Macmillan, London, 2004.

European Union Enlargement, A Comparative History, Wolfram Kaiser and Jürgen Elvert, Routledge, London and New York, 2004.

European Union Enlargement, Law and Socio-Economic Changes, Nanette Neuwahl, Les éditions thémis, Chaire Jean Monnet, Montréal, 2004.

Europe Undivided, Democracy, Leverage & Integration after Communism, Milada Anna Vachudova, Oxford University Press, Oxford, 2005.

EU Enlargement: A Legal Approach, Christophe Hillion, Hart Publishing, Oxford and Portland, Ore., 2004.

EU Enlargement versus Social Europe? The Uncertain Future of the European Social Model, Daniel C. Vaughan Whitehead, Edward Elgar, Cheltenham, UK and Northampton, MA, USA, 2003.

Institutional Challenges in the European Union, Madeleine O. Hosli, Adrian van Deemen and Mika Widgrén, Routledge, London and New York, 2002.

Integration and Transition in Europe, The Economic Geography of Interaction, George Petrakos, Gunther Maier, Grzegorz Gorzelak, Routledge, London and New York, 2000.

New Europe in Transition, Peter J. Anderson, Georg Wiessala and Christopher Williams, Continuum, London and New York, 2000.

Politics in the European Union, Stephen George and Ian Bache, Oxford University Press, Oxford, 2001.

Remaking Europe, The European Union and the Transition Economies, Jozef M. van Brabant, Rowman and Littlefield Publishers Inc., Lanham, Boulder, New York and Oxford, 1999.

Sceptical Essays on Human Rights, T. Campbell, K. Ewing and A. Tomkins (eds), Oxford University Press, Oxford, 1992.

Second Treatise of Government, J. Locke, [1690], republished by Prometheus Books, New York, 1986.

The Enlarged European Union, Diversity and Adaptation, Peter Mair and Jan Zielonka, Frank Cass, London, Portland, Or, 2002.

The Enlargement of the European Union, Marise Cremona, Academy of European Law, European University Institute, Oxford University Press, Oxford, 2003.

The Enlargement of the EU, Issues and Strategies, Victoria Curzon Price, Alice Landau and Richard G. Whitman, Routledge Studies in the European Economy, London, 2000.

The Enlargement of the European Union and NATO, Ordering from the Menu in Central Europe, Wade Jacoby, Cambridge University Press, Cambridge, 2004.

The Europeanisation of Law: The Legal Effects of European Integration, Francis Snyder, Hart Publishing, Oxford and Portland Ore., 2000.

The European Union and Central and Eastern Europe, The Implications of Enlargement in Stages, Susan Senior Nello and Karen E. Smith, Ashgate, Aldershot and Brookfield, USA, 1998.

The European Union in the wake of Eastern Enlargement, Institutional and Policy Making Challenges, Amy Verdun and Osvaldo Croci, Manchester University Press, Manchester and New York, 2005.

The European Union Transformed, Community Method and Institutional Evolution from the Schuman Plan to the Constitution for Europe, Youri Devuyst and P.I.E. Peter Lang, Bruxelles, Bern, Berlin, Frankfurt am Main, New York, Oxford and Wien, 2005.

The Future of Europe, Integration and Enlargement, Fraser Cameron, Routledge, London and New York, 2004.

The Integration Process between Eastern and Western Europe, Daniel Piazolo, Springer, Berlin and Heidelberg, 2001.

The Leviathan, Thomas Hobbes, [1660], republished by University of Oregan, 1999.

The Political Economy of Transition, Coming to Grips with History and Methodology, Jozef M. van Brabant, Routledge, London and New York, 1998.

The Politics of Europeanisation, Kevin Featherstone and Claudio M. Radaelli, Oxford University Press, Oxford, 2003.

The Politics of European Union Enlargement, Theoretical Approaches, Frank Schimmelfennig and Ulrich Sedelmeier, Routledge, London and New York, 2005.

The Return to Europe, The Reintegration of Eastern Europe into the European Economy, Alan Smith, Macmillan Press Ltd, Basingstoke, 2000.

The World We're In, W. Hutton, Little Brown, London, 2002.
This Blessed Plot: Britain and Europe from Churchill to Blair, Hugo Young, Macmillan, London, 1999.
Through the Paper Curtain, Insiders and Outsiders in the New Europe, Julie Smith and Charles Jenkins, The Royal Institute of International Affairs, Chatham House Papers, Blackwell Publishing, Oxford, 2003.
Towards a New Europe, Stops and Starts in Regional Integration, Gerald Schneider, Patricia A. Weitsman and Thomas Bernauer, Praeger, Westport, Connecticut, London, 1995.
What Kind of Europe?, Loukas Tsoukalis, Oxford University Press, Oxford, 2003 and Potamos, Athens, 2004.
Why did the Socialist System Collapse in Central and Eastern Europe?, Jan Adam, Macmillan Press, London, 1995.

ARTICLES

Bartol Letica, 'Reflections on a New Europe, Europe's Second Chance: European Union Enlargement to Croatia and the Western Balkans', *Fletcher Forum of World Affairs Journal*, 28, 2004.
Cesare Pinelli, 'Conditionality and Enlargement in Light of EU Constitutional Developments', *European Law Journal*, 10(3), May 2004.
Christine Juliet Sohar, 'The European Union's Legal Integration, A Case Study of Living up to the Denver Summit of Eight', *Denver Journal of International Law and Policy*, 27, 1999.
Christophe Hillion, 'The European Union is Dead. Long Live the European Union, A Commentary on the Treaty of Accession 2003', *European Law Review*, 29(5), 2004.
Claus Dieter Ehlermann, Director General of Legal Service, European Commission, European Community: 'How Flexible is Community Law? An Unusual Approach to the Concept of "Two Speeds" ', *Michigan Law Review*, 82, 1984.
Clements W. Carson, 'A More Perfect Union? Eastern Enlargement and the Institutional Challenges of the Czech Republic's Accession to the European Union', *Syracuse Journal of International Law and Commerce*, 29, 2002.
Daniel T. Murphy, 'Closer or Enhanced Co-operation: Amsterdam or Nice', *Georgia Journal of International and Comparative Law*, 31, 2003.
David O'Keeffe, 'Current Issues in European Integration', *Pace International Law Review*, 7, 1995.
Eneko Landaburu, Director General of DG Enlargement, European Commission, European Union Law Essay, 'The Fifth Enlargement of the European Union: The Power of Example', *Fordham International Law Journal*, 26(1), 2002.

Eritja Mar Campins, 'The New Accessions to the European Union from the Central and Eastern European Countries: The Strategy of Accession and its Implications on the Environmental European Community Policy', *ILSA Journal of International and Comparative Law*, 6, 2005.

Geoana Mircea, Eighth Annual Philip D. Reed Memorial Issue: Essay 'Romania: Euro-Atlantic Integration and Economic Reform', *Fordham International Law Journal*, 27, 1997.

Heather Grabbe, 'European Union Conditionality and the Acquis Communautaire', *International Political Science Review*, 23(3), 2002.

Helen E. Hartnell, 'Subregional Coalescence in European Regional Integration', *Wisconsin International Law Journal*, 16, 1997.

Ian Ward, *Temple International and Comparative Law Journal*, 15, 2001.

Inga Markovits, 'Exporting Law Reform, But Will It Travel?', *Cornell International Law Journal*, 37, 2004.

Jill Parker, 'Comment: West Meets East: A Discussion of European Union Enlargement and Human Rights', *Tulsa Journal of Comparative and International Law*, 11, 2004.

Jirí Pribán, 'European Union Constitution Making, Political Identity and Central European Reflections', *European Law Journal*, 11(2), March 2005.

John Richardson, Head of the Delegation of the European Commission to the United Nations, European Union Law Essay 'The European Union in the World, A Community of Values', *Fordham International Law Journal*, 26, 2003.

Katharina Pistor, 'The Standardisation of Law and its Effect on Developing Economies', *American Journal of Comparative Law*, 50, 2002.

Loïc Azoulai, 'The Acquis of the European Union and International Organisations', *European Law Journal*, 11(2), March 2005.

Marcin Zaborowski, 'Westernising the East: External Influences in the Post Communist Transformation of Eastern and Central Europe', *The Journal of Communist Studies and Transition Politics*, 21, March 2005, no. 1, Special Issue on Policy Transfer and Programmic Change in the Communist Successor Parties of Eastern and Central Europe, edited by Dan Hough, William E. Paterson and James Sloam, Routledge, New York.

Marise Cremona, 'EU Enlargement: Solidarity and Conditionality', *European Law Review*, 30(1), 2005.

Markus G. Puder, 'Constitutionalising the EU', *Fordham International Law Journal*, 26, 2003.

Neil Walker, 'Constitutionalising Enlargement, Enlarging Constitutionalism', *European Law Journal*, 9(3), Blackwell Publishing, July 2003.

Nicholas C. Kyriazis and Michel S. Zouboulakis, 'Modeling Institutional Change in transition Economies', *Communist and Post-Communist Studies*, 38, 2005.

R. Burchill, 'The EU and Social Democracy on Democracy with a Social Dimension', *Canadian Journal of Law and Jurisprudence on Social Democracy*, 185 at 186.

Rachel Sabates Wheeler, 'Legal Transfer and the Legitimisation of Law: Implications of Farm Family Property Provisions in Albanian Legislation', *The Journal of East European Law*, 9(1), 2002.

Rilka O. Dragneva and Thomas N. Jersild, 'Perspectives on Company Law Reform in Central and Eastern Europe: An Introduction', *Review of Central and East European Law*, 27(1), 2001.

Roger J. Goebel, 'The European Union Grows: The Constitutional Impact of the Accession of Austria, Finland and Sweden', *Fordham International Law Journal*, 18, 1995.

Roland Kobia, 'Reflections on the Effects of Future Enlargements of the EU on Industrial Property: The Case of Trade Marks', *European Intellectual Property Review*, 20(5), 1998.

Sadurski Wojciech, 'Accession's Democracy Dividend: The Impact of the EU Enlargement upon Democracy in the New Member States of Central and Eastern Europe', *European Law Journal*, 10(4), July 2004.

Simon Helm, 'Intellectual Property in Transition Economies: Assessing the Latvian Experience', *Fordham Intellectual Property, Media and Entertainment Law Journal*, 14, 2003.

Stanimir Alexandrov and Latchezar Petkov, 'Paving the Way for Bulgaria's Accession to the European Union', *Fordham International Law Journal*, 21, 1998.

PRESS ARTICLES

Le Monde, 'La Persistence de l'attachement à l'Identité Nationale', 3 June 2005.

Geremek Bronislaw, former minister of foreign affairs of Poland, *The Wall Street Journal*, 30 May 2005.

Le Monde, 'Les Néerlandais ont rejeté massivement la Constitution européenne', 2 June 2005.

Independent, 'What Now for Europe', Stephen Castle and Colin Brown, 2 June 2005.

Financial Times, 'Dutch Join French in Rejecting EU Treaty', Ian Bickerstone, 1 June 2005.

Washington Times, 'French Voters Reject EU Treaty', Nicholas Kralev, 30 May 2005.

International Herald Tribune, 'Politicus: After French "No" Vote, All Bets are Off on EU', John Vinocur, 31 May 2005.

Le Figaro, 'Le non des Pays Bas, nouveau choc européen', François Hauter, 2 June 2005.
El Mundo, 'Holanda rechaza la Constitutción Europea con un no aún más rotundo que Francia', 2 June 2005.
Le Monde, 'Une révolte contre une Europe qui va trop vite, trop loin et coûte trop cher', 1 June 2005.
Washington Times, 'Politicians Try to Turn Tide for EU Constitution', David Rennie, 1 June 2005.
Le Monde, 'Le rejet de la Constitution par 61, 6% des Néerlandais révèle l'ampleur du fosse qui separe l'Europe des citoyens', 2 June 2005.
The Times, 'Goodbye Treaty, Goodbye Chirac but Europe will Muddle on', Bronwen Maddox, 30 May 2005.
La Liberation, 'Le fosse qui s'élargit entre les nantis et les autres est un vrai débat', Nathalie Dubois, 2 June 2005.
Abc, 'Francia rechaza la Constitución europea y sume a la UE en una crisis sin precedents', Juan Pedro Qiuiñonero, 30 May 2005.
Le Figaro, 'Ankara pèse les consequences du rejet français', Marie Michèle Martinet, 31 May 2005.
Guardian, 'Dutch Say Devastating "No" to EU Constitution', 2 June 2005.
Ute Schaeffer, 'A Small Chance for Europe', *Deutsche Welle*, 1 June 2005, see: www.dw-world.de/dw/article/0,1564,1602667,00.html.
El Mundo, 'Moratinos cree que el no holandés y francés a la Constitutión va a afectar a la ampliación', 2 June 2005.
International Herald Tribune, 'Villepin Unveils Plan to Cut Jobless Rates', 8 June 2005.
Le Figaro, 'Sarkozy relie le "non" du 29 mai au soutien à l'adhésion de la Turquie', 10 July 2005.
Le Figaro, 'L'Europe assommée par les deux non', 3 June 2005.
The Times, 'Blair Puts Boot in Over Rebate by Marching to Moral High Ground', Charles Bremner, 15 June 2005.
The Times, 'Flat Tax Revolution Shakes up Europe', Anthony Browne, 19 March 2005.
The Economist, 'The Impact of Central Europe's Tax Revolution', 5 March 2005.
New York Times, 'Fear of Regression in a Growing EU', Craig S. Smith, 19 May 2005.
Greek Financial Newspaper *Naftemporiki*, 30 May 2005.
Le Figaro, 'Le Fabuleux destin du petit plombier polonaise', Arielle Thedrel, 31 May 2005.
Polish Daily *Zycie Warszawy*, 30 May 2005.
Greek Daily *Kathimerini*, 'The Polish Plumber', Konstantinos Kallergis, 29 May 2005.

The Economist, 'A severe crise d'identité', 28 May 2005.

Le Monde, 'La crainte pour l'emploi est la raison principale du rejet de la Constitution par les Français', 30 May 2005.

Guardian, 'Chirac Takes Aim at EU Liberals in Race to Win Yes Vote', Nicholas Watt, David Gow, 24 March 2005.

International Herald Tribune, 'Chirac urges French to back EU Charter', Graham Bowley and James Kanter, 24 March 2005.

The Times, 'Liberalisation of EU Services Hits Political Delays', Aine Gallagher, 27 March 2005.

Le Monde, 'Il n'existe pas de modèle social européenne. Chaque pays a ses traditions', Günter Verheugen, 2 September 2005.

La Tribune, Sir John Holmes, 2 June 2005.

The Times, 'As Luxembourg Wavers, Poles and Czechs Wobble', Anthony Browne and Rosemary Bennett, 2 June 2005.

New York Times, 'French No Vote on European Constitution Rattles Continent', Elaine Sciolino, 31 May 2005.

Le Monde, ' "Trop liberal, trop inégalitaire", la Constitution a été rejetée par les nombreux enseignants', 31 May 2005.

Libération, 'La Hollande, l'autre pays du non', Nathalie Dubois, 1 June 2005.

Independent, 'Chirac Seeks to Overcome Rejection with New Cabinet', John Lichfield, 31 May 2005.

Le Monde, 'Le non souligne les difficultés de l'élargissement', 30 May 2005.

Greek Newspaper *Kathimerini*, 'Why the French Said "No" to Chirac', 31 May 2005.

The Economist, 'So Whose Bright Idea was the Constitution in the First Place?', p. 52, 28 May 2005.

The Times, 'Europe Turmoil as Treaty Collapses', Philip Webster, David Charter and Anthony Browne, 14 June 2005.

Independent, 'Blair Rejects EU Rebate Freeze', Jon Smith, 14 June 2005.

Guardian, 'Sharp Disagreement at Blair Chirac Talks', Matthew Tempest, 14 June 2005.

El Mundo, 'Blair dice que existen intensas diferencias sobre los presupuestos se l'Unión Europea', 14 June 2005.

Le Monde, 'Tony Blair parle d'un profond désaccord sur le budget européen', 14 June 2005.

Le Monde, 'Budget de l'UE: Tony Blair juge "inacceptable" un gel du rabais britannique', 14 June 2005.

Le Figaro, 'Budget UE: Blair parle d'un "désaccord aigu" avec Chirac', 14 June 2005.

Le Figaro, 'Blair ne cède rien sur l'Europe et s'attaque au tandem Chirac-Schröder', 14 June 2005.

International Herald Tribune, 'Blair Calls for Debate on Direction of EU', 14 June 2005.

European Commissioner for Agriculture Mariann Fischer Boel in the Greek newspaper *Kathimerini*, 17 July 2005.
Spanish secretary of state for the European Union Alberto Navarro in *Financial Times*, 'Leslie Crawford, Spain will Accept EU Cuts if UK Rebate Pared', 9 June 2005.
El Mundo, 'El gobierno considera que es major volver sin acuerdo que con uno que perjudique a España', 18 June 2005.
Independent, 'Pathetic, Tragic, Embarrassing. And Then Things Got Really Nasty', 19 June 2005.
Polish newspaper *Rzeczpospolita*, 'London does not want to pay for the expansion of the EU', 19 June 2005.
Guardian, 'Rebate Row Wrecks EU Summit', Nicholas Watt and Patrick Wintour, 18 June 2005.
International Herald Tribune, 'Shame and Anger as EU Budget Talks Collapse', Elaine Sciolino, 20 June 2005.
Der Spiegel, 'Brussels in Crisis, EU Summit Collapse in Historic Failure', Hans-Jürgen Schlamp and Frank Dohmen, 20 June 2005.
Independent, 'New Members Review Relations with Britain after Rebate Row', Stephen Castle, 21 June 2005.
Financial Times, 'Poles Hit Out at National Egoism', Jan Cienski and James Blitz, 19 June 2005.
International Herald Tribune, 'German Minister Warns of a Conflict Ridden EU', Judy Dempsey, 22 June 2005.
Le Monde, 'Le risque de détricolage du projet européene est grave', Interview of the former minister of foreign affairs, 21 June 2005.
International Herald Tribune, 'Rival Views on the Future of Europe', Judy Dempsey, 21 June 2005.
Le Figaro, 'Blair défend sa vision d'une Europe moderne', Pierre Avril, 24 June 2005.
International Herald Tribune, 'EU Must Reform or It Will Risk Massive Failure Blair Warns', Anthony Browne, 24 June 2005.
Adam Rotfeld, Foreign Minister of Poland, in *International Herald Tribune*, 'Blair's Vision of a Changed EU Gains Support', Judy Dempsey, 24 June 2005.
Wall Street Journal, 'Europe Revisited', 31 May 2005.
The Economist, 'How Britain Unexpectedly Emerged Victorious from Votes on the EU Constitution', 4 June 2005.
The Economist, 'Tony Blair's Battle for Europe', 28 May 2005.
Independent, 'Which Way for Europe', 31 May 2005.
The Times, 'Eleventh Hour Vall for EU to Halt its Talks with Turkey', Anthony Browne, 28 June 2005.
The Times, 'New Obstacle blocks Turkish Road to EU', Adam Sage, 3 August 2005.

Le Figaro, 'La question chypriote est une cause nationale, Ankara rejette les conditions françaises', Marie Michèle Martinet, 5 August 2005.

Le Monde, 'La Turquie déplore officiellement la position française sur Chypre', 4 August 2005.

Le Monde, 'Les declarations de Villepin sur la Turquie sèment le trouble', 4 August 2005.

The Economist, 'Bazaar Bargaining', 3 September 2005.

Le Monde, 'Le ton entre Ankara et Paris à propos de Chypre', 2 August 2005.

Financial Times, 'European Public Struck by Sense of Foreboding over Ankara EU Entry', Daniel Dombey, Friederike Tiesenhausen Cave and Vincent Boland, 7 September 2005.

Financial Times, 'European Public Anxious over Ankara Entry', 6 September 2005.

Le Monde, 'Les Vingt Cinq vont adresser un rappel à l'ordre à la Turquie', 2 September 2005.

Le Monde, 'Les Turcs estiment que la question de Chypre n'est qu'un prétexte brandi par leurs adversaries', 31 August 2005.

FILES, REPORTS, SITES AND OTHER DOCUMENTS

European Commission publications on Enlargement at: http://europa.eu.int/comm/publications/booklets/move/41/en.pdf

European Commission site at: http://www.europa.eu.int/comm/enlargement/arguments/index.htm#Benefits

Presidency Conclusions, Copenhagen European Council 21–22 June 1993, see: http://www.europarl.eu.int/enlargement/ec/pdf/cop_en.pdf#search='copenhagen%20%20council%201993'

Dublin European Council, Presidency Conclusions, 25 and 26 June 1990, see: http://www.europarl.eu.int/summits/dublin/du1_en.pdf

European Council in Rome, 27 and 28 October 1990, Presidency Conclusions, see: http://www.europarl.eu.int/summits/rome1/ro1_en.pdf

European Council in Rome, 14 and 15 December 1990, Presidency Conclusions, see: http://www.europarl.eu.int/summits/rome2/rd2_en.pdf

Maastricht European Council, 9 and 10 December 1991, Presidency conclusions, see: http://www.europarl.eu.int/summits/maastricht/ma1_en.pdf

European Council in Essen, 9 and 10 December 1994, see: http://www.europarl.eu.int/summits/ess1_en.htm#ext

NATO Enlargement: http://www.nato.int/docu/basictxt/enl-9501.htm

Olli Rehn, member of the European Commission, responsible for Enlargement, 'EU Enlargement under Stress: The Policy of Consolidation, Conditionality and Communication', Speech at the Institute for European

Policy, Berlin, 12 July 2005. SPEECE/05/438. Accessed also at: http://europa.eu.int/comm/commission_barroso/rehn/speeches/pdf/s05_438.en.pdf

Olli Rehn, Commissioner responsible for Enlargement, 'The Balkans, Europe and Reconciliation', Debate in Sarajevo University, Sarajevo 11 July 2005, SPEECH/05/434, accessed also at: http://europa.eu.int/comm/commission_barroso/rehn/speeches/pdf/s05_434.en.pdf

Treaty of Athens: See its content at: http://europa.eu.int/eur-lex/en/archive/2003/l_23620030923en.html

Dominique de Villepin, speech at: http://www.latribune.fr/Tribune/Articles.nsf/ArticlesWeb/ ID05196A7503538215C125701A00492BC3?OpenDocument, accessed 8 June 2005.

Economic relevant data at: http://www.factbook.net/GDP_Comparison_data.htm, accessed 12 June 2005.

Data on economic growth: Eurostat news release 12 May 2005, accessed at: http://epp.eurostat.cec.eu.int/pls/portal/docs/PAGE/PGP_PRD_CAT_PREREL/PGE_CAT_PREREL_YEAR_2005/PGE_CAT_PREREL_YEAR_2005_MONTH_05/2-12052005-EN-AP.PDF

See the survey of the Federation of the European Employers at: ttp://www.fedee.com/payinasia.shtml, accessed 12 June 2005.

Minimum wage data: The Eurostat report at: http://epp.eurostat.cec.eu.int/cache/ITY_OFFPUB/KS-NK-03-010/EN/KS-NK-03-010-EN.PDF#search='minimum%20wages%20and%20EU', accessed 12 June 2005.

The European Social Charter signed in the framework of the Council of Europe for 'the purpose of safeguarding and realising the ideals and principles which are [its members'] common heritage and of facilitating their economic and social progress' http://conventions.coe.int/treaty/en/treaties/html/163.htm

Act of Accession: http://europa.eu.int/comm/enlargement/negotiations/treaty_of_accession_2003/ treaty_accession_28.htm

The Bolkenstein Directive: http://europa.eu.int/eur-lex/en/com/pdf/2004/com2004_0002en03.pdf, accessed 13 June 2005.

Information about the Bolkenstein Directive: the DG Internal Market of the European Commission at: http://europa.eu.int/comm/internal_market/services/services-dir/faq/200410-faq-point06_en.htm#63

Olli Rehn, European Commissioner for Enlargement, 'Europe at a Crossroads: Enlargement, Constitution and the Future of the EU, Speech to the Transatlantic Institute, Brussels, 30 June 2005, SPEECH/05/363, accessed also at: http://europa.eu.int/comm/commission_barroso/rehn/speeches/pdf/s05_363.en.pdf

Data on the referendum on the Constitutional Treaty in France: the survey conducted by Canal Ipsos, accessed at: www.ipsos.fr/CanalIpsos/articles/1608.asp?rubId=19, 30 May 2005.

Olli Rehn, European Commissioner for Enlargement, 'Is the Future Enlargement of the EU in Peril?', Speech to the European Policy Centre, Brussels, 20 June 2005, SPEECH/05/362

Tony Blair. His speech at the European Parliament: http://www.number-10.gov.uk/output/Page7714.asp

Council Regulation (EC) No. 1260/1999 of 21 June 1999 laying down general provisions on the Structural Funds, *Official Journal* L 161, 26/06/1999 P. 0001–0042. It can be also accessed at: http://europa.eu.int/eur-lex/lex/LexUriServ/LexUriServ.do?uri=CELEX:31999R1260:EN:HTML

Structural Funds data: the European Commission site at: http://europa.eu.int/scadplus/leg/en/lvb/l60014.htm, accessed 14 June 2005.

Eurostat, Regional Breakdown of GDP per capita, Percentage of EU 25 average, accessed at: http://epp.eurostat.cec.eu.int/portal/page?_ pageid=1996, 39140985&_dad=portal&_schema=PORTAL&screen=detailref& language=en&product=sdi_ed&root=sdi_ed/sdi_ed/sdi_ed_inv/sdi_ed 1130 on 14 June 2005.

Council Regulation (EC) No. 1164/94 of 16 May 1994 establishing a Cohesion Fund *Official Journal* L 130, 25/05/1994 P. 0001–0013. Accessed also at: http://europa.eu.int/smartapi/cgi/sga_doc?smartapi!celexplus! prod!DocNumber&lg=en&type_doc=Regulation&an_doc=1994&nu_ doc=1164

Council Regulation (EC) No. 1264/1999 of 21 June 1999 amending Regulation (EC) No. 1164/94 establishing a Cohesion Fund, *Official Journal* L 161, 26/06/1999 p. 0057–0061, accessed also at: http://europa.eu.int/eur-lex/lex/LexUriServ/LexUriServ.do?uri=CELEX: 31999R1264:EN:HTML

Council Regulation (EC) No. 1265/1999 of 21 June 1999 amending Annex II to Regulation (EC) No. 1164/94 establishing a Cohesion Fund, *Official Journal* L 161, 26/06/1999 p. 0062–0067. Accessed also at: http://europa.eu.int/smartapi/cgi/sga_doc?smartapi!celexplus!prod!DocNumber&lg=en&type_doc=Regulation&an_doc=1999&nu_doc=1265

European Commission site on the Cohesion Fund, http://europa.eu.int/scadplus/leg/en/lvb/l60018.htm, accessed 14 June 2005.

Debate for the Future of the Cohesion Policy over 2006: http://europa.eu.int/comm/regional_policy/debate/contri_member_en.htm

The Conclusion of the Italian Presidency in Rome, 20 October 2003: http://europa.eu.int/comm/regional_policy/debate/document/futur/member /rome_201003.pdf, accessed 14 June 2005.

The Euobserver, Core Europe Idea Resurfaces, Honor Mahony, 2 June 2005, see: http://www.euobserver.com/?aid=19224, accessed 2 June 2005.

Glossary in the EU site: http://www.europa.eu.int/scadplus/glossary/variable-geometry_europe_en.htm

Treaty of Rome, accessed at the European Union site at: http://europa.eu.int/eur-lex/en/treaties/selected/livre2_c.html

European Community of Coal and Steel. The Treaty: http://www.europa.eu.int/abc/obj/treaties/en/entoc29.htm, accessed 25 June 2005.

Robert Schuman declaration of 9 May 1950: http://www.europa.eu.int/abc/symbols/9-may/decl_en.htm, accessed on 25 June 2005.

The Treaty establishing the European Community at: http://europa.eu.int/abc/obj/treaties/en/entoc05.htm

The European Atomic Energy Community. The treaty: http://europa.eu.int/abc/obj/treaties/en/entoc38.htm

President Charles de Gaulle at his fifteenth press conference on 16 May 1967, access at: http://www.fordham.edu/halsall/mod/1967-degaulle-non-uk.html or http://www.cartage.org.lb/en/themes/GeogHist/histories/histdocts/Biblio20/A20/deGaulle/1967-degaulle-non-uk.html

The Hague Summit, *Bulletin of the European Communities*, No. 1 1970.

The Final Communiqué of the Hague Summit, 2 December 1969.

Paris Summit, 19 to 21 October 1972, *Bulletin of the European Communities*, No. 10 1972.

Opinion on Greek application for membership, transmitted to the Council by the Commission, 29 January 1976, COM (76) 30 final, *Bulletin of the European Communities*, Supplement 2/76.

Opinion on Portuguese application for membership, transmitted to Council by the Commission, 19 May 1978, COM (78) 220, *Bulletin of the European Communities*, supplement 5/78.

General Considerations on the Problems of Enlargement, Communication sent by the Commission to the Council, 20 April 1978, COM (78) 120 final, *Bulletin of the European Communities*, Supplement 1/78.

Enlargement of the Community, transitional period and institutional implications, *Bulletin of the European Communities*, COM (78) 190, supplement 2/78.

Solemn Declaration on European Union, European Council, Stuttgart 19 June 1983, *Bulletin of the European Communities*, No. 6/1983.

European Council, 28 and 29 June 1985 in Milan, Draft Concerning the Reform of the Treaty establishing the European Economic Community, *Bulletin of the European Parliament*, 8 July 1985. Alternatively access at: http://www.europarl.eu.int/summits/milan/mil_en.pdf

Commission of the European Communities, COM (85) 310 final, Brussels 14 June 1985, Completing the Internal Market, White Paper from the Commission to the European Council, Milan, 28–29 June 1985. Alternatively at: http://europa.eu.int/comm/off/pdf/1985_0310_f_en.pdf

European Council, 9 and 10 December 1994, Essen, Presidency Conclusions, *Bulletin of the European Communities*, 12/1994.

Single European Act: http://europa.eu.int/abc/obj/treaties/en/entoc113.htm
Special Meeting of the European Council, Dublin, 28 April 1990, *Bulletin of the European Communities*, No. 4/1990, Presidency Conclusions.
European Council in Edinburgh, 11 and 12 December 1992, *Bulletin of the European Communities*, 12/1992, Presidency Conclusions.
Treaty of Maastricht: http://europa.eu.int/eur-lex/en/treaties/dat/EU_treaty.html
Presidency Conclusions, European Council at Corfu, 24–5 June 1994. See the conclusions at: http://www.europarl.eu.int/summits/cor1_en.htm#into
European Commission Opinion on the Intergovernmental Conference in 1996, Reinforcing Political Union and Preparing for Enlargement, 28 February 1996, accessed at: http://europa.eu.int/en/agenda/igc-home/eu-doc/commissn/avis-en.html on 28 June 2005.
Report on a Strategy for Europe, Brussels, 5 December 1995, at: http://europa.eu.int/en/agenda/igc-home/eu-doc/reflect/final.html, accessed 28 June 2005.
European Summit in Corfu, 24–5 June 1994, Presidency Conclusions, access at: http://www.europarl.eu.int/summits/cor1_en.htm#igc
Resolution on Parliament's opinion on the convening of the Intergovernmental Conference; and evaluation of the work of the Reflection Group and definition of the political priorities of the European Parliament with a view to the Intergovernmental Conference. Based on the DURY/MAIJ-WEGGEN report (A4-0068/96), 13 March 1996. Accessed at: http://europa.eu.int/en/agenda/igc-home/eu-doc/parlment/opinion.html#1, 28 June 2005.
The Treaty of Amsterdam: : http://europa.eu.int/eur-lex/lex/en/treaties/dat/11997E/htm/11997E.html#0001010001
The Final Act (Treaty of Nice) at the European Union site at: http://europa.eu.int/eur-lex/lex/en/treaties/dat/12001C/htm/C_2001080EN.007001.html
Protocol on the Enlargement of the EU annexed to the Treaty of Nice at: http://www.europa.eu.int/eur-lex/en/treaties/dat/C_2002325EN.016301. html
Olli Rehn the Commissioner for Enlargement and his speech to the Transatlantic Institute, 20 June 2005: http://europa.eu.int/rapid/pressReleasesAction.do?reference=SPEECH/05/363&format=HTML&aged=0&language= EN&guiLanguage=en
The reply to Morocco's application for entry: the European Parliament: http://www.europarl.eu.int/factsheets/6_3_1_en.htm, accessed 23 June 2005.
The European Council, Copenhagen, 7–8 April 1978, *Bulletin of the European Communities*, 3/1978. See also: Joint Declaration by the European Parliament, the Council and the Commission on Fundamental Rights of 5 April 1977, OJ C 103, 27. 4. 1977.

The transitional period and the institutional implications of enlargement (Commission Communication to the Council further to the Communication sent on 20 April 1978). COM (78) 190, 24 April 1978, *Bulletin of the European Communities*, Supplement 2/78.

General considerations on the problems of enlargement (Communication sent by the Commission to the Council on 20 April 1978). COM (78) 120.

Economic and Sectoral Aspects. Commission analyses supplementing its views on enlargement. COM (78) 200, 27 April 1978, Part II.

Economic and sectoral aspects. Commission analyses supplementing its views on enlargement (Communication from the Commission, sent to the Council on 20 April 1978). COM (78) 200, 27 April 1978. Part I. Bulletin of the European Communities, Supplement 3/78.

Consultation on Migration Policies vis-à-vis Third Countries (Communication of the Commission to the Council). COM (79) 115, 23 March 1979.

Spain and the European Community [May 1978]. Europe Information. External Relations, 5/78.

Portugal and the European Community [May 1978]. Europe Information. External Relations, 7/78.

European Commission, Report to the Council, Europe and the Challenge of Enlargement, Brussels, 24 June 1992.

European Council, Copenhagen, 21–22 June 1993. Access at: http://www.europarl.eu.int/summits/copenhagen/co_en.pdf

Madrid European Council, 15 and 16 December 2005, Presidency Conclusions, III. A Europe Open to the World, Enjoying Stability, Security Freedom and Solidarity, A. Enlargement.

European Commission, Composite Paper, Reports on Progress towards Accession by each of the candidate countries, 13 October 1999. DG Enlargement: http://europa.eu.int/comm/enlargement/report_10_99/pdf/en/composite_en.pdf, accessed 29 June 2005.

Helsinki European Council, 10 and 11 December 1999. Presidency Conclusions. I Preparing for Enlargement.

The Euroobserver, 'Member States Struggle on Cyprus Counter Declaration', Mark Beunderman, 9 September 2005. On the net at: http://euobserver.com/?aid=19820&print=1, accessed 9 September 2005.

Opinion poll on the enlargement: *Eurobarometer*, 63, Publication July 2005, accessed at: http://europa.eu.int/comm/public_opinion/archives/eb/eb63/eb63.4_en_first.pdf

European Commission's Press Release, 'Commission Presents a Rigorous Draft Framework for Accession Negotiations with Turkey', Reference: IP/05/807, Brussels, 29/06/2005. Available at: http://europa.eu.int/rapid/pressReleasesAction.do?reference=IP/05/807&format=HTML&aged=0&language=en&guiLanguage=en

European Council, Brussels, 16 and 17 December 2004, Presidency Conclusions.

European Council in Copenhagen Presidency Conclusions, 21 and 22 June *Bulletin of the European Communities*, No. 6/1993.

European Council in Madrid, 15 and 16 December 1995, Presidency Conclusions, *Bulletin of the European Communities*, No. 12/1995.

European Council in Luxembourg, 12 and 13 December 1997, Presidency Conclusions, *Bulletin of the European Communities*, No. 12/1997.

European Council in Cologne, 3 and 4 June 1999, Presidency Conclusions, Access at the European Council site at: http://europa.eu.int/council/off/conclu/june99/june99_en.htm

European Council in Nice, 7 to 9 December 2000, Presidency Conclusions, Access at the site of the European Parliament at: http://www.europarl.eu.int/summits/nice1_en.htm

European Commission, 'Agenda 2000 – Volume I – Communication: For a Stronger and Wider Union', DOC/97/6.

Official position of the European Parliament, Resolution on the Communication from the Commission 'Agenda 2000 – for a stronger and wider Union' (COM (97) 2000 – C4-0371/97), accessed at the European Parliament's site at: http://www.europarl.eu.int/enlargement/positionep/resolutions/041297a_en.htm

Meeting of the Heads of State or Government, The Hague, 1–2 December 1969, *Bulletin of the European Communities*, No. 1/1970, Final Communiqué of the Conference, 2 December 1969.

Olli Rehn, Member of the European Commission, responsible for Enlargement, 'The European Union as a Global Actor?', Speech to the Bucerius/Die Zeit Summer School, Die Zeit Foundation, Hamburg, 9 August 2005, SPEECH/05/465, accessed also at: http://europa.eu.int/comm/commission_barroso/rehn/speeches/pdf/s05_465.en.pdf

Regular Report on the Enlargement Process: at the site of the DG Enlargement of the European Commission at: http://europa.eu.int/comm/enlargement/report_10_99/#1.%20Progress%20Reports and http://europa.eu.int/comm/enlargement/ docs/

European Council in Madrid, 15 and 16 December 1995, Presidency Conclusions, *Bulletin of the European Communities*, No. 12/1995.

European Council in Luxembourg, 12 and 13 December 1997, Presidency Conclusions, *Bulletin of the European Communities*, No. 12/1997.

Helsinki European Council, 10 and 11 December 1999, Presidency Conclusions, access at: http://www.europarl.eu.int/summits/hel1_en.htm#a

The Eurostat news release 164/2005 – 20 December 2005 on the GDP per capita in purchasing power standards in the EU.

Financial Perspectives 2007–2013, Document 15915/05, Council of the European Union, Brussels, 19 December 2005, CADREFIN 268.

Communication from the Commission, Commission Opinion on the application from the Former Yugoslav Republic of Macedonia for membership of the European Union. Brussels, 9 November 2005, COM (2005) 562.

The Parliament's position on the budget at: http://www.europarl.eu.int/news/expert/infopress_page/034-4219-37-2-6-905-20060112IPR04218-06-02-2006-2006—false/default_en.htm

The same: http://www.europarl.eu.int/news/expert/infopress_page/034-4415-18-1-3-905-20060118IPR04414-18-01-2006-2006—true/default_en.htm

Jose Manuel Barroso in Greek newspaper *Kathimerini*, 'European Union: A Budget Fair for All', 4 December 2005.

Jacques Chirac, *Kathimerini*, 26 October 2005.

Eurostat news release 47/2005 of 7 April 2005 on the Regional GDP per Capita in the EU25.

Speech by Olli Rehn, 'Accesssion Negotiations with Turkey: The Journey is as Important as the Final Destination', European Parliament Plenary Session, Strasbourg, 28 September 2005. Speech/05/556.

Council of the European Union, Enlargement: Turkey, Declaration by the European Community and its Member States, Document 12541/05 (Presse 243), 21 September 2005.

Eurobarometer, 63, Publication July 2005, accessed at: http://europa.eu.int/comm/public_opinion/archives/eb/eb63/eb63.4_en_first.pdf

Eurobarometer, 64 published December 2005.

Council of the European Union, Document 12514/05 (Presse 241), Press Release, 2678th Council Meeting, General Affairs and External Relations, General Affairs, Luxembourg, 3 October 2005.

Declaration of the President of the European Commission José Manuel Barroso on the opening of accession negotiations with Turkey, Brussels, 3 October 2005, IP/05/1219, accessed also at: http://www.europa.eu.int/comm/external_relations/news/barroso/sp05_1210.htm

Texts Adopted by the Parliament, 28 September 2005, P6_TA-PROV(2005)0350.

Index